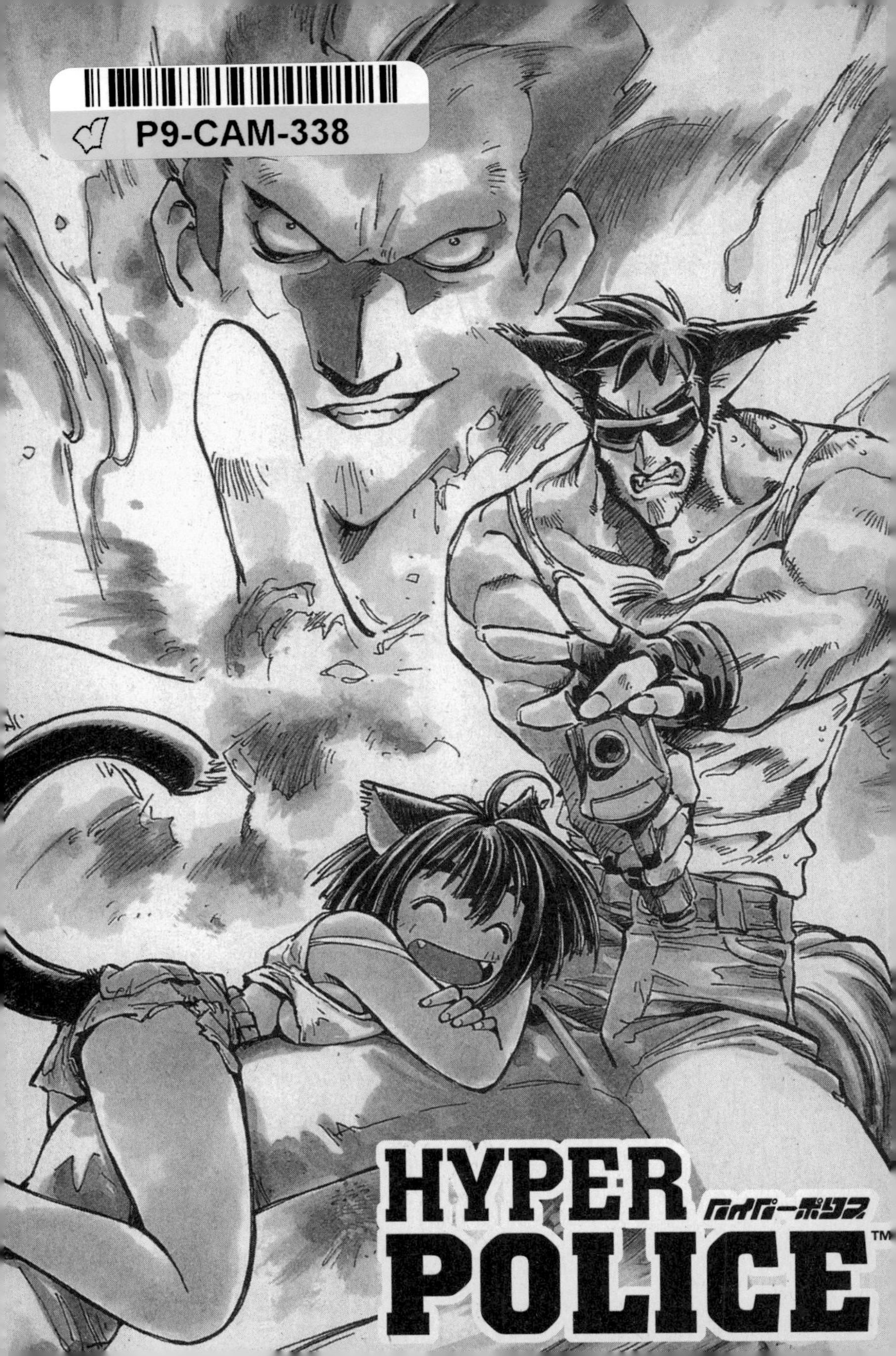
HYPER POLICE™
ハイパーポリス

Hyper Police Vol. 8
Created By MEE

Translation - Nan Rymer
English Adaption - Aaron Sparrow
Layout and Lettering - Star Print Brokers
Production Artist - Kitty Orchard
Cover Layout - James Lee

Editor - Katherine Schilling
Digital Imaging Manager - Chris Buford
Pre-Production Supervisor - Erika Terriquez
Art Director - Anne Marie Horne
Managing Editor - Vy Nguyen
Production Manager - Elisabeth Brizzi
VP of Production - Ron Klamert
Editor-in-Chief - Rob Tokar
Publisher - Mike Kiley
President and C.O.O. - John Parker
C.E.O. and Chief Creative Officer - Stuart Levy

A  Manga

TOKYOPOP Inc.
5900 Wilshire Blvd. Suite 2000
Los Angeles, CA 90036

E-mail: info@TOKYOPOP.com
Come visit us online at www.TOKYOPOP.com

HYPER POLICE 8 ©MEE 2002
First published in Japan in 2002 by KADOKAWA SHOTEN
PUBLISHING CO., LTD., Tokyo. English translation rights
arranged with KADOKAWA SHOTEN PUBLISHING CO., LTD.,
Tokyo through TUTTLE–MORI AGENCY, INC., Tokyo.
English text copyright © 2007 TOKYOPOP Inc.

ISBN: 978-1-59532-301-9

First TOKYOPOP printing: January 2007
10 9 8 7 6 5 4 3 2 1
Printed in the USA

HYPER POLICE ™

ハイパーポリス

by

MEE

Volume 8

HAMBURG // LONDON // LOS ANGELES // TOKYO

HYPER POLICE ハイパーポリス

The Story So Far...

It is the year 22 H.C. (Holy Century), and the human race has all but disappeared. The Japanese city of Shinjuku has become a haven for "monsters"—intelligent creatures that possess human-like anatomy with distinctly animal features. While most monsters are benevolent, all possess the ability to cause destruction, due largely to an internal struggle that is both constant and unwavering. Their evolved minds recognize the necessity for order and respect the sanctity of life, but the animal inside each of them is never too far beneath the surface...

Natsuki Sasahara is one such monster. A rookie at Police Company, a private police organization, she makes her living as a bounty hunter. She was scouted for the position by Batanen Fujioka, a werewolf who harbors a secret attraction for the young cat girl. Cool under pressure and stunningly efficient, Batanen is a seasoned veteran of the hunter trade. With his partner Tomy, Batanen always tops the list of monthly arrests. Recently, Police Company welcomed a new officer to their ranks. Sakura is part nine-tailed fox—or rather she WOULD be if her ninth tail would finish growing in. Partnered with Natsuki, Sakura has formed an uneasy friendship with the young cat girl. While Sakura has come to depend on Natsuki as a partner and roommate, she also hides a vicious desire to eat her. It is her hope that the strong magical essence Natsuki possesses will finally allow Sakura's stumpy tail to grow.

While the team was enjoying their steamy summer (and we aren't just talking about the heat,) a sneaky brigade of mice was starting a revolution of their own. And now that they've completed their fake Natsuki doll, what sort of trouble are they ready to unleash on the city... and Natsuki's reputation?

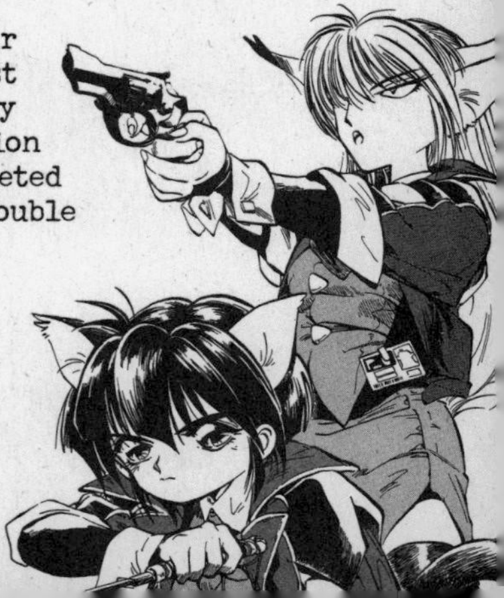

CHARACTERS

Natsuki

A rookie bounty hunter with magical powers and wicked sword skills. Her magic manifests itself as electrical energy capable of frying anything in sight, and is further amplified through the assistance of her two pet parasites, Raijin and Fujin.

Natsuki's partner and a fellow rookie, Sakura is a nine-tailed fox whose ninth tail has yet to grow in. To trigger its growth, Sakura plans to eat the highly magical Natsuki...as soon as she can figure out how.

Sakura

Batanen

A clean shot and a brutal brawler, Batanen is one of the best hunters in the biz. He was Police Company's pride and joy, and has been equally successful as a freelancer, largely due to his possession of something the others lack: a license.

Resourceful, quiet and clever, Tomy prefers to keep busy behind the scenes. He's proven to be an efficient yin to Batanen's yang, often accompanying the great hunter on some of his greatest hunts.

Tomy

CONTENTS

HYPER POLICE

Report #64

Cat Out of The Bag

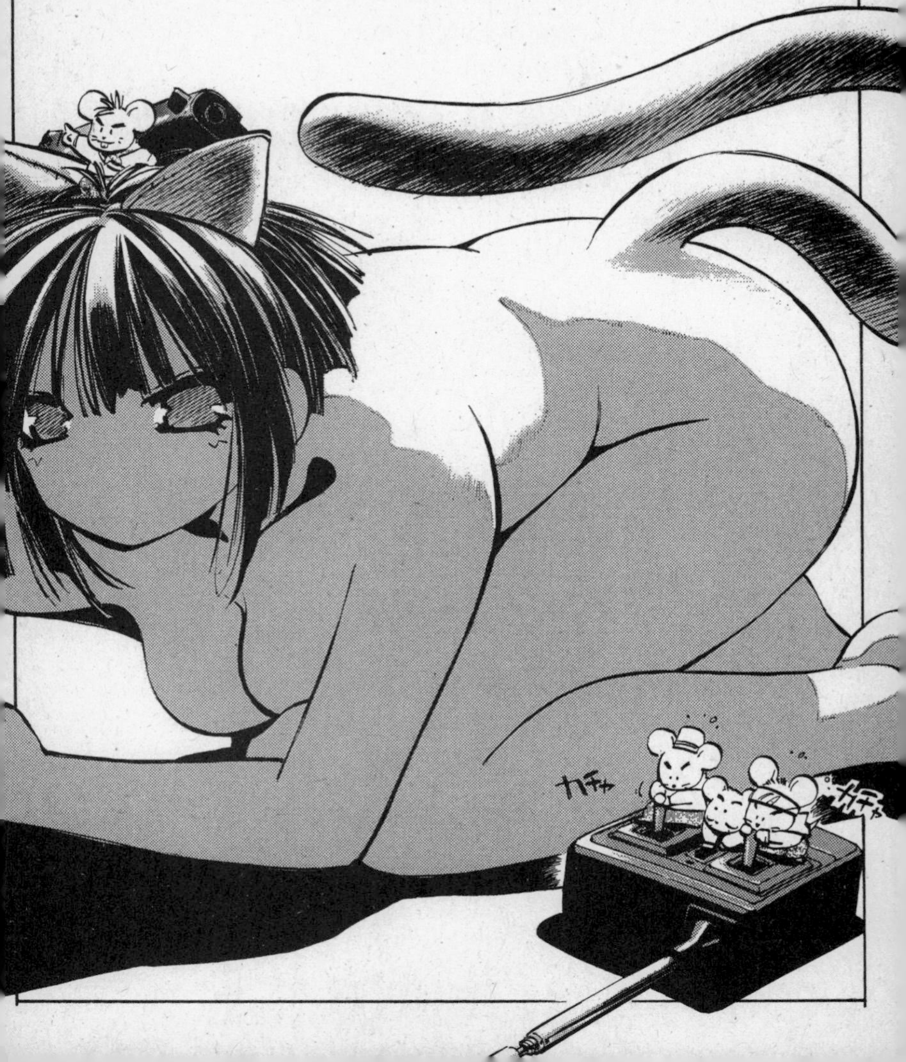
カチャ
カチャ

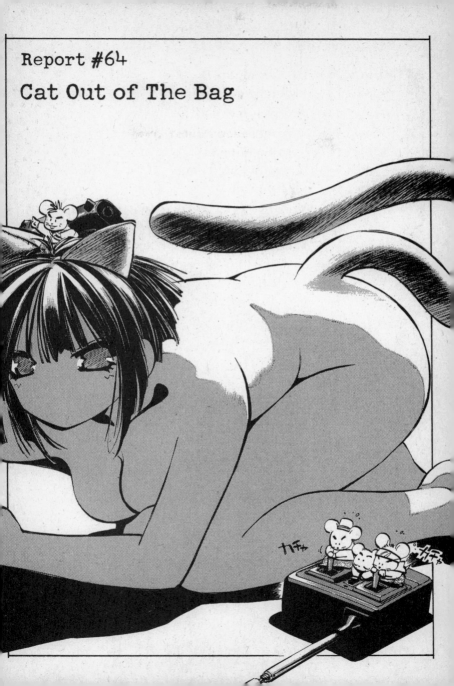

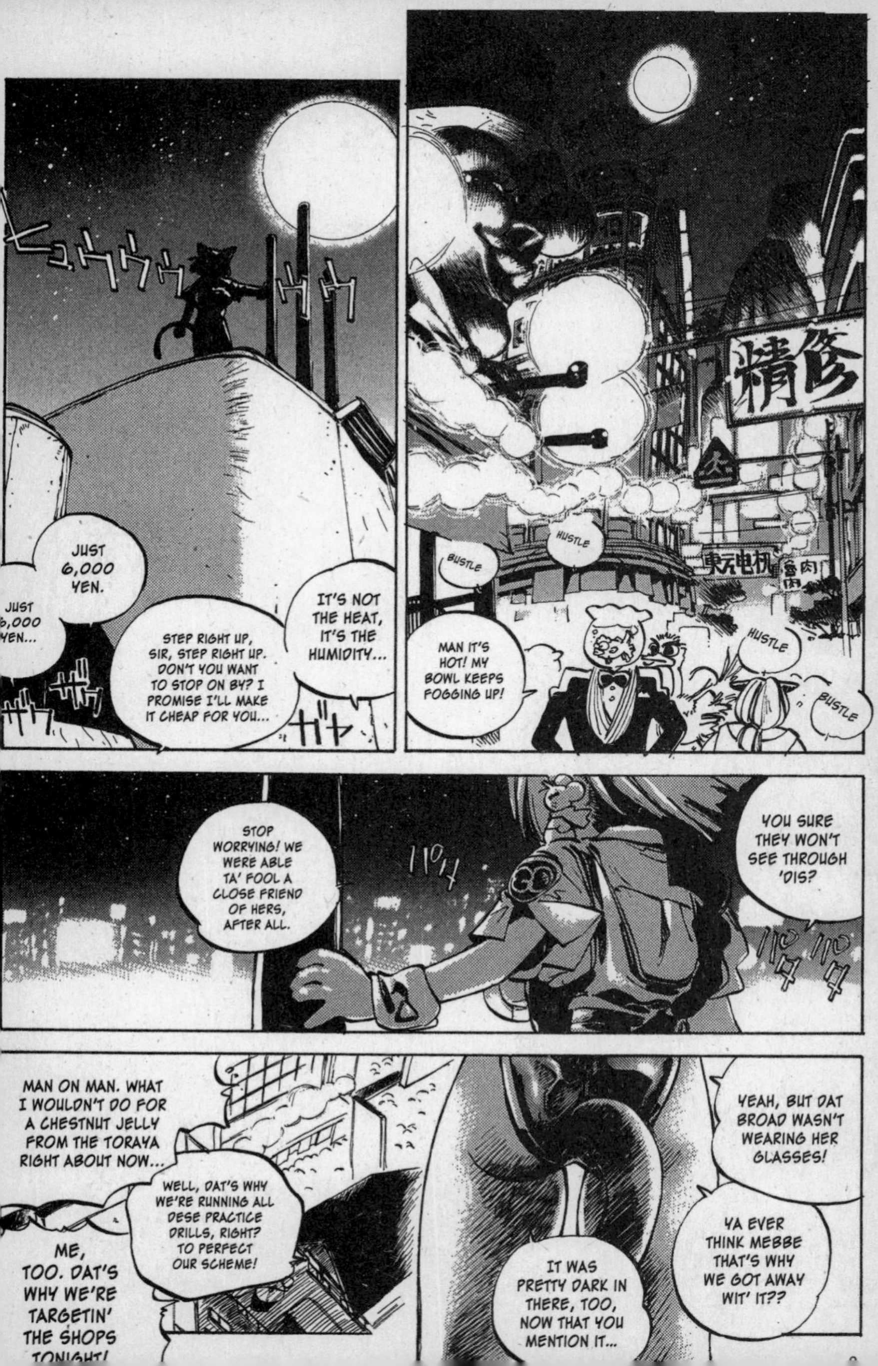
HUSTLE
BUSTLE
HUSTLE
BUSTLE
MAN IT'S HOT! MY BOWL KEEPS FOGGING UP!
IT'S NOT THE HEAT, IT'S THE HUMIDITY...
JUST 6,000 YEN.
STEP RIGHT UP, SIR, STEP RIGHT UP. DON'T YOU WANT TO STOP ON BY? I PROMISE I'LL MAKE IT CHEAP FOR YOU...
JUST 6,000 YEN...
YOU SURE THEY WON'T SEE THROUGH 'DIS?
STOP WORRYING! WE WERE ABLE TA' FOOL A CLOSE FRIEND OF HERS, AFTER ALL.
YEAH, BUT DAT BROAD WASN'T WEARING HER GLASSES!
YA EVER THINK MEBBE THAT'S WHY WE GOT AWAY WIT' IT??
IT WAS PRETTY DARK IN THERE, TOO, NOW THAT YOU MENTION IT...
MAN ON MAN. WHAT I WOULDN'T DO FOR A CHESTNUT JELLY FROM THE TORAYA RIGHT ABOUT NOW...
WELL, DAT'S WHY WE'RE RUNNING ALL DESE PRACTICE DRILLS, RIGHT? TO PERFECT OUR SCHEME!
ME, TOO. DAT'S WHY WE'RE TARGETIN' THE SHOPS

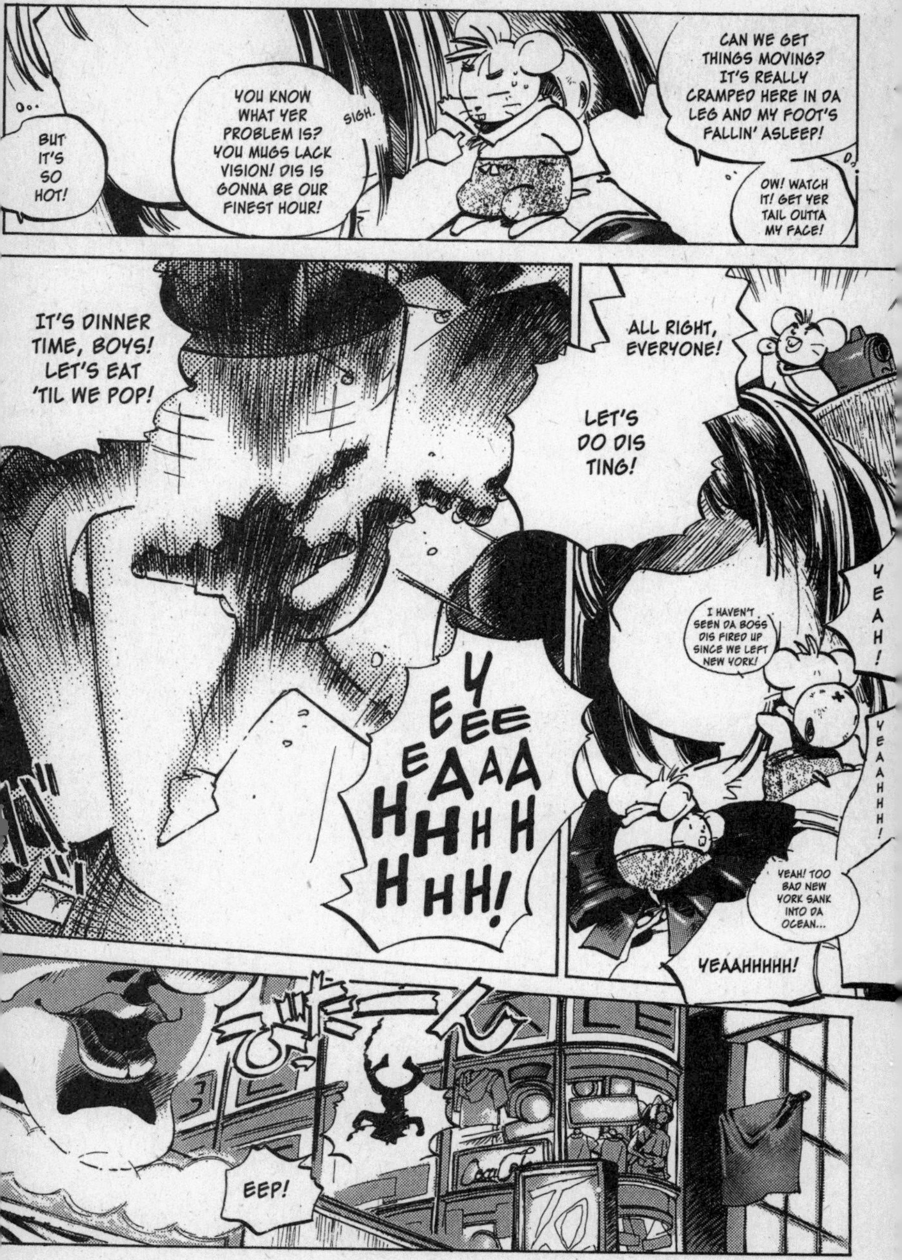
CAN WE GET THINGS MOVING? IT'S REALLY CRAMPED HERE IN DA LEG AND MY FOOT'S FALLIN' ASLEEP!
OW! WATCH IT! GET YER TAIL OUTTA MY FACE!
SIGH.
YOU KNOW WHAT YER PROBLEM IS? YOU MUGS LACK VISION! DIS IS GONNA BE OUR FINEST HOUR!
O..
BUT IT'S SO HOT!
ALL RIGHT, EVERYONE!
LET'S DO DIS TING!
YEAH!
I HAVEN'T SEEN DA BOSS DIS FIRED UP SINCE WE LEFT NEW YORK!
YEAAHHHH!
YEAH! TOO BAD NEW YORK SANK INTO DA OCEAN...
YEAAHHHHH!
IT'S DINNER TIME, BOYS! LET'S EAT 'TIL WE POP!
YEEEEAAAAHHHHHHHH!
EEP!

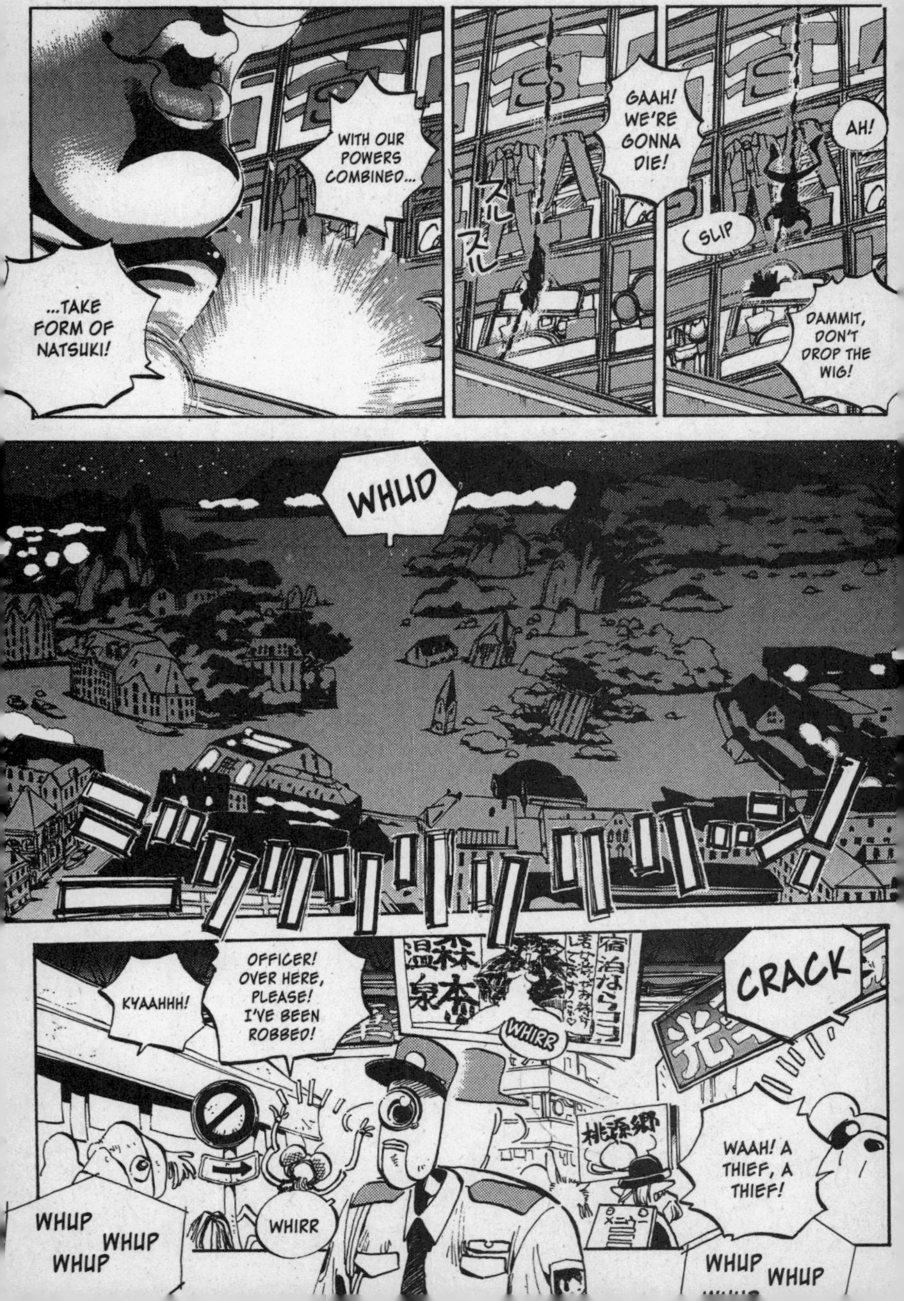
AH!
SLIP
DAMMIT, DON'T DROP THE WIG!
スルスル
GAAH! WE'RE GONNA DIE!
WITH OUR POWERS COMBINED...
...TAKE FORM OF NATSUKI!
WHUD
CRACK
WAAH! A THIEF, A THIEF!
WHUP WHUP
宿泊ならココ
森本温泉
WHIRR
OFFICER! OVER HERE, PLEASE! I'VE BEEN ROBBED!
KYAAHHH!
WHIRR
WHUP WHUP WHUP

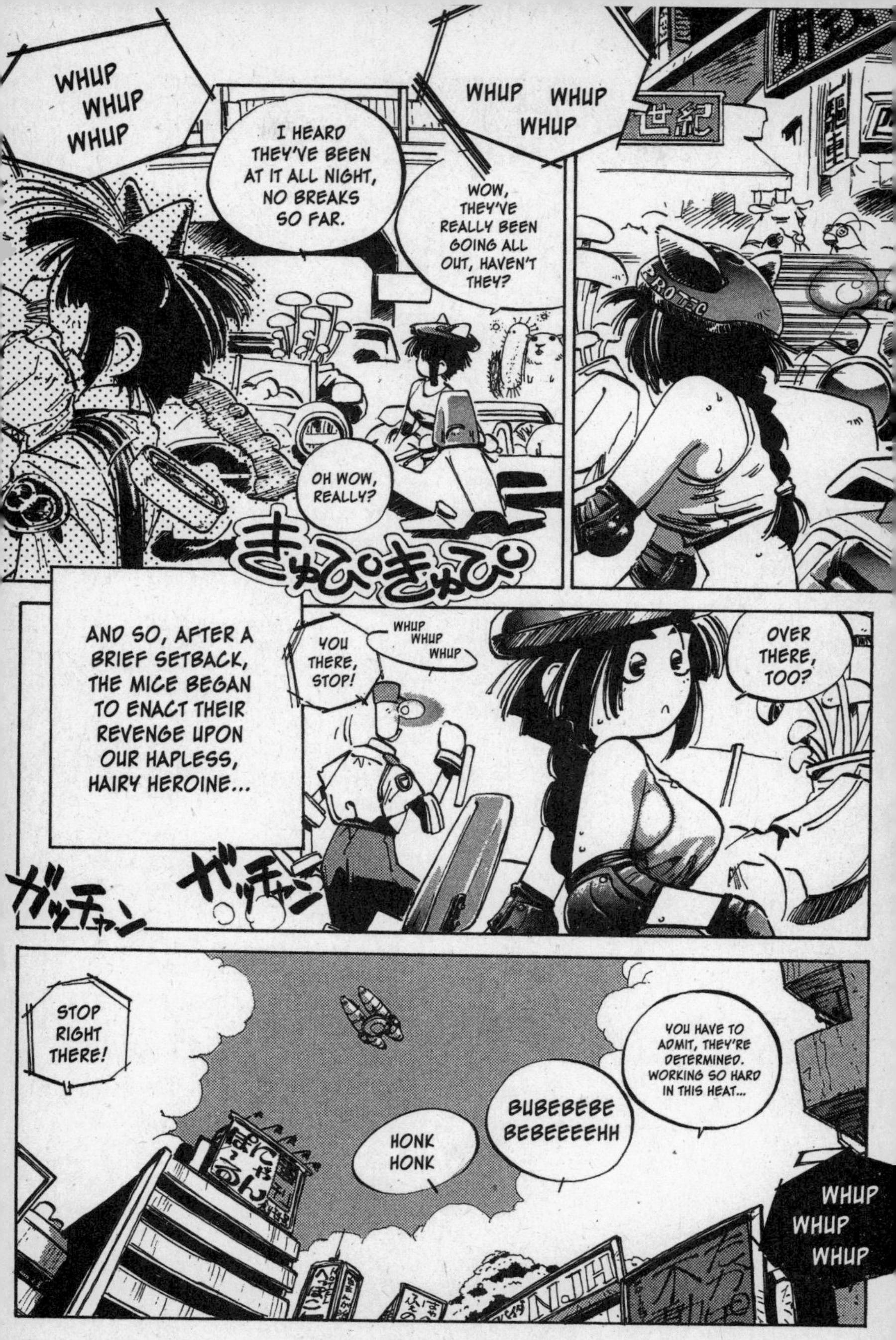
WHUP WHUP WHUP
PROTEC
世紀
WHUP WHUP WHUP
I HEARD THEY'VE BEEN AT IT ALL NIGHT, NO BREAKS SO FAR.
WOW, THEY'VE REALLY BEEN GOING ALL OUT, HAVEN'T THEY?
OH WOW, REALLY?
きゅぴきゅぴ
OVER THERE, TOO?
WHUP WHUP WHUP
YOU THERE, STOP!
ガッチャン
ガッチャン
AND SO, AFTER A BRIEF SETBACK, THE MICE BEGAN TO ENACT THEIR REVENGE UPON OUR HAPLESS, HAIRY HEROINE...
WHUP WHUP WHUP
YOU HAVE TO ADMIT, THEY'RE DETERMINED. WORKING SO HARD IN THIS HEAT...
BUBEBEBE BEBEEEEHH
HONK HONK
STOP RIGHT THERE!
N.JH

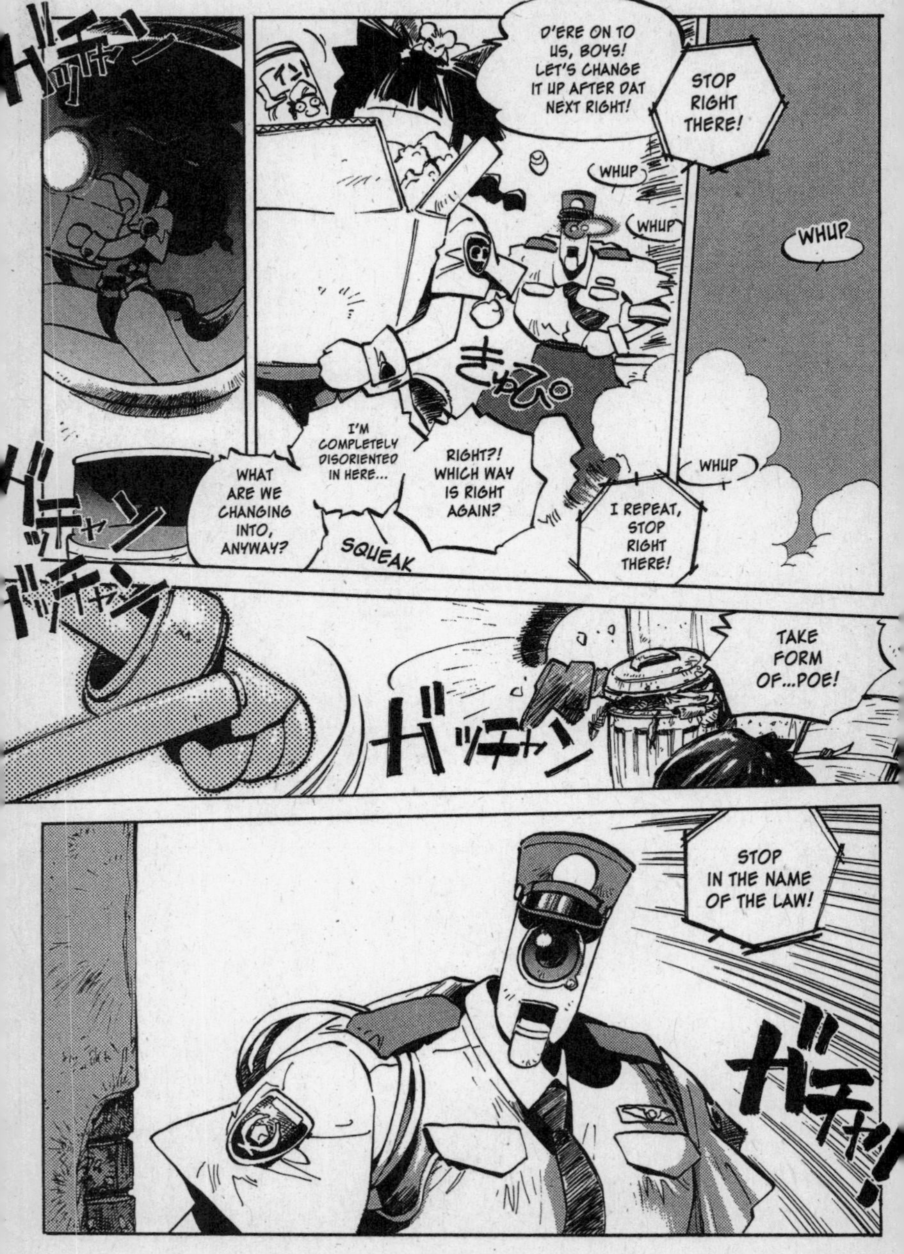

STOP RIGHT THERE!
D'ERE ON TO US, BOYS! LET'S CHANGE IT UP AFTER DAT NEXT RIGHT!
WHUP
WHUP
WHUP
WHUP
I REPEAT, STOP RIGHT THERE!
きゅぴ
RIGHT?! WHICH WAY IS RIGHT AGAIN?
I'M COMPLETELY DISORIENTED IN HERE...
WHAT ARE WE CHANGING INTO, ANYWAY?
SQUEAK
TAKE FORM OF...POE!
ガッチャン
STOP IN THE NAME OF THE LAW!

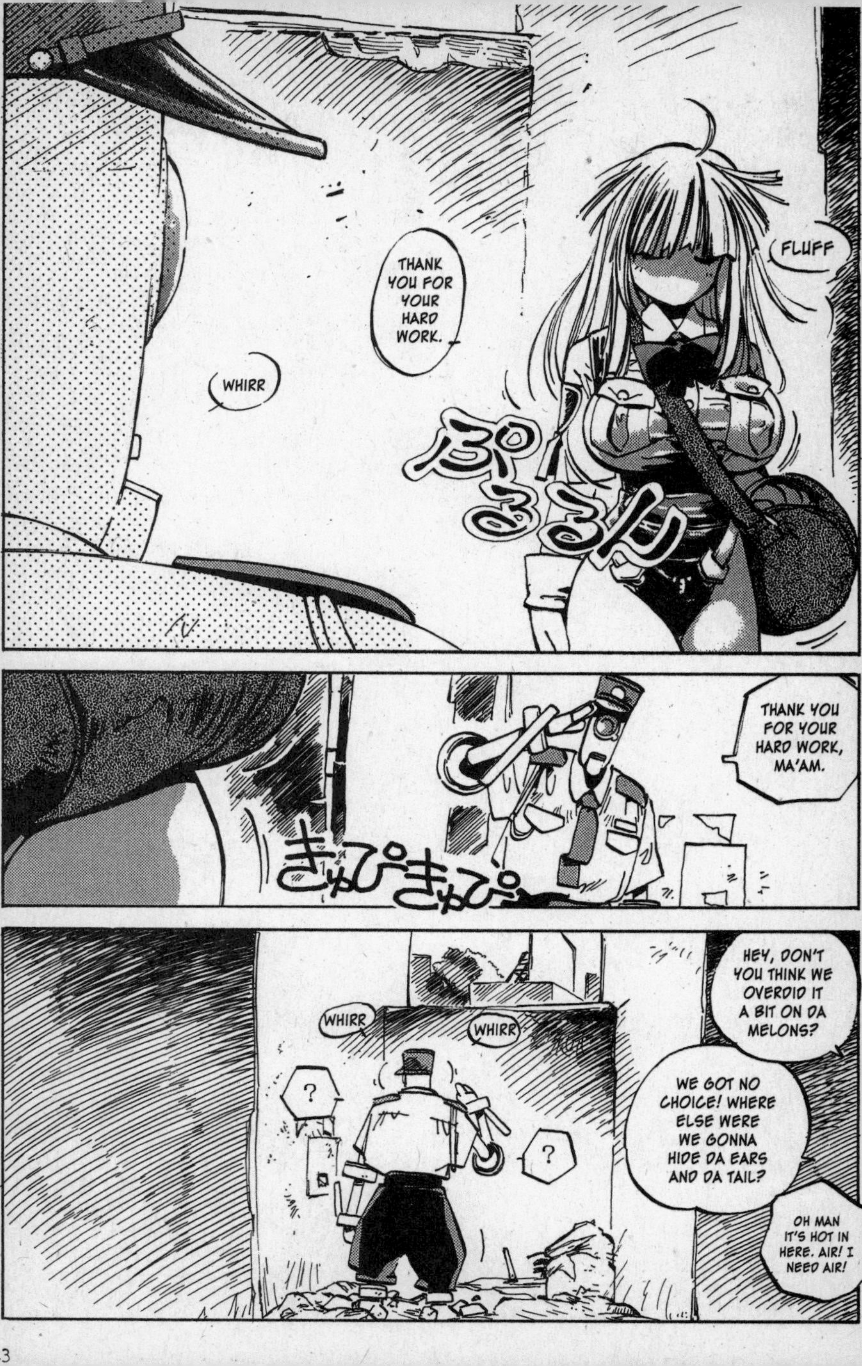
FLUFF
ぷるるん
THANK YOU FOR YOUR HARD WORK.
WHIRR
THANK YOU FOR YOUR HARD WORK, MA'AM.
きゅぴきゅぴ
HEY, DON'T YOU THINK WE OVERDID IT A BIT ON DA MELONS?
WE GOT NO CHOICE! WHERE ELSE WERE WE GONNA HIDE DA EARS AND DA TAIL?
OH MAN IT'S HOT IN HERE. AIR! I NEED AIR!
WHIRR
WHIRR
?
?

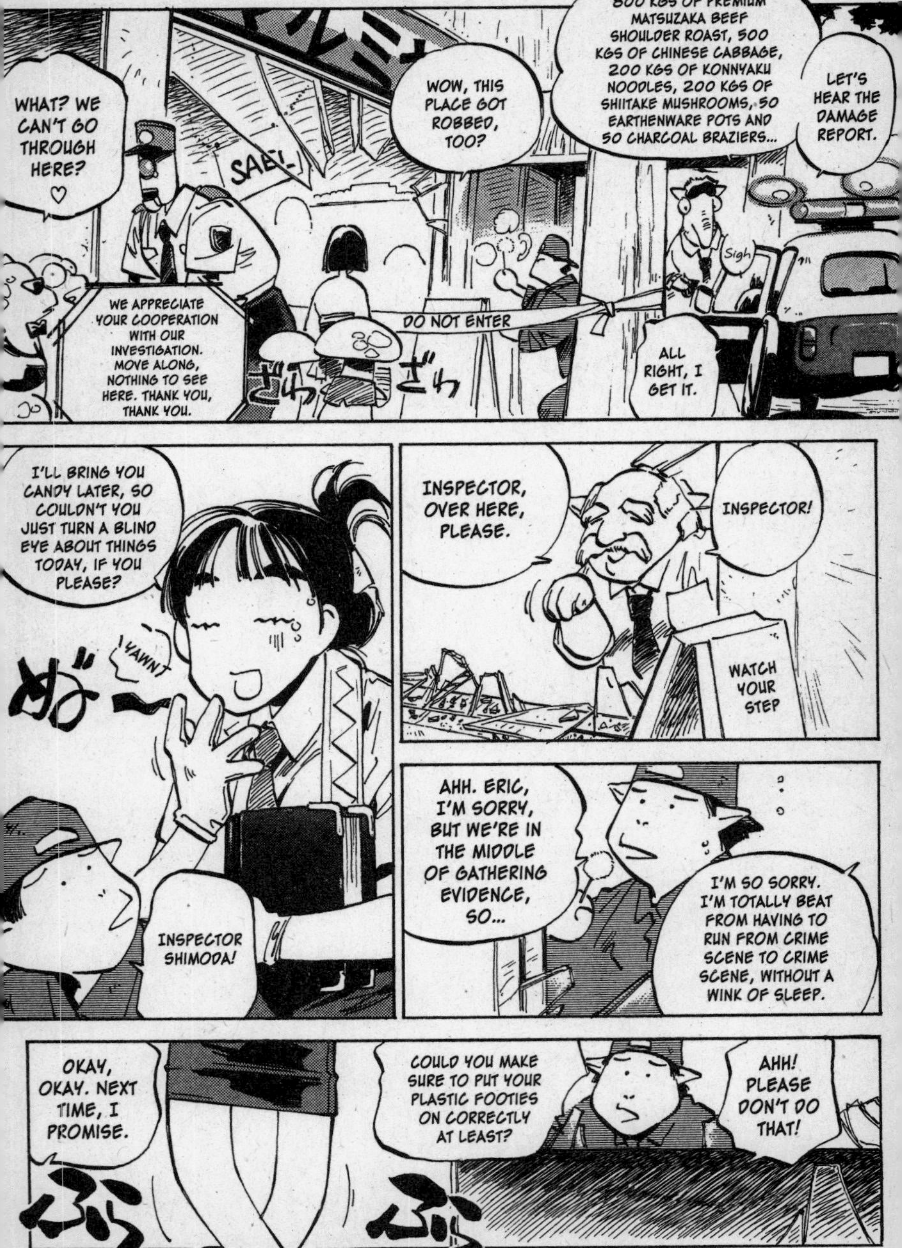
LET'S HEAR THE DAMAGE REPORT.
800 KGS OF PREMIUM MATSUZAKA BEEF SHOULDER ROAST, 500 KGS OF CHINESE CABBAGE, 200 KGS OF KONNYAKU NOODLES, 200 KGS OF SHIITAKE MUSHROOMS, 50 EARTHENWARE POTS AND 50 CHARCOAL BRAZIERS...
WOW, THIS PLACE GOT ROBBED, TOO?
WHAT? WE CAN'T GO THROUGH HERE? ♡
Sigh
ALL RIGHT, I GET IT.
DO NOT ENTER
ざわ
ざわ
WE APPRECIATE YOUR COOPERATION WITH OUR INVESTIGATION. MOVE ALONG, NOTHING TO SEE HERE. THANK YOU, THANK YOU.
INSPECTOR!
INSPECTOR, OVER HERE, PLEASE.
WATCH YOUR STEP
I'M SO SORRY. I'M TOTALLY BEAT FROM HAVING TO RUN FROM CRIME SCENE TO CRIME SCENE, WITHOUT A WINK OF SLEEP.
AHH. ERIC, I'M SORRY, BUT WE'RE IN THE MIDDLE OF GATHERING EVIDENCE, SO...
I'LL BRING YOU CANDY LATER, SO COULDN'T YOU JUST TURN A BLIND EYE ABOUT THINGS TODAY, IF YOU PLEASE?
YAWN
めぇ～
INSPECTOR SHIMODA!
AHH! PLEASE DON'T DO THAT!
COULD YOU MAKE SURE TO PUT YOUR PLASTIC FOOTIES ON CORRECTLY AT LEAST?
ふら
OKAY, OKAY. NEXT TIME, I PROMISE.
ふら

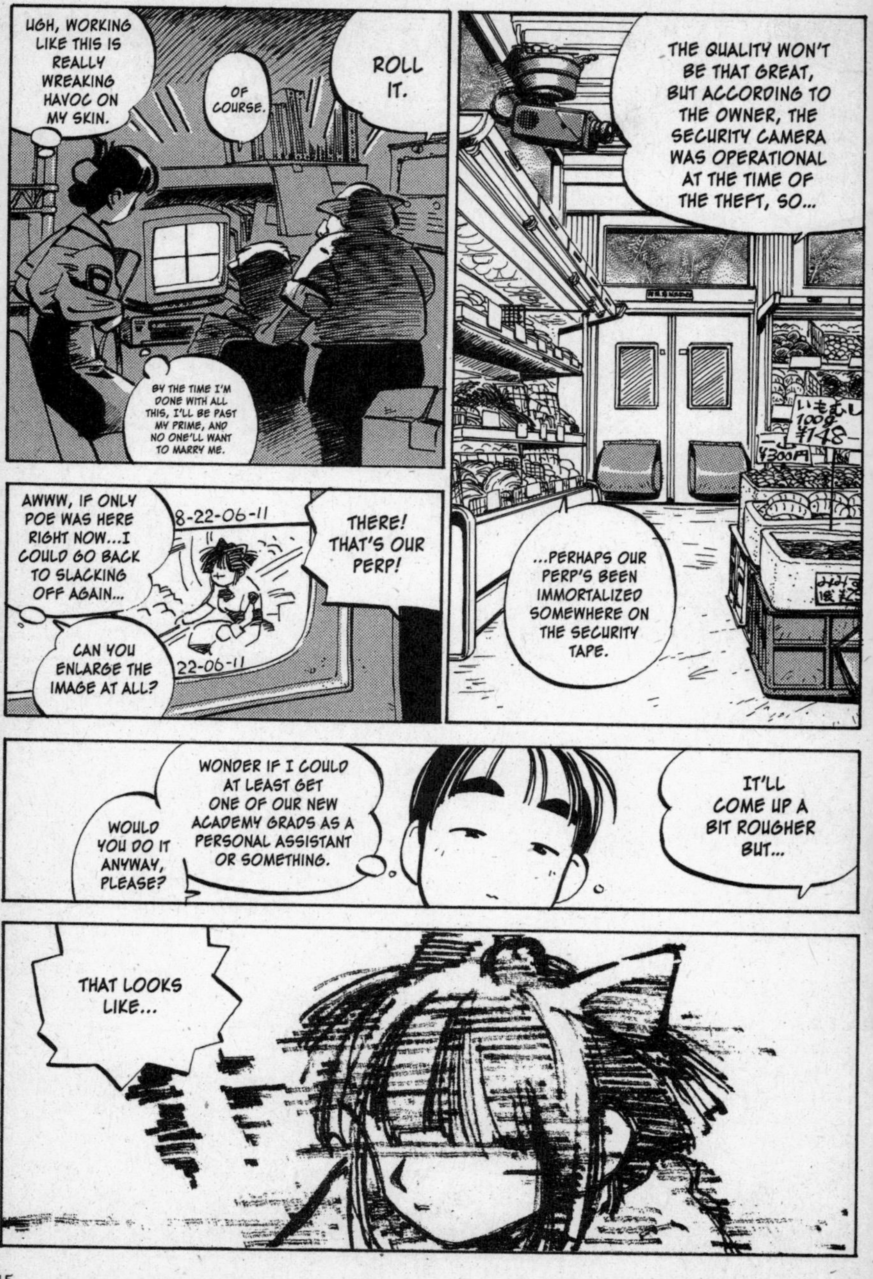
THE QUALITY WON'T BE THAT GREAT, BUT ACCORDING TO THE OWNER, THE SECURITY CAMERA WAS OPERATIONAL AT THE TIME OF THE THEFT, SO...
¥148
¥300円
...PERHAPS OUR PERP'S BEEN IMMORTALIZED SOMEWHERE ON THE SECURITY TAPE.
ROLL IT.
OF COURSE.
UGH, WORKING LIKE THIS IS REALLY WREAKING HAVOC ON MY SKIN.
BY THE TIME I'M DONE WITH ALL THIS, I'LL BE PAST MY PRIME, AND NO ONE'LL WANT TO MARRY ME.
THERE! THAT'S OUR PERP!
AWWW, IF ONLY POE WAS HERE RIGHT NOW...I COULD GO BACK TO SLACKING OFF AGAIN...
8-22-06-11
22-06-11
CAN YOU ENLARGE THE IMAGE AT ALL?
IT'LL COME UP A BIT ROUGHER BUT...
WONDER IF I COULD AT LEAST GET ONE OF OUR NEW ACADEMY GRADS AS A PERSONAL ASSISTANT OR SOMETHING.
WOULD YOU DO IT ANYWAY, PLEASE?
THAT LOOKS LIKE...

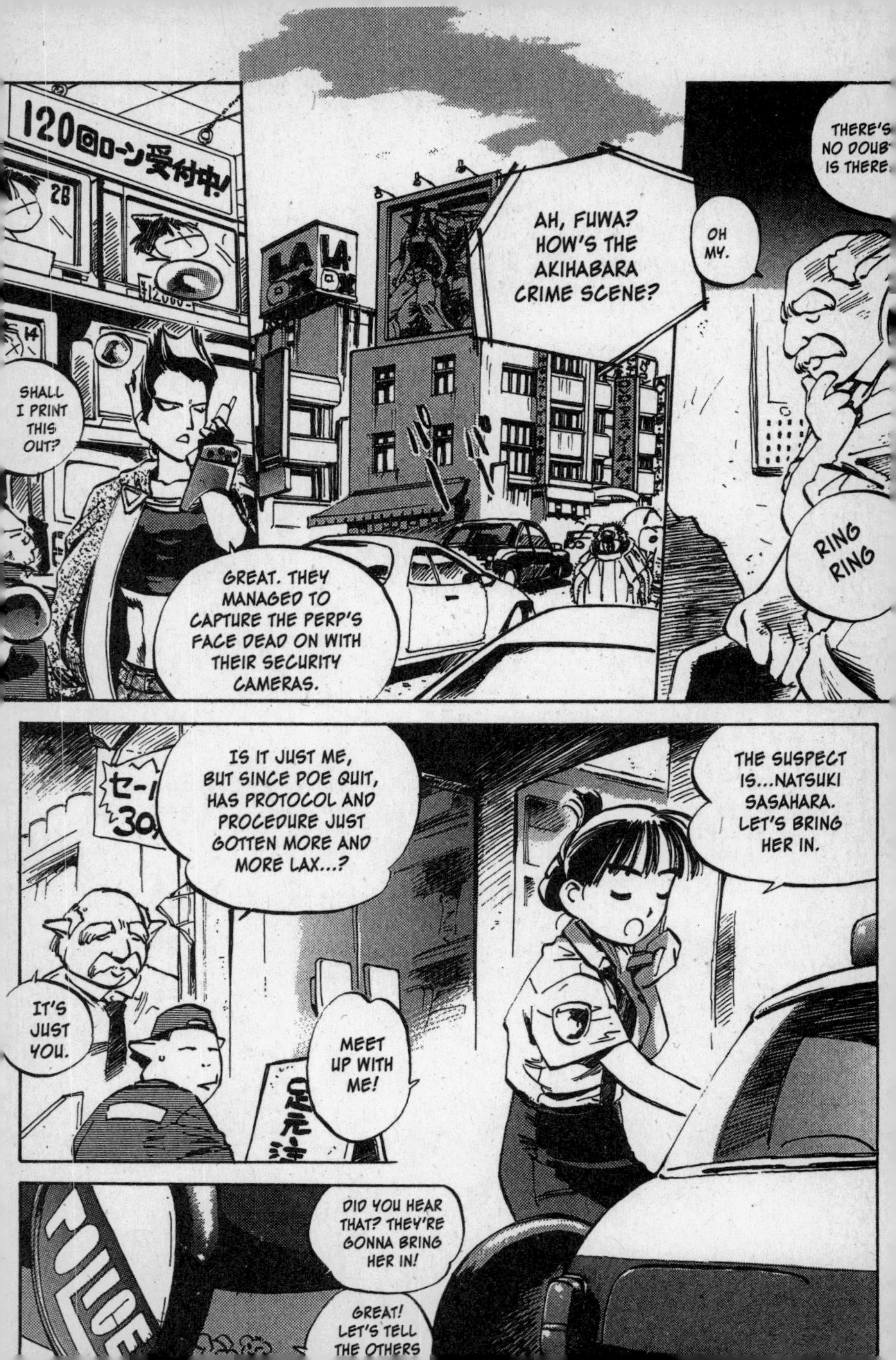

THERE'S NO DOUB IS THERE
OH MY.
RING RING
120回ローン受付中!
AH, FUWA? HOW'S THE AKIHABARA CRIME SCENE?
GREAT. THEY MANAGED TO CAPTURE THE PERP'S FACE DEAD ON WITH THEIR SECURITY CAMERAS.
SHALL I PRINT THIS OUT?
THE SUSPECT IS...NATSUKI SASAHARA. LET'S BRING HER IN.
IS IT JUST ME, BUT SINCE POE QUIT, HAS PROTOCOL AND PROCEDURE JUST GOTTEN MORE AND MORE LAX...?
IT'S JUST YOU.
MEET UP WITH ME!
DID YOU HEAR THAT? THEY'RE GONNA BRING HER IN!
GREAT! LET'S TELL THE OTHERS

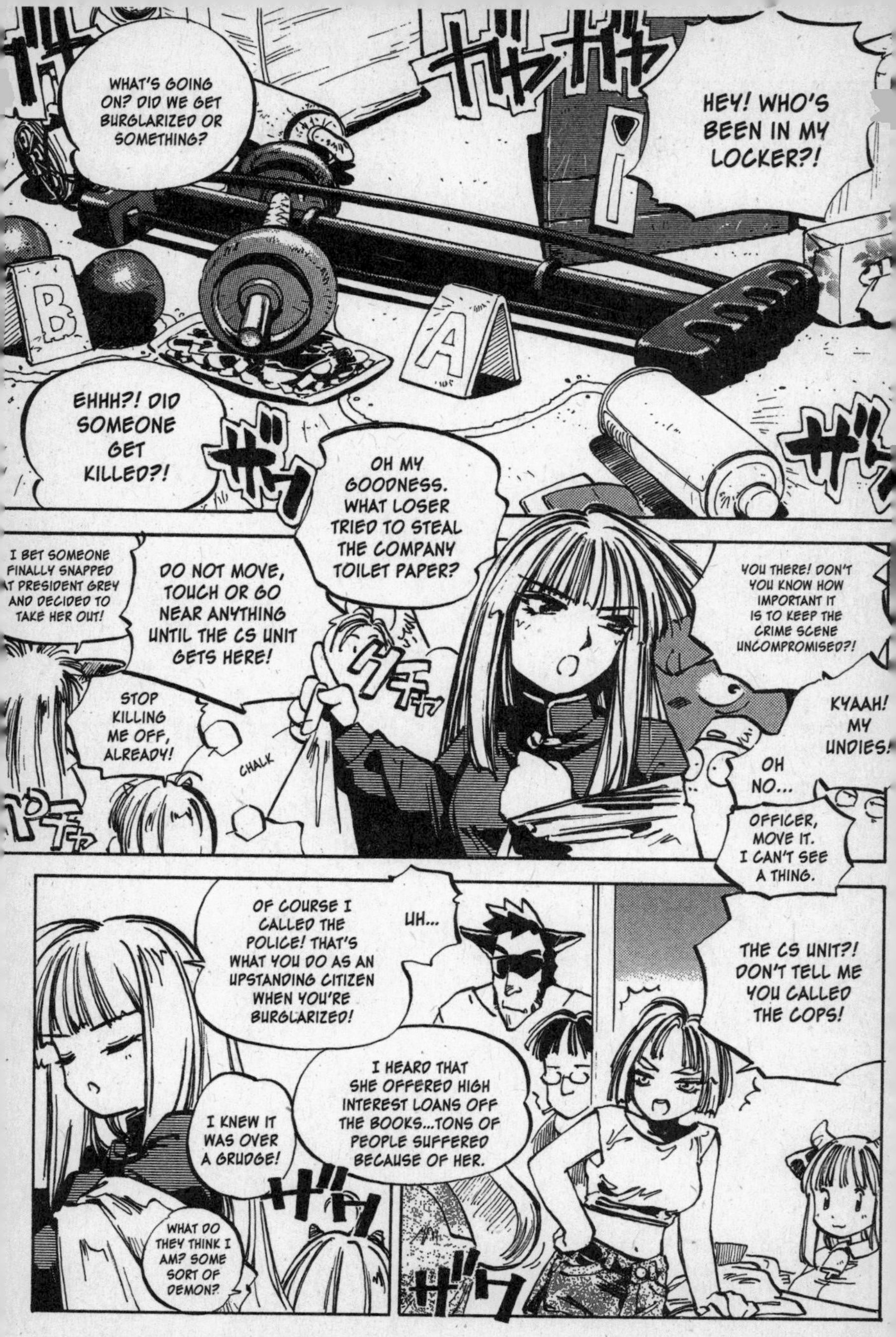

HEY! WHO'S BEEN IN MY LOCKER?!
WHAT'S GOING ON? DID WE GET BURGLARIZED OR SOMETHING?
EHHH?! DID SOMEONE GET KILLED?!
YOU THERE! DON'T YOU KNOW HOW IMPORTANT IT IS TO KEEP THE CRIME SCENE UNCOMPROMISED?!
KYAAH! MY UNDIES!
OH NO...
OFFICER, MOVE IT. I CAN'T SEE A THING.
OH MY GOODNESS. WHAT LOSER TRIED TO STEAL THE COMPANY TOILET PAPER?
DO NOT MOVE, TOUCH OR GO NEAR ANYTHING UNTIL THE CS UNIT GETS HERE!
I BET SOMEONE FINALLY SNAPPED AT PRESIDENT GREY AND DECIDED TO TAKE HER OUT!
STOP KILLING ME OFF, ALREADY!
CHALK
THE CS UNIT?! DON'T TELL ME YOU CALLED THE COPS!
UH...
OF COURSE I CALLED THE POLICE! THAT'S WHAT YOU DO AS AN UPSTANDING CITIZEN WHEN YOU'RE BURGLARIZED!
I HEARD THAT SHE OFFERED HIGH INTEREST LOANS OFF THE BOOKS...TONS OF PEOPLE SUFFERED BECAUSE OF HER.
I KNEW IT WAS OVER A GRUDGE!
WHAT DO THEY THINK I AM? SOME SORT OF DEMON?

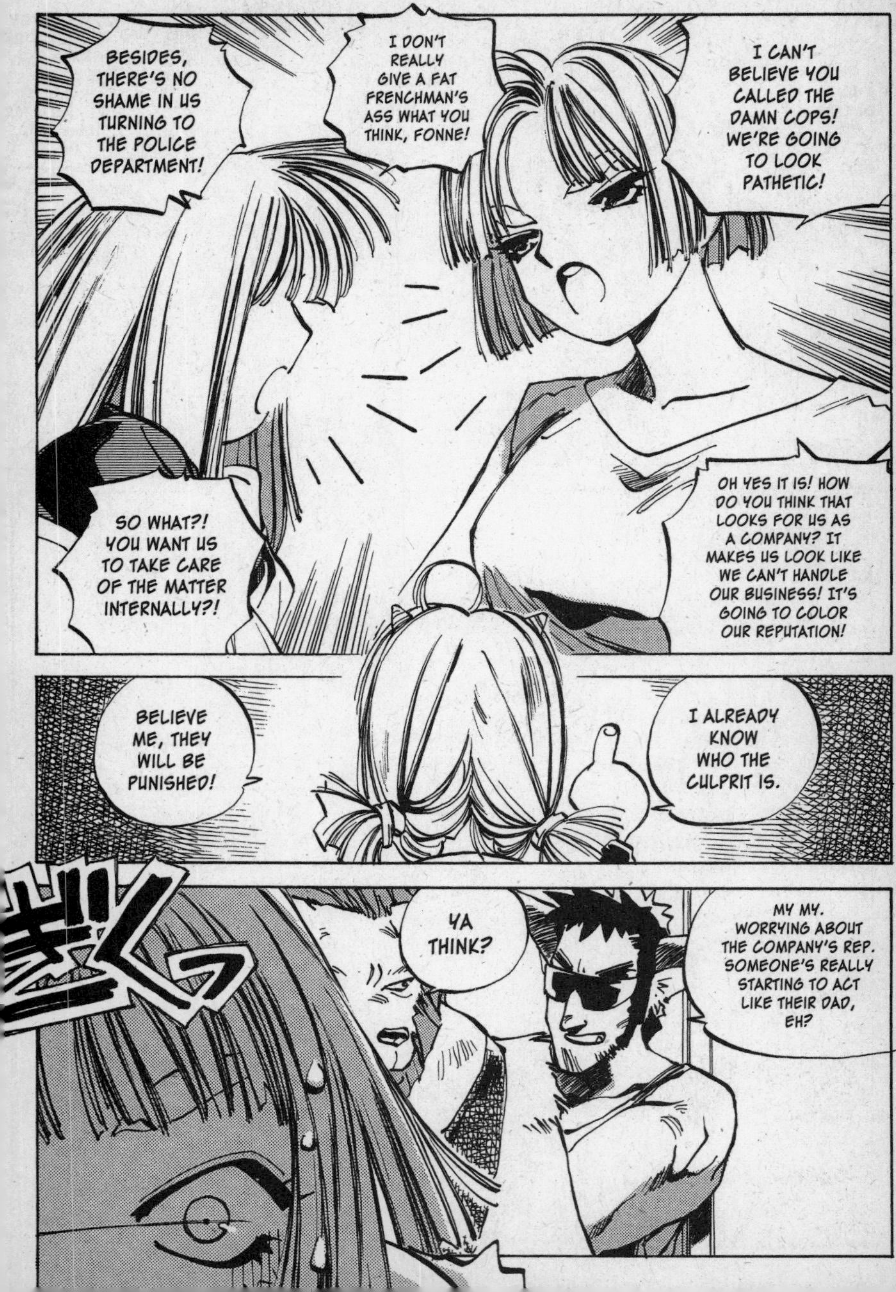
I CAN'T BELIEVE YOU CALLED THE DAMN COPS! WE'RE GOING TO LOOK PATHETIC!
I DON'T REALLY GIVE A FAT FRENCHMAN'S ASS WHAT YOU THINK, FONNE!
BESIDES, THERE'S NO SHAME IN US TURNING TO THE POLICE DEPARTMENT!
OH YES IT IS! HOW DO YOU THINK THAT LOOKS FOR US AS A COMPANY? IT MAKES US LOOK LIKE WE CAN'T HANDLE OUR BUSINESS! IT'S GOING TO COLOR OUR REPUTATION!
SO WHAT?! YOU WANT US TO TAKE CARE OF THE MATTER INTERNALLY?!
I ALREADY KNOW WHO THE CULPRIT IS.
BELIEVE ME, THEY WILL BE PUNISHED!
MY MY. WORRYING ABOUT THE COMPANY'S REP. SOMEONE'S REALLY STARTING TO ACT LIKE THEIR DAD, EH?
YA THINK?

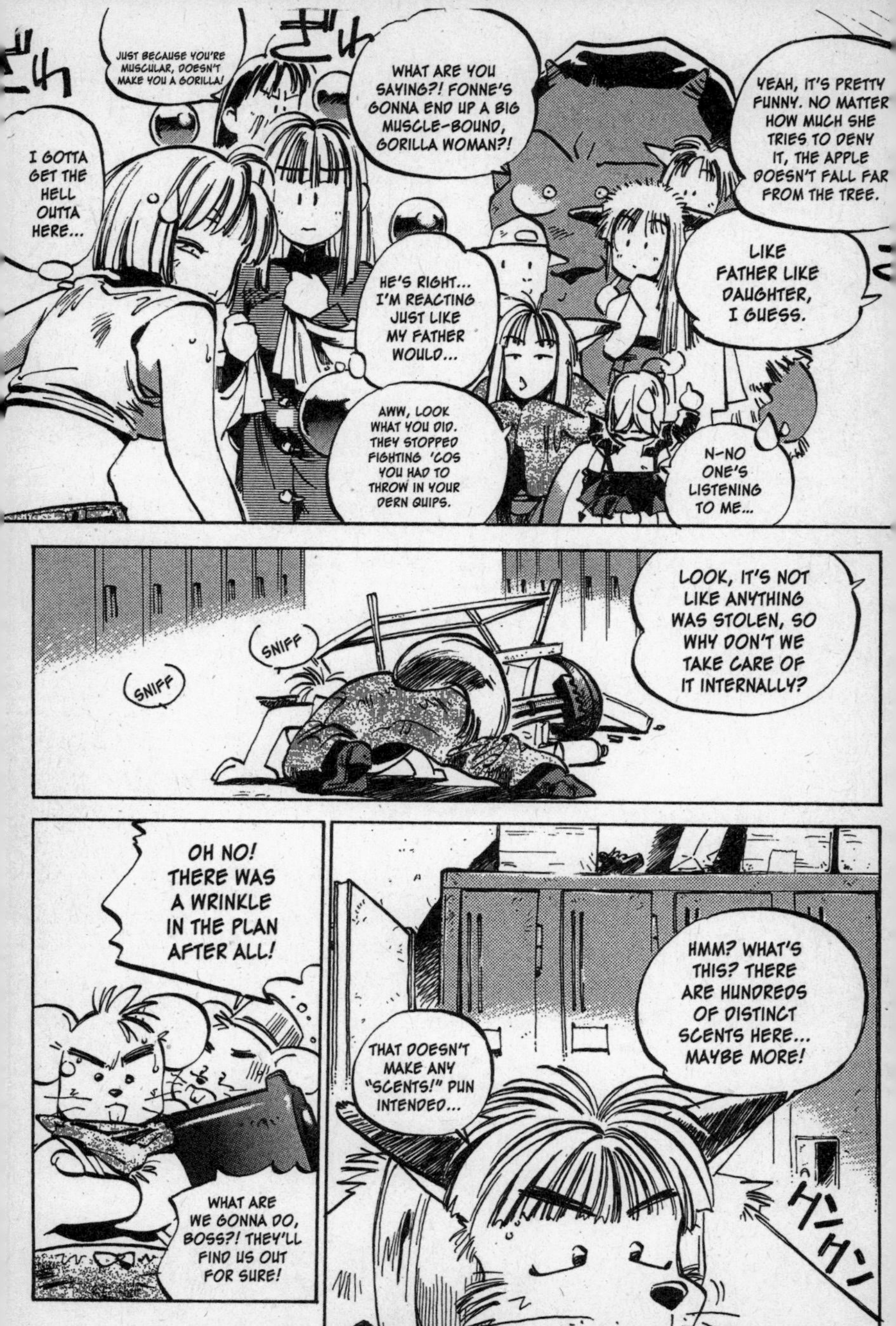
YEAH, IT'S PRETTY FUNNY. NO MATTER HOW MUCH SHE TRIES TO DENY IT, THE APPLE DOESN'T FALL FAR FROM THE TREE.
WHAT ARE YOU SAYING?! FONNE'S GONNA END UP A BIG MUSCLE-BOUND, GORILLA WOMAN?!
ざわ
JUST BECAUSE YOU'RE MUSCULAR, DOESN'T MAKE YOU A GORILLA!
ざわ
I GOTTA GET THE HELL OUTTA HERE...
LIKE FATHER LIKE DAUGHTER, I GUESS.
HE'S RIGHT... I'M REACTING JUST LIKE MY FATHER WOULD...
N-NO ONE'S LISTENING TO ME...
AWW, LOOK WHAT YOU DID. THEY STOPPED FIGHTING 'COS YOU HAD TO THROW IN YOUR DERN QUIPS.
LOOK, IT'S NOT LIKE ANYTHING WAS STOLEN, SO WHY DON'T WE TAKE CARE OF IT INTERNALLY?
SNIFF
SNIFF
HMM? WHAT'S THIS? THERE ARE HUNDREDS OF DISTINCT SCENTS HERE... MAYBE MORE!
クンクン
THAT DOESN'T MAKE ANY "SCENTS!" PUN INTENDED...
OH NO! THERE WAS A WRINKLE IN THE PLAN AFTER ALL!
WHAT ARE WE GONNA DO, BOSS?! THEY'LL FIND US OUT FOR SURE!

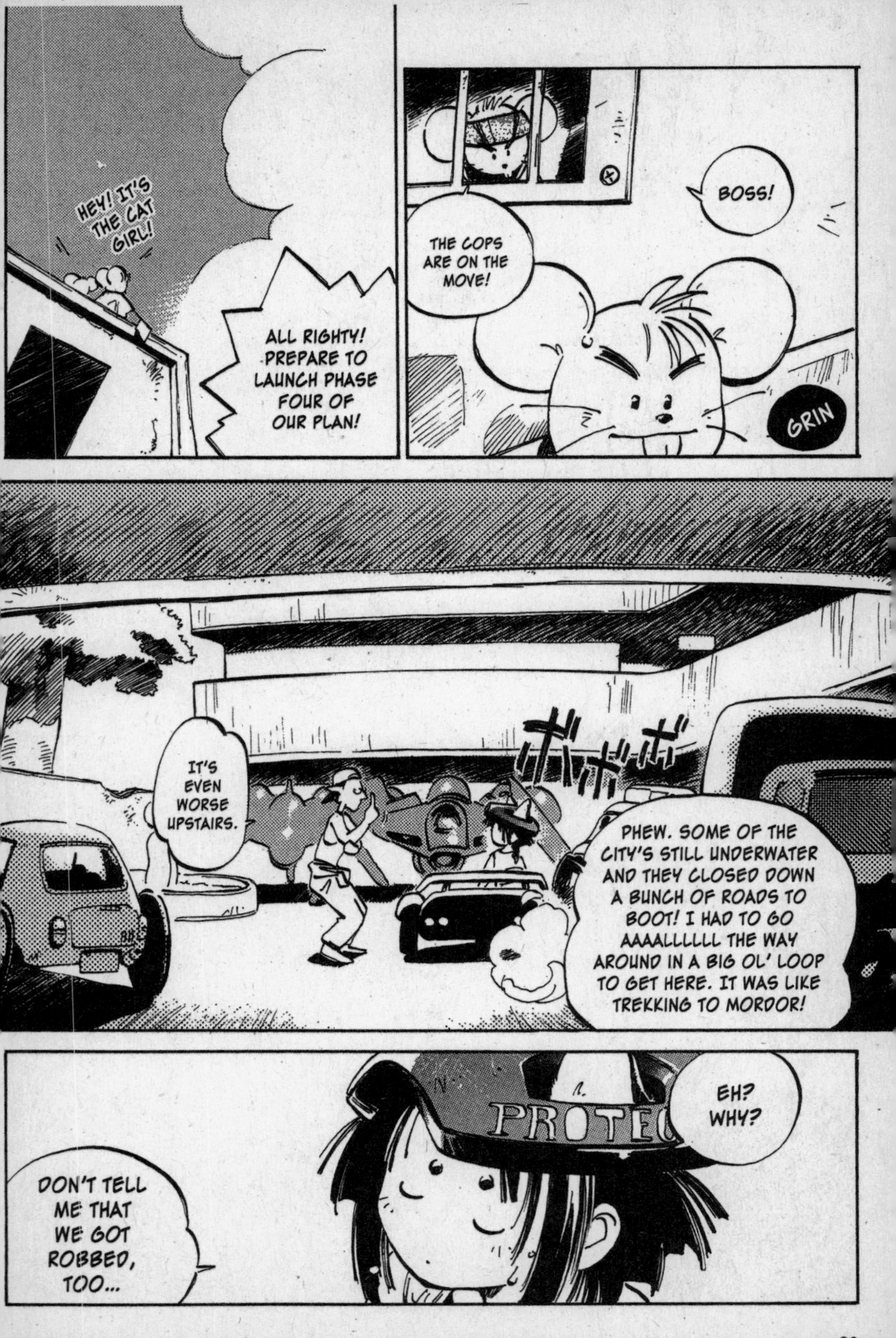
BOSS!
THE COPS ARE ON THE MOVE!
GRIN
HEY! IT'S THE CAT GIRL!
ALL RIGHTY! PREPARE TO LAUNCH PHASE FOUR OF OUR PLAN!
ボボボ
PHEW. SOME OF THE CITY'S STILL UNDERWATER AND THEY CLOSED DOWN A BUNCH OF ROADS TO BOOT! I HAD TO GO AAAALLLLLL THE WAY AROUND IN A BIG OL' LOOP TO GET HERE. IT WAS LIKE TREKKING TO MORDOR!
IT'S EVEN WORSE UPSTAIRS.
EH? WHY?
PROTEC
DON'T TELL ME THAT WE GOT ROBBED, TOO...

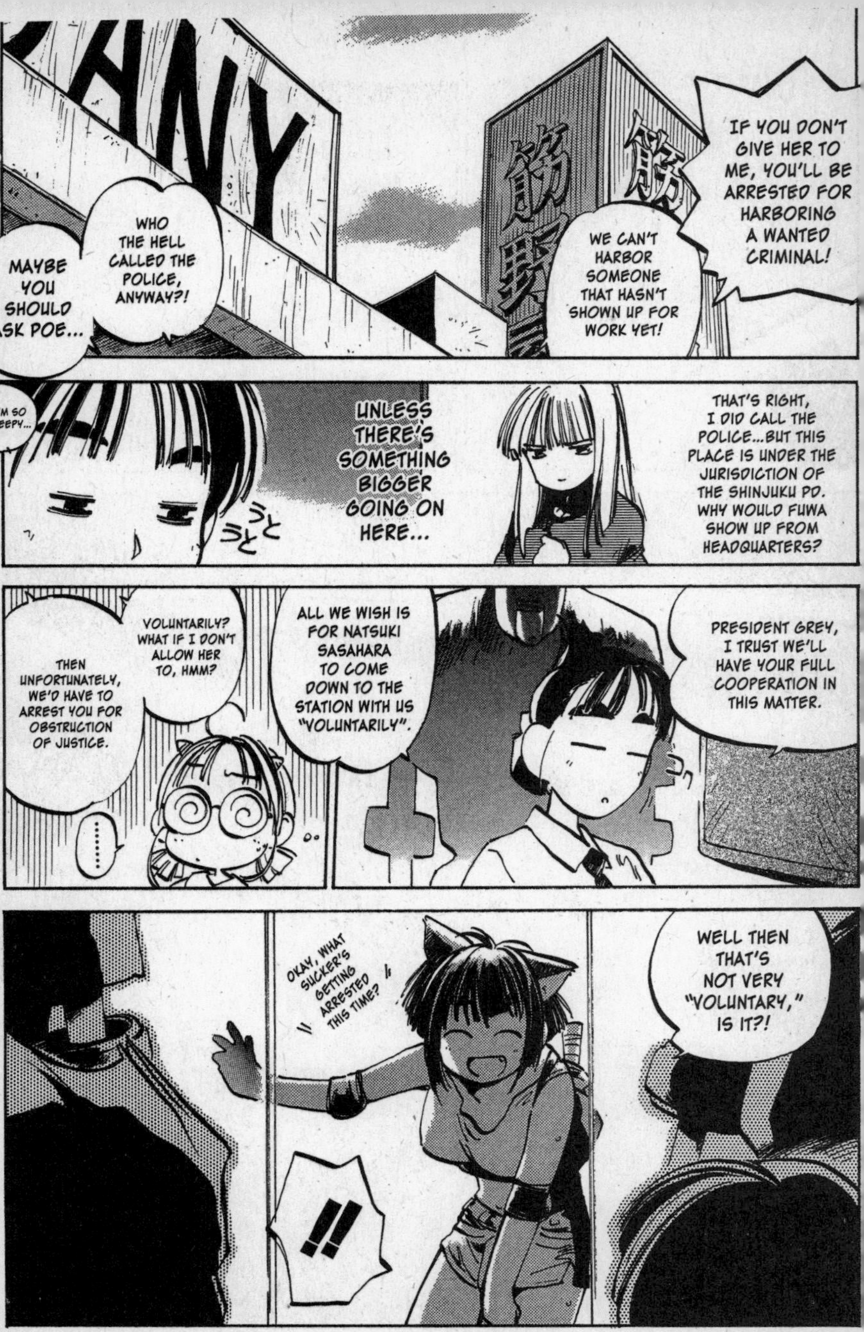
IF YOU DON'T GIVE HER TO ME, YOU'LL BE ARRESTED FOR HARBORING A WANTED CRIMINAL!
WE CAN'T HARBOR SOMEONE THAT HASN'T SHOWN UP FOR WORK YET!
WHO THE HELL CALLED THE POLICE, ANYWAY?!
MAYBE YOU SHOULD ASK POE...
THAT'S RIGHT, I DID CALL THE POLICE...BUT THIS PLACE IS UNDER THE JURISDICTION OF THE SHINJUKU PD. WHY WOULD FUWA SHOW UP FROM HEADQUARTERS?
UNLESS THERE'S SOMETHING BIGGER GOING ON HERE...
うとうと
I'M SO SLEEPY...
PRESIDENT GREY, I TRUST WE'LL HAVE YOUR FULL COOPERATION IN THIS MATTER.
ALL WE WISH IS FOR NATSUKI SASAHARA TO COME DOWN TO THE STATION WITH US "VOLUNTARILY".
VOLUNTARILY? WHAT IF I DON'T ALLOW HER TO, HMM?
THEN UNFORTUNATELY, WE'D HAVE TO ARREST YOU FOR OBSTRUCTION OF JUSTICE.
......
WELL THEN THAT'S NOT VERY "VOLUNTARY," IS IT?!
OKAY, WHAT SUCKER'S GETTING ARRESTED THIS TIME?
!!

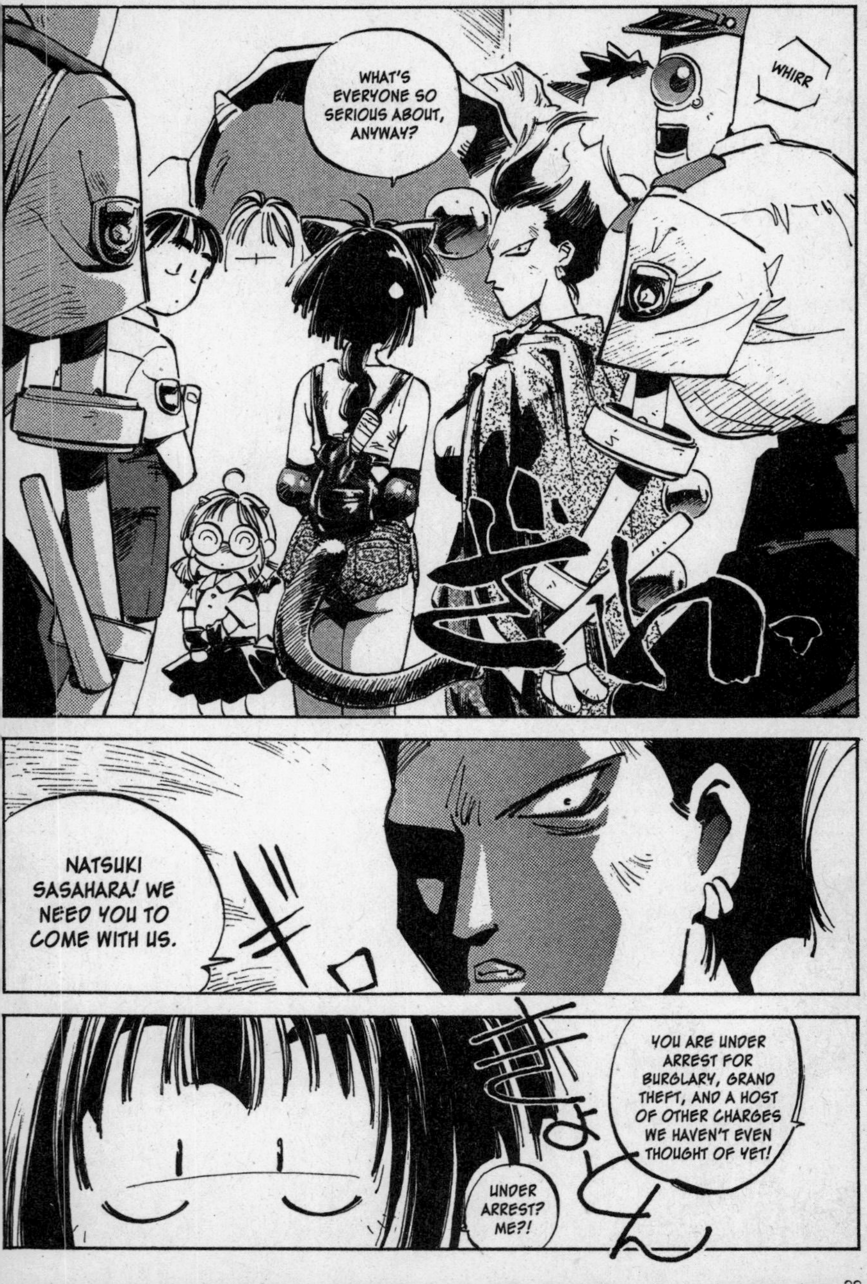
WHIRR
WHAT'S EVERYONE SO SERIOUS ABOUT, ANYWAY?
NATSUKI SASAHARA! WE NEED YOU TO COME WITH US.
YOU ARE UNDER ARREST FOR BURGLARY, GRAND THEFT, AND A HOST OF OTHER CHARGES WE HAVEN'T EVEN THOUGHT OF YET!
UNDER ARREST? ME?!

Report #65
Height of Summer!

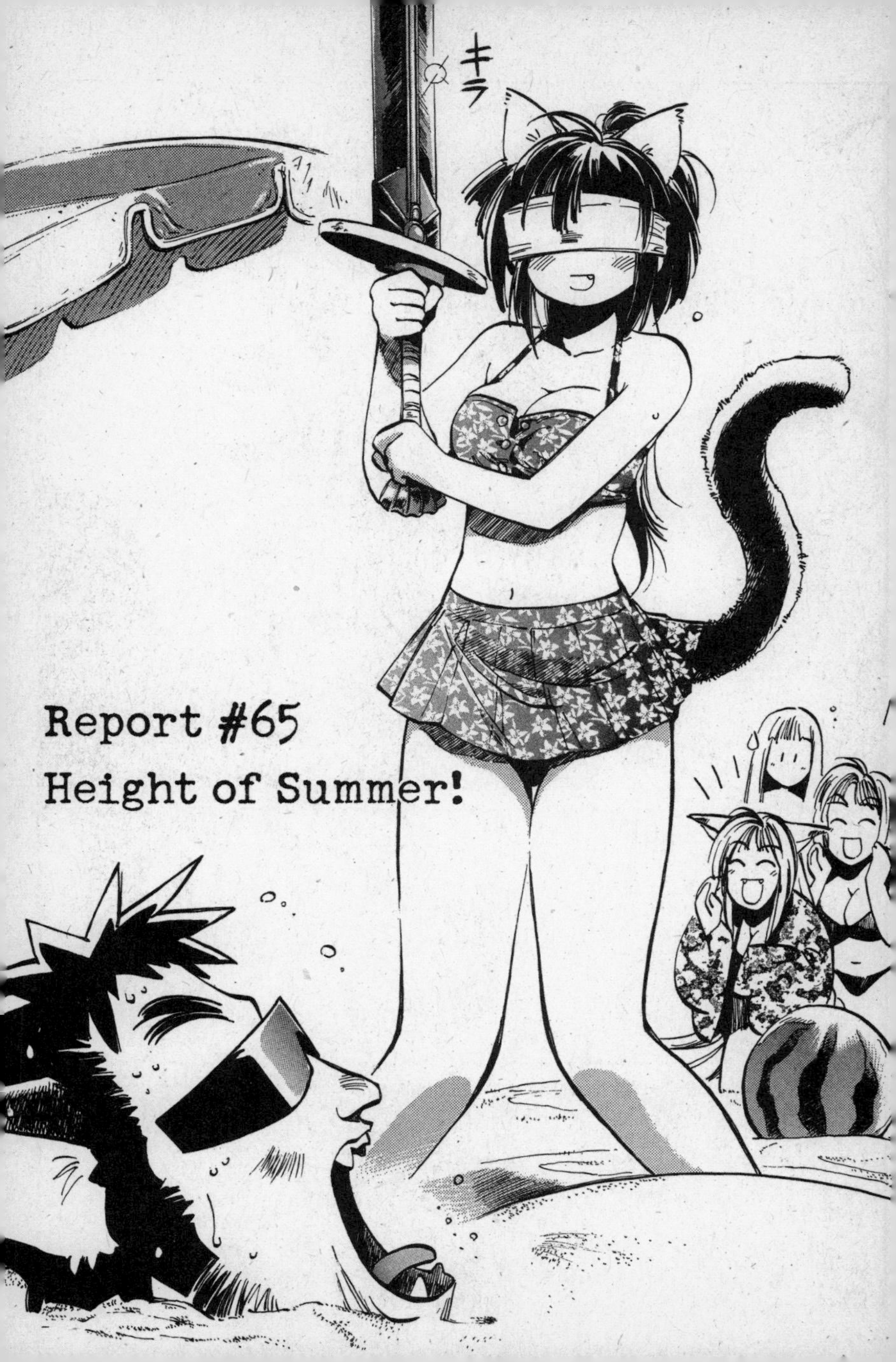
キラ

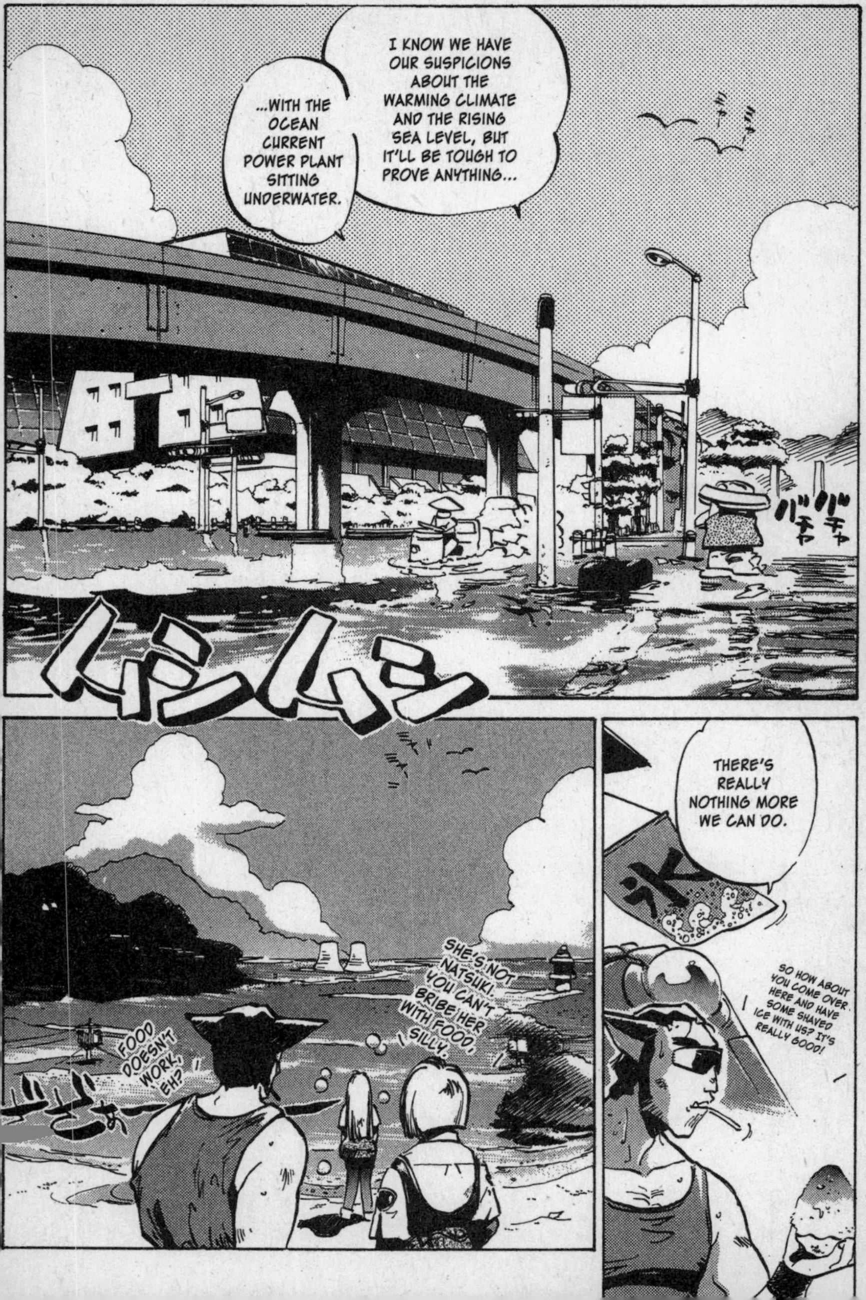
I KNOW WE HAVE OUR SUSPICIONS ABOUT THE WARMING CLIMATE AND THE RISING SEA LEVEL, BUT IT'LL BE TOUGH TO PROVE ANYTHING...
...WITH THE OCEAN CURRENT POWER PLANT SITTING UNDERWATER.
THERE'S REALLY NOTHING MORE WE CAN DO.
SO HOW ABOUT YOU COME OVER HERE AND HAVE SOME SHAVED ICE WITH US? IT'S REALLY GOOD!
SHE'S NOT NATSUKI. YOU CAN'T BRIBE HER WITH FOOD, SILLY.
FOOD DOESN'T WORK, EH?

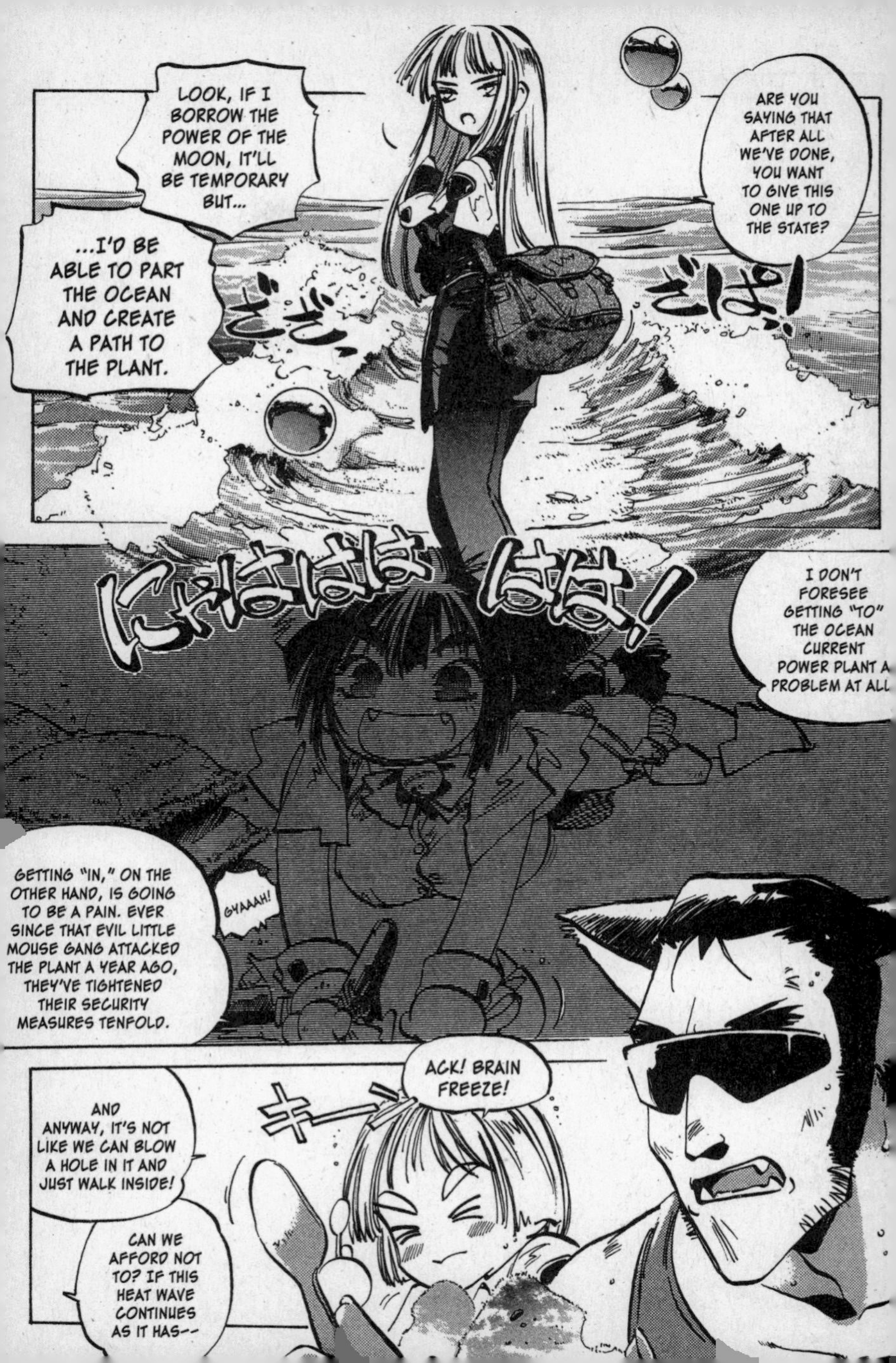
ARE YOU SAYING THAT AFTER ALL WE'VE DONE, YOU WANT TO GIVE THIS ONE UP TO THE STATE?
ざぱ!
LOOK, IF I BORROW THE POWER OF THE MOON, IT'LL BE TEMPORARY BUT...
...I'D BE ABLE TO PART THE OCEAN AND CREATE A PATH TO THE PLANT.
ざざ
I DON'T FORESEE GETTING "TO" THE OCEAN CURRENT POWER PLANT A PROBLEM AT ALL
にゃははは はは!
GETTING "IN," ON THE OTHER HAND, IS GOING TO BE A PAIN. EVER SINCE THAT EVIL LITTLE MOUSE GANG ATTACKED THE PLANT A YEAR AGO, THEY'VE TIGHTENED THEIR SECURITY MEASURES TENFOLD.
GYAAAH!
ACK! BRAIN FREEZE!
キー
AND ANYWAY, IT'S NOT LIKE WE CAN BLOW A HOLE IN IT AND JUST WALK INSIDE!
CAN WE AFFORD NOT TO? IF THIS HEAT WAVE CONTINUES AS IT HAS--

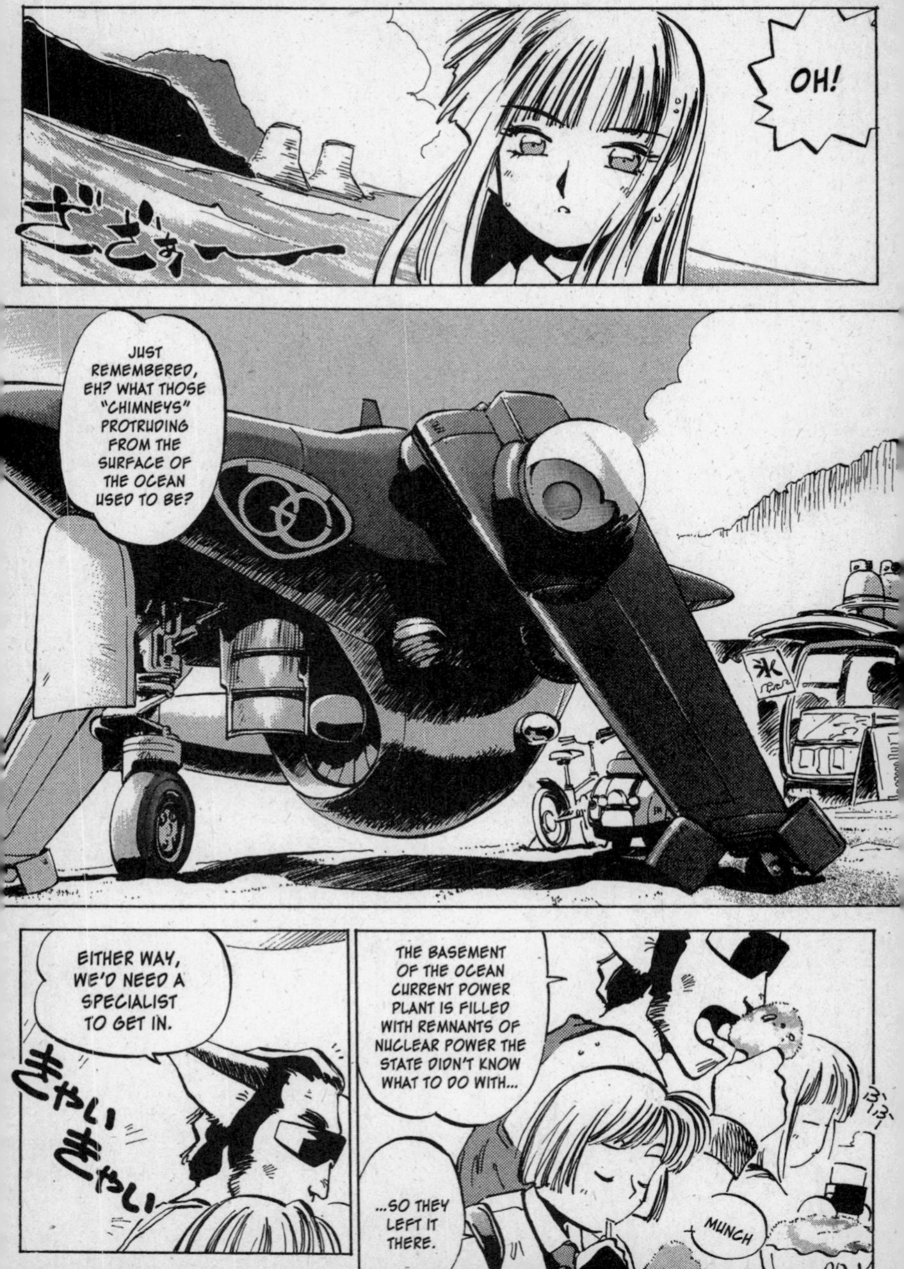
OH!
ざざぁ〜
JUST REMEMBERED, EH? WHAT THOSE "CHIMNEYS" PROTRUDING FROM THE SURFACE OF THE OCEAN USED TO BE?
THE BASEMENT OF THE OCEAN CURRENT POWER PLANT IS FILLED WITH REMNANTS OF NUCLEAR POWER THE STATE DIDN'T KNOW WHAT TO DO WITH...
...SO THEY LEFT IT THERE.
MUNCH
EITHER WAY, WE'D NEED A SPECIALIST TO GET IN.
きゃいきゃい

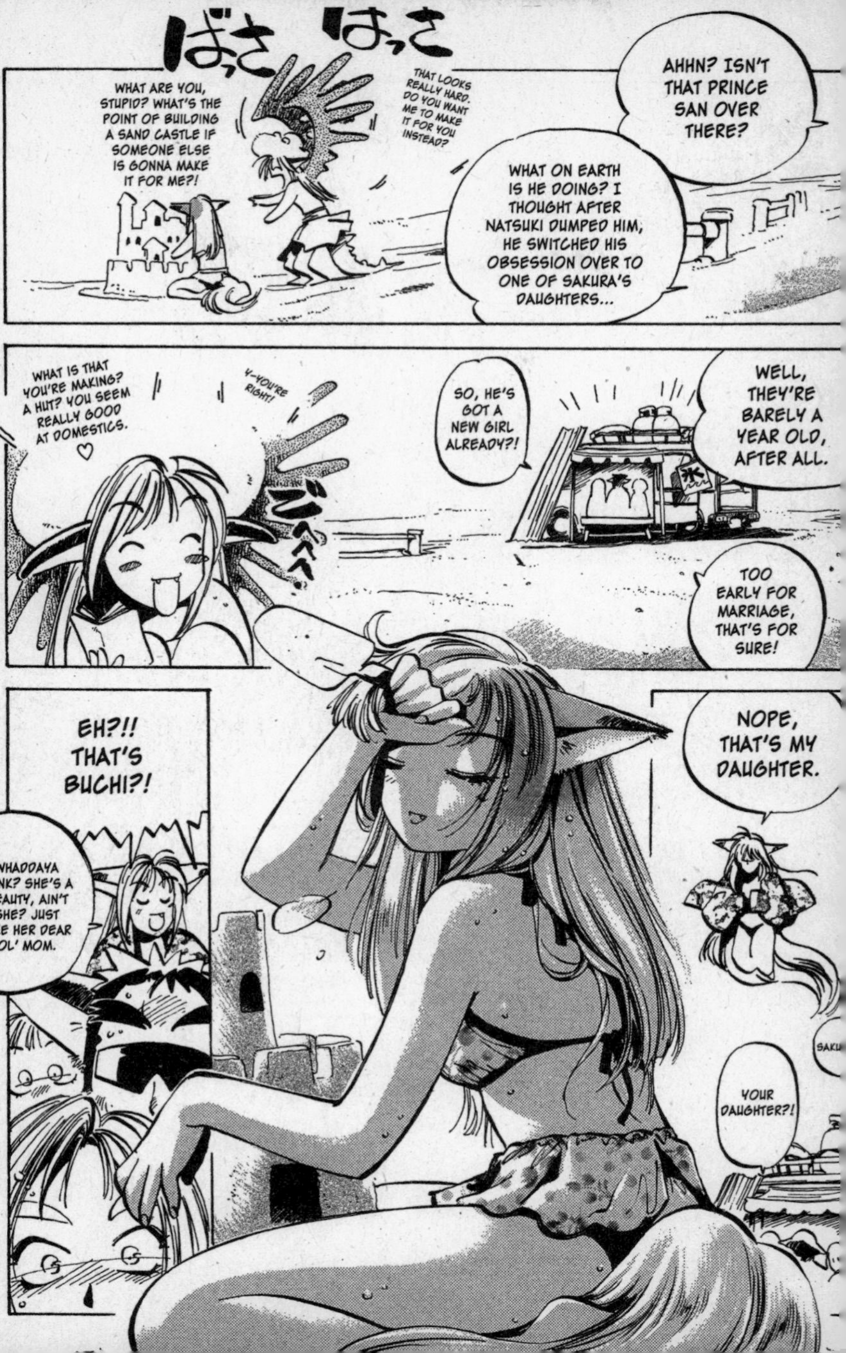
ばっさ はっさ
AHHN? ISN'T THAT PRINCE SAN OVER THERE?
WHAT ON EARTH IS HE DOING? I THOUGHT AFTER NATSUKI DUMPED HIM, HE SWITCHED HIS OBSESSION OVER TO ONE OF SAKURA'S DAUGHTERS...
THAT LOOKS REALLY HARD. DO YOU WANT ME TO MAKE IT FOR YOU INSTEAD?
WHAT ARE YOU, STUPID? WHAT'S THE POINT OF BUILDING A SAND CASTLE IF SOMEONE ELSE IS GONNA MAKE IT FOR ME?!
WELL, THEY'RE BARELY A YEAR OLD, AFTER ALL.
SO, HE'S GOT A NEW GIRL ALREADY?!
TOO EARLY FOR MARRIAGE, THAT'S FOR SURE!
Y-YOU'RE RIGHT!
WHAT IS THAT YOU'RE MAKING? A HUT? YOU SEEM REALLY GOOD AT DOMESTICS. ♡
NOPE, THAT'S MY DAUGHTER.
YOUR DAUGHTER?!
EH?!! THAT'S BUCHI?!
WHADDAYA THINK? SHE'S A BEAUTY, AIN'T SHE? JUST LIKE HER DEAR OL' MOM.

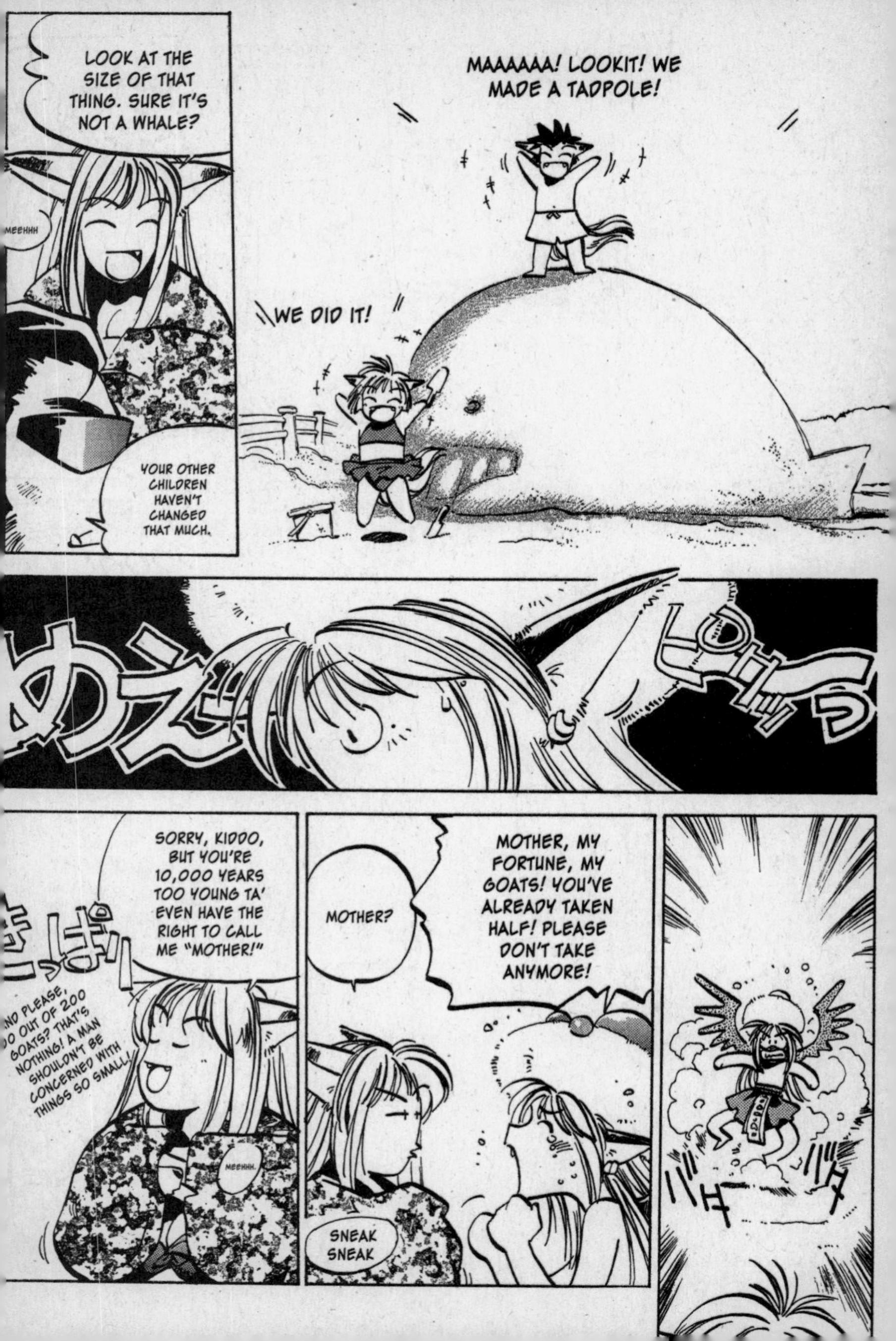
MAAAAAA! LOOKIT! WE MADE A TADPOLE!
WE DID IT!
LOOK AT THE SIZE OF THAT THING. SURE IT'S NOT A WHALE?
MEEHHH
YOUR OTHER CHILDREN HAVEN'T CHANGED THAT MUCH.
MOTHER, MY FORTUNE, MY GOATS! YOU'VE ALREADY TAKEN HALF! PLEASE DON'T TAKE ANYMORE!
MOTHER?
SNEAK SNEAK
SORRY, KIDDO, BUT YOU'RE 10,000 YEARS TOO YOUNG TA' EVEN HAVE THE RIGHT TO CALL ME "MOTHER!"
GOATS? THAT'S NOTHING! A MAN SHOULDN'T BE CONCERNED WITH THINGS SO SMALL!
MEEHHH.

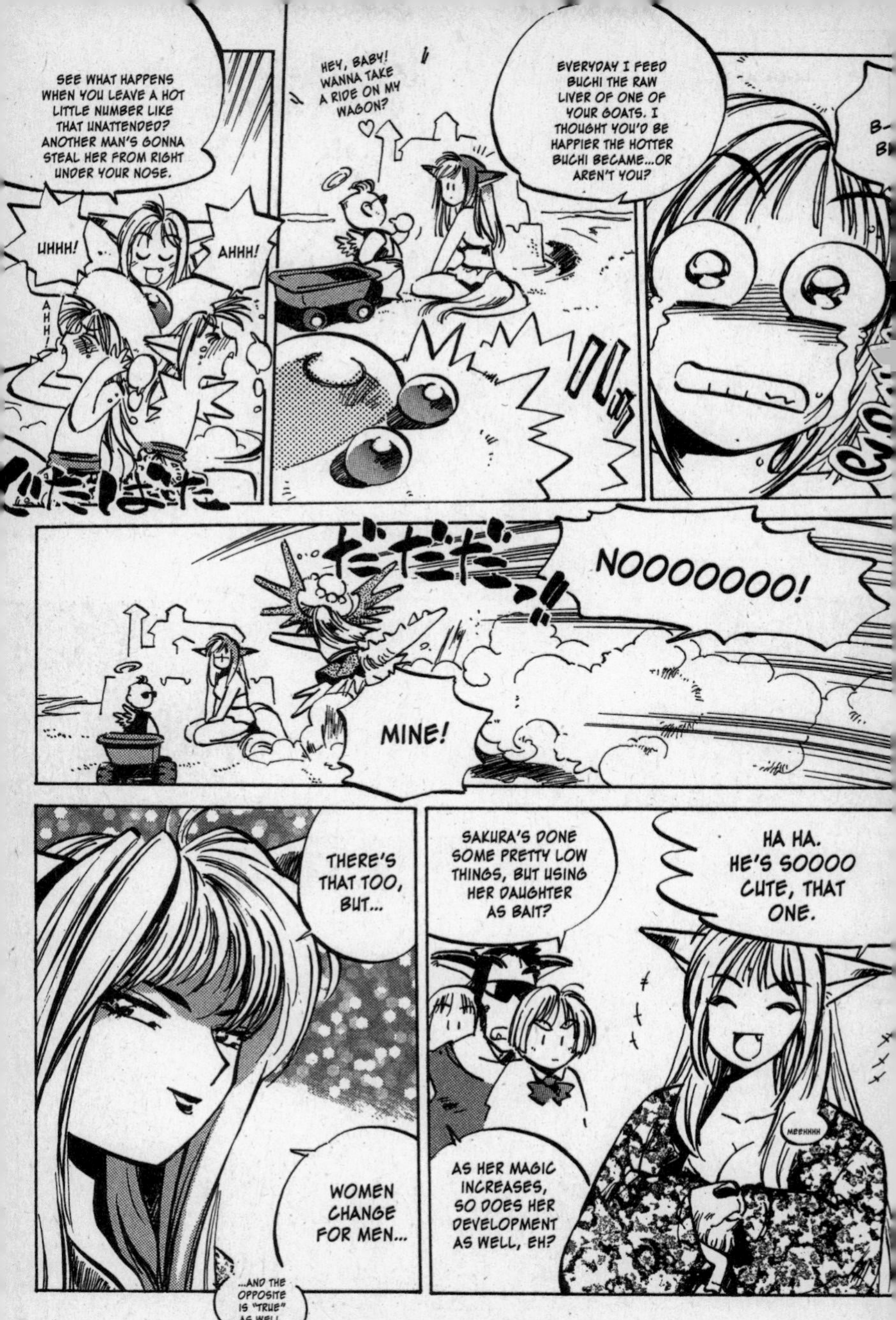
EVERYDAY I FEED BUCHI THE RAW LIVER OF ONE OF YOUR GOATS. I THOUGHT YOU'D BE HAPPIER THE HOTTER BUCHI BECAME...OR AREN'T YOU?
B-
B
HEY, BABY! WANNA TAKE A RIDE ON MY WAGON?
SEE WHAT HAPPENS WHEN YOU LEAVE A HOT LITTLE NUMBER LIKE THAT UNATTENDED? ANOTHER MAN'S GONNA STEAL HER FROM RIGHT UNDER YOUR NOSE.
AHHH!
UHHH!
AHH!
NOOOOOOO!
MINE!
HA HA. HE'S SOOOO CUTE, THAT ONE.
SAKURA'S DONE SOME PRETTY LOW THINGS, BUT USING HER DAUGHTER AS BAIT?
MEEHHHH
AS HER MAGIC INCREASES, SO DOES HER DEVELOPMENT AS WELL, EH?
THERE'S THAT TOO, BUT...
WOMEN CHANGE FOR MEN...
...AND THE OPPOSITE IS "TRUE" AS WELL.

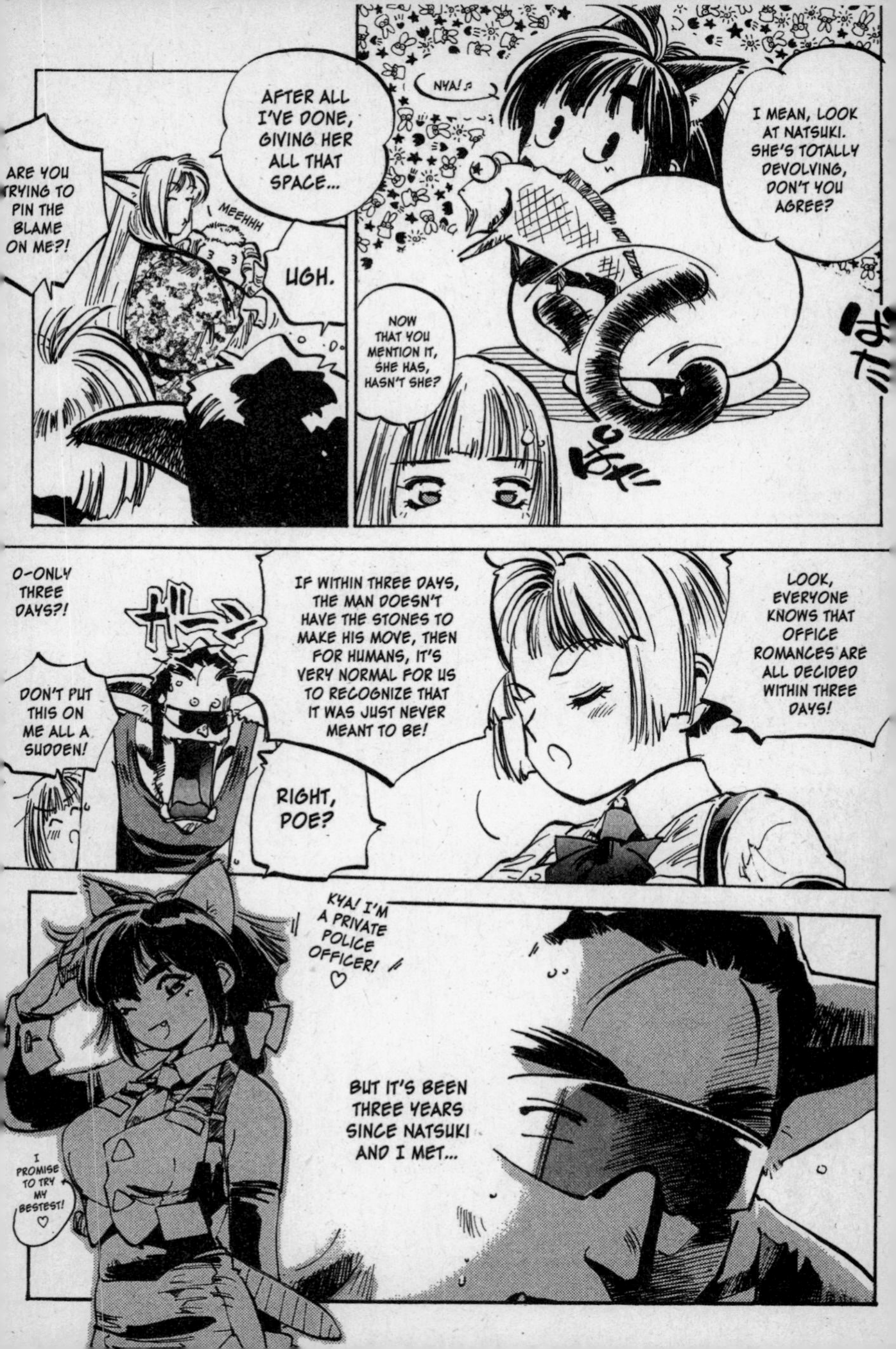
I MEAN, LOOK AT NATSUKI. SHE'S TOTALLY DEVOLVING, DON'T YOU AGREE?
NYA! ♪
NOW THAT YOU MENTION IT, SHE HAS, HASN'T SHE?
AFTER ALL I'VE DONE, GIVING HER ALL THAT SPACE...
ARE YOU TRYING TO PIN THE BLAME ON ME?!
MEEHHH
UGH.
LOOK, EVERYONE KNOWS THAT OFFICE ROMANCES ARE ALL DECIDED WITHIN THREE DAYS!
IF WITHIN THREE DAYS, THE MAN DOESN'T HAVE THE STONES TO MAKE HIS MOVE, THEN FOR HUMANS, IT'S VERY NORMAL FOR US TO RECOGNIZE THAT IT WAS JUST NEVER MEANT TO BE!
RIGHT, POE?
O-ONLY THREE DAYS?!
DON'T PUT THIS ON ME ALL A SUDDEN!
BUT IT'S BEEN THREE YEARS SINCE NATSUKI AND I MET...
KYA! I'M A PRIVATE POLICE OFFICER! ♡
I PROMISE TO TRY MY BESTEST! ♡

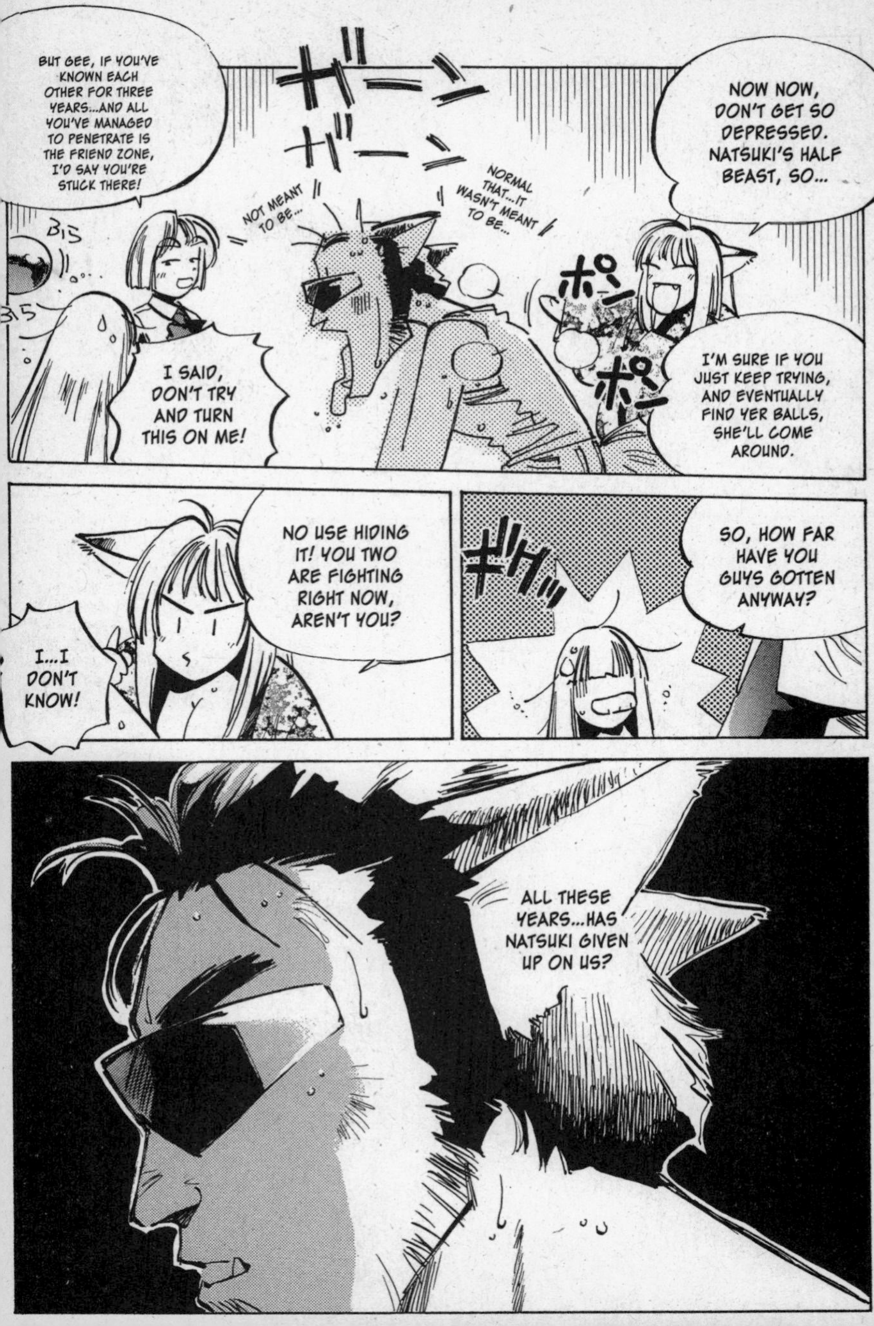
NOW NOW, DON'T GET SO DEPRESSED. NATSUKI'S HALF BEAST, SO...
ガーン
ガーン
NORMAL THAT...IT WASN'T MEANT TO BE...
NOT MEANT TO BE...
BUT GEE, IF YOU'VE KNOWN EACH OTHER FOR THREE YEARS...AND ALL YOU'VE MANAGED TO PENETRATE IS THE FRIEND ZONE, I'D SAY YOU'RE STUCK THERE!
ポーン
ポーン
I'M SURE IF YOU JUST KEEP TRYING, AND EVENTUALLY FIND YER BALLS, SHE'LL COME AROUND.
I SAID, DON'T TRY AND TURN THIS ON ME!
SO, HOW FAR HAVE YOU GUYS GOTTEN ANYWAY?
ギクッ
NO USE HIDING IT! YOU TWO ARE FIGHTING RIGHT NOW, AREN'T YOU?
I...I DON'T KNOW!
ALL THESE YEARS...HAS NATSUKI GIVEN UP ON US?

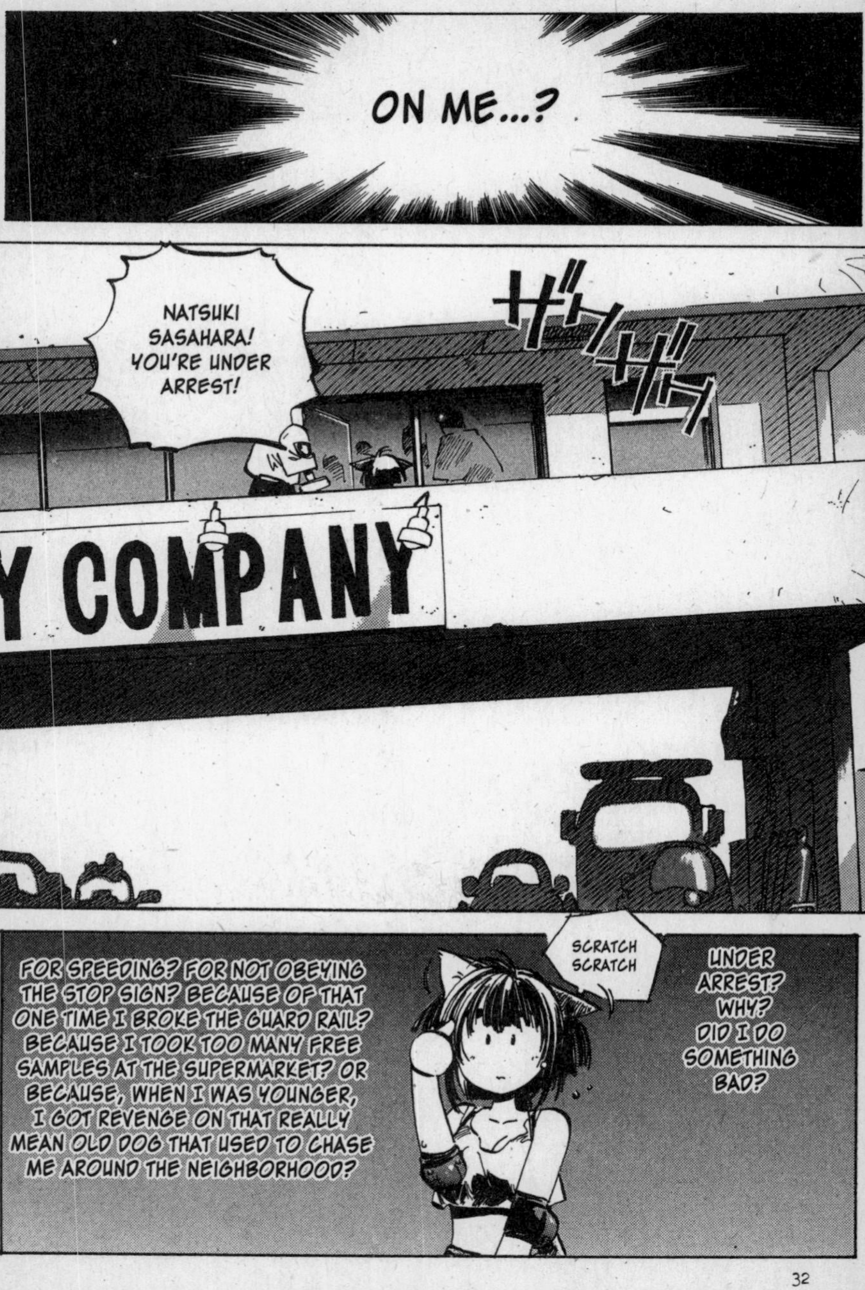
ON ME...?
ザワザワ
NATSUKI SASAHARA! YOU'RE UNDER ARREST!
Y COMPANY
UNDER ARREST? WHY? DID I DO SOMETHING BAD?
SCRATCH SCRATCH
FOR SPEEDING? FOR NOT OBEYING THE STOP SIGN? BECAUSE OF THAT ONE TIME I BROKE THE GUARD RAIL? BECAUSE I TOOK TOO MANY FREE SAMPLES AT THE SUPERMARKET? OR BECAUSE, WHEN I WAS YOUNGER, I GOT REVENGE ON THAT REALLY MEAN OLD DOG THAT USED TO CHASE ME AROUND THE NEIGHBORHOOD?

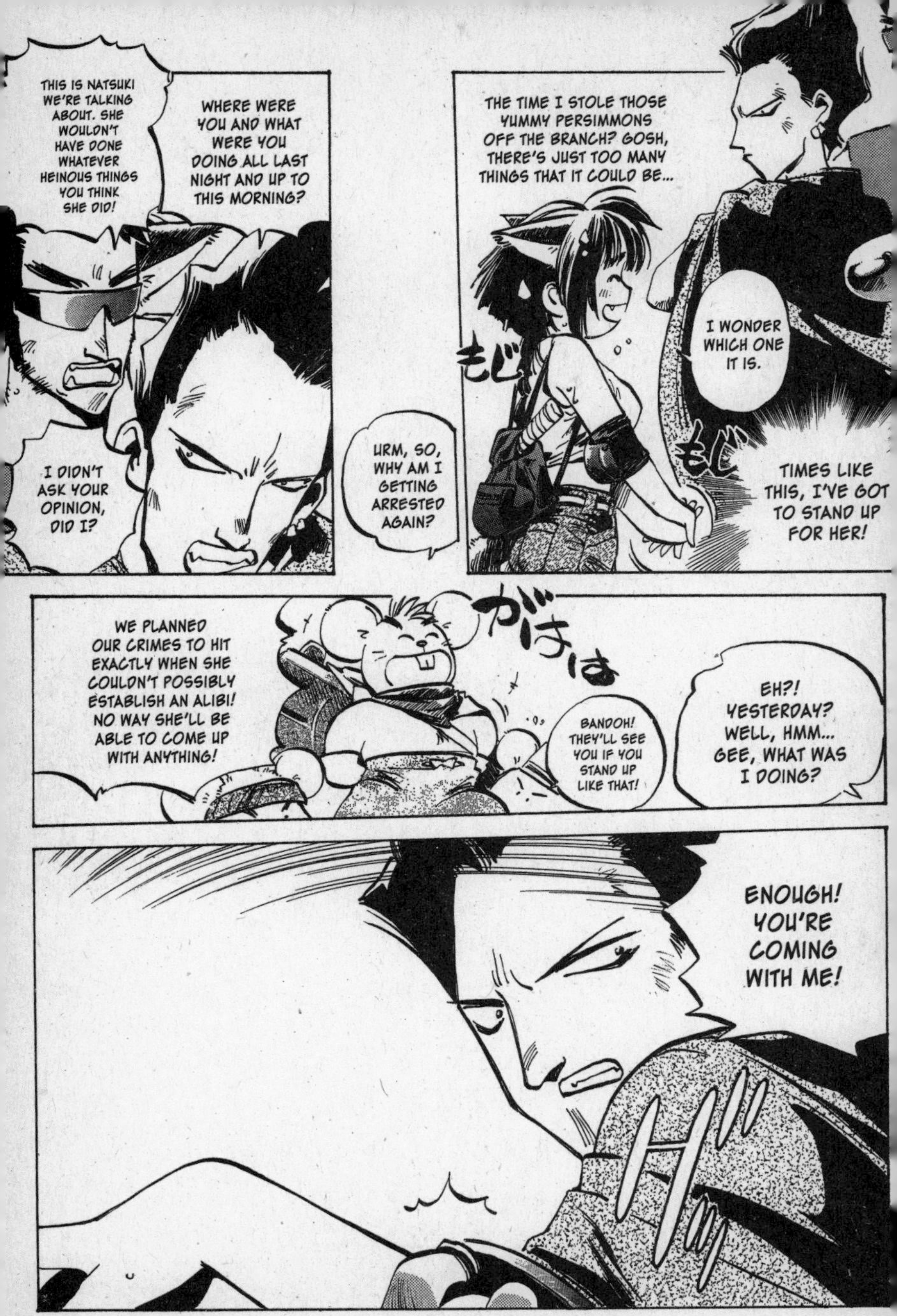
THE TIME I STOLE THOSE YUMMY PERSIMMONS OFF THE BRANCH? GOSH, THERE'S JUST TOO MANY THINGS THAT IT COULD BE...
I WONDER WHICH ONE IT IS.
もじ
もじ
TIMES LIKE THIS, I'VE GOT TO STAND UP FOR HER!
URM, SO, WHY AM I GETTING ARRESTED AGAIN?
WHERE WERE YOU AND WHAT WERE YOU DOING ALL LAST NIGHT AND UP TO THIS MORNING?
THIS IS NATSUKI WE'RE TALKING ABOUT. SHE WOULDN'T HAVE DONE WHATEVER HEINOUS THINGS YOU THINK SHE DID!
I DIDN'T ASK YOUR OPINION, DID I?
EH?! YESTERDAY? WELL, HMM... GEE, WHAT WAS I DOING?
BANDOH! THEY'LL SEE YOU IF YOU STAND UP LIKE THAT!
WE PLANNED OUR CRIMES TO HIT EXACTLY WHEN SHE COULDN'T POSSIBLY ESTABLISH AN ALIBI! NO WAY SHE'LL BE ABLE TO COME UP WITH ANYTHING!
ENOUGH! YOU'RE COMING WITH ME!

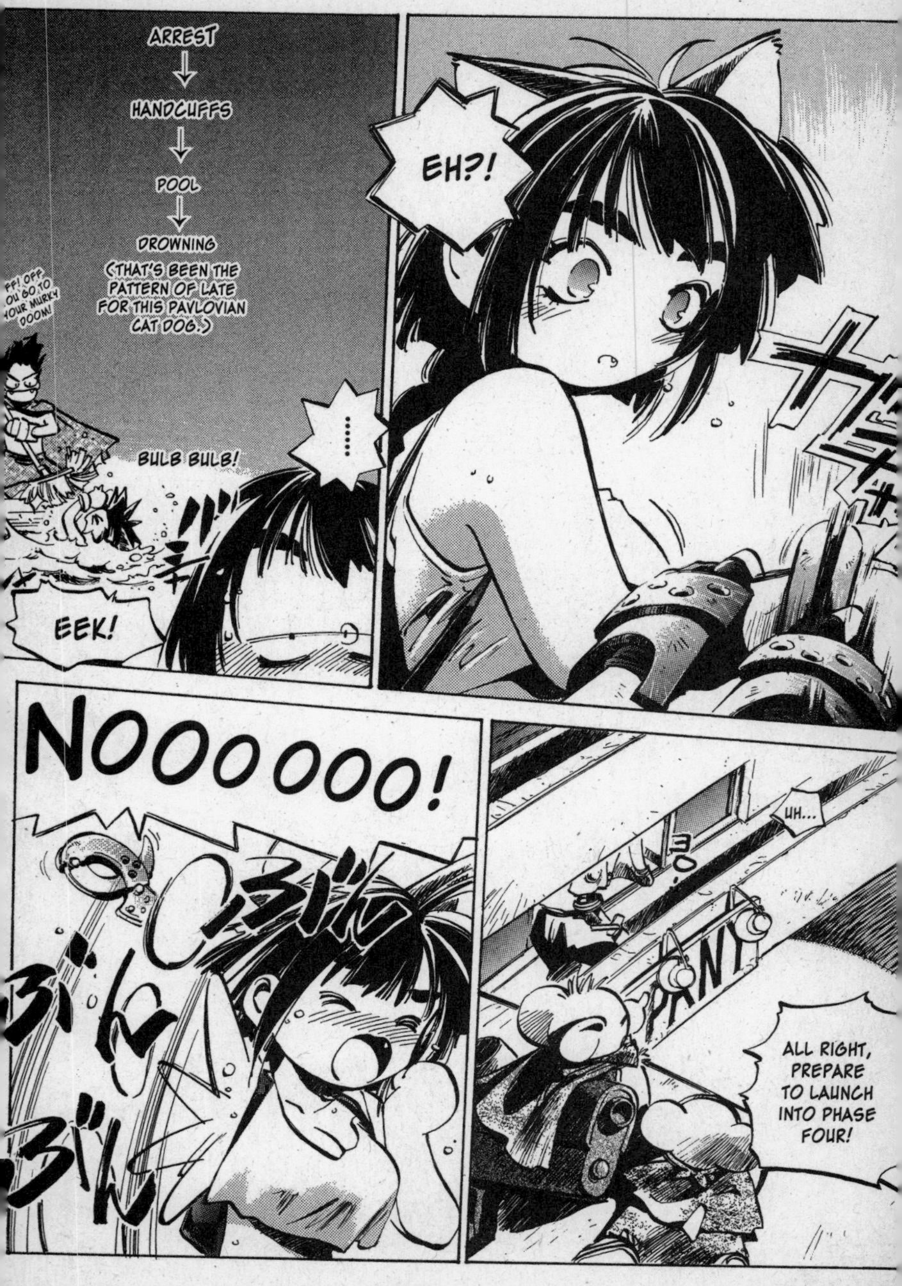

EH?!
ARREST
HANDCUFFS
POOL
DROWNING
(THAT'S BEEN THE PATTERN OF LATE FOR THIS PAVLOVIAN CAT DOG.)
FF! OFF OU GO TO OUR MURKY DOOM!
......
BULB BULB!
EEK!
UH...
PANT
ALL RIGHT, PREPARE TO LAUNCH INTO PHASE FOUR!
NOOOOOOO!

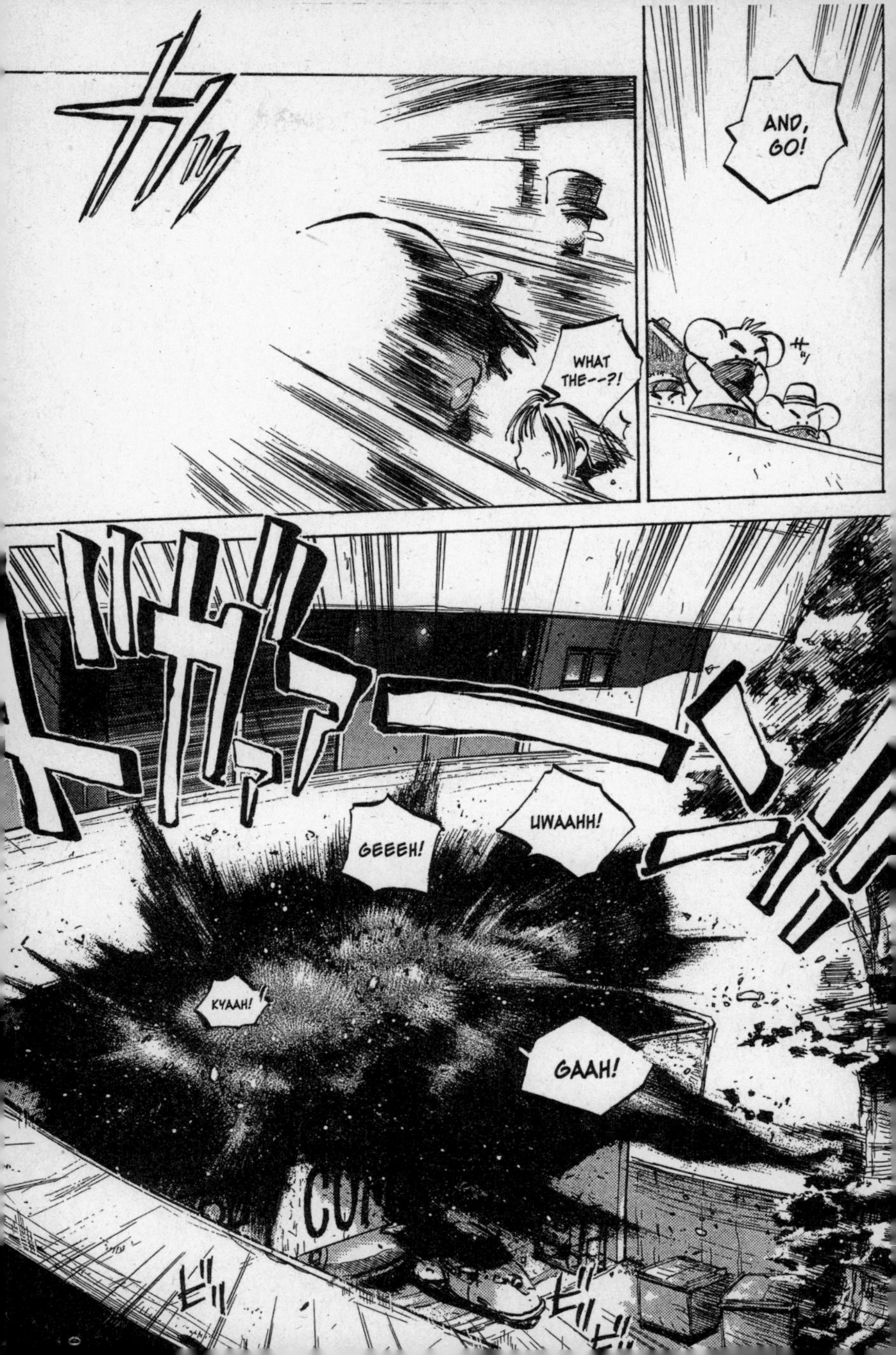
AND, GO!
WHAT THE--?!
UWAAHH!
GEEEH!
GAAH!
KYAAH!

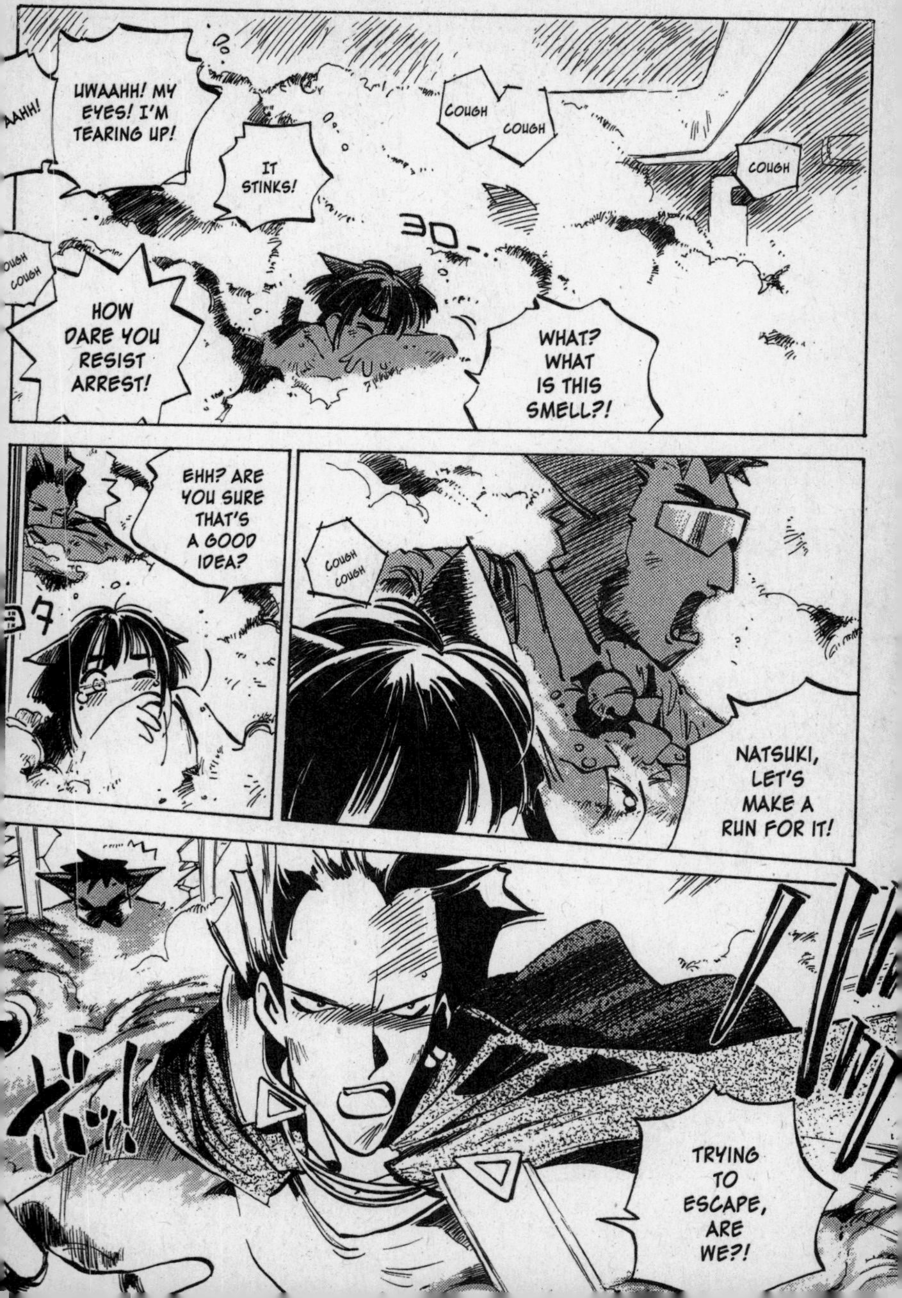
COUGH
COUGH COUGH
WHAT? WHAT IS THIS SMELL?!
IT STINKS!
UWAAHH! MY EYES! I'M TEARING UP!
AAHH!
COUGH COUGH
HOW DARE YOU RESIST ARREST!
COUGH COUGH
NATSUKI, LET'S MAKE A RUN FOR IT!
EHH? ARE YOU SURE THAT'S A GOOD IDEA?
TRYING TO ESCAPE, ARE WE?!

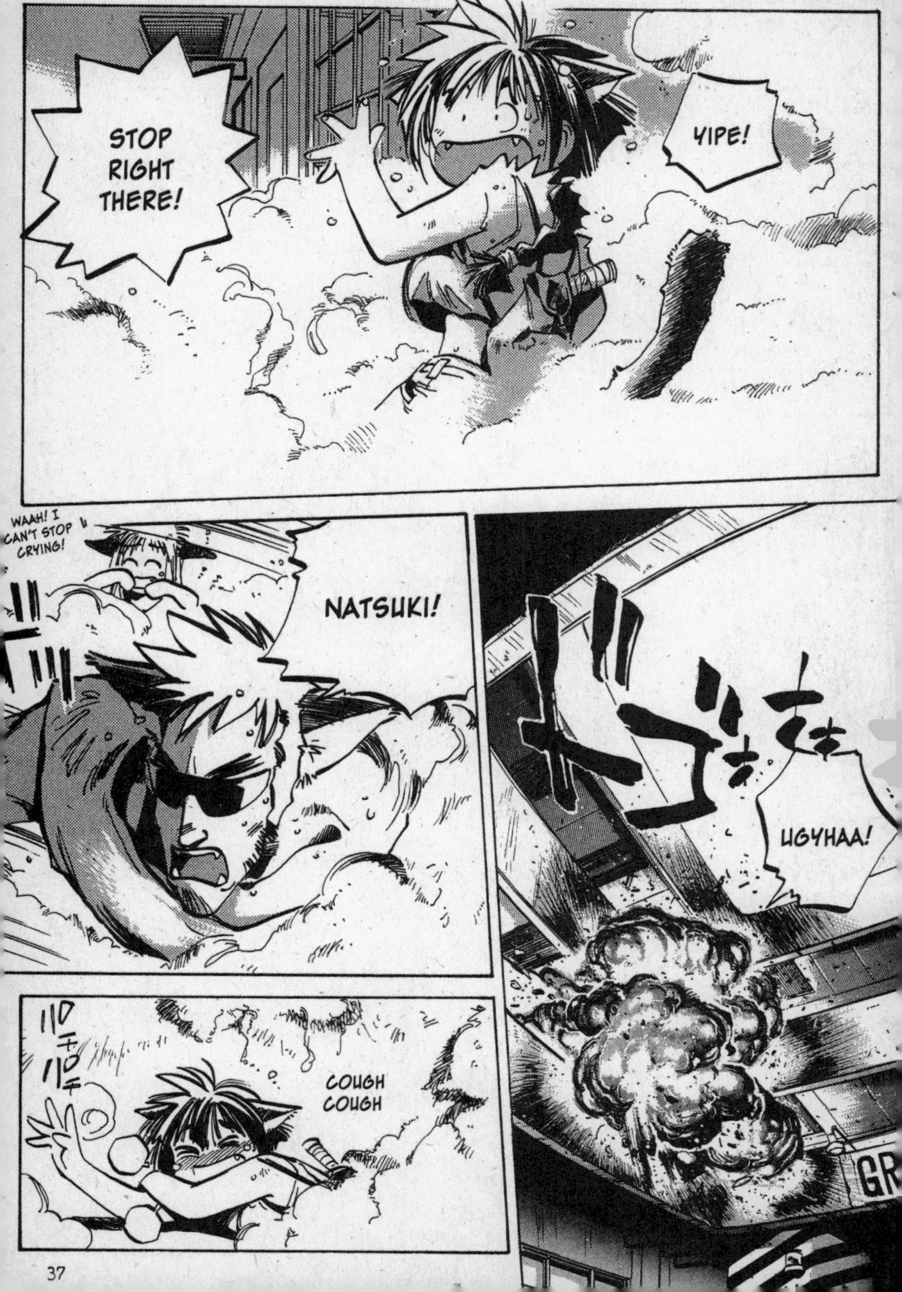
YIPE!
STOP RIGHT THERE!
UGYHAA!
GR
WAAH! I CAN'T STOP CRYING!
NATSUKI!
COUGH COUGH

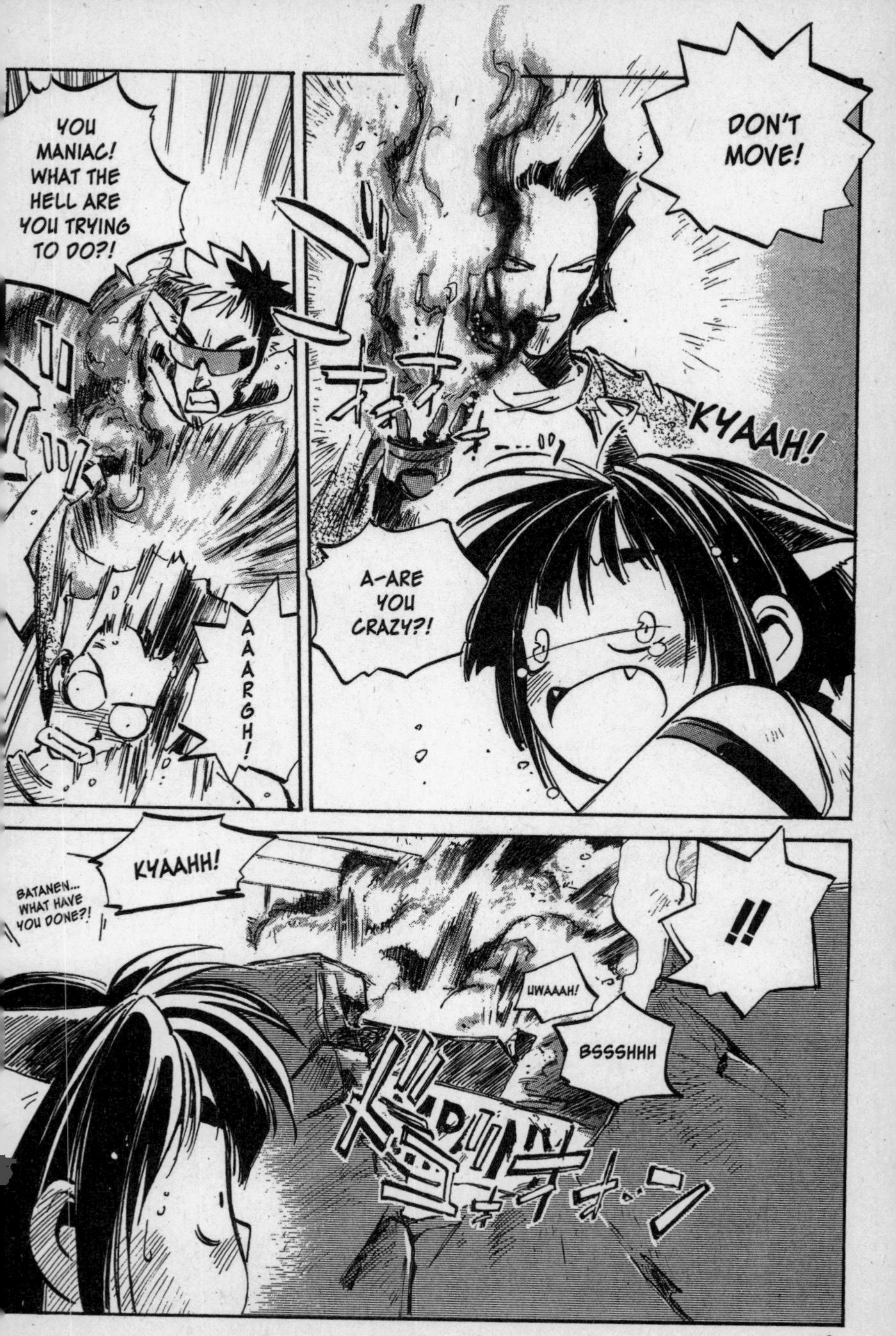
DON'T MOVE!
KYAAH!
A-ARE YOU CRAZY?!
YOU MANIAC! WHAT THE HELL ARE YOU TRYING TO DO?!
AAARGH!
!!
UWAAAH!
BSSSHHH
KYAAHH!
BATANEN... WHAT HAVE YOU DONE?!

HYPER POLICE™
ハイパーポリス

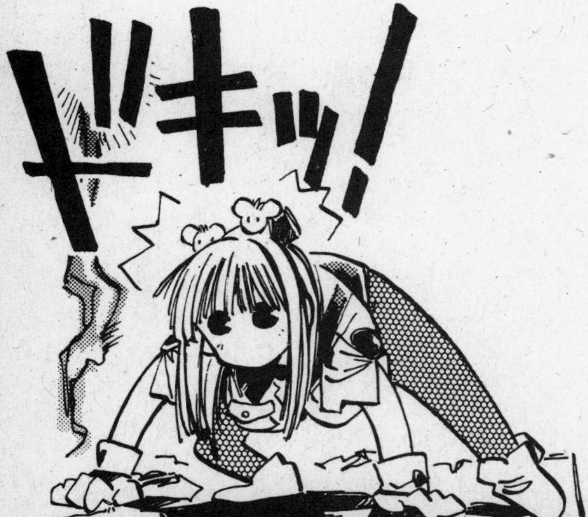
ドキッ!

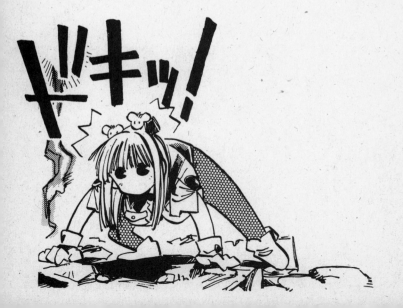

HYPER POLICE™

ハイパーポリス

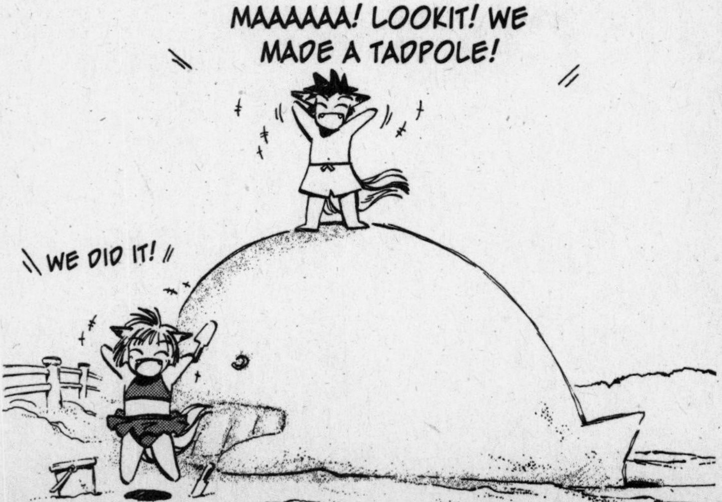
MAAAAAA! LOOKIT! WE MADE A TADPOLE!
WE DID IT!

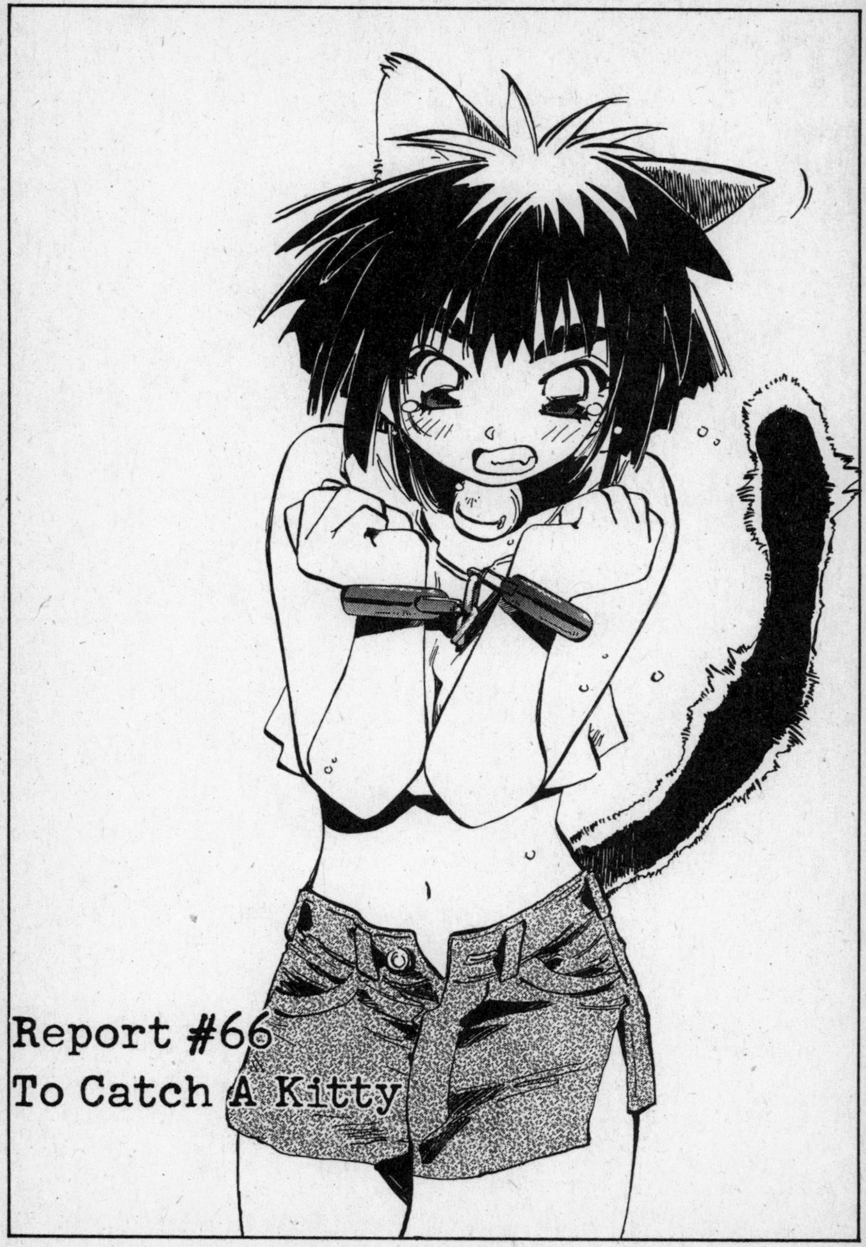
Report #66
To Catch A Kitty

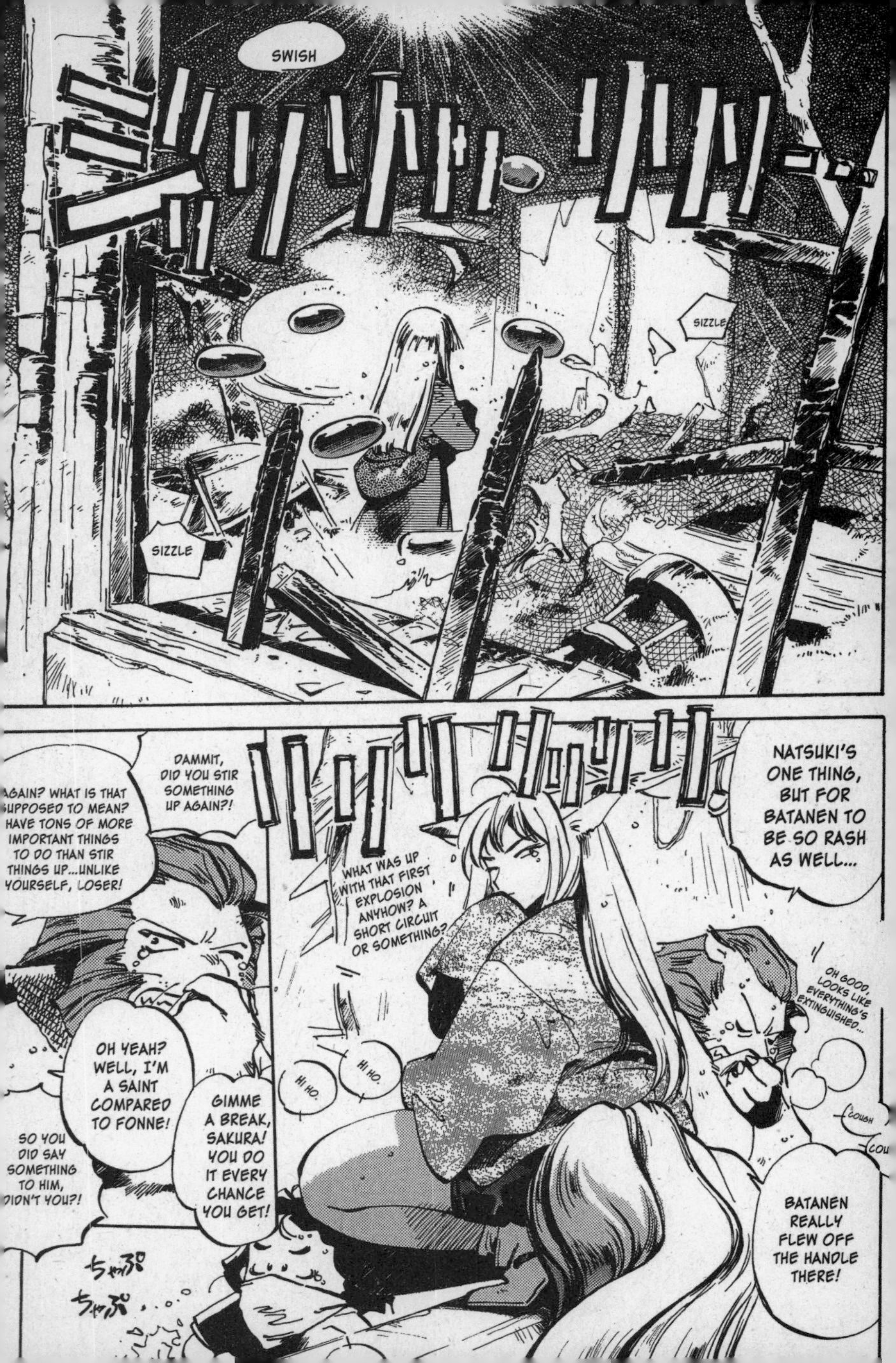
SWISH
SIZZLE
SIZZLE
NATSUKI'S ONE THING, BUT FOR BATANEN TO BE SO RASH AS WELL...
WHAT WAS UP WITH THAT FIRST EXPLOSION ANYHOW? A SHORT CIRCUIT OR SOMETHING?
OH GOOD, LOOKS LIKE EVERYTHING'S EXTINGUISHED...
COUGH
COU
HI HO.
HI HO.
BATANEN REALLY FLEW OFF THE HANDLE THERE!
DAMMIT, DID YOU STIR SOMETHING UP AGAIN?!
AGAIN? WHAT IS THAT UPPOSED TO MEAN? HAVE TONS OF MORE IMPORTANT THINGS TO DO THAN STIR THINGS UP...UNLIKE YOURSELF, LOSER!
OH YEAH? WELL, I'M A SAINT COMPARED TO FONNE!
GIMME A BREAK, SAKURA! YOU DO IT EVERY CHANCE YOU GET!
SO YOU DID SAY SOMETHING TO HIM, IDN'T YOU?!
ちゃぷ
ちゃぷ...

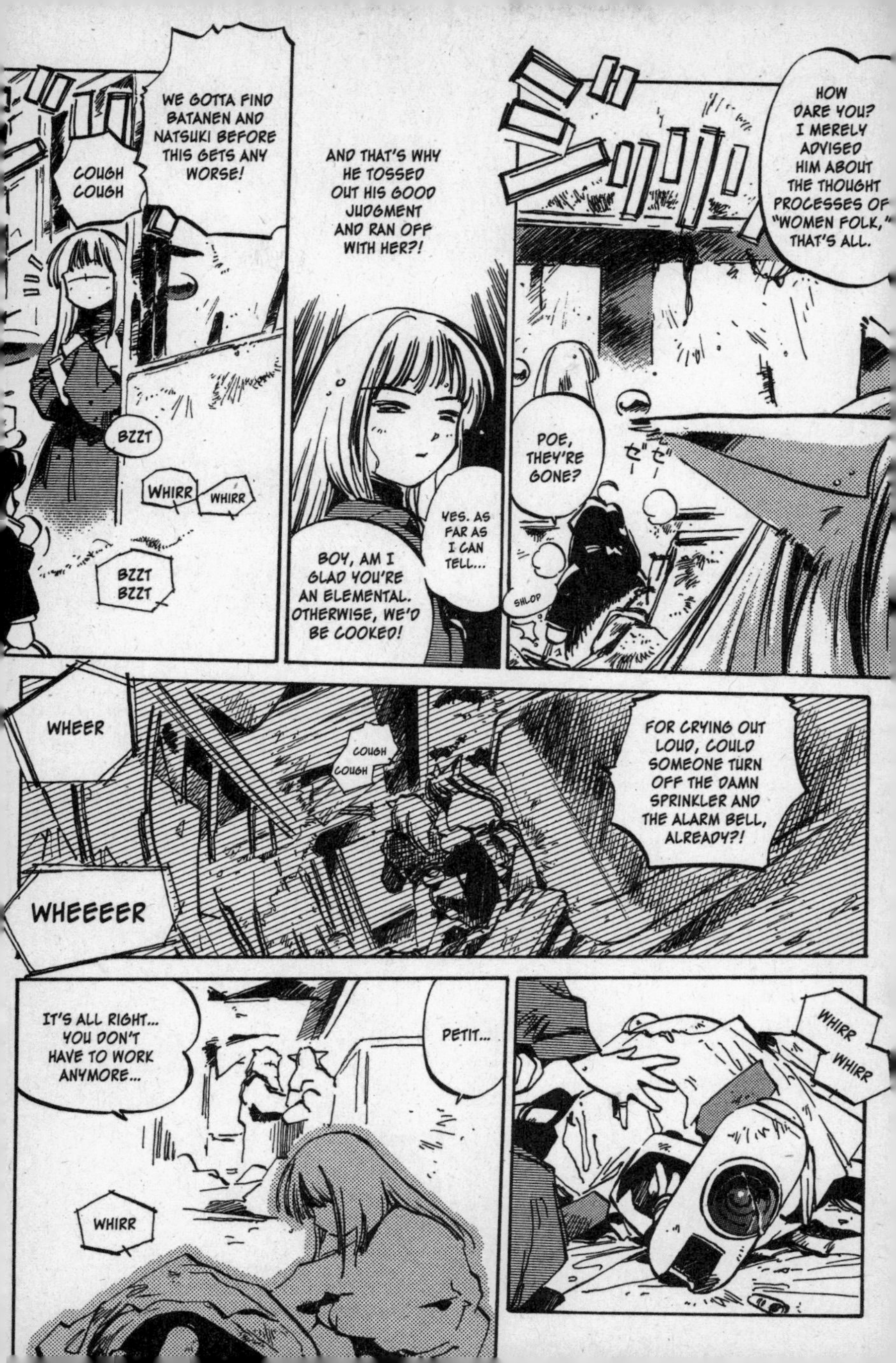
HOW DARE YOU? I MERELY ADVISED HIM ABOUT THE THOUGHT PROCESSES OF "WOMEN FOLK," THAT'S ALL.
POE, THEY'RE GONE?
SHLOP
AND THAT'S WHY HE TOSSED OUT HIS GOOD JUDGMENT AND RAN OFF WITH HER?!
YES. AS FAR AS I CAN TELL...
BOY, AM I GLAD YOU'RE AN ELEMENTAL. OTHERWISE, WE'D BE COOKED!
WE GOTTA FIND BATANEN AND NATSUKI BEFORE THIS GETS ANY WORSE!
COUGH COUGH
BZZT
WHIRR
WHIRR
BZZT BZZT
FOR CRYING OUT LOUD, COULD SOMEONE TURN OFF THE DAMN SPRINKLER AND THE ALARM BELL, ALREADY?!
COUGH
COUGH
WHEER
WHEEEER
WHIRR
WHIRR
PETIT...
IT'S ALL RIGHT... YOU DON'T HAVE TO WORK ANYMORE...
WHIRR

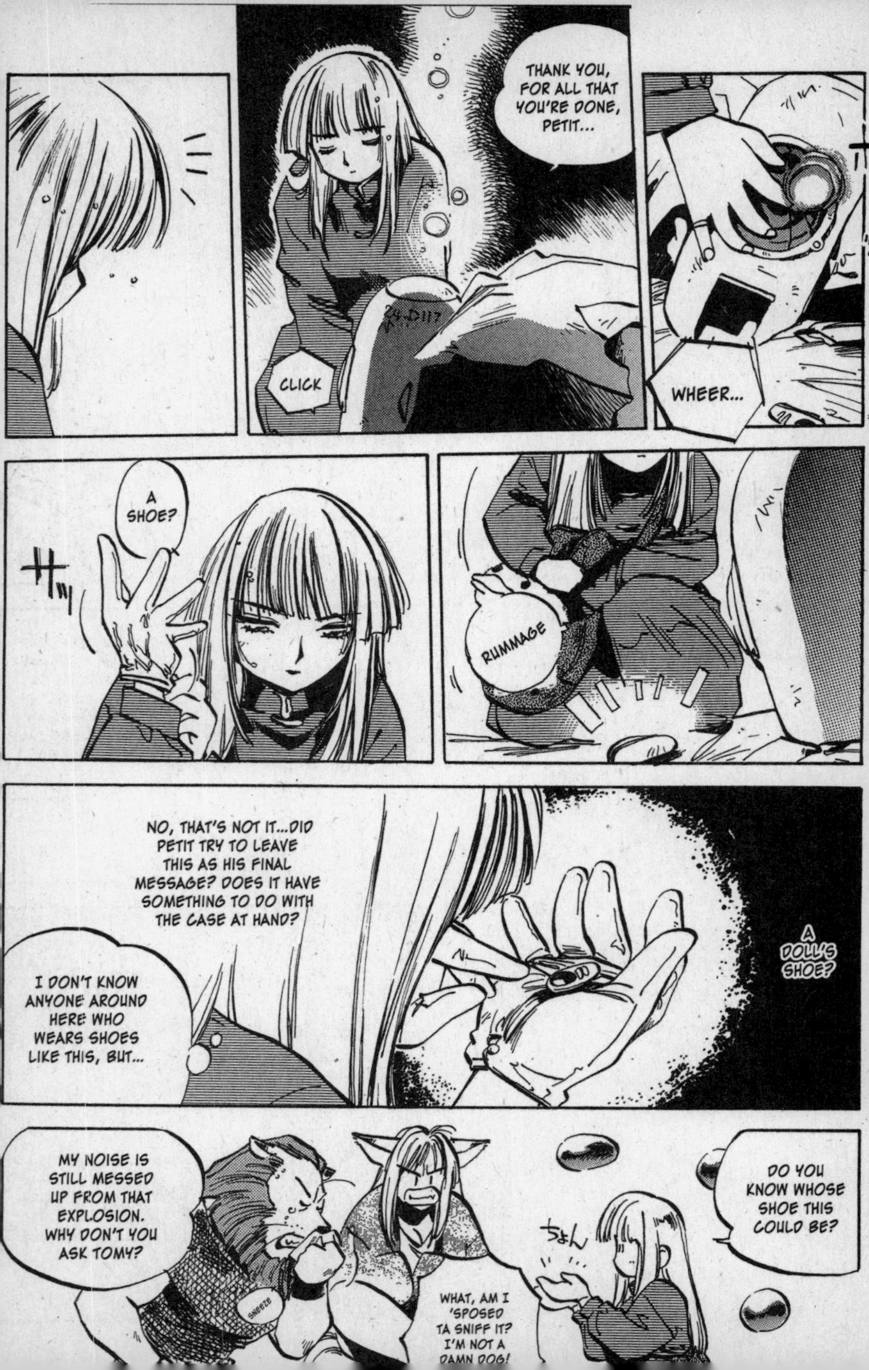
WHEER...
THANK YOU, FOR ALL THAT YOU'RE DONE, PETIT...
CLICK
RUMMAGE
A SHOE?
A DOLL'S SHOE?
NO, THAT'S NOT IT...DID PETIT TRY TO LEAVE THIS AS HIS FINAL MESSAGE? DOES IT HAVE SOMETHING TO DO WITH THE CASE AT HAND?
I DON'T KNOW ANYONE AROUND HERE WHO WEARS SHOES LIKE THIS, BUT...
DO YOU KNOW WHOSE SHOE THIS COULD BE?
ちょん
WHAT, AM I 'SPOSED TA SNIFF IT? I'M NOT A DAMN DOG!
MY NOISE IS STILL MESSED UP FROM THAT EXPLOSION. WHY DON'T YOU ASK TOMY?
SNEEZE

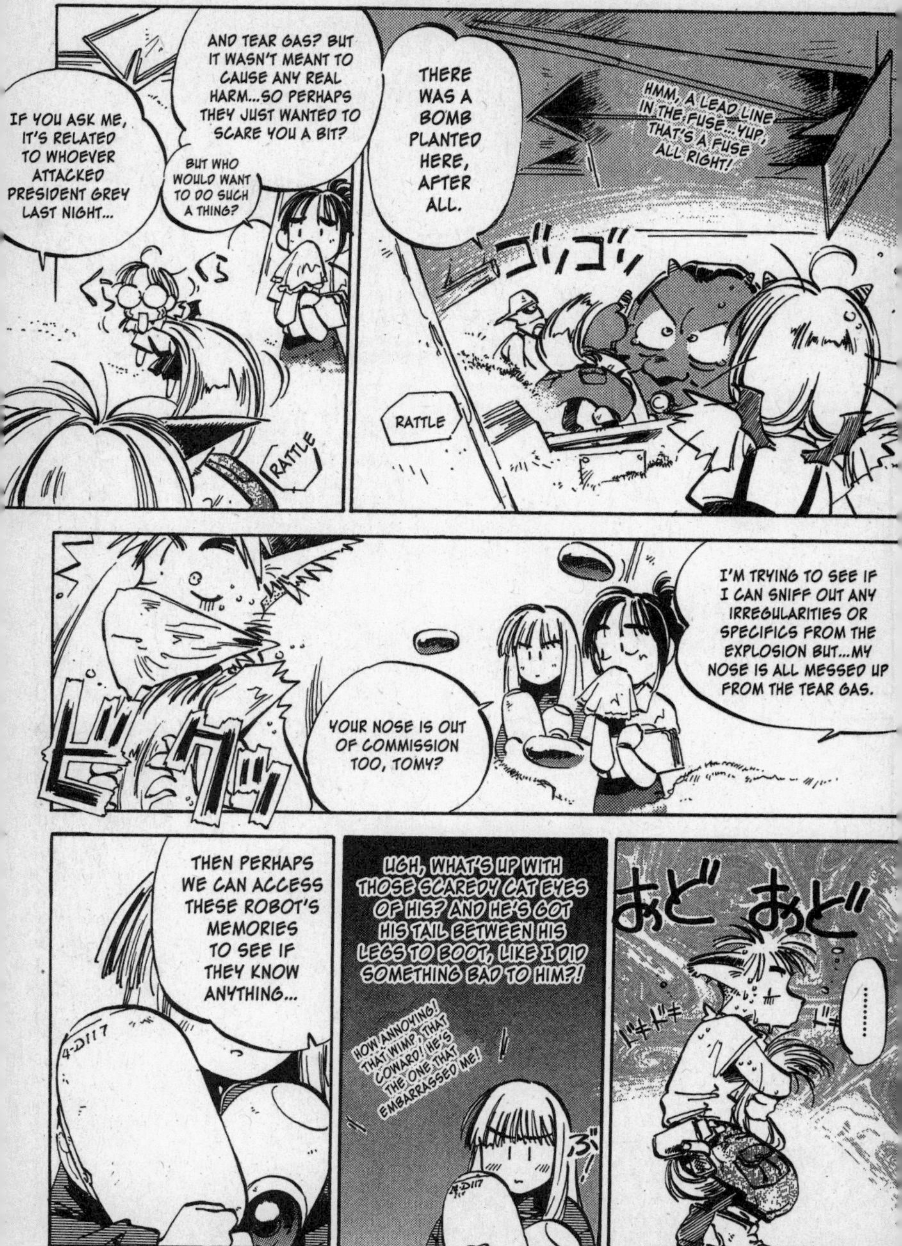
HMM, A LEAD LINE IN THE FUSE...YUP, THAT'S A FUSE ALL RIGHT!
THERE WAS A BOMB PLANTED HERE, AFTER ALL.
ゴソゴソ
RATTLE
AND TEAR GAS? BUT IT WASN'T MEANT TO CAUSE ANY REAL HARM...SO PERHAPS THEY JUST WANTED TO SCARE YOU A BIT?
IF YOU ASK ME, IT'S RELATED TO WHOEVER ATTACKED PRESIDENT GREY LAST NIGHT...
BUT WHO WOULD WANT TO DO SUCH A THING?
くらくら
RATTLE
I'M TRYING TO SEE IF I CAN SNIFF OUT ANY IRREGULARITIES OR SPECIFICS FROM THE EXPLOSION BUT...MY NOSE IS ALL MESSED UP FROM THE TEAR GAS.
YOUR NOSE IS OUT OF COMMISSION TOO, TOMY?
ビクッ
おど おど
......
ドキドキ
UGH, WHAT'S UP WITH THOSE SCAREDY CAT EYES OF HIS? AND HE'S GOT HIS TAIL BETWEEN HIS LEGS TO BOOT, LIKE I DID SOMETHING BAD TO HIM?!
HOW ANNOYING! THAT WIMP, THAT COWARD! HE'S THE ONE THAT EMBARRASSED ME!
ぶ
THEN PERHAPS WE CAN ACCESS THESE ROBOT'S MEMORIES TO SEE IF THEY KNOW ANYTHING...
4-D117

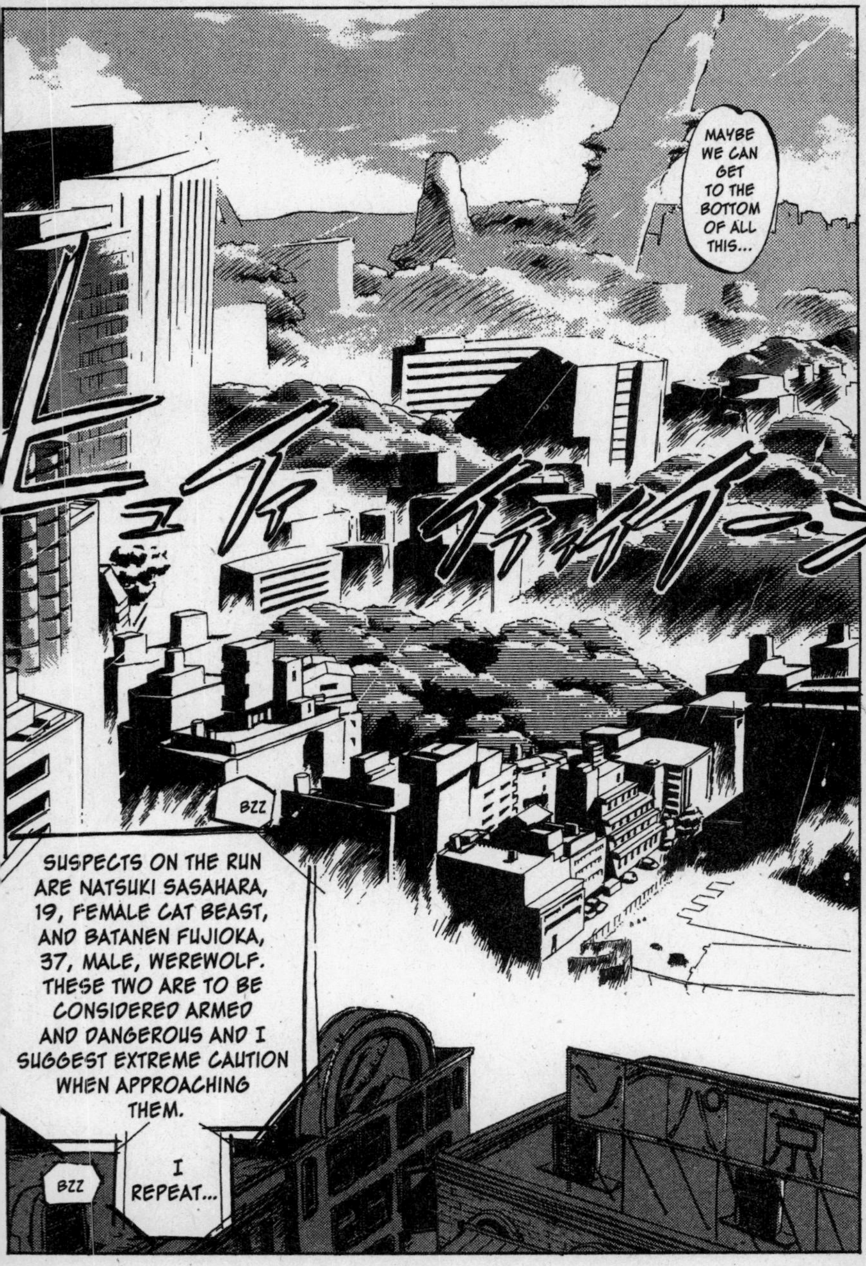
MAYBE WE CAN GET TO THE BOTTOM OF ALL THIS...
BZZ
SUSPECTS ON THE RUN ARE NATSUKI SASAHARA, 19, FEMALE CAT BEAST, AND BATANEN FUJIOKA, 37, MALE, WEREWOLF. THESE TWO ARE TO BE CONSIDERED ARMED AND DANGEROUS AND I SUGGEST EXTREME CAUTION WHEN APPROACHING THEM.
BZZ
I REPEAT...

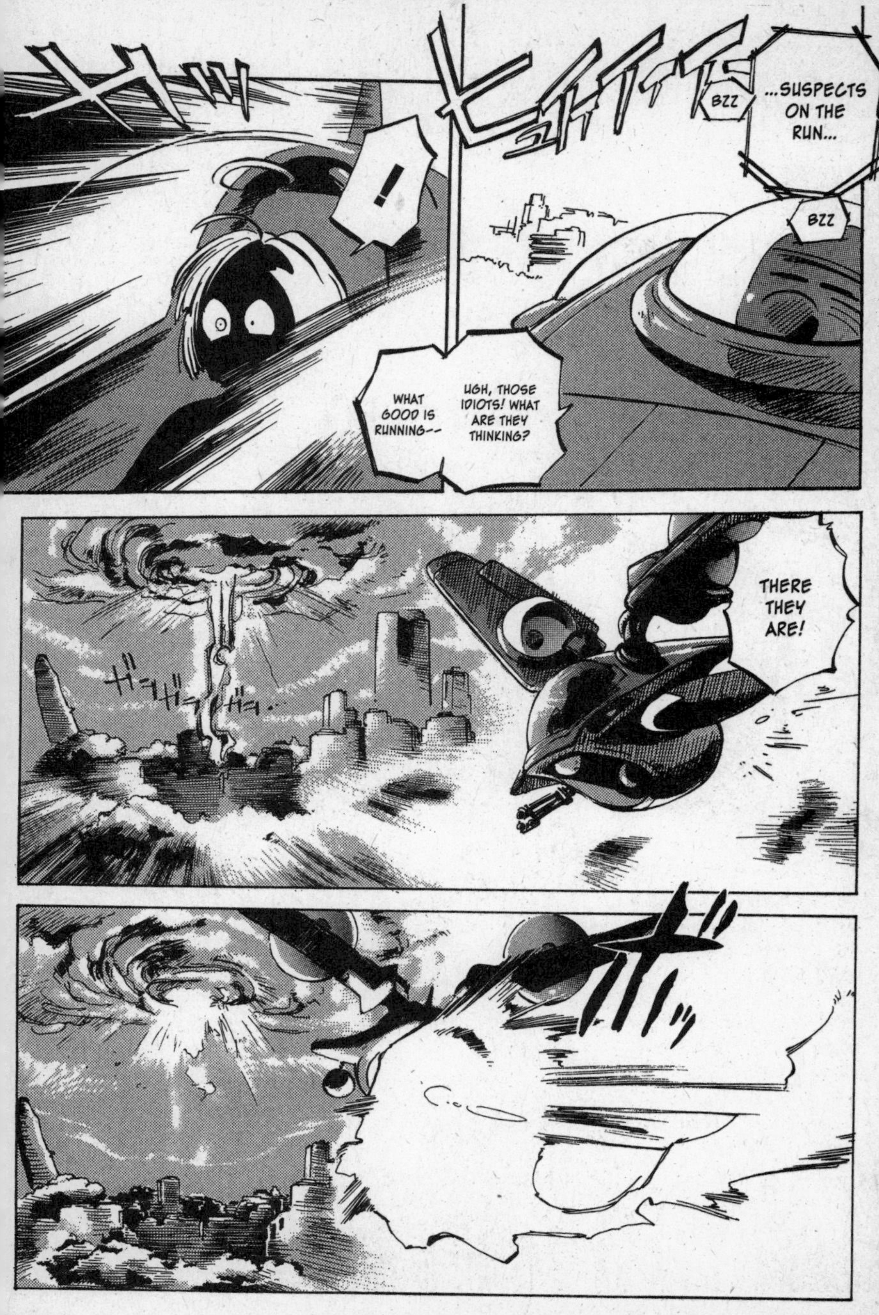

BZZ
...SUSPECTS ON THE RUN...
BZZ
UGH, THOSE IDIOTS! WHAT ARE THEY THINKING?
WHAT GOOD IS RUNNING--
!
THERE THEY ARE!

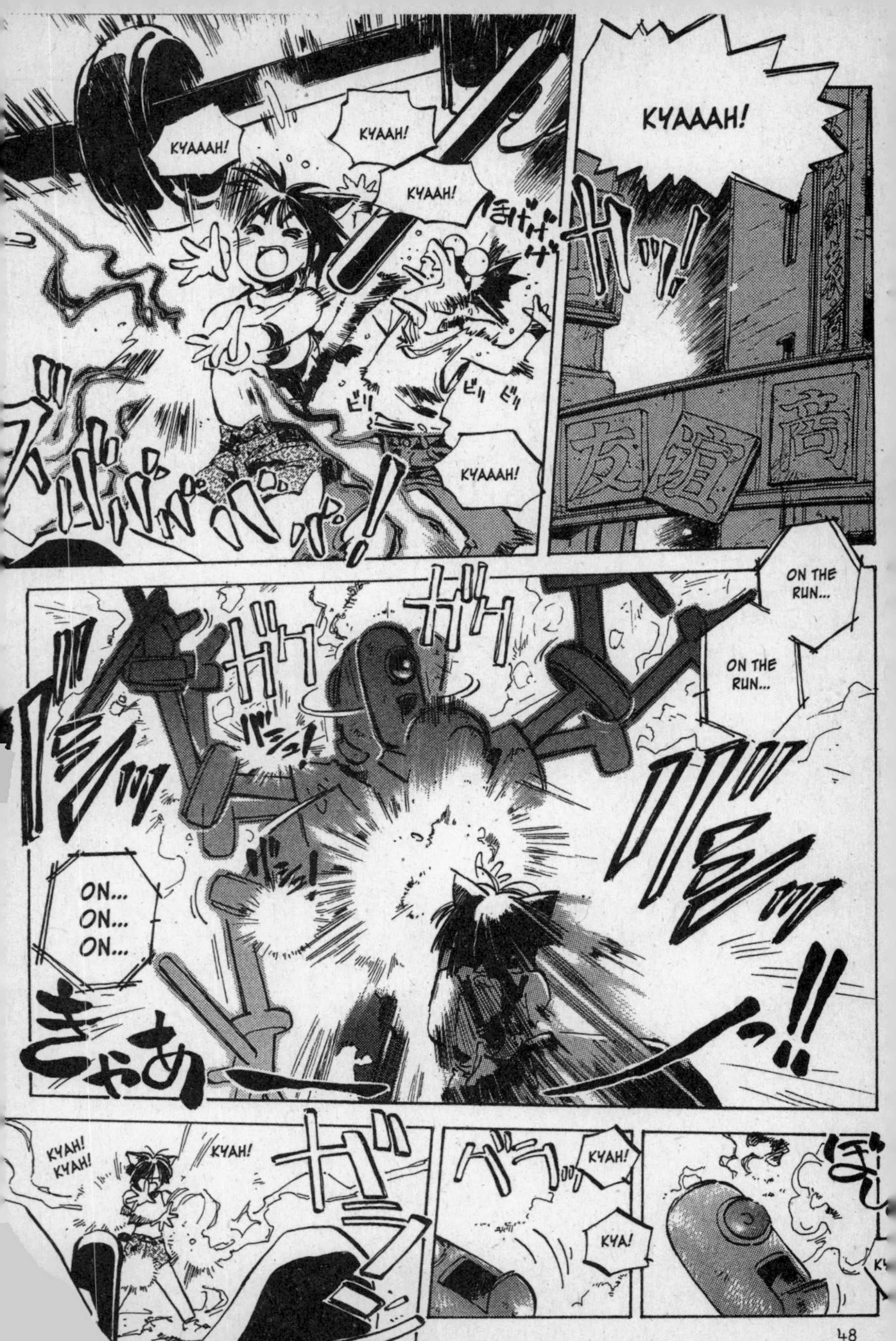
KYAAAH!
KYAAH!
KYAAH!
KYAAAH!
KYAAAH!
ON THE RUN...
ON THE RUN...
ON... ON... ON...
KYAH!
KYA!
KYAH!
KYAH! KYAH!

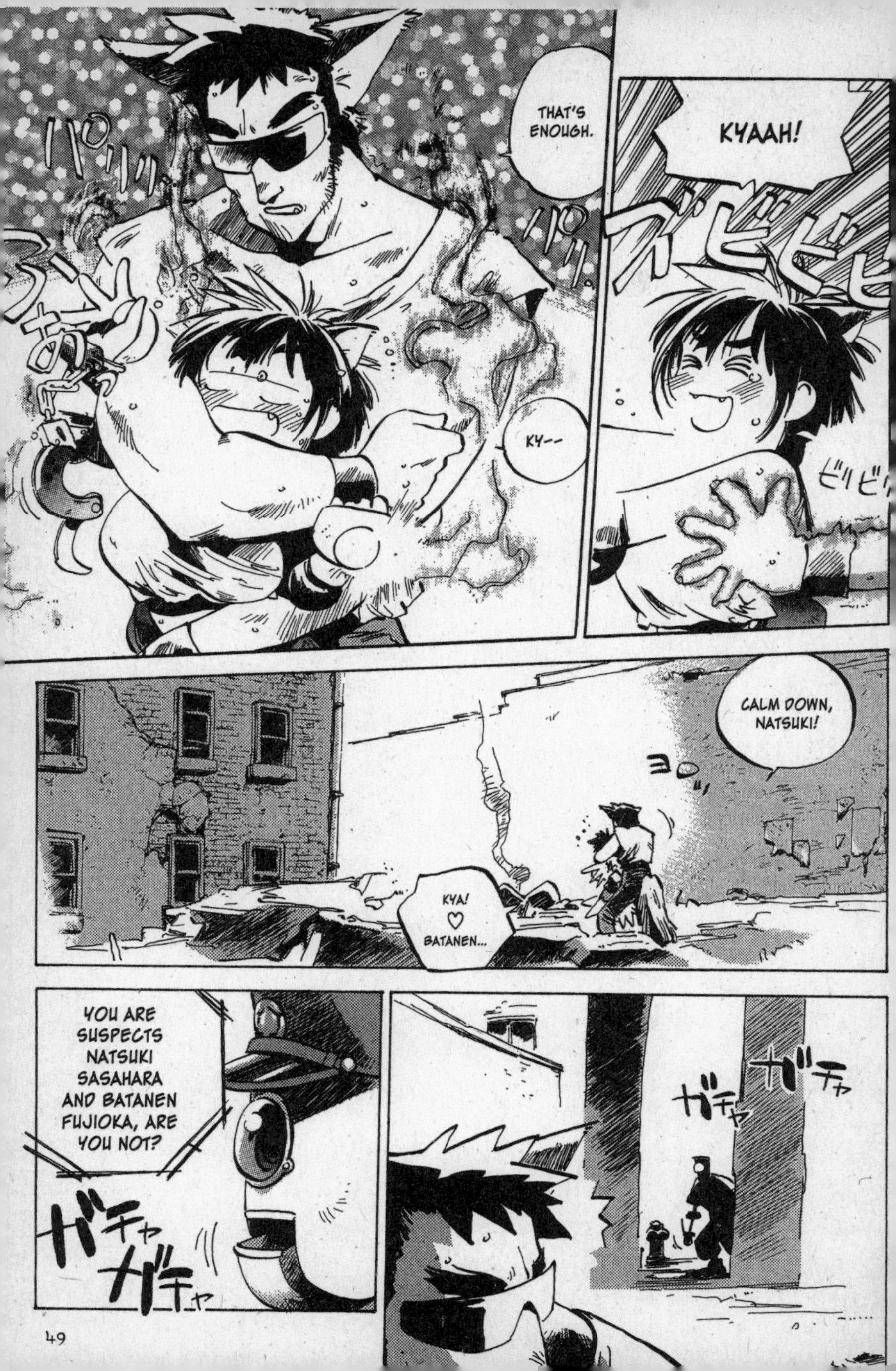
KYAAH!
THAT'S ENOUGH.
KY--
CALM DOWN, NATSUKI!
KYA! ♡ BATANEN...
YOU ARE SUSPECTS NATSUKI SASAHARA AND BATANEN FUJIOKA, ARE YOU NOT?

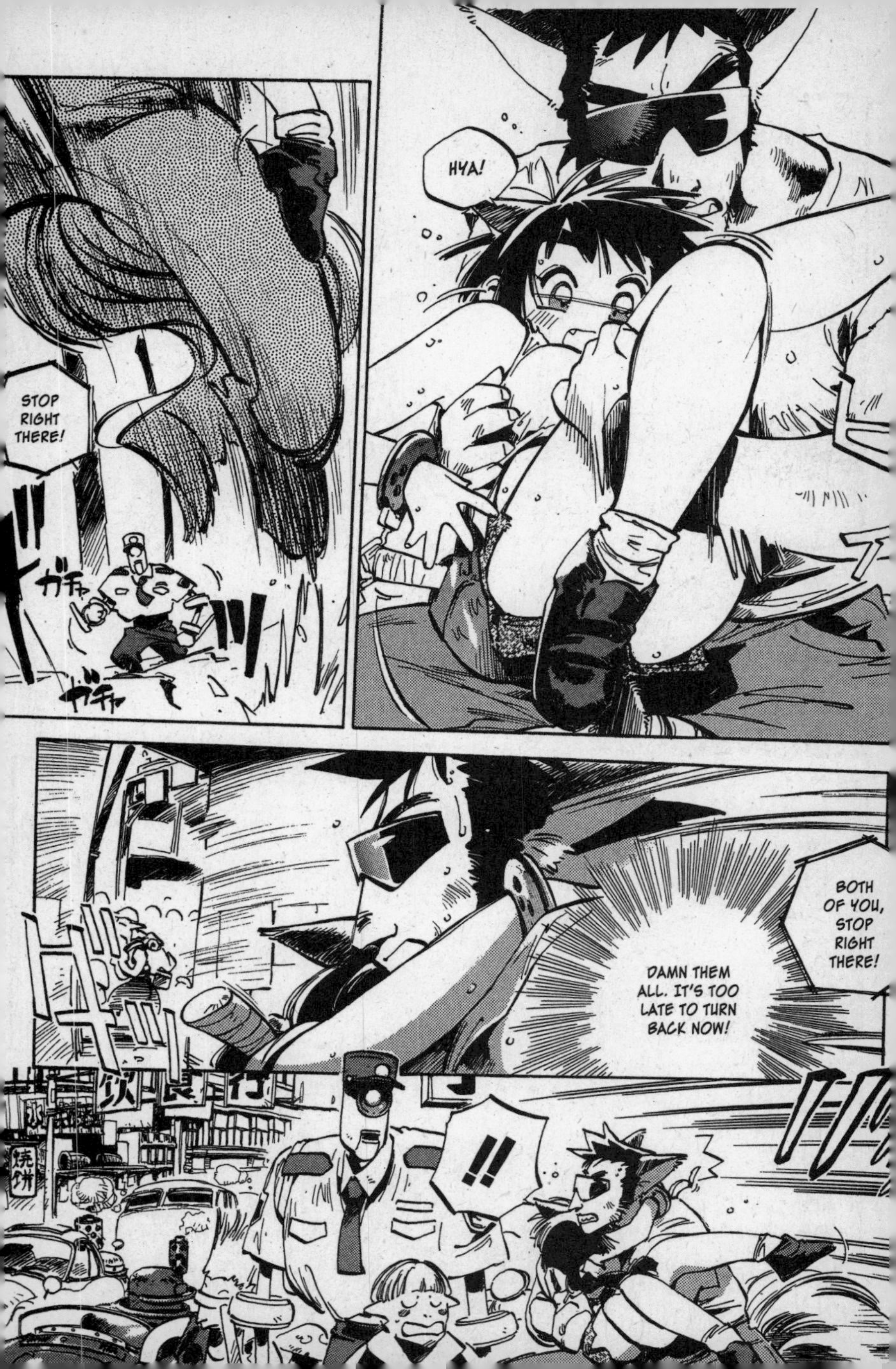
HYA!
STOP RIGHT THERE!
ガチャ
ガチャ
BOTH OF YOU, STOP RIGHT THERE!
DAMN THEM ALL. IT'S TOO LATE TO TURN BACK NOW!
!!
焼餅

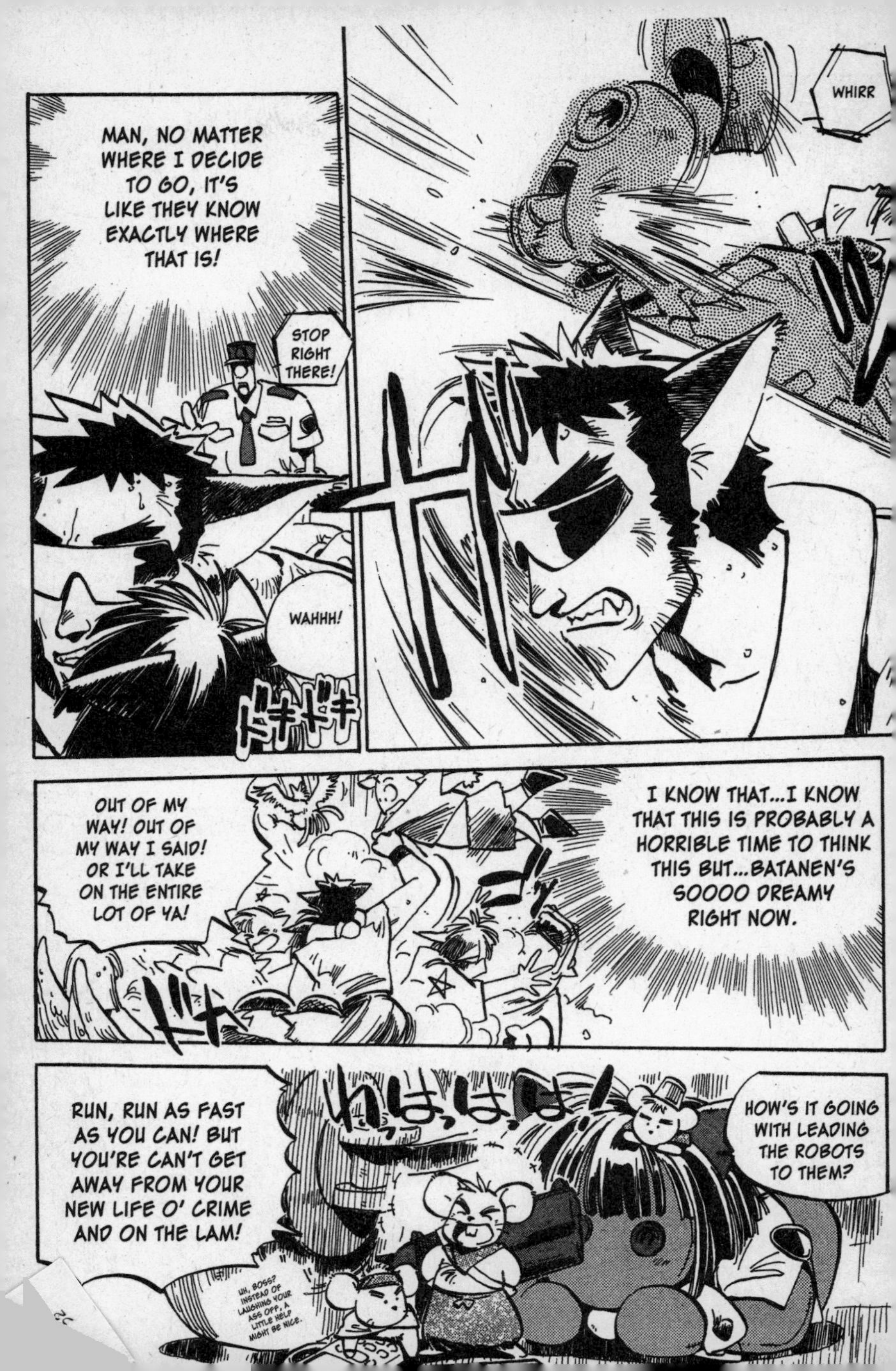
WHIRR
MAN, NO MATTER WHERE I DECIDE TO GO, IT'S LIKE THEY KNOW EXACTLY WHERE THAT IS!
STOP RIGHT THERE!
WAHHH!
I KNOW THAT...I KNOW THAT THIS IS PROBABLY A HORRIBLE TIME TO THINK THIS BUT...BATANEN'S SOOOO DREAMY RIGHT NOW.
OUT OF MY WAY! OUT OF MY WAY I SAID! OR I'LL TAKE ON THE ENTIRE LOT OF YA!
HOW'S IT GOING WITH LEADING THE ROBOTS TO THEM?
RUN, RUN AS FAST AS YOU CAN! BUT YOU'RE CAN'T GET AWAY FROM YOUR NEW LIFE O' CRIME AND ON THE LAM!
UH, BOSS? INSTEAD OF LAUGHING YOUR ASS OFF, A LITTLE HELP MIGHT BE NICE.

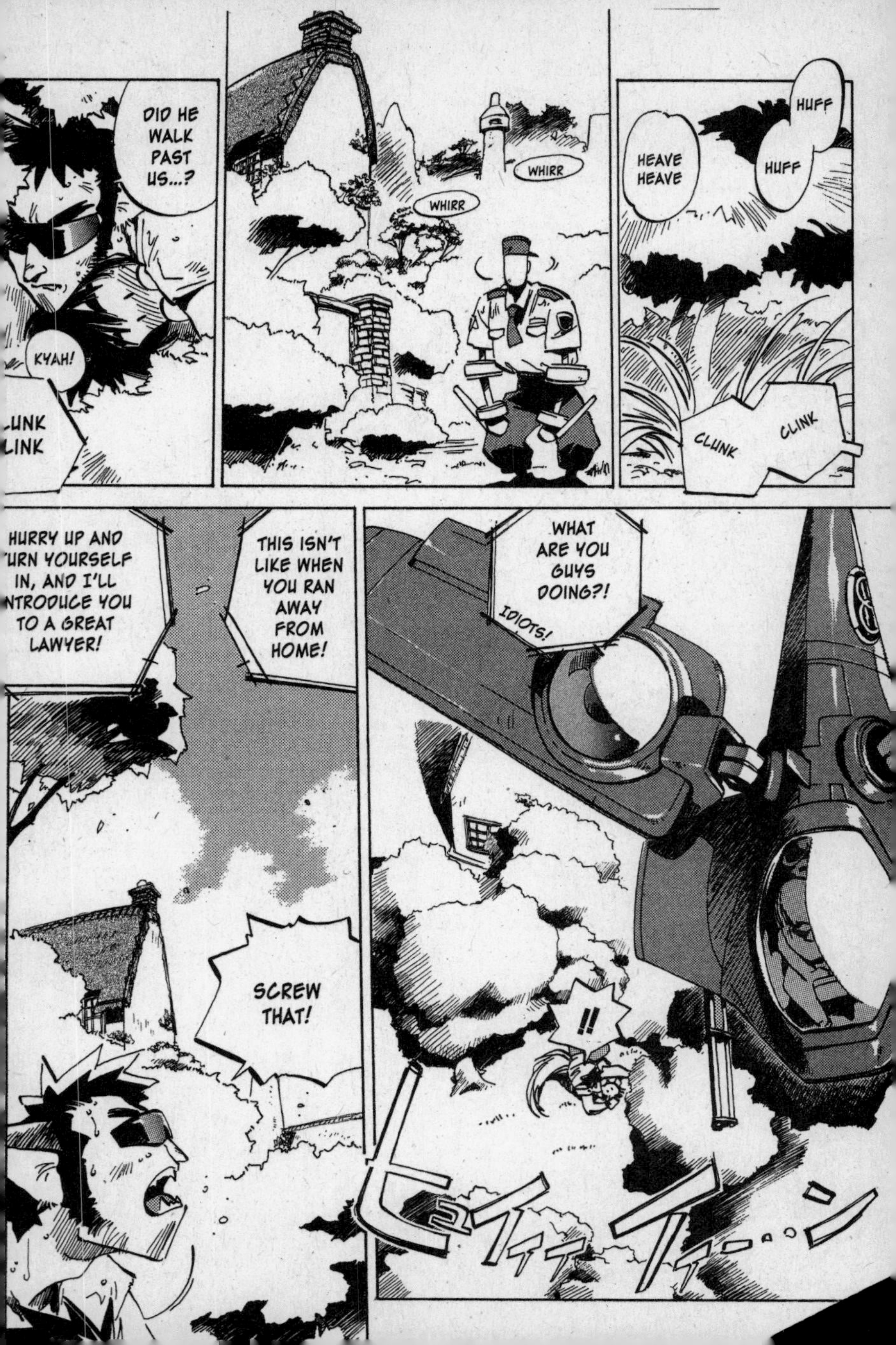
HUFF
HUFF
HEAVE HEAVE
CLINK
CLUNK
WHIRR
WHIRR
DID HE WALK PAST US...?
KYAH!
UNK
LINK
WHAT ARE YOU GUYS DOING?!
IDIOTS!
!!
THIS ISN'T LIKE WHEN YOU RAN AWAY FROM HOME!
HURRY UP AND URN YOURSELF IN, AND I'LL NTRODUCE YOU TO A GREAT LAWYER!
SCREW THAT!

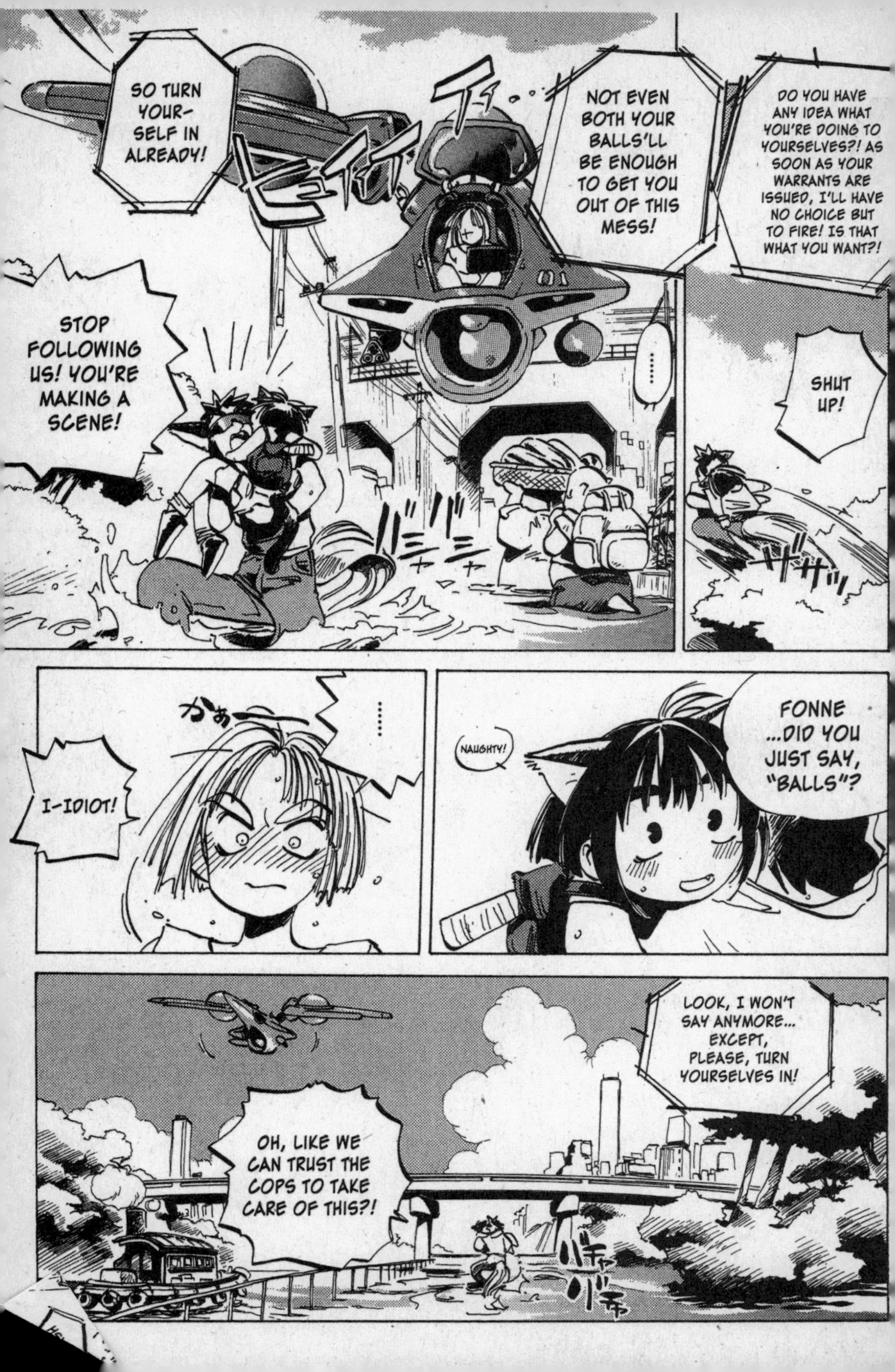
DO YOU HAVE ANY IDEA WHAT YOU'RE DOING TO YOURSELVES?! AS SOON AS YOUR WARRANTS ARE ISSUED, I'LL HAVE NO CHOICE BUT TO FIRE! IS THAT WHAT YOU WANT?!
SHUT UP!
NOT EVEN BOTH YOUR BALLS'LL BE ENOUGH TO GET YOU OUT OF THIS MESS!
SO TURN YOUR-SELF IN ALREADY!
......
STOP FOLLOWING US! YOU'RE MAKING A SCENE!
FONNE ...DID YOU JUST SAY, "BALLS"?
NAUGHTY!
......
I-IDIOT!
LOOK, I WON'T SAY ANYMORE... EXCEPT, PLEASE, TURN YOURSELVES IN!
OH, LIKE WE CAN TRUST THE COPS TO TAKE CARE OF THIS?!

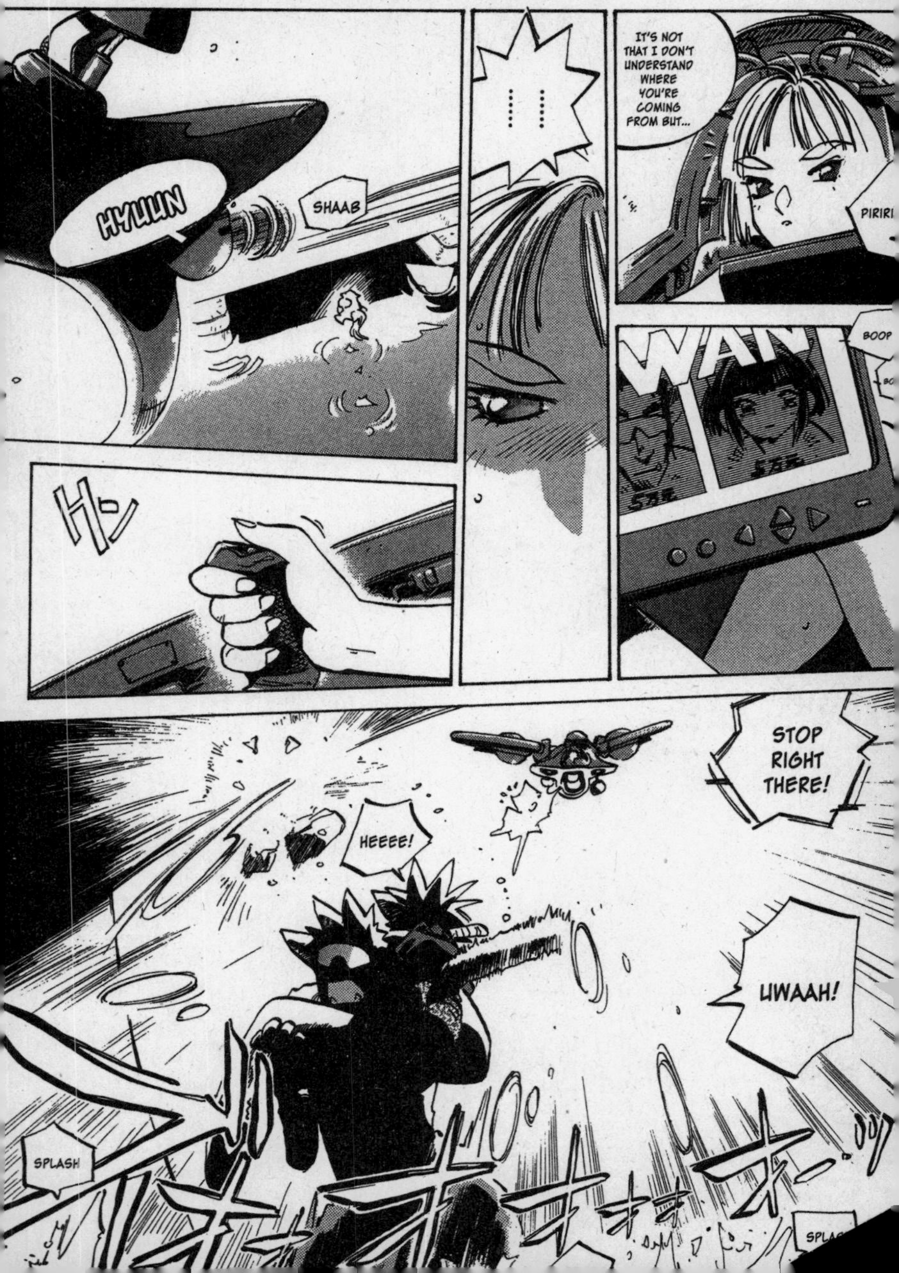

IT'S NOT THAT I DON'T UNDERSTAND WHERE YOU'RE COMING FROM BUT...
PIRIRI
WAN
BOOP
....
HYUUN
SHAAB
STOP RIGHT THERE!
HEEEE!
UWAAH!
SPLASH

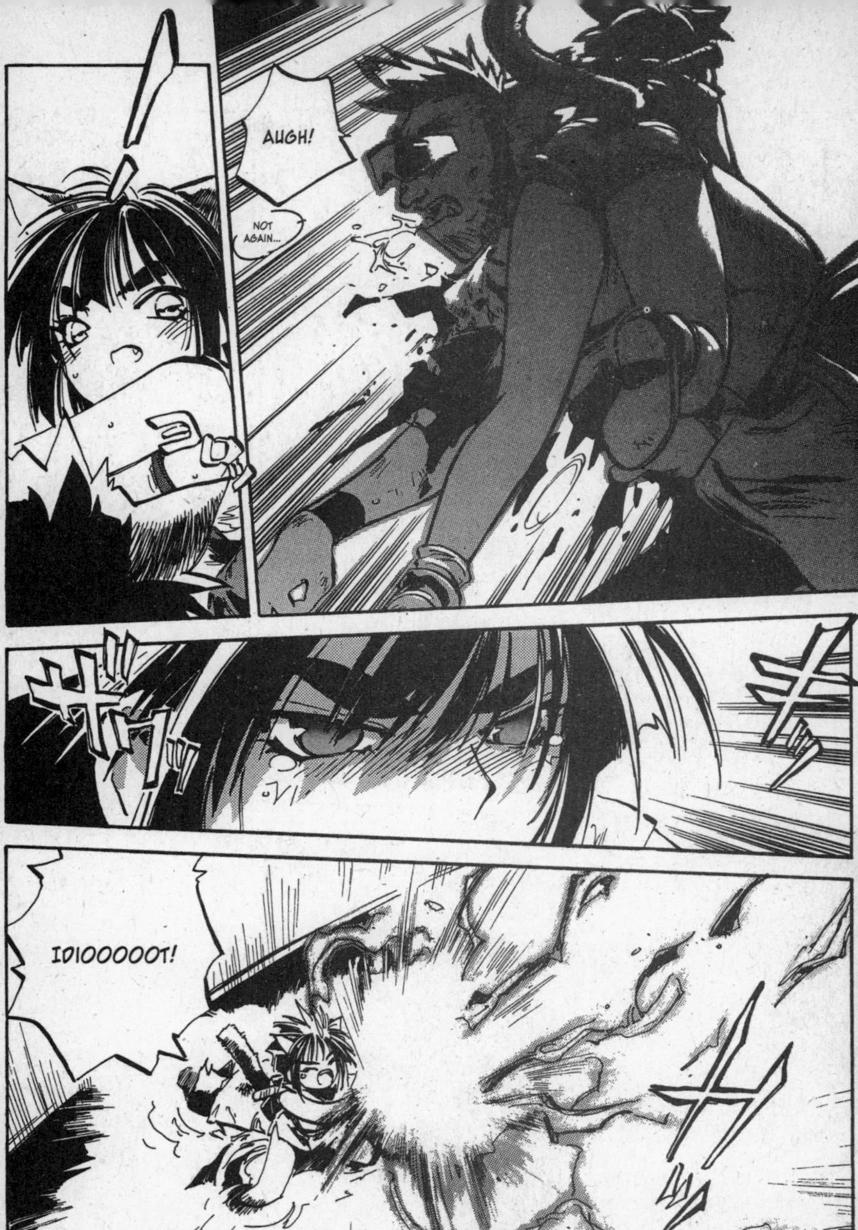
AUGH!
NOT AGAIN...
IDIOOOOOT!

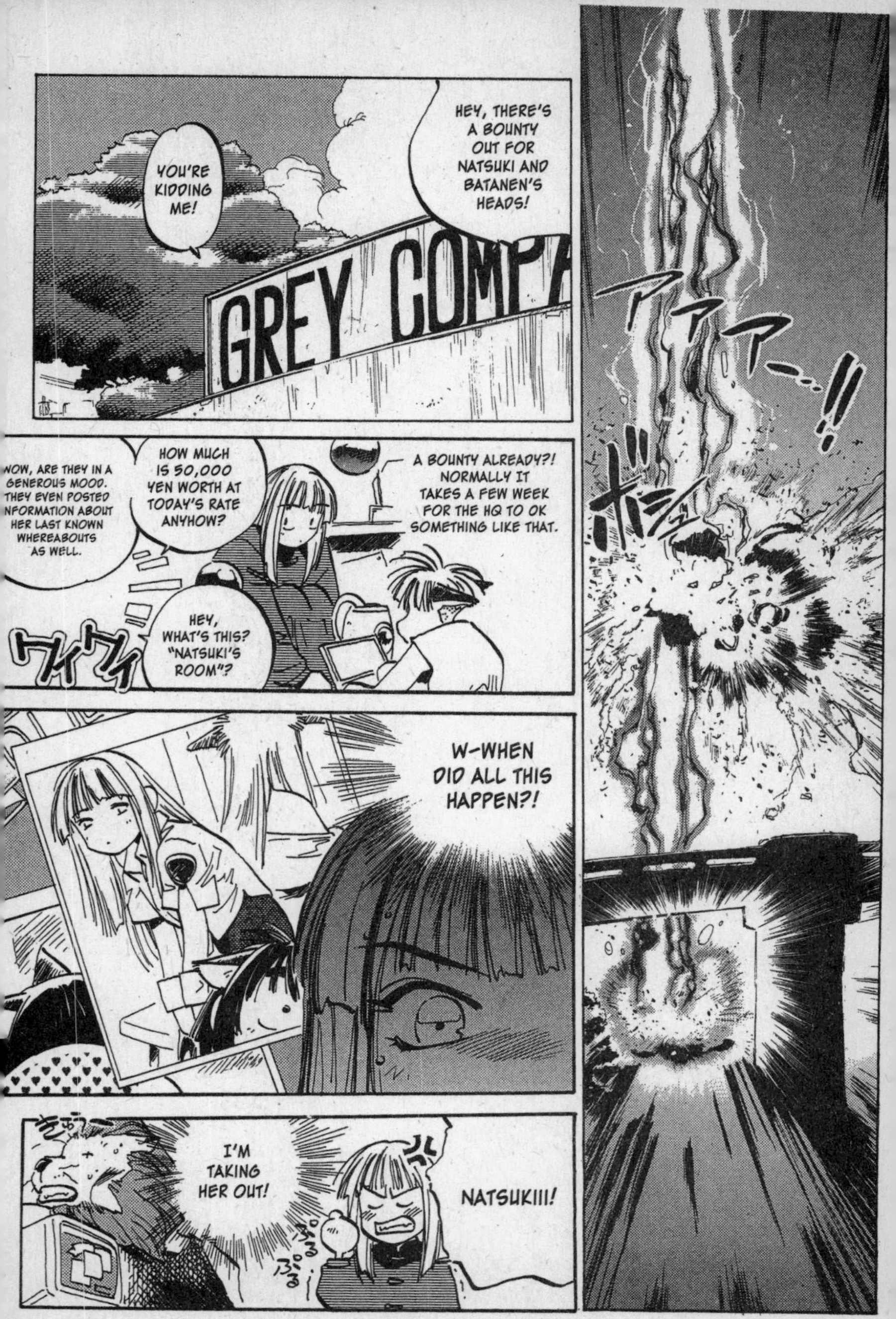
アアアー…!!
ボシュ
HEY, THERE'S A BOUNTY OUT FOR NATSUKI AND BATANEN'S HEADS!
YOU'RE KIDDING ME!
A BOUNTY ALREADY?! NORMALLY IT TAKES A FEW WEEK FOR THE HQ TO OK SOMETHING LIKE THAT.
HOW MUCH IS 50,000 YEN WORTH AT TODAY'S RATE ANYHOW?
NOW, ARE THEY IN A GENEROUS MOOD. THEY EVEN POSTED NFORMATION ABOUT HER LAST KNOWN WHEREABOUTS AS WELL.
HEY, WHAT'S THIS? "NATSUKI'S ROOM"?
ウィウィ
W-WHEN DID ALL THIS HAPPEN?!
NATSUKIII!
I'M TAKING HER OUT!

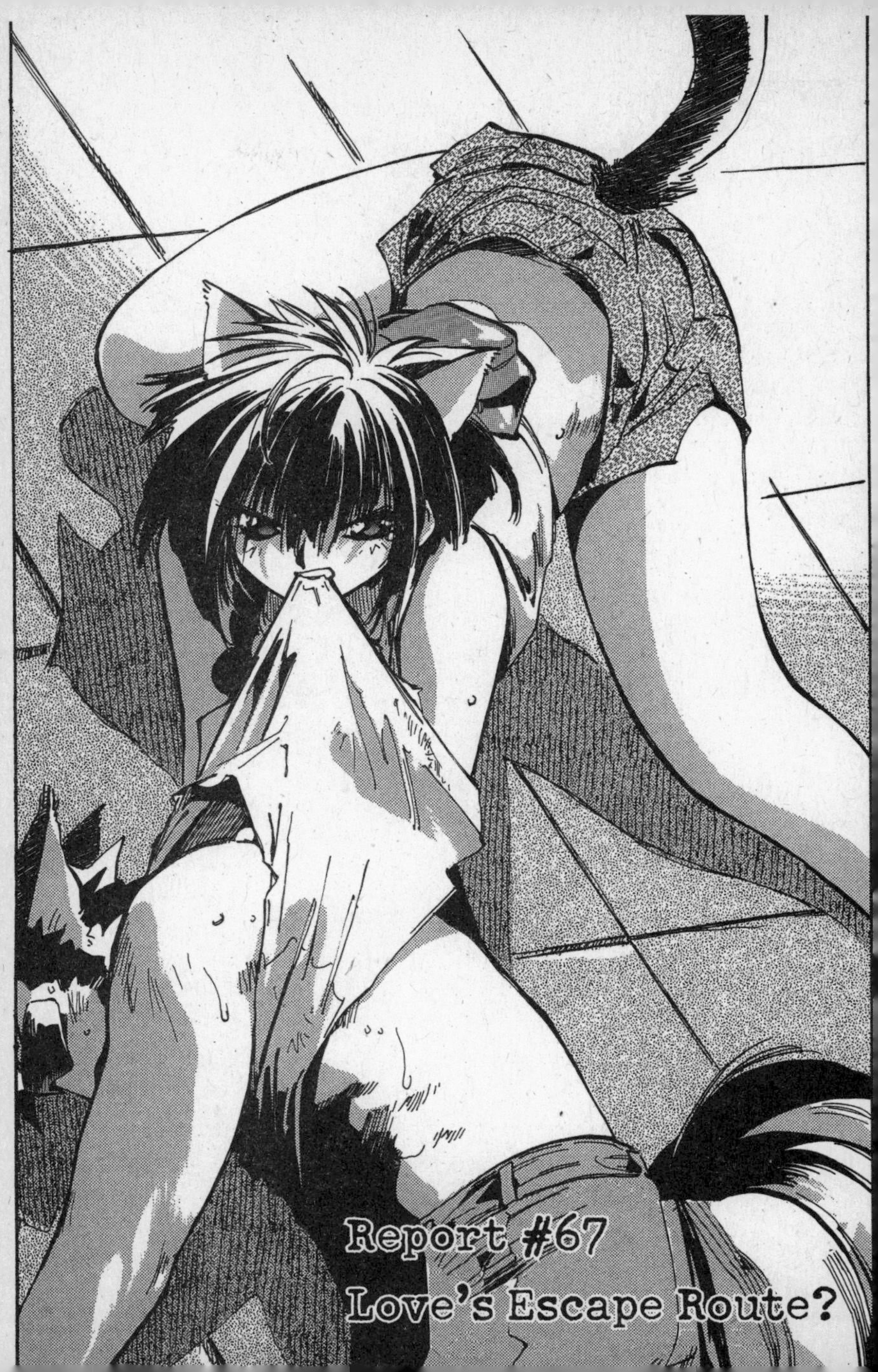
Report #67
Love's Escape Route?

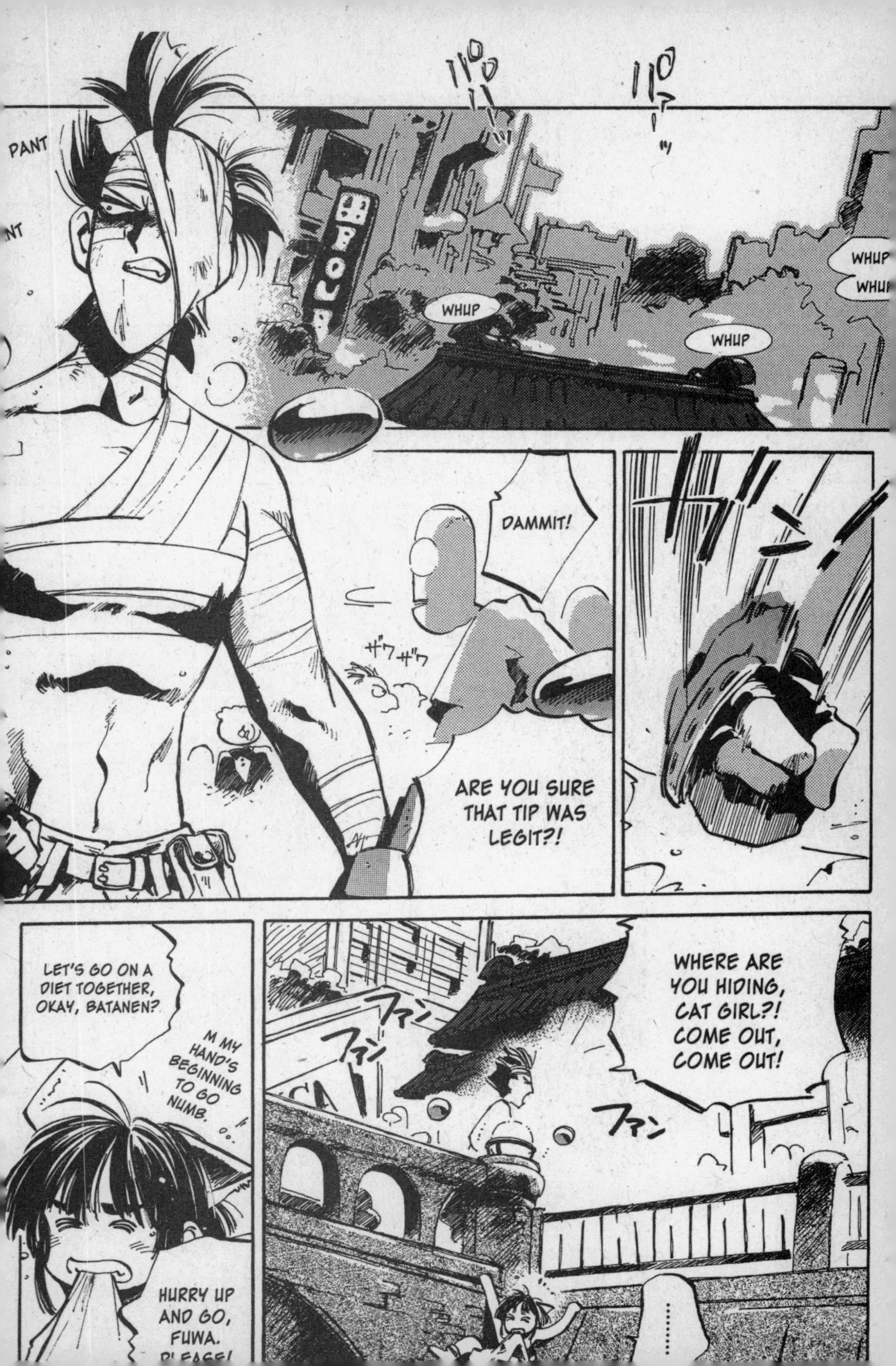
WHUP
WHUP
WHUP
PANT
DAMMIT!
ザワザワ
ARE YOU SURE THAT TIP WAS LEGIT?!
WHERE ARE YOU HIDING, CAT GIRL?! COME OUT, COME OUT!
ファン
ファン
ファン
LET'S GO ON A DIET TOGETHER, OKAY, BATANEN?
M MY HAND'S BEGINNING TO GO NUMB.
HURRY UP AND GO, FUWA.

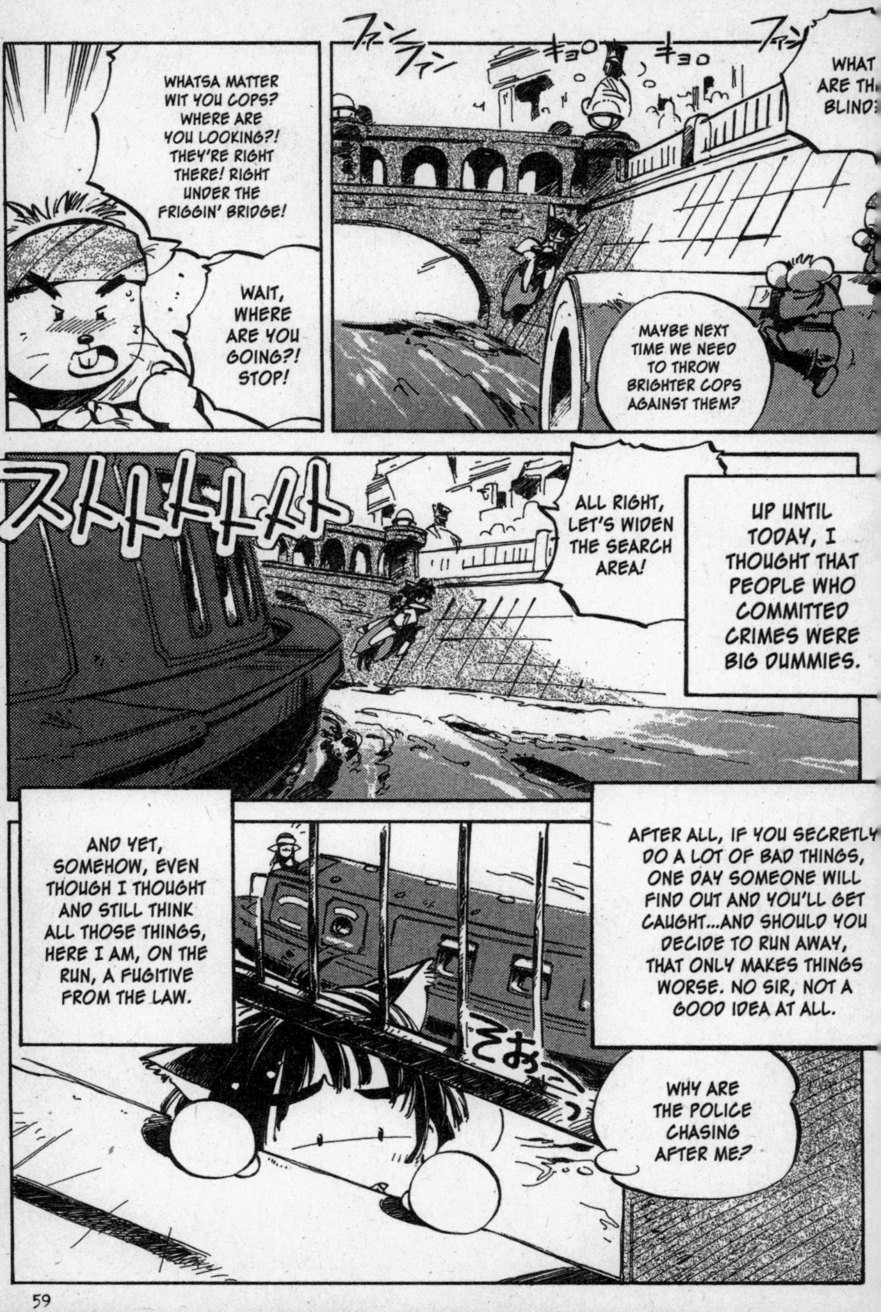
ファン ファン
キョロ キョロ
ファン
WHAT ARE TH BLIND
MAYBE NEXT TIME WE NEED TO THROW BRIGHTER COPS AGAINST THEM?
WHATSA MATTER WIT YOU COPS? WHERE ARE YOU LOOKING?! THEY'RE RIGHT THERE! RIGHT UNDER THE FRIGGIN' BRIDGE!
WAIT, WHERE ARE YOU GOING?! STOP!
UP UNTIL TODAY, I THOUGHT THAT PEOPLE WHO COMMITTED CRIMES WERE BIG DUMMIES.
ALL RIGHT, LET'S WIDEN THE SEARCH AREA!
ストトトトトト
AFTER ALL, IF YOU SECRETLY DO A LOT OF BAD THINGS, ONE DAY SOMEONE WILL FIND OUT AND YOU'LL GET CAUGHT...AND SHOULD YOU DECIDE TO RUN AWAY, THAT ONLY MAKES THINGS WORSE. NO SIR, NOT A GOOD IDEA AT ALL.
AND YET, SOMEHOW, EVEN THOUGH I THOUGHT AND STILL THINK ALL THOSE THINGS, HERE I AM, ON THE RUN, A FUGITIVE FROM THE LAW.
そぉー
WHY ARE THE POLICE CHASING AFTER ME?

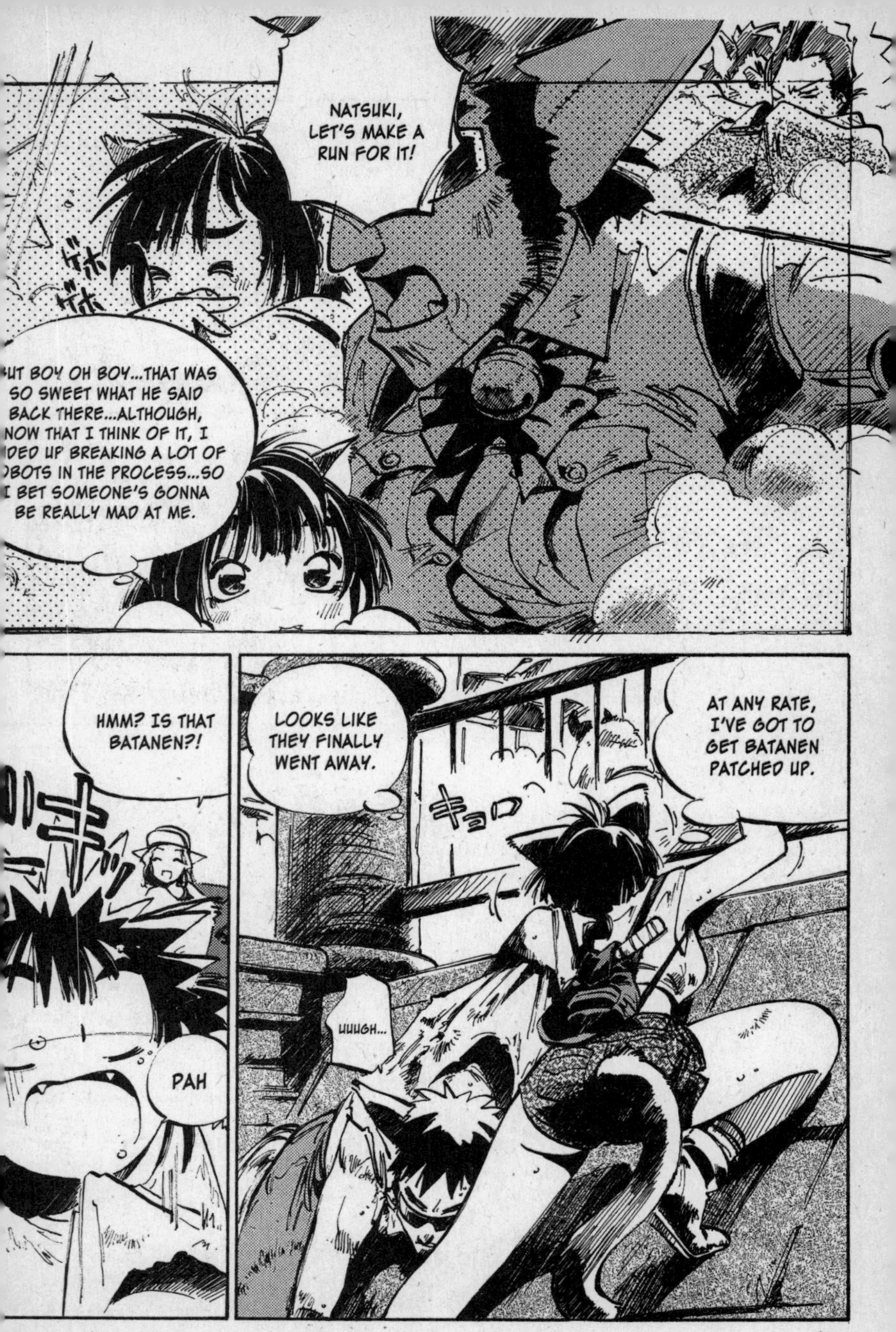
NATSUKI, LET'S MAKE A RUN FOR IT!
ゲホ ゲホ
UT BOY OH BOY...THAT WAS SO SWEET WHAT HE SAID BACK THERE...ALTHOUGH, NOW THAT I THINK OF IT, I IDED UP BREAKING A LOT OF OBOTS IN THE PROCESS...SO I BET SOMEONE'S GONNA BE REALLY MAD AT ME.
AT ANY RATE, I'VE GOT TO GET BATANEN PATCHED UP.
LOOKS LIKE THEY FINALLY WENT AWAY.
キョロ
UUUGH...
HMM? IS THAT BATANEN?!
ギキッ
PAH

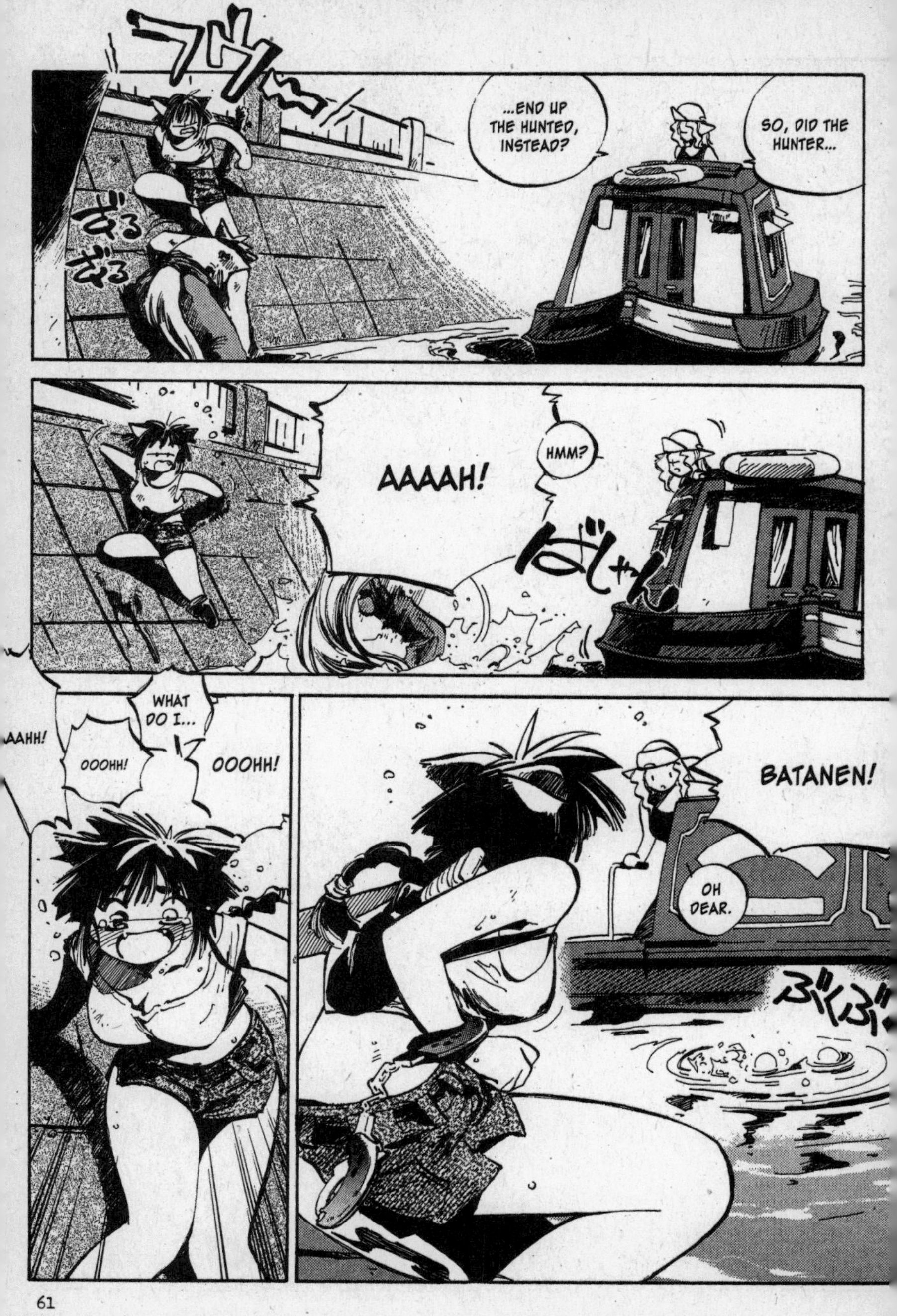

SO, DID THE HUNTER...
...END UP THE HUNTED, INSTEAD?
HMM?
ばしゃん
AAAAH!
BATANEN!
OH DEAR.
ぶくぶ
WHAT DO I...
OOOHH!
OOOHH!
AAHH!

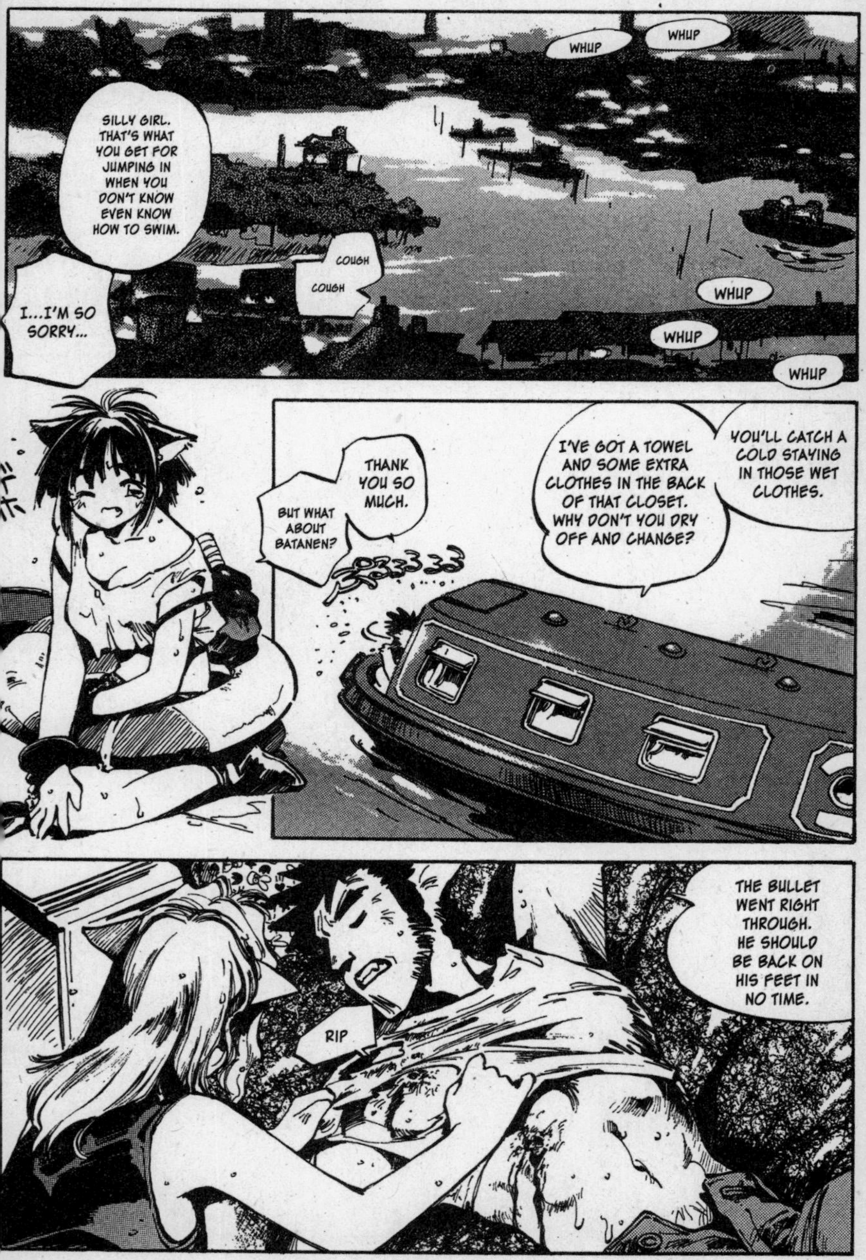
WHUP
WHUP
SILLY GIRL. THAT'S WHAT YOU GET FOR JUMPING IN WHEN YOU DON'T KNOW EVEN KNOW HOW TO SWIM.
COUGH
COUGH
WHUP
I...I'M SO SORRY...
WHUP
WHUP
YOU'LL CATCH A COLD STAYING IN THOSE WET CLOTHES.
I'VE GOT A TOWEL AND SOME EXTRA CLOTHES IN THE BACK OF THAT CLOSET. WHY DON'T YOU DRY OFF AND CHANGE?
THANK YOU SO MUCH.
BUT WHAT ABOUT BATANEN?
THE BULLET WENT RIGHT THROUGH. HE SHOULD BE BACK ON HIS FEET IN NO TIME.
RIP

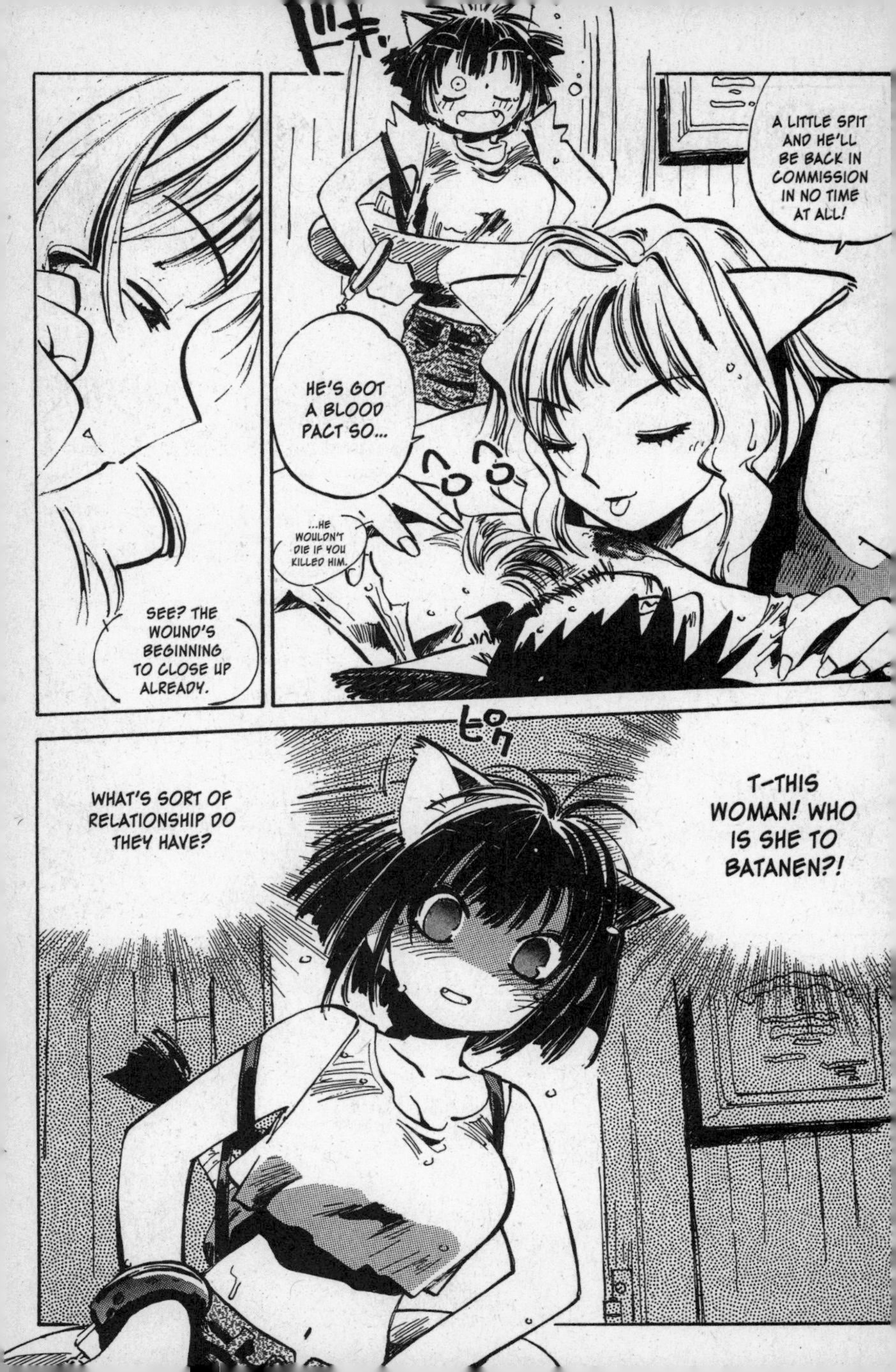
ドキッ
A LITTLE SPIT AND HE'LL BE BACK IN COMMISSION IN NO TIME AT ALL!
HE'S GOT A BLOOD PACT SO...
...HE WOULDN'T DIE IF YOU KILLED HIM.
SEE? THE WOUND'S BEGINNING TO CLOSE UP ALREADY.
ピクッ
T-THIS WOMAN! WHO IS SHE TO BATANEN?!
WHAT'S SORT OF RELATIONSHIP DO THEY HAVE?

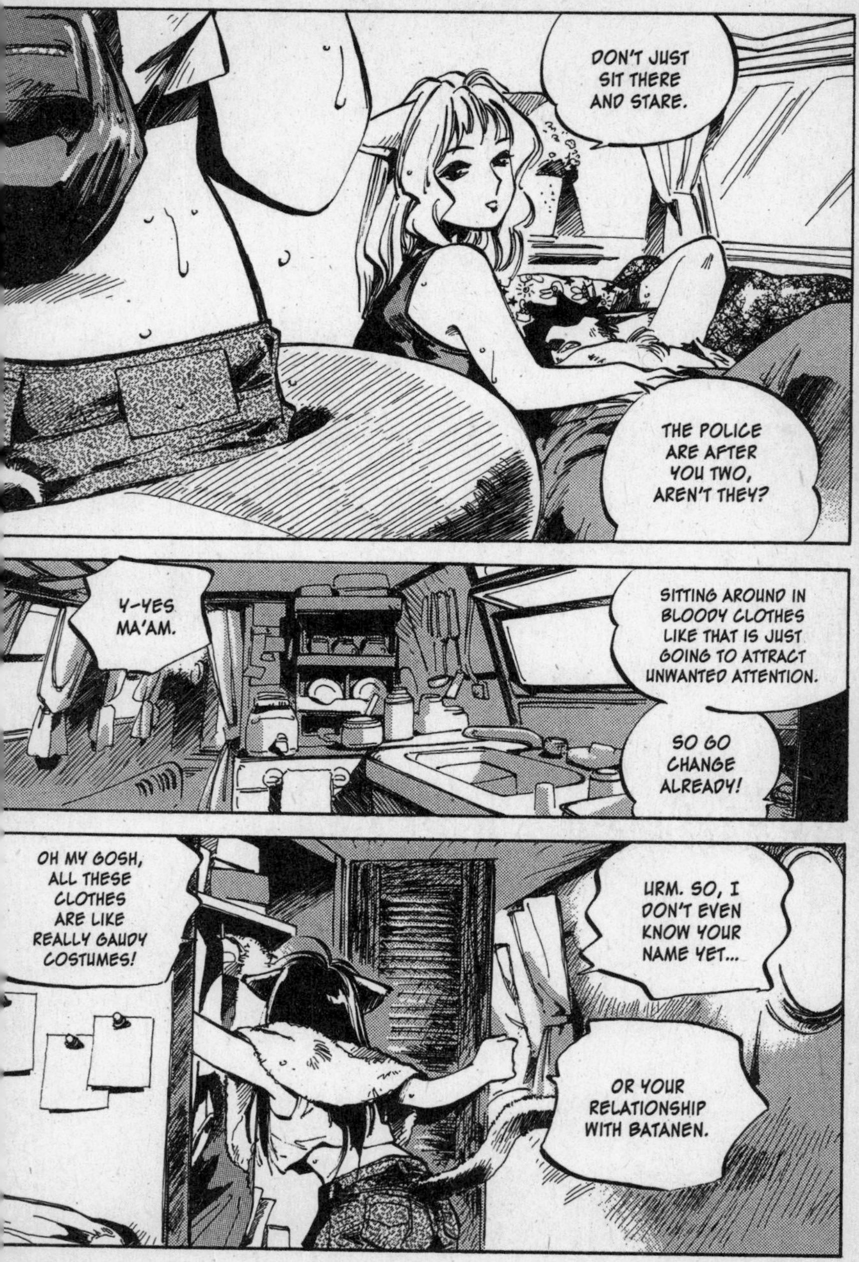
DON'T JUST SIT THERE AND STARE.
THE POLICE ARE AFTER YOU TWO, AREN'T THEY?
SITTING AROUND IN BLOODY CLOTHES LIKE THAT IS JUST GOING TO ATTRACT UNWANTED ATTENTION.
SO GO CHANGE ALREADY!
Y-YES MA'AM.
URM. SO, I DON'T EVEN KNOW YOUR NAME YET...
OR YOUR RELATIONSHIP WITH BATANEN.
OH MY GOSH, ALL THESE CLOTHES ARE LIKE REALLY GAUDY COSTUMES!

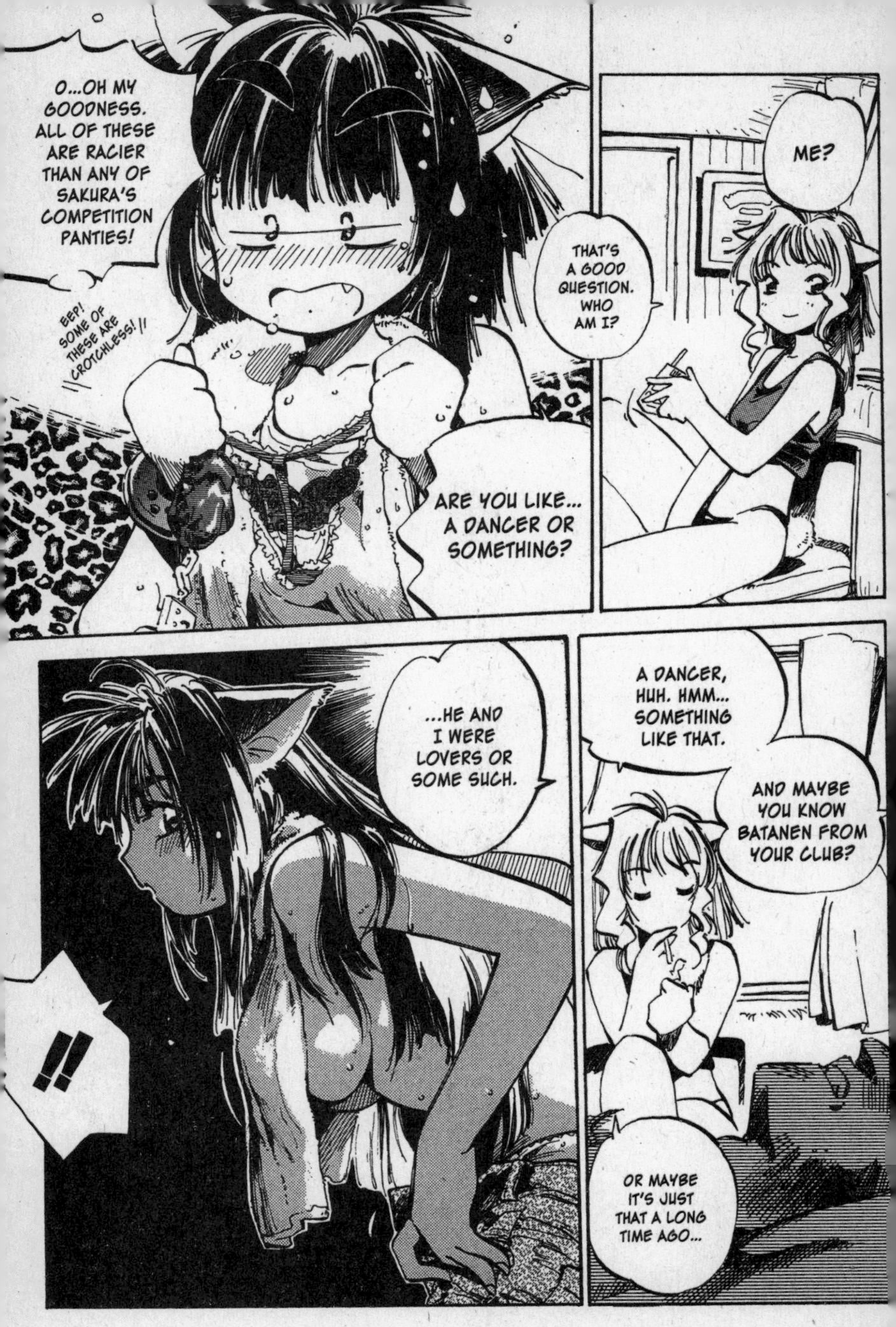
ME?
THAT'S A GOOD QUESTION. WHO AM I?
O...OH MY GOODNESS. ALL OF THESE ARE RACIER THAN ANY OF SAKURA'S COMPETITION PANTIES!
EEP! SOME OF THESE ARE CROTCHLESS!
ARE YOU LIKE... A DANCER OR SOMETHING?
A DANCER, HUH. HMM... SOMETHING LIKE THAT.
AND MAYBE YOU KNOW BATANEN FROM YOUR CLUB?
OR MAYBE IT'S JUST THAT A LONG TIME AGO...
...HE AND I WERE LOVERS OR SOME SUCH.
!!

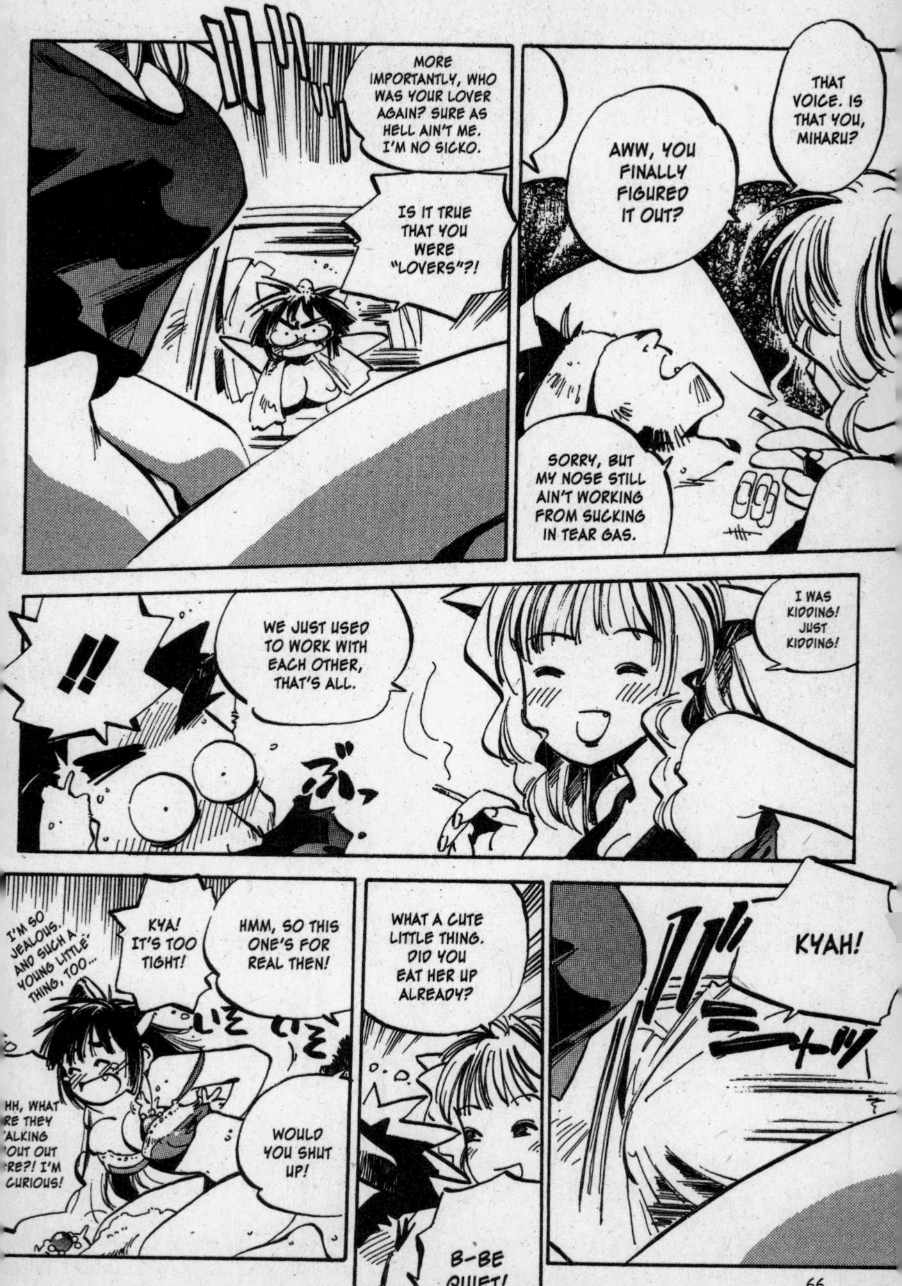
THAT VOICE. IS THAT YOU, MIHARU?
AWW, YOU FINALLY FIGURED IT OUT?
SORRY, BUT MY NOSE STILL AIN'T WORKING FROM SUCKING IN TEAR GAS.
MORE IMPORTANTLY, WHO WAS YOUR LOVER AGAIN? SURE AS HELL AIN'T ME. I'M NO SICKO.
IS IT TRUE THAT YOU WERE "LOVERS"?!
I WAS KIDDING! JUST KIDDING!
WE JUST USED TO WORK WITH EACH OTHER, THAT'S ALL.
!!
KYAH!
WHAT A CUTE LITTLE THING. DID YOU EAT HER UP ALREADY?
WOULD YOU SHUT UP!
B-BE QUIET!
HMM, SO THIS ONE'S FOR REAL THEN!
KYA! IT'S TOO TIGHT!
I'M SO JEALOUS. AND SUCH A YOUNG LITTLE THING, TOO...
HH, WHAT RE THEY ALKING OUT OUT RE?! I'M CURIOUS!

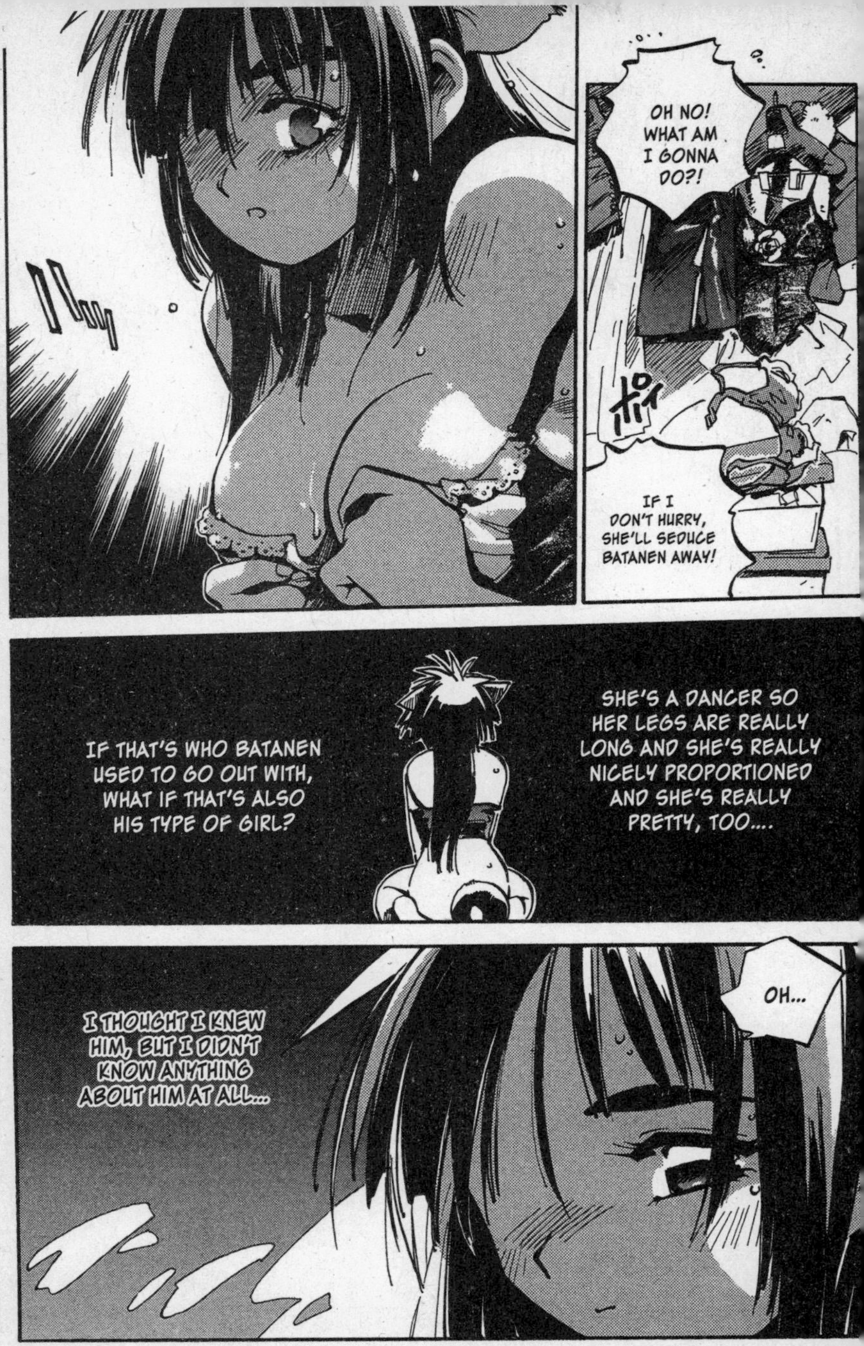
OH NO! WHAT AM I GONNA DO?!
IF I DON'T HURRY, SHE'LL SEDUCE BATANEN AWAY!
SHE'S A DANCER SO HER LEGS ARE REALLY LONG AND SHE'S REALLY NICELY PROPORTIONED AND SHE'S REALLY PRETTY, TOO....
IF THAT'S WHO BATANEN USED TO GO OUT WITH, WHAT IF THAT'S ALSO HIS TYPE OF GIRL?
OH...
I THOUGHT I KNEW HIM, BUT I DIDN'T KNOW ANYTHING ABOUT HIM AT ALL...

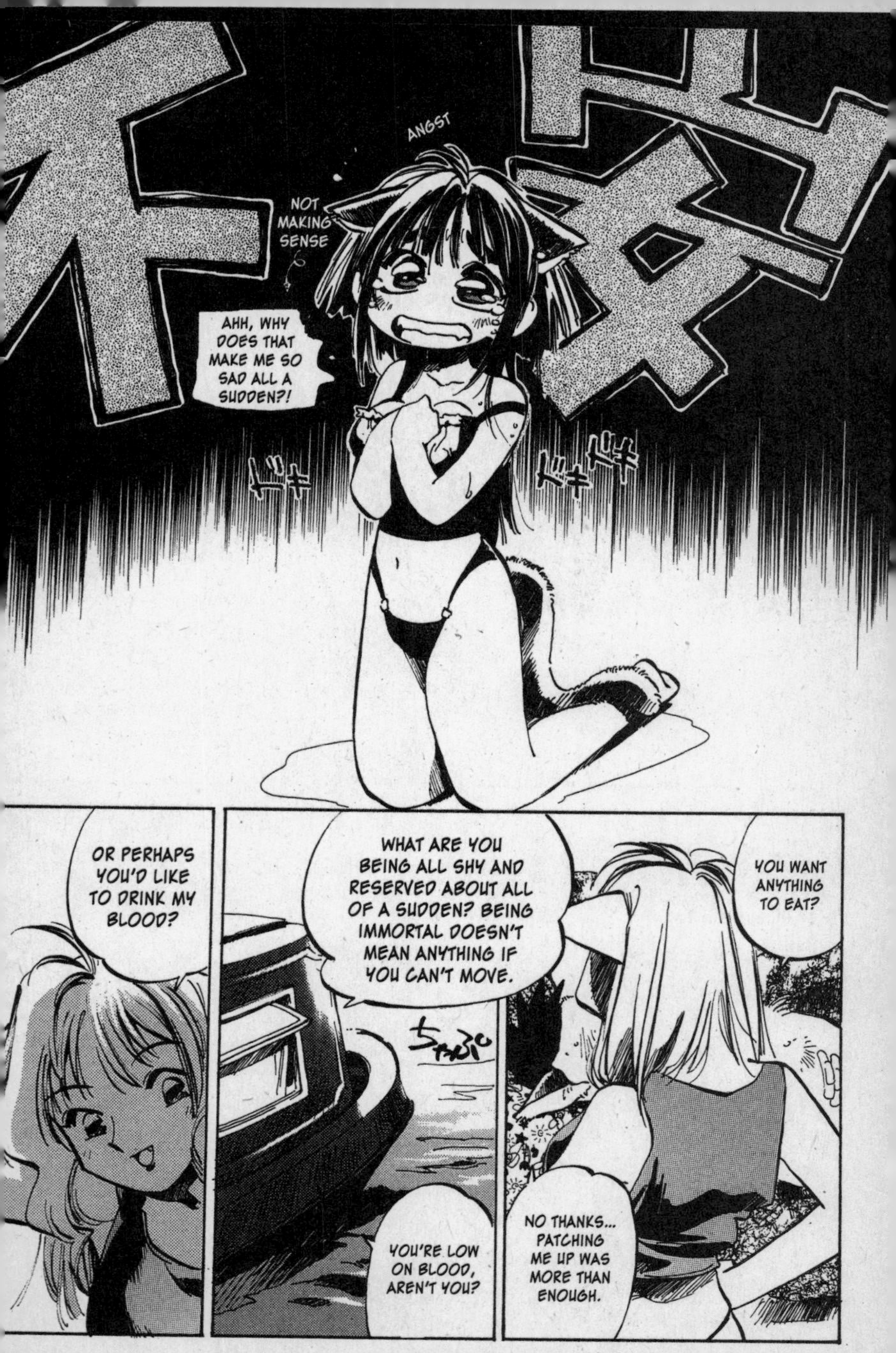
ANGST
NOT MAKING SENSE
AHH, WHY DOES THAT MAKE ME SO SAD ALL A SUDDEN?!
YOU WANT ANYTHING TO EAT?
NO THANKS... PATCHING ME UP WAS MORE THAN ENOUGH.
WHAT ARE YOU BEING ALL SHY AND RESERVED ABOUT ALL OF A SUDDEN? BEING IMMORTAL DOESN'T MEAN ANYTHING IF YOU CAN'T MOVE.
YOU'RE LOW ON BLOOD, AREN'T YOU?
OR PERHAPS YOU'D LIKE TO DRINK MY BLOOD?

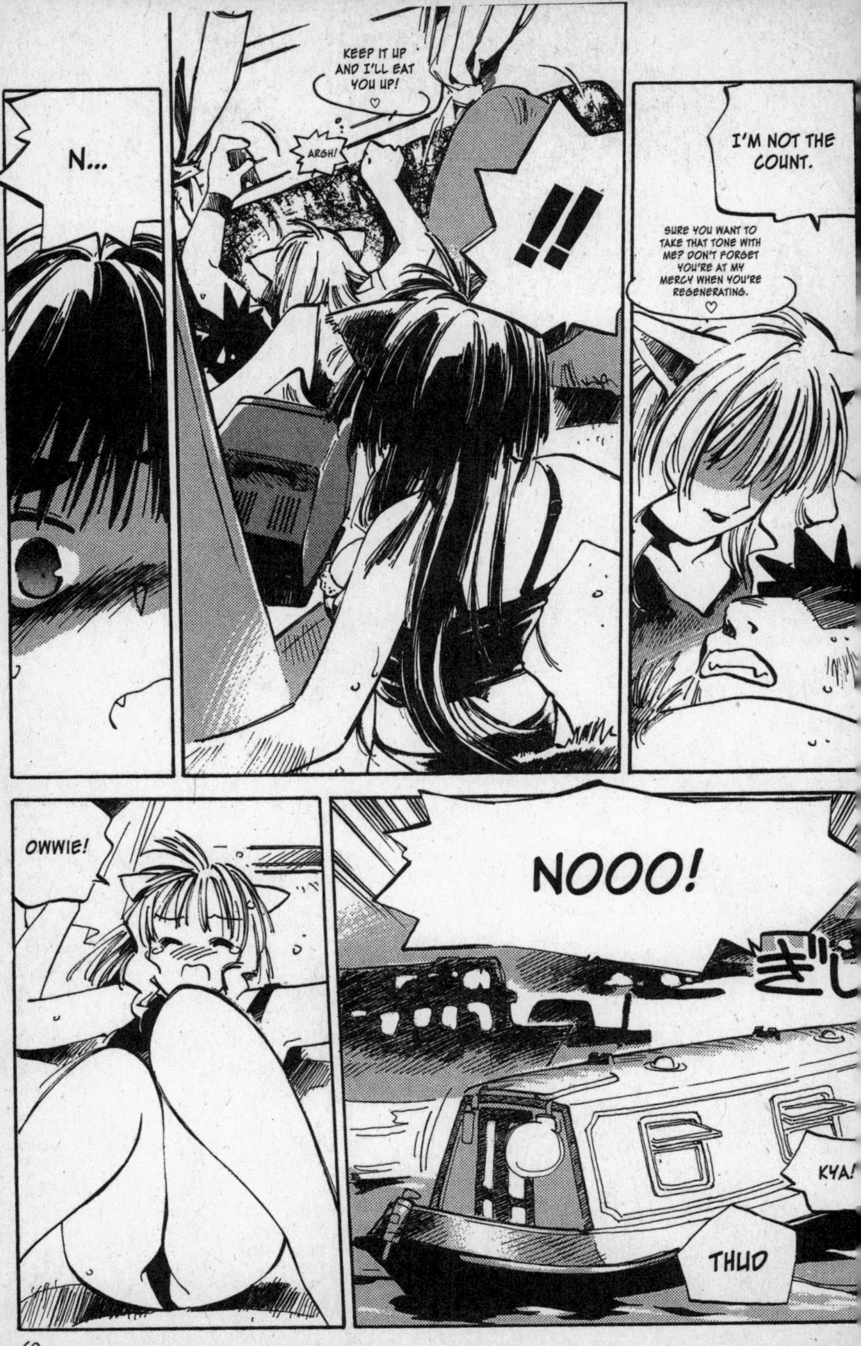

I'M NOT THE COUNT.
SURE YOU WANT TO TAKE THAT TONE WITH ME? DON'T FORGET YOU'RE AT MY MERCY WHEN YOU'RE REGENERATING. ♡
KEEP IT UP AND I'LL EAT YOU UP! ♡
ARGH!
!!
N...
NOOO!
ぎし
KYA!
THUD
OWWIE!

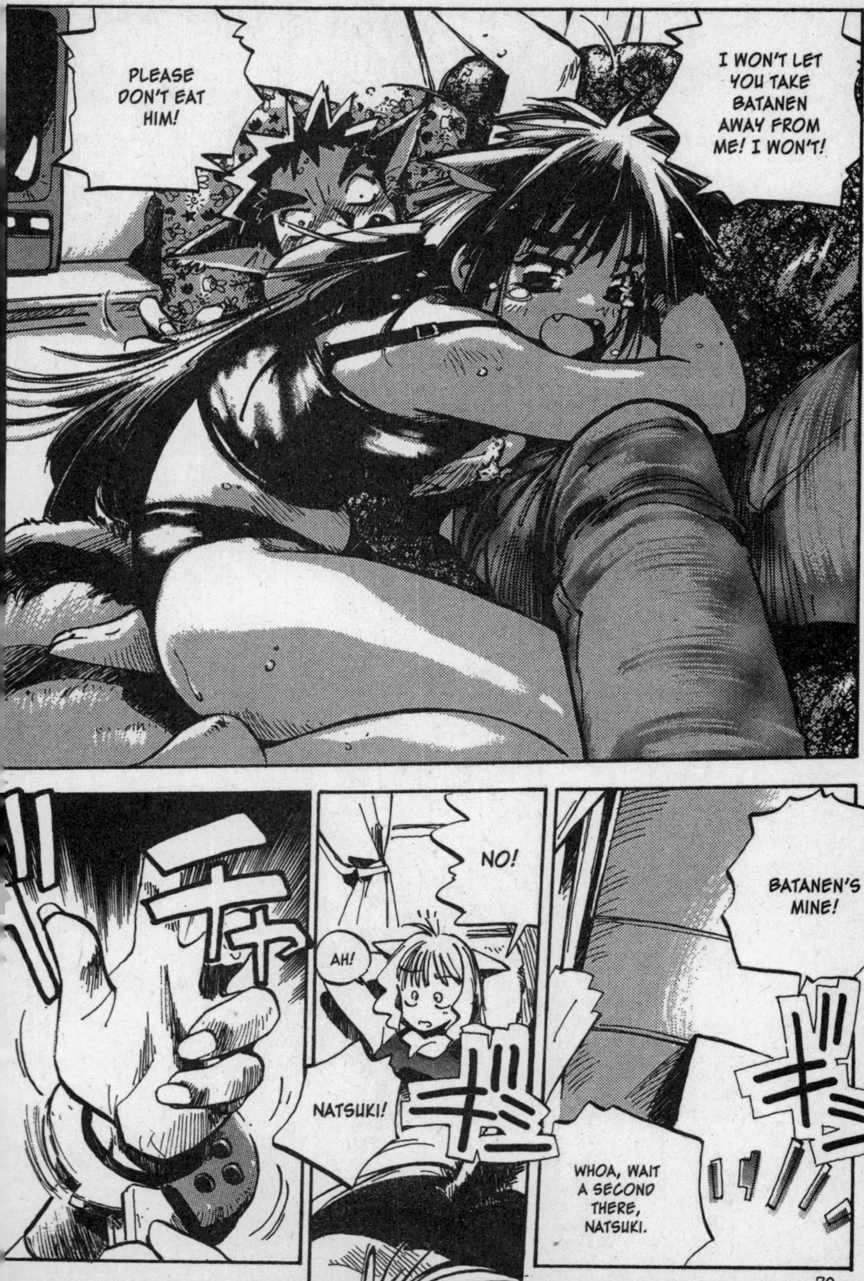
I WON'T LET YOU TAKE BATANEN AWAY FROM ME! I WON'T!
PLEASE DON'T EAT HIM!
BATANEN'S MINE!
WHOA, WAIT A SECOND THERE, NATSUKI.
NO!
AH!
NATSUKI!

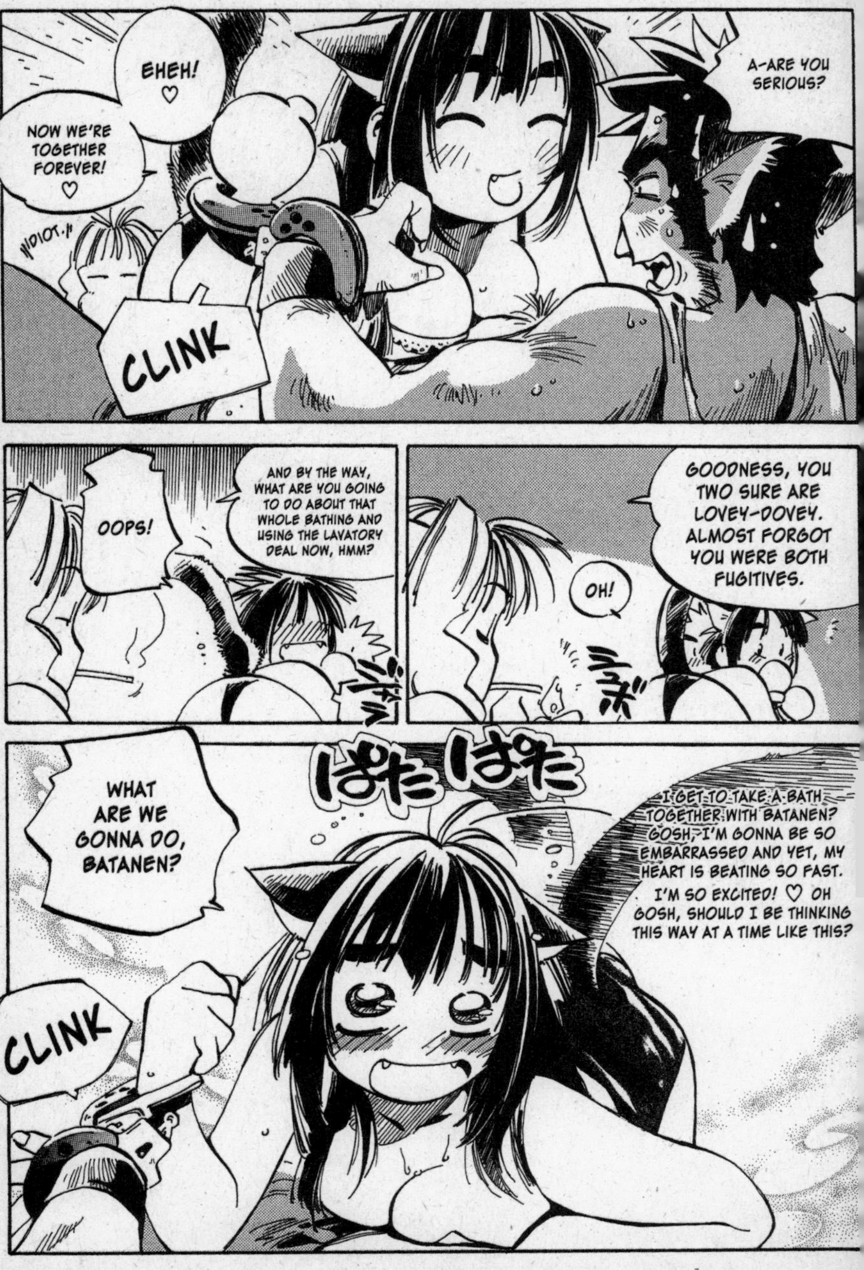
A-ARE YOU SERIOUS?
EHEH! ♡
NOW WE'RE TOGETHER FOREVER! ♡
IDIOT..!!
CLINK
GOODNESS, YOU TWO SURE ARE LOVEY-DOVEY. ALMOST FORGOT YOU WERE BOTH FUGITIVES.
OH!
AND BY THE WAY, WHAT ARE YOU GOING TO DO ABOUT THAT WHOLE BATHING AND USING THE LAVATORY DEAL NOW, HMM?
OOPS!
I GET TO TAKE A BATH TOGETHER WITH BATANEN? GOSH, I'M GONNA BE SO EMBARRASSED AND YET, MY HEART IS BEATING SO FAST. I'M SO EXCITED! ♡ OH GOSH, SHOULD I BE THINKING THIS WAY AT A TIME LIKE THIS?
ぱた ぱた
WHAT ARE WE GONNA DO, BATANEN?
CLINK

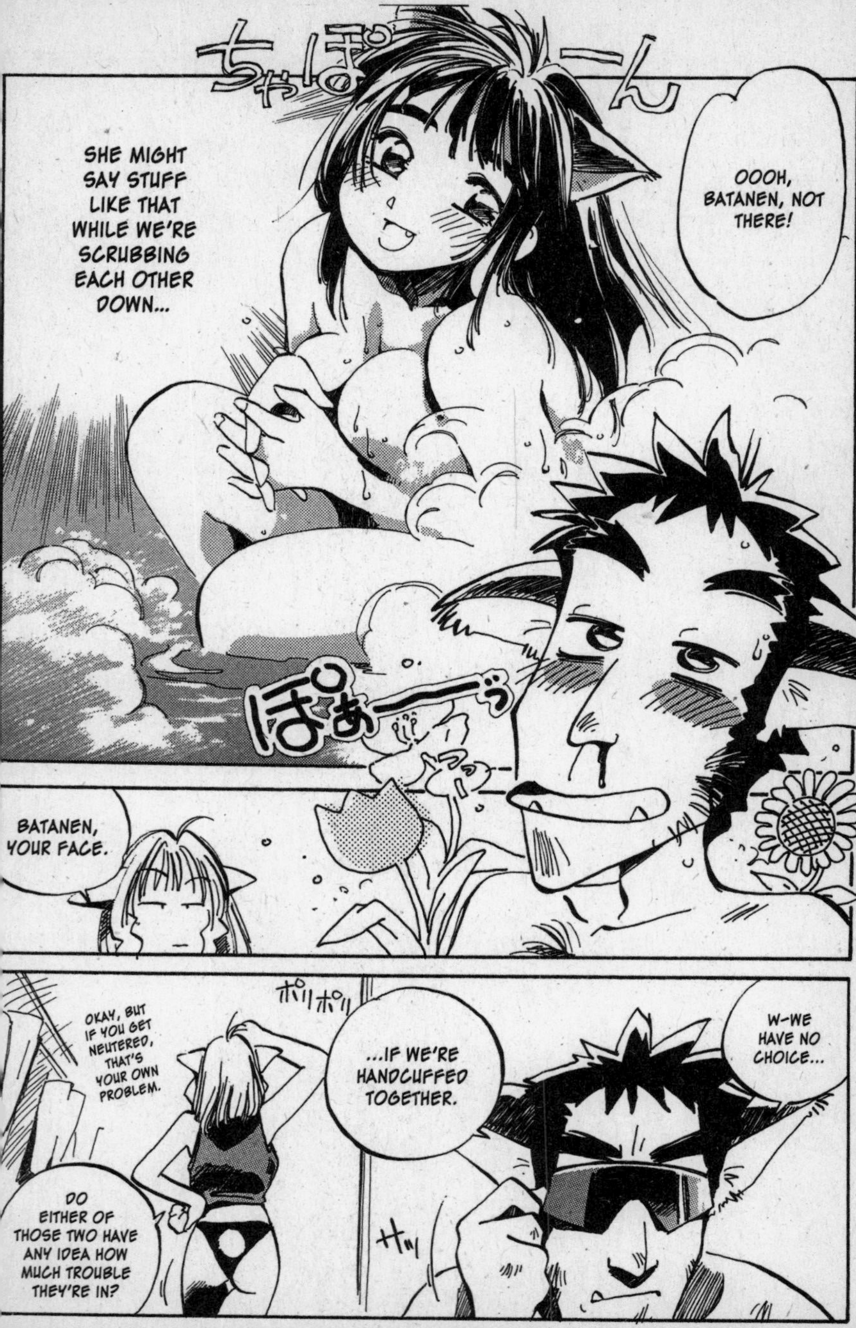

ちゃぽーーん
OOOH, BATANEN, NOT THERE!
SHE MIGHT SAY STUFF LIKE THAT WHILE WE'RE SCRUBBING EACH OTHER DOWN...
ぽあーーっ
BATANEN, YOUR FACE.
W-WE HAVE NO CHOICE...
...IF WE'RE HANDCUFFED TOGETHER.
ポリポリ
OKAY, BUT IF YOU GET NEUTERED, THAT'S YOUR OWN PROBLEM.
DO EITHER OF THOSE TWO HAVE ANY IDEA HOW MUCH TROUBLE THEY'RE IN?

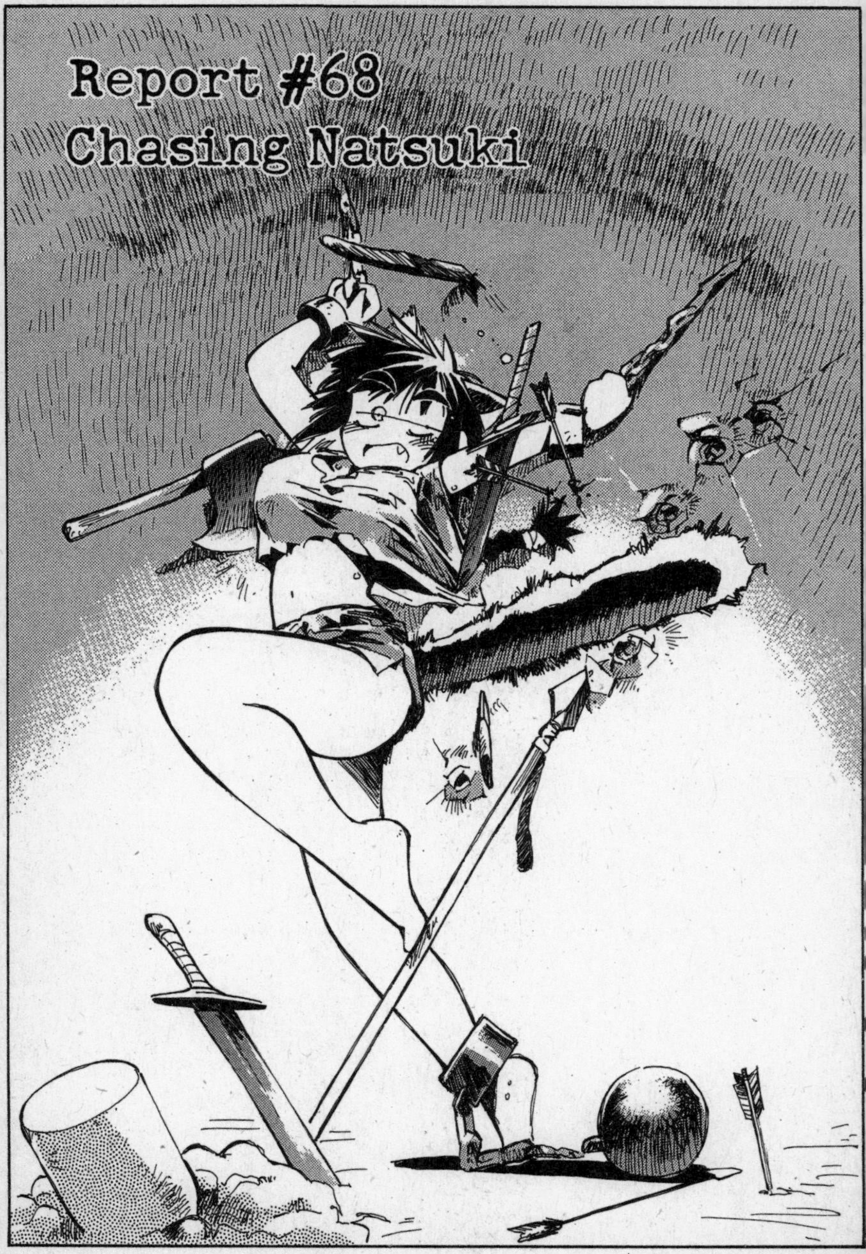
Report #68
Chasing Natsuki

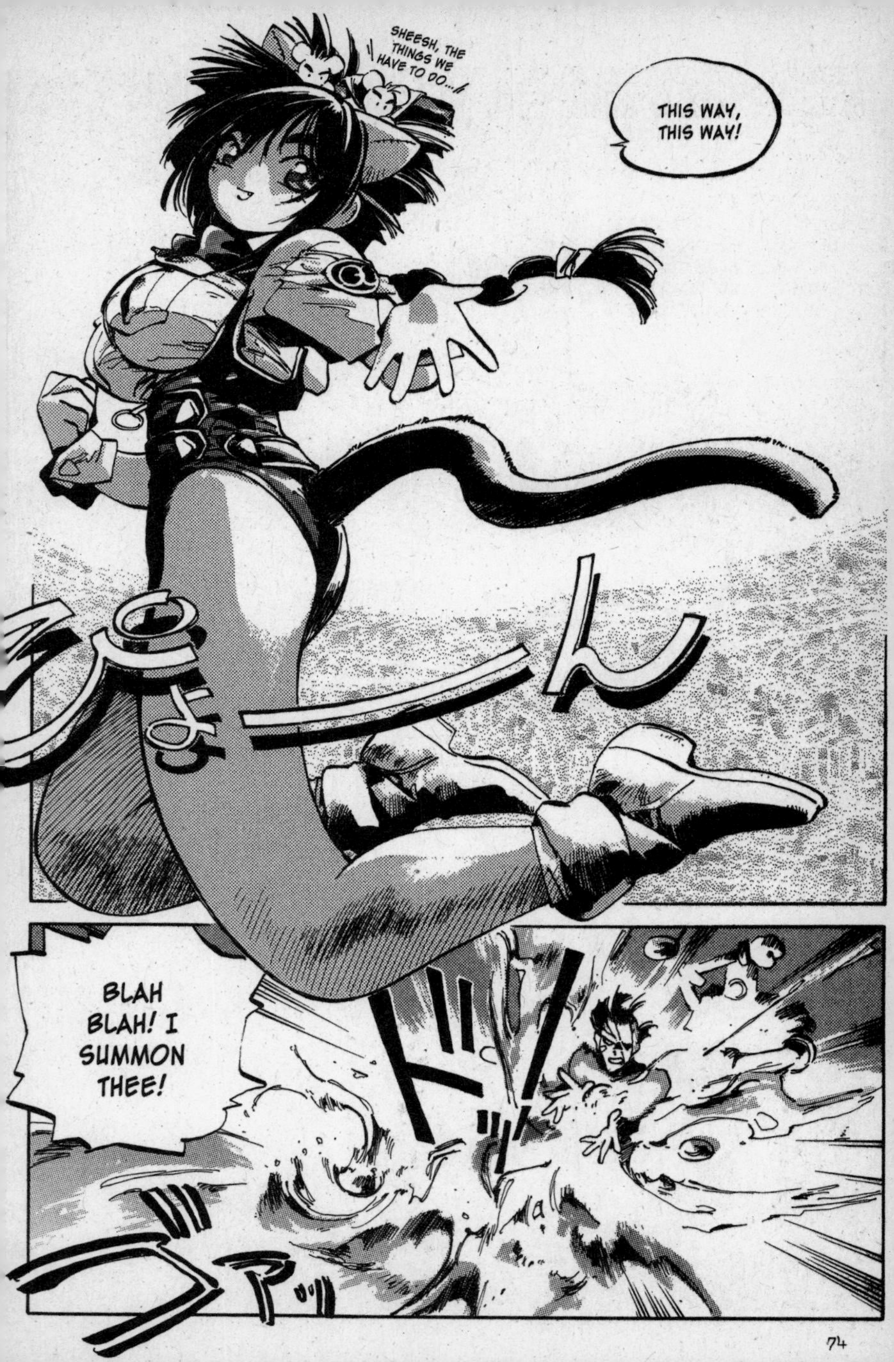
THIS WAY, THIS WAY!
SHEESH, THE THINGS WE HAVE TO DO...!
BLAH BLAH! I SUMMON THEE!

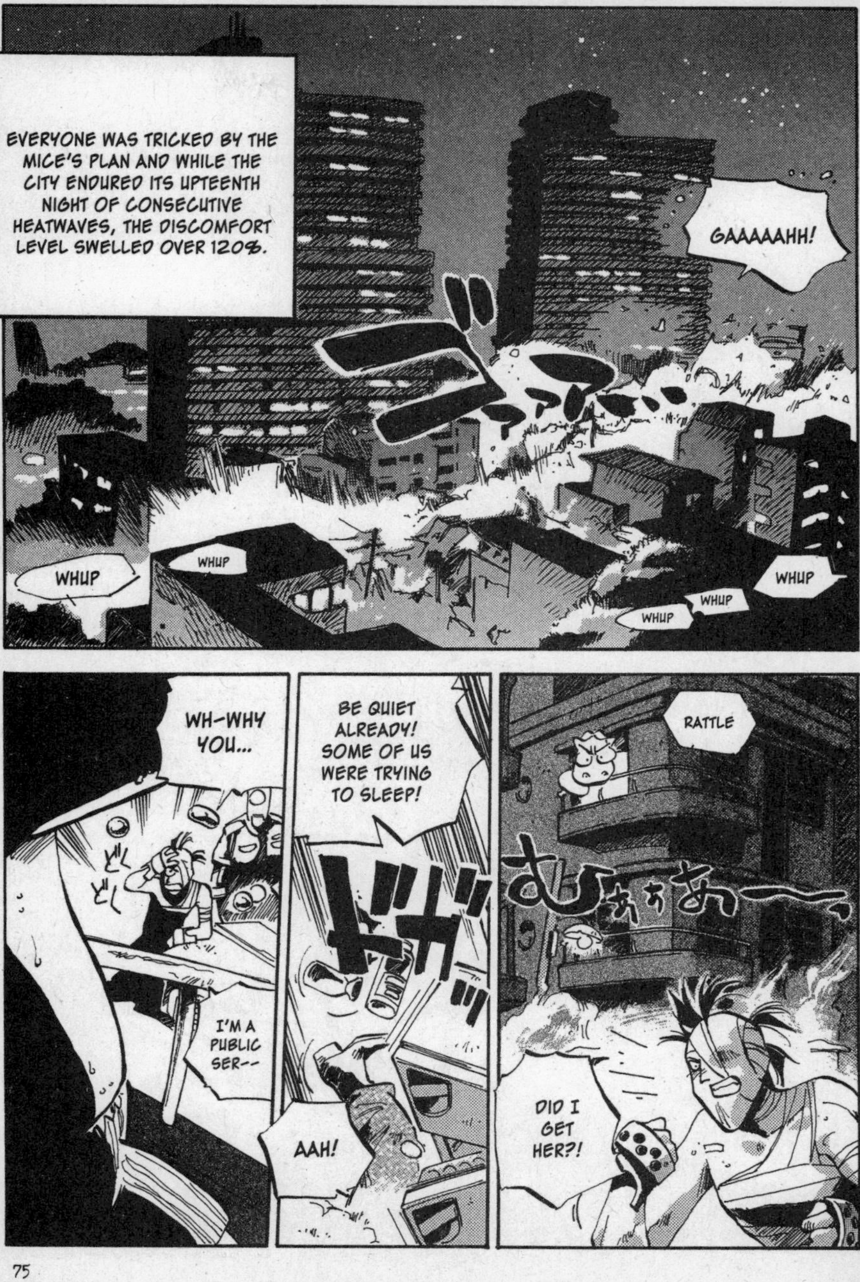
EVERYONE WAS TRICKED BY THE MICE'S PLAN AND WHILE THE CITY ENDURED ITS UPTEENTH NIGHT OF CONSECUTIVE HEATWAVES, THE DISCOMFORT LEVEL SWELLED OVER 120%.
GAAAAAHH!
WHUP
WHUP
WHUP
WHUP
WHUP
RATTLE
DID I GET HER?!
BE QUIET ALREADY! SOME OF US WERE TRYING TO SLEEP!
AAH!
WH-WHY YOU...
I'M A PUBLIC SER--
どし
どし

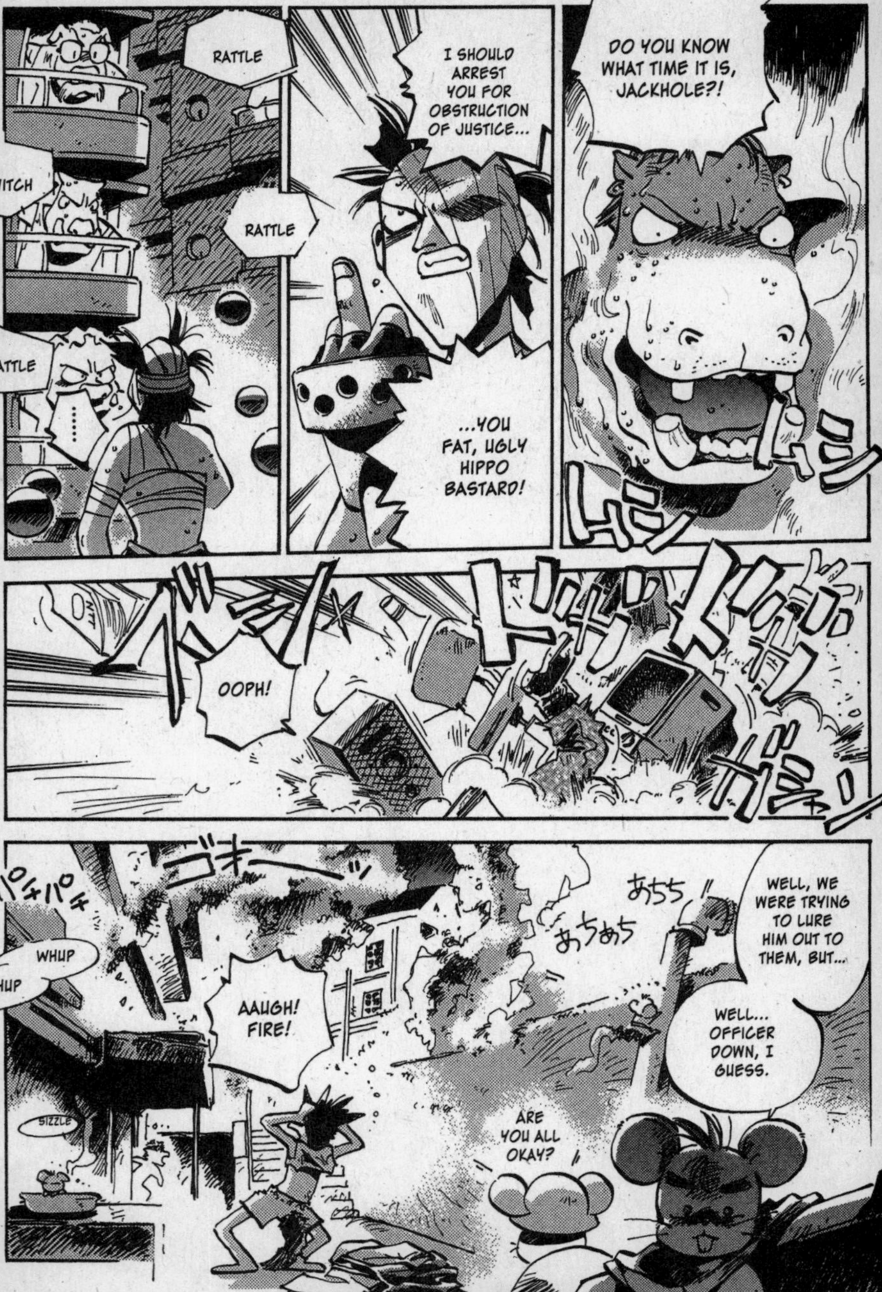
DO YOU KNOW WHAT TIME IT IS, JACKHOLE?!
I SHOULD ARREST YOU FOR OBSTRUCTION OF JUSTICE...
...YOU FAT, UGLY HIPPO BASTARD!
RATTLE
WITCH
RATTLE
ATTLE
OOPH!
WELL, WE WERE TRYING TO LURE HIM OUT TO THEM, BUT...
WELL... OFFICER DOWN, I GUESS.
あちち
あちあち
ARE YOU ALL OKAY?
AAUGH! FIRE!
パチパチ
WHUP
HUP
SIZZLE

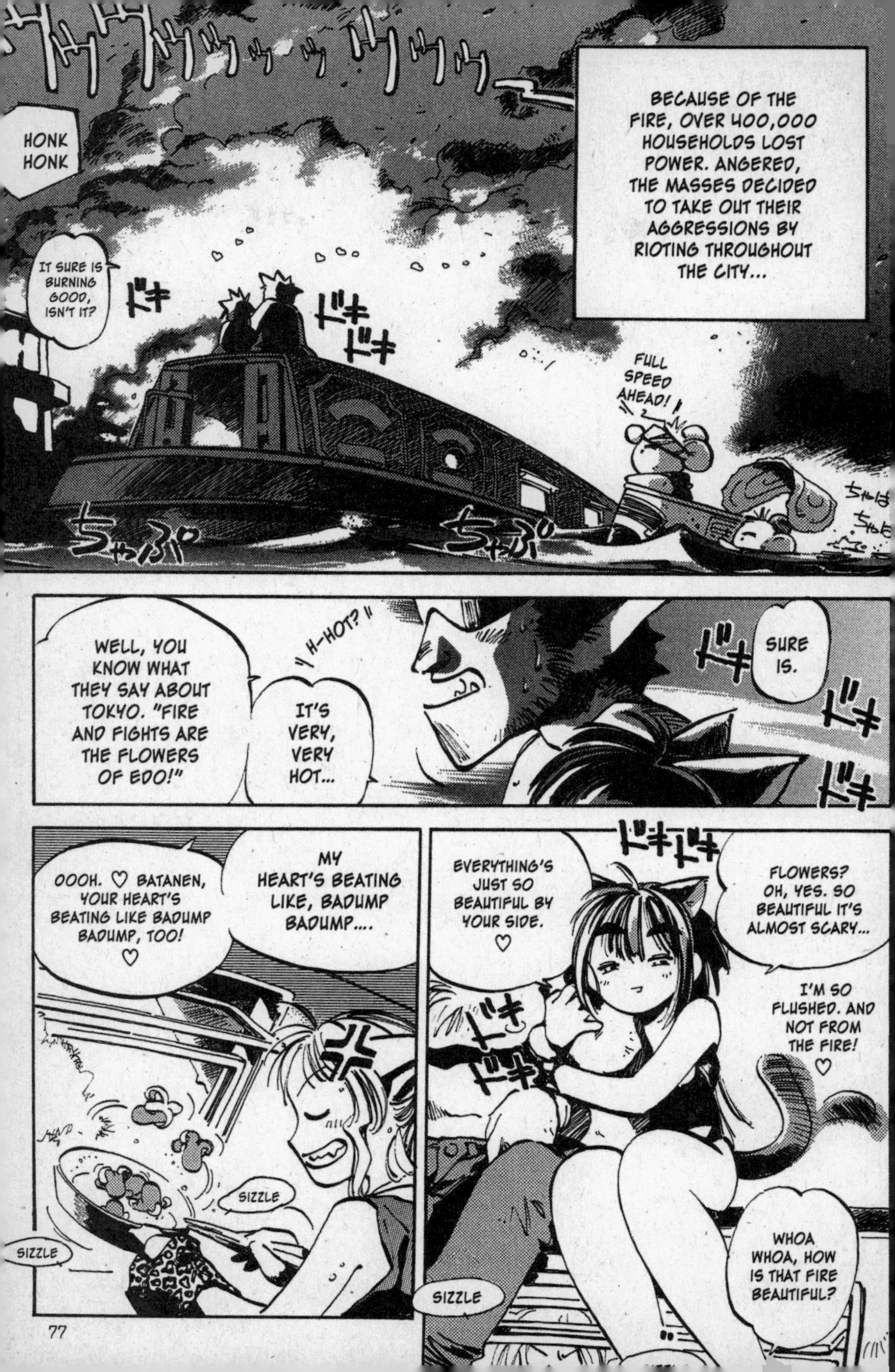
BECAUSE OF THE FIRE, OVER 400,000 HOUSEHOLDS LOST POWER. ANGERED, THE MASSES DECIDED TO TAKE OUT THEIR AGGRESSIONS BY RIOTING THROUGHOUT THE CITY...
FULL SPEED AHEAD!
ドキ ドキ
IT SURE IS BURNING GOOD, ISN'T IT?
ドキ
HONK HONK
ちゃぷ
ちゃぷ
SURE IS.
ドキ
ドキ
ドキ
H-HOT?!!
IT'S VERY, VERY HOT...
WELL, YOU KNOW WHAT THEY SAY ABOUT TOKYO. "FIRE AND FIGHTS ARE THE FLOWERS OF EDO!"
ドキドキ
FLOWERS? OH, YES. SO BEAUTIFUL IT'S ALMOST SCARY...
EVERYTHING'S JUST SO BEAUTIFUL BY YOUR SIDE. ♡
I'M SO FLUSHED. AND NOT FROM THE FIRE! ♡
ドキ
ドキ
WHOA WHOA, HOW IS THAT FIRE BEAUTIFUL?
SIZZLE
MY HEART'S BEATING LIKE, BADUMP BADUMP....
OOOH. ♡ BATANEN, YOUR HEART'S BEATING LIKE BADUMP BADUMP, TOO! ♡
SIZZLE
SIZZLE

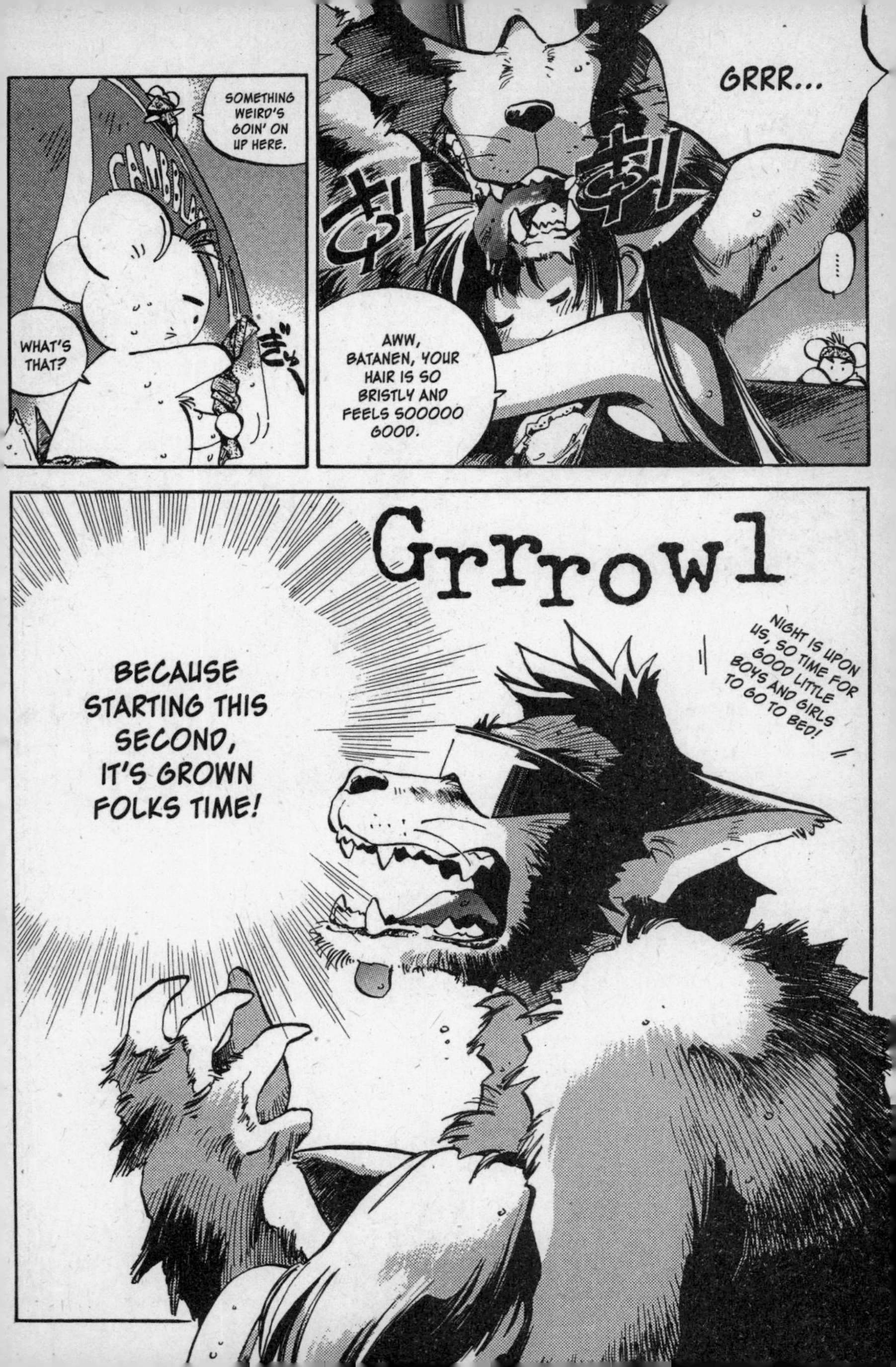
GRRR...
......
AWW, BATANEN, YOUR HAIR IS SO BRISTLY AND FEELS SOOOOO GOOD.
SOMETHING WEIRD'S GOIN' ON UP HERE.
WHAT'S THAT?
ぎゅ～
Grrrowl
NIGHT IS UPON US, SO TIME FOR GOOD LITTLE BOYS AND GIRLS TO GO TO BED!
BECAUSE STARTING THIS SECOND, IT'S GROWN FOLKS TIME!

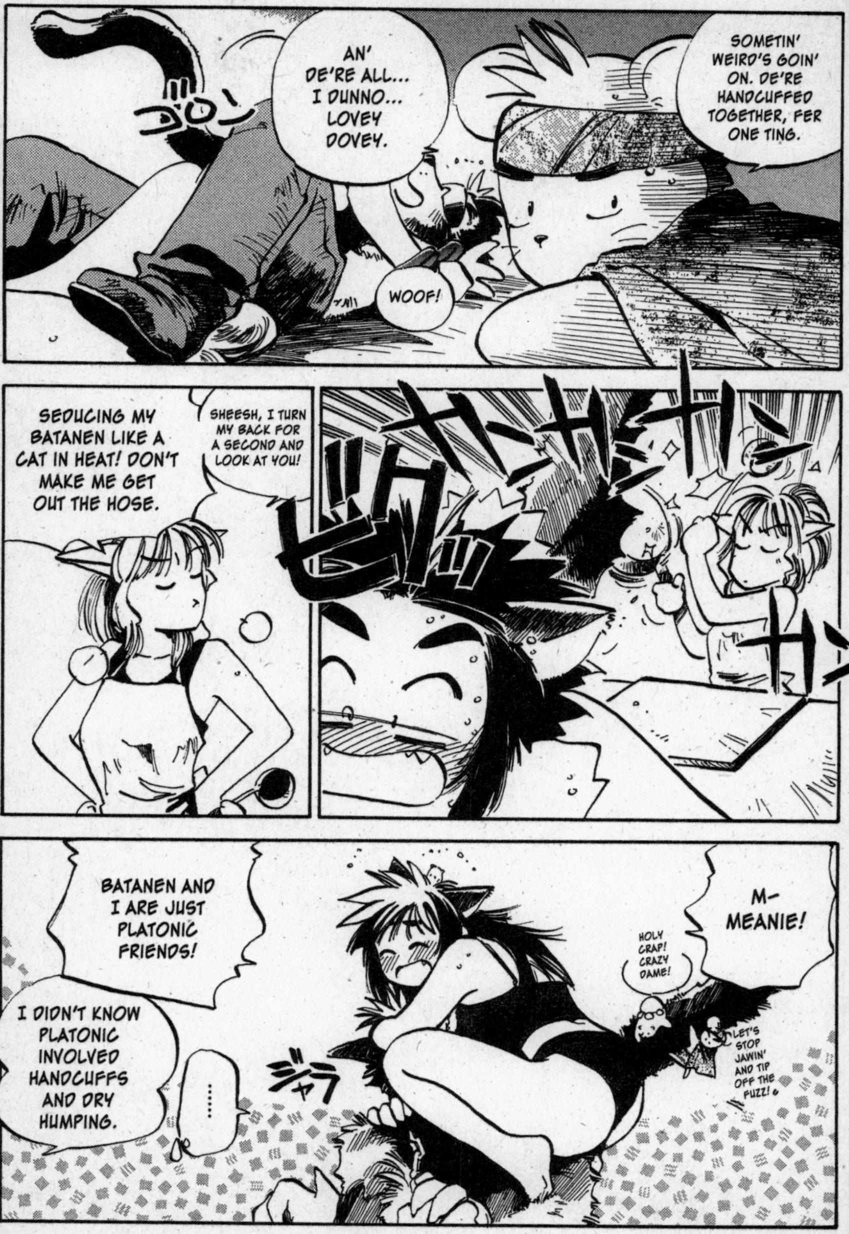
SOMETIN' WEIRD'S GOIN' ON. DE'RE HANDCUFFED TOGETHER, FER ONE TING.
AN' DE'RE ALL... I DUNNO... LOVEY DOVEY.
WOOF!
SHEESH, I TURN MY BACK FOR A SECOND AND LOOK AT YOU!
SEDUCING MY BATANEN LIKE A CAT IN HEAT! DON'T MAKE ME GET OUT THE HOSE.
M-MEANIE!
HOLY CRAP! CRAZY DAME!
LET'S STOP JAWIN' AND TIP OFF THE FUZZ!
BATANEN AND I ARE JUST PLATONIC FRIENDS!
I DIDN'T KNOW PLATONIC INVOLVED HANDCUFFS AND DRY HUMPING.
......

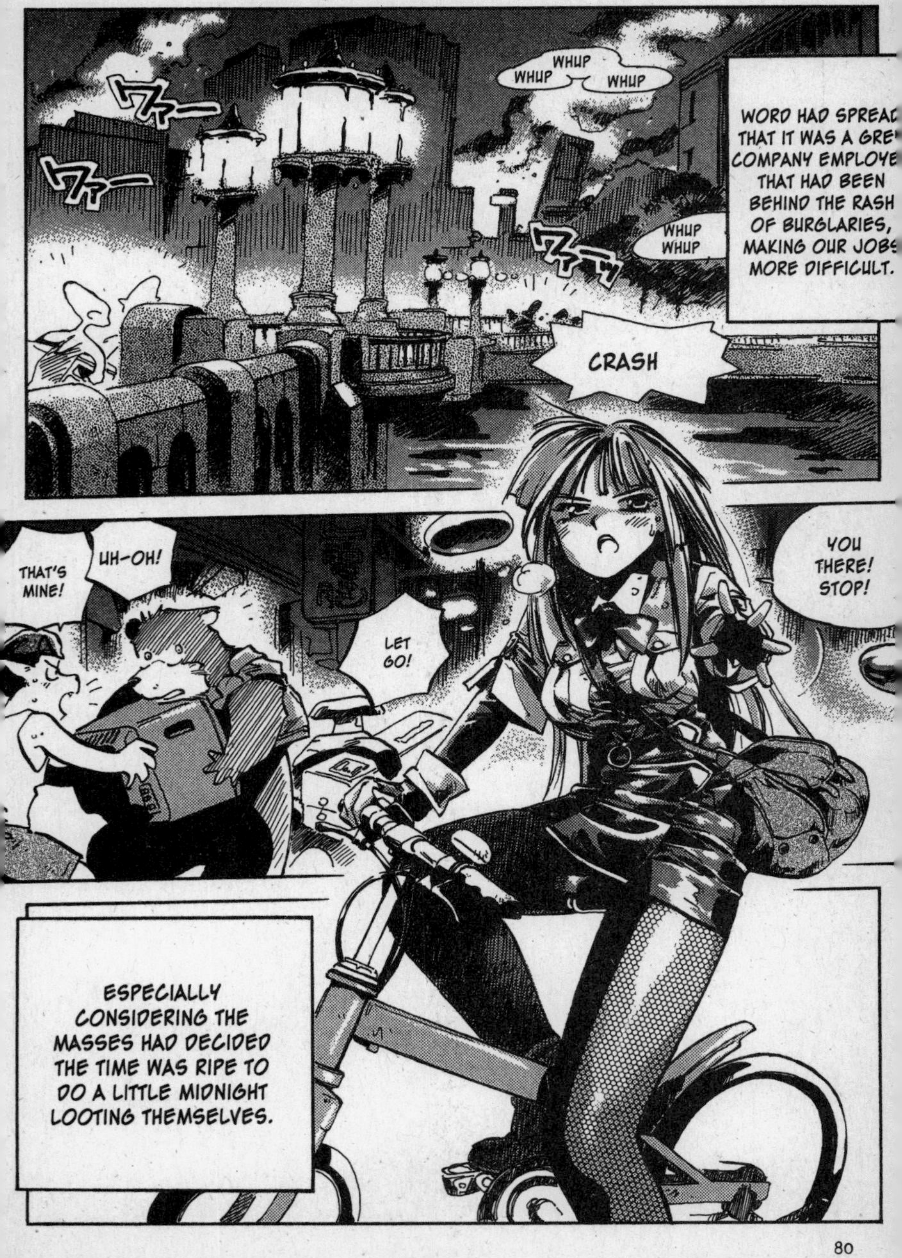
WORD HAD SPREAD THAT IT WAS A GRE COMPANY EMPLOYE THAT HAD BEEN BEHIND THE RASH OF BURGLARIES, MAKING OUR JOBS MORE DIFFICULT.
WHUP WHUP
WHUP WHUP WHUP
ワァーッ
ワァー
ワァー
CRASH
YOU THERE! STOP!
LET GO!
UH-OH!
THAT'S MINE!
ESPECIALLY CONSIDERING THE MASSES HAD DECIDED THE TIME WAS RIPE TO DO A LITTLE MIDNIGHT LOOTING THEMSELVES.

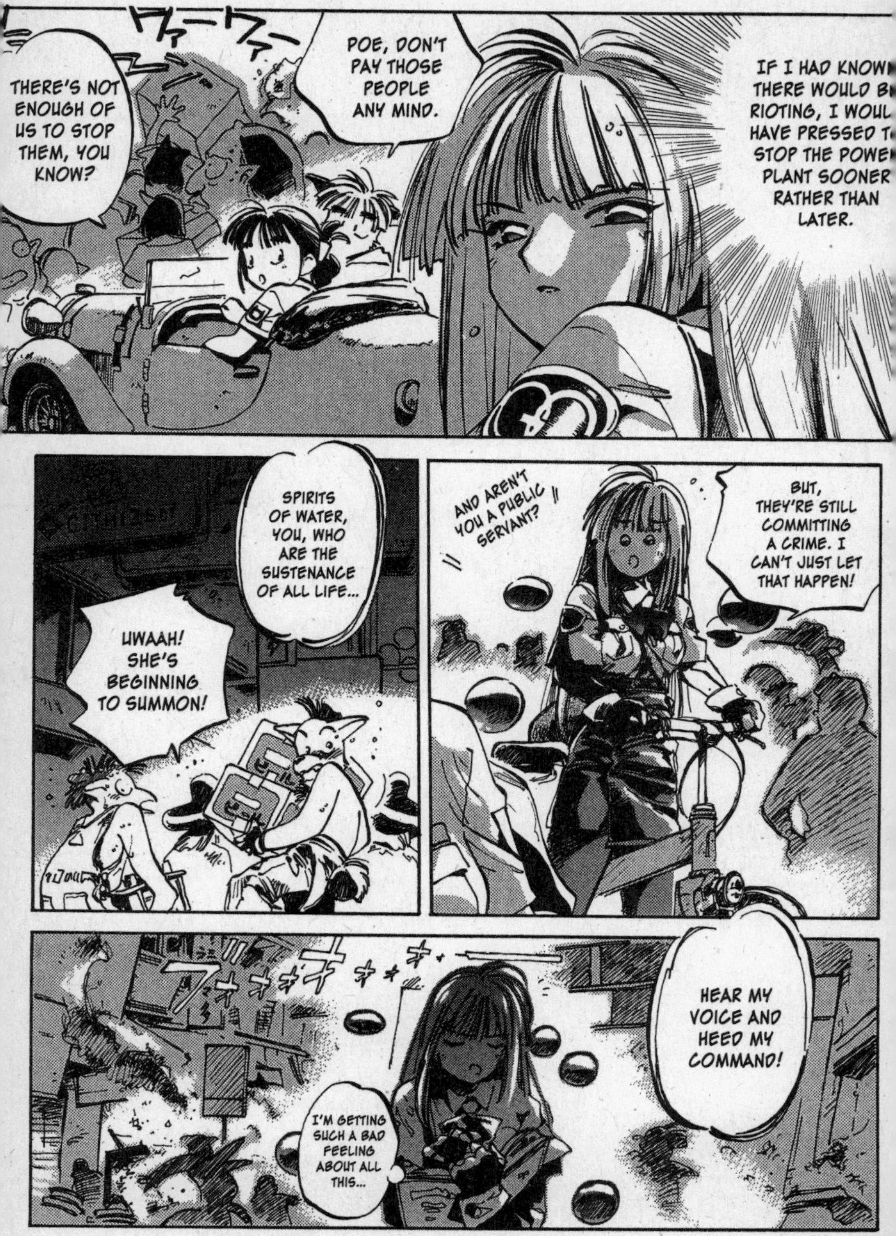
IF I HAD KNOWN THERE WOULD B RIOTING, I WOUL HAVE PRESSED T STOP THE POWE PLANT SOONER RATHER THAN LATER.
POE, DON'T PAY THOSE PEOPLE ANY MIND.
THERE'S NOT ENOUGH OF US TO STOP THEM, YOU KNOW?
BUT, THEY'RE STILL COMMITTING A CRIME. I CAN'T JUST LET THAT HAPPEN!
AND AREN'T YOU A PUBLIC SERVANT?
SPIRITS OF WATER, YOU, WHO ARE THE SUSTENANCE OF ALL LIFE...
UWAAH! SHE'S BEGINNING TO SUMMON!
HEAR MY VOICE AND HEED MY COMMAND!
I'M GETTING SUCH A BAD FEELING ABOUT ALL THIS...

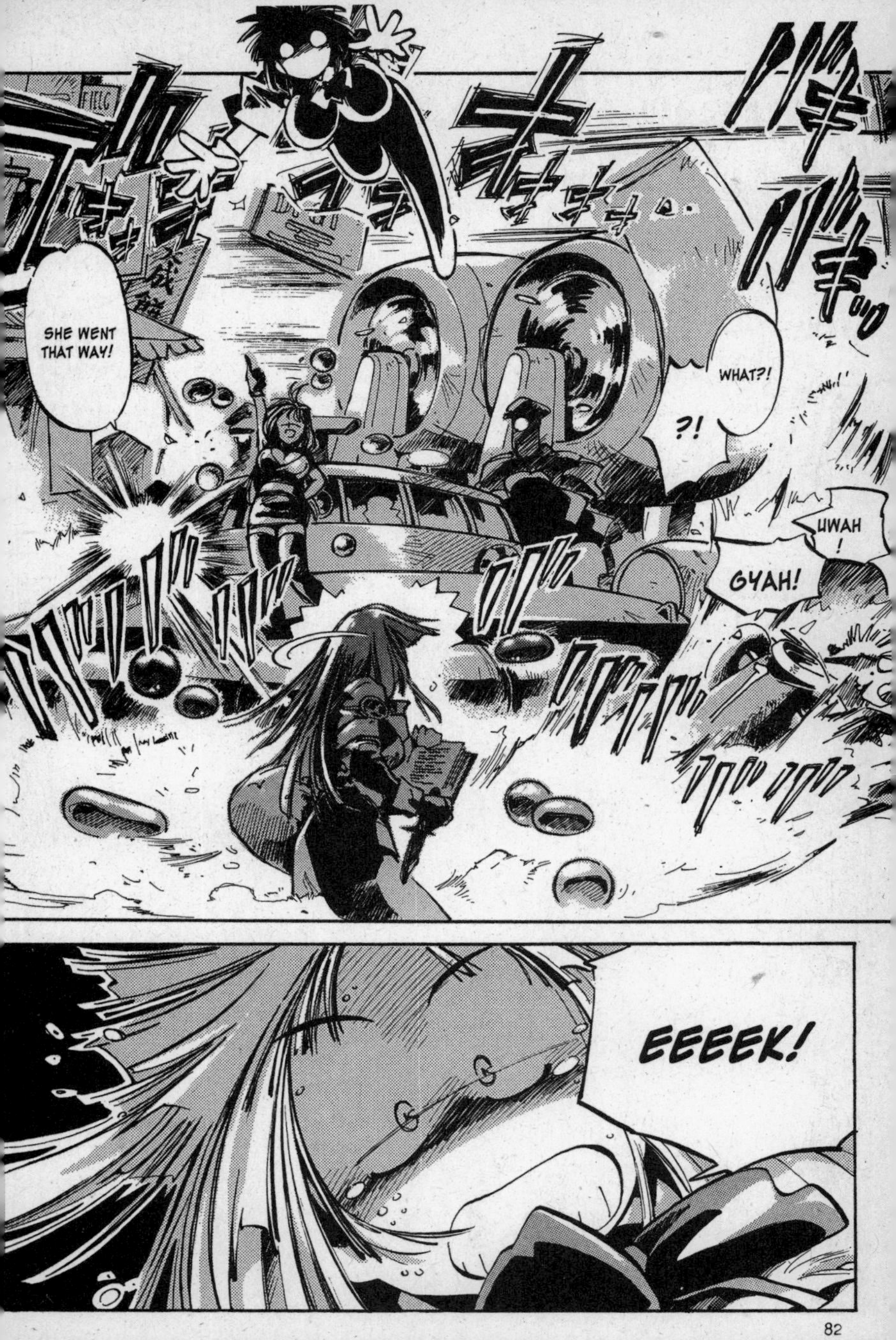
WHAT?!
?!
UWAH!
GYAH!
SHE WENT THAT WAY!
EEEEK!

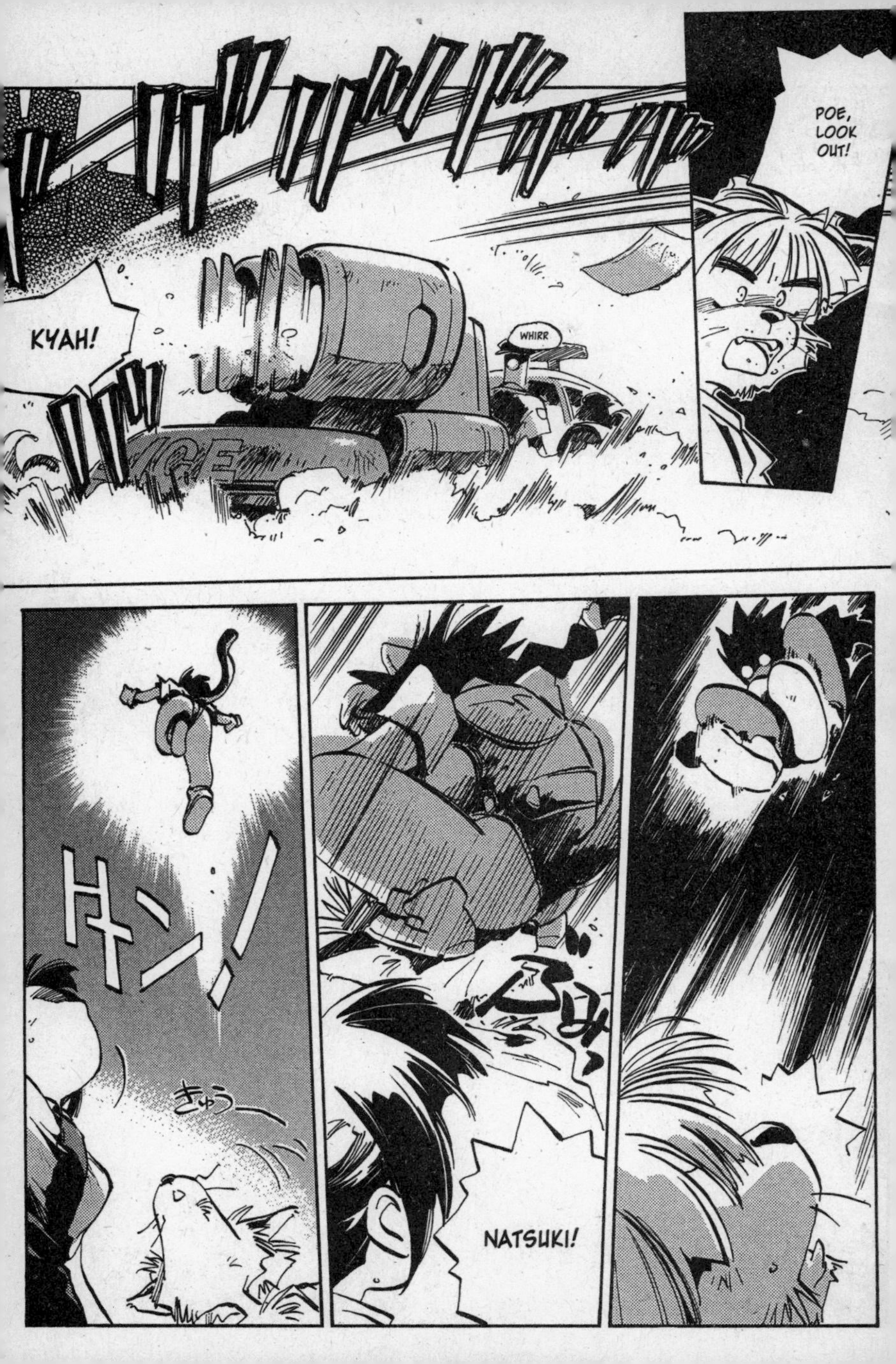
POE, LOOK OUT!
KYAH!
WHIRR
NATSUKI!

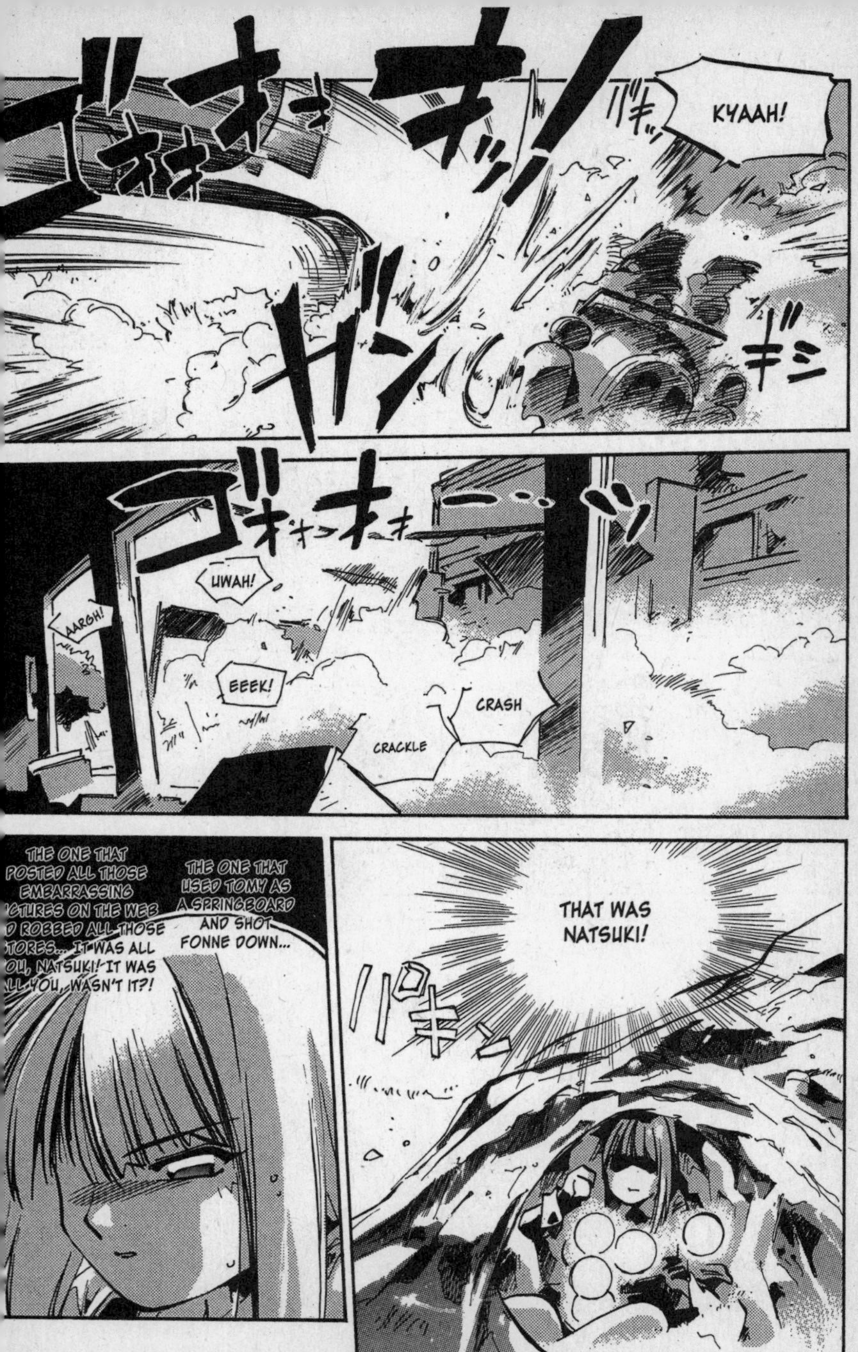
KYAAH!
UWAH!
AARGH!
CRASH
EEEK!
CRACKLE
THAT WAS NATSUKI!
THE ONE THAT USED TOMY AS A SPRINGBOARD AND SHOT FONNE DOWN...
THE ONE THAT POSTED ALL THOSE EMBARRASSING CTURES ON THE WEB D ROBBED ALL THOSE TORES... IT WAS ALL OU, NATSUKI! IT WAS LL YOU, WASN'T IT?!

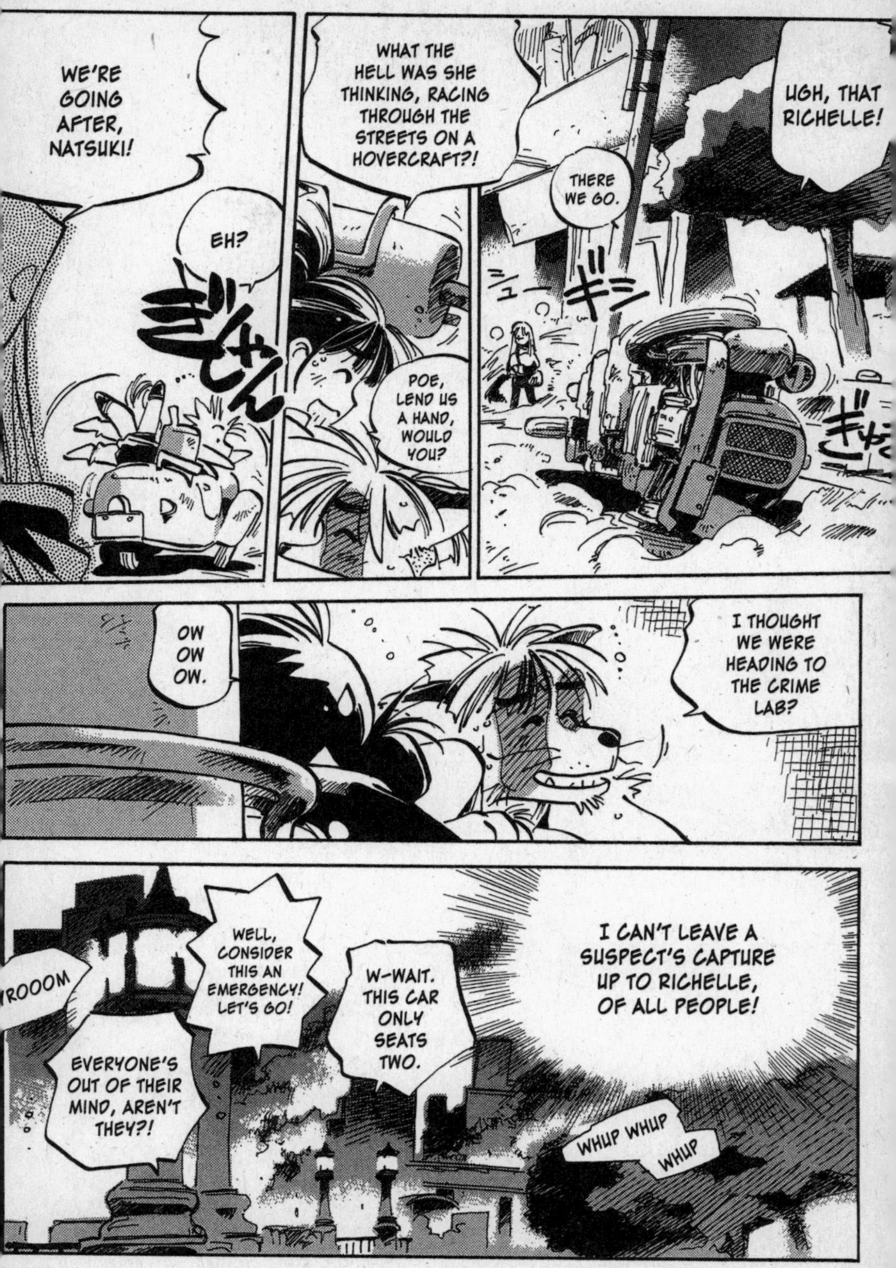
UGH, THAT RICHELLE!
THERE WE GO.
WHAT THE HELL WAS SHE THINKING, RACING THROUGH THE STREETS ON A HOVERCRAFT?!
POE, LEND US A HAND, WOULD YOU?
WE'RE GOING AFTER, NATSUKI!
EH?
I THOUGHT WE WERE HEADING TO THE CRIME LAB?
OW OW OW.
I CAN'T LEAVE A SUSPECT'S CAPTURE UP TO RICHELLE, OF ALL PEOPLE!
WHUP WHUP
WHUP
W-WAIT. THIS CAR ONLY SEATS TWO.
WELL, CONSIDER THIS AN EMERGENCY! LET'S GO!
EVERYONE'S OUT OF THEIR MIND, AREN'T THEY?!
ROOOM

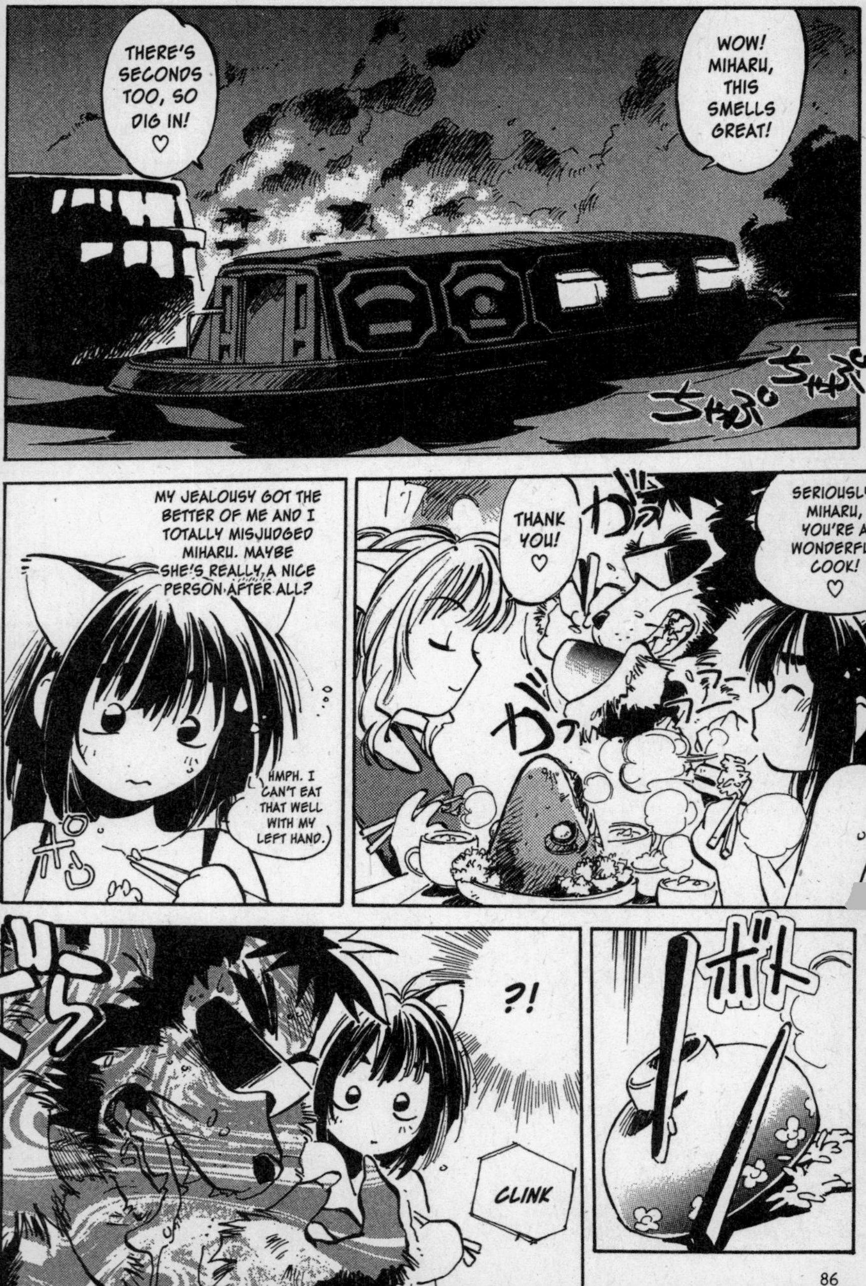
WOW! MIHARU, THIS SMELLS GREAT!
THERE'S SECONDS TOO, SO DIG IN! ♡
ちゃぷ ちゃぷ
SERIOUSLY, MIHARU, YOU'RE A WONDERFUL COOK! ♡
THANK YOU! ♡
MY JEALOUSY GOT THE BETTER OF ME AND I TOTALLY MISJUDGED MIHARU. MAYBE SHE'S REALLY A NICE PERSON AFTER ALL?
HMPH. I CAN'T EAT THAT WELL WITH MY LEFT HAND.
ボト
CLINK
?!

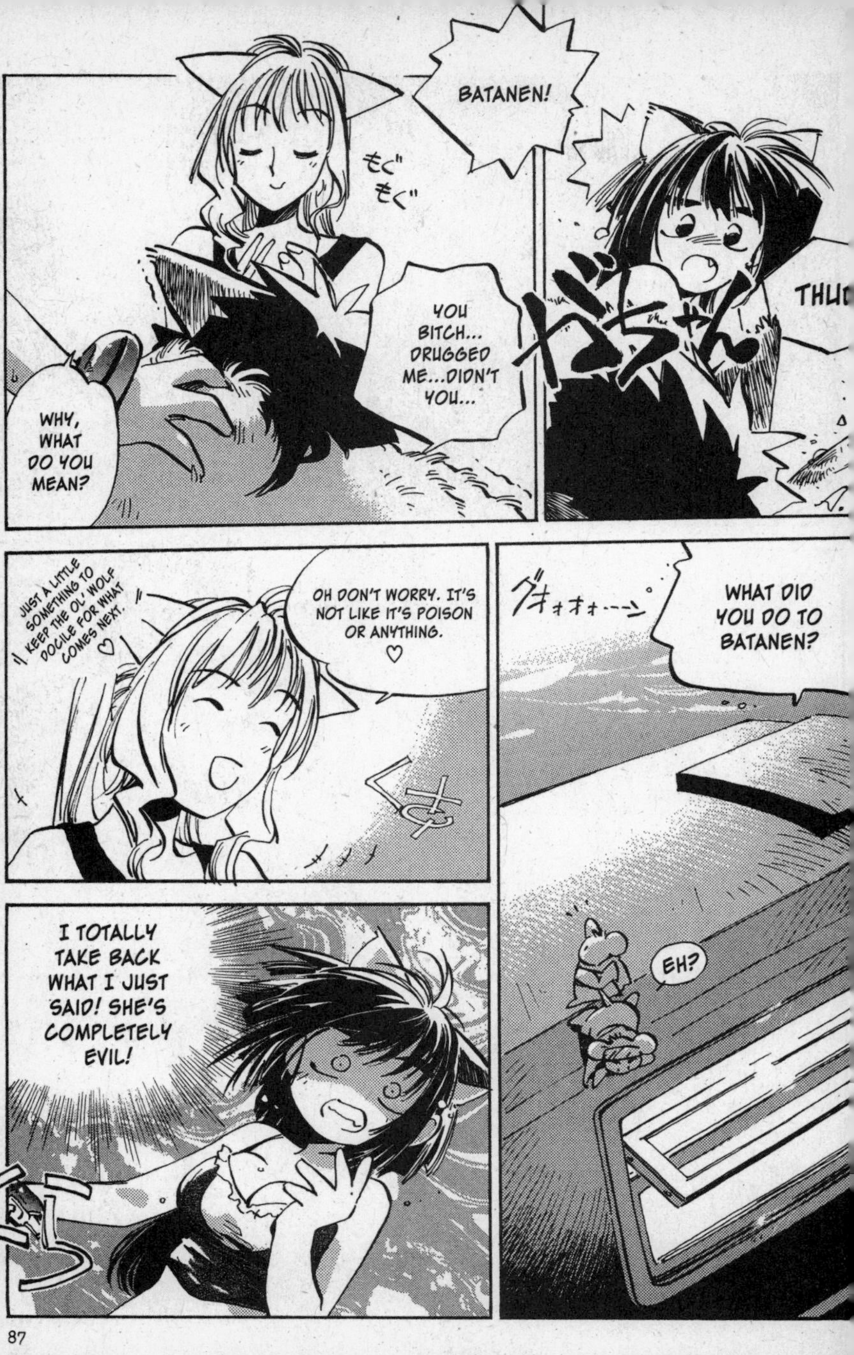
BATANEN!
THUD
YOU BITCH... DRUGGED ME...DIDN'T YOU...
WHY, WHAT DO YOU MEAN?
もぐ もぐ
WHAT DID YOU DO TO BATANEN?
EH?
OH DON'T WORRY. IT'S NOT LIKE IT'S POISON OR ANYTHING. ♡
JUST A LITTLE SOMETHING TO KEEP THE OL' WOLF DOCILE FOR WHAT COMES NEXT. ♡
I TOTALLY TAKE BACK WHAT I JUST SAID! SHE'S COMPLETELY EVIL!

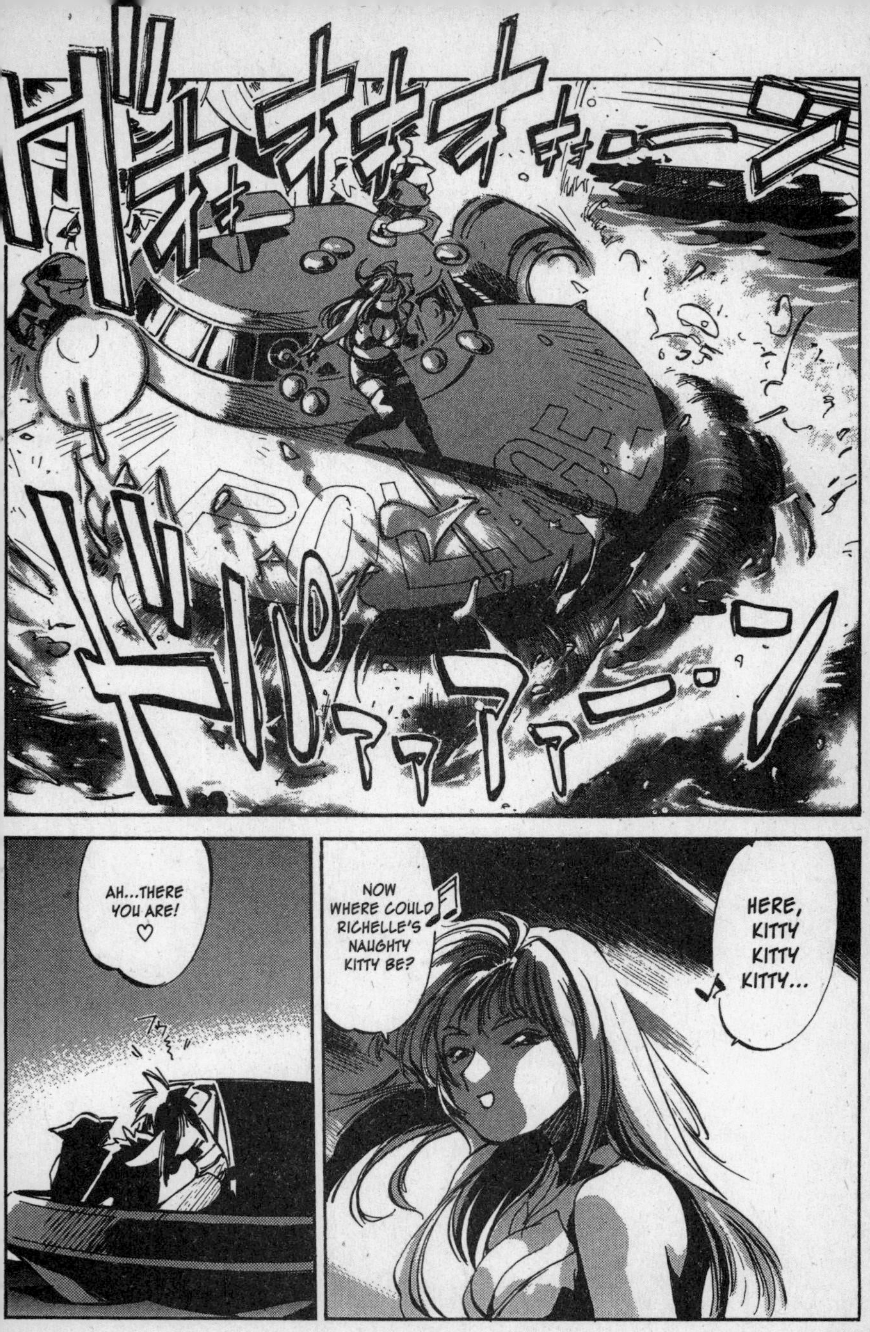
HERE, KITTY KITTY KITTY...
NOW WHERE COULD RICHELLE'S NAUGHTY KITTY BE?
AH...THERE YOU ARE! ♡

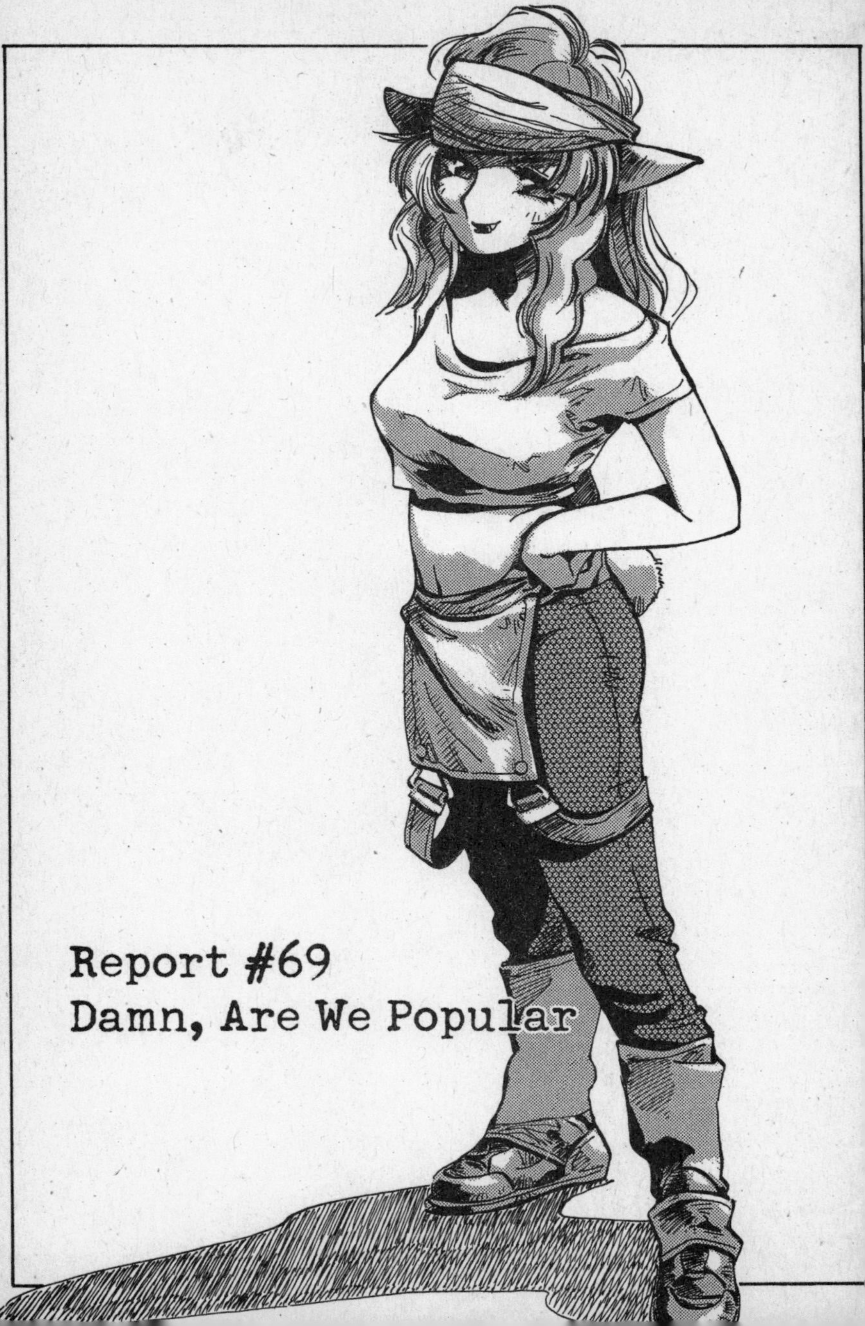

Report #69
Damn, Are We Popular

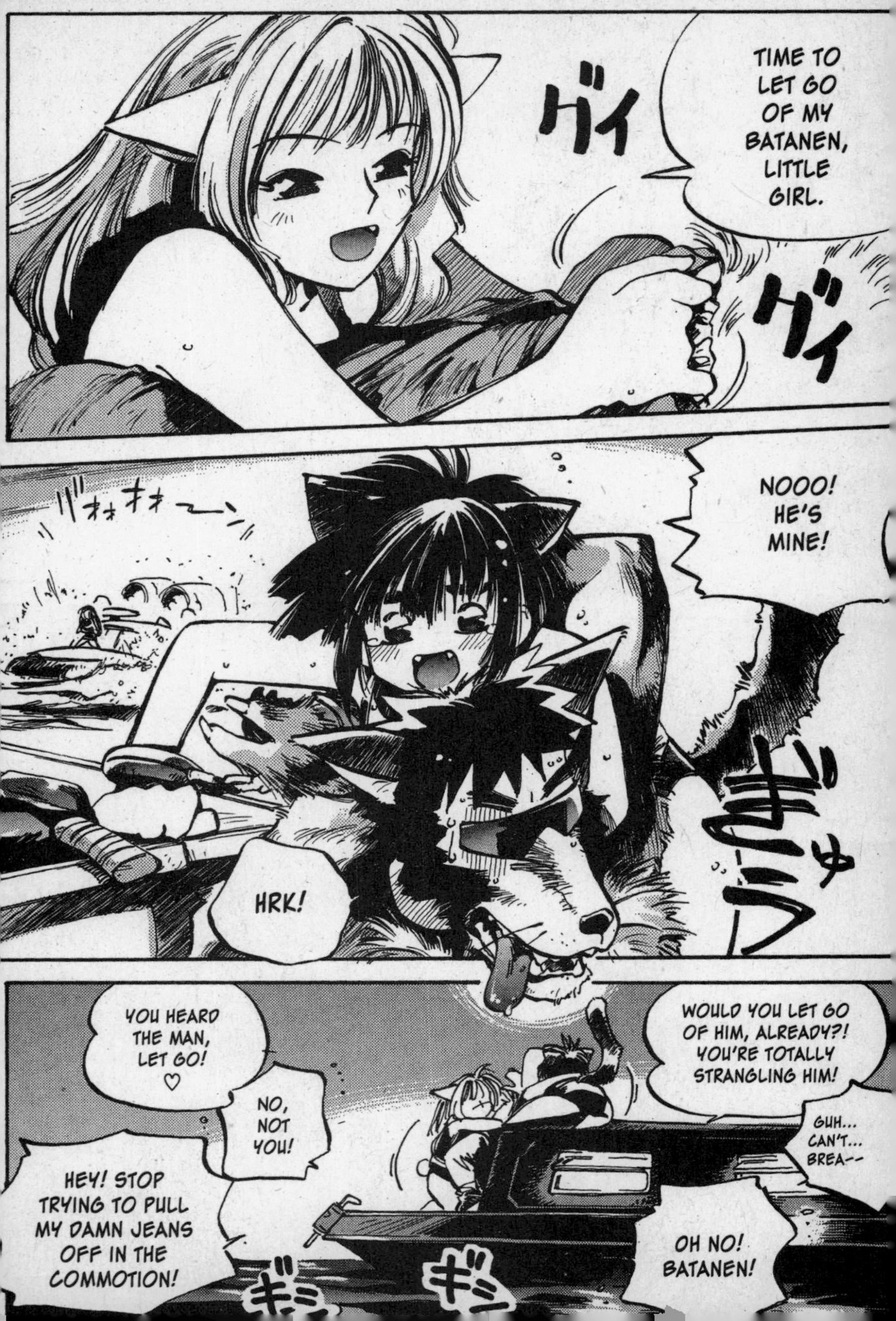
TIME TO LET GO OF MY BATANEN, LITTLE GIRL.
グイ
グイ
NOOO! HE'S MINE!
HRK!
WOULD YOU LET GO OF HIM, ALREADY?! YOU'RE TOTALLY STRANGLING HIM!
GUH... CAN'T... BREA--
YOU HEARD THE MAN, LET GO! ♡
NO, NOT YOU!
OH NO! BATANEN!
HEY! STOP TRYING TO PULL MY DAMN JEANS OFF IN THE COMMOTION!
ギシ
ギシ

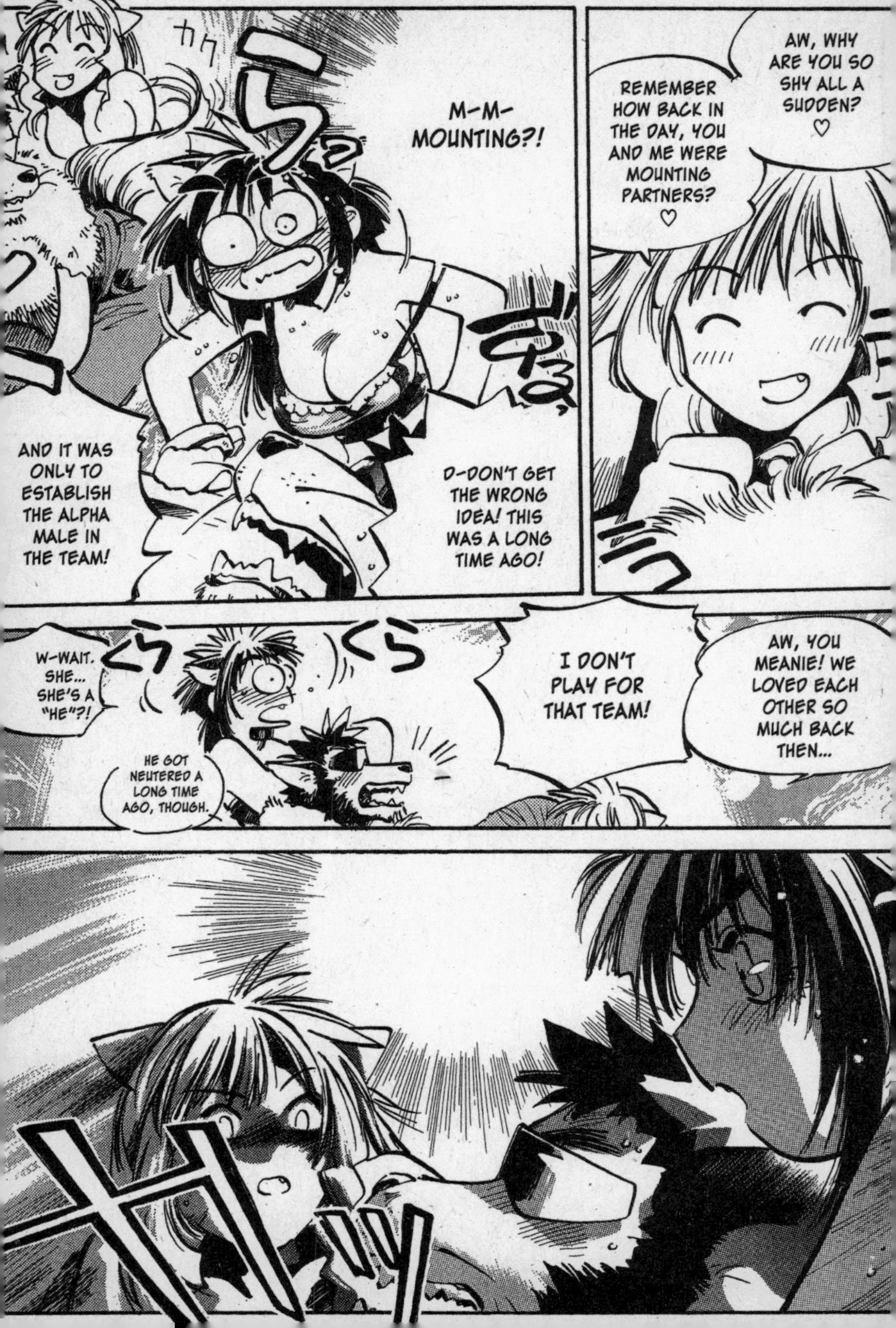
AW, WHY ARE YOU SO SHY ALL A SUDDEN? ♡
REMEMBER HOW BACK IN THE DAY, YOU AND ME WERE MOUNTING PARTNERS? ♡
M-M-MOUNTING?!
D-DON'T GET THE WRONG IDEA! THIS WAS A LONG TIME AGO!
AND IT WAS ONLY TO ESTABLISH THE ALPHA MALE IN THE TEAM!
AW, YOU MEANIE! WE LOVED EACH OTHER SO MUCH BACK THEN...
I DON'T PLAY FOR THAT TEAM!
くら
くら
W-WAIT. SHE... SHE'S A "HE"?!
HE GOT NEUTERED A LONG TIME AGO, THOUGH.

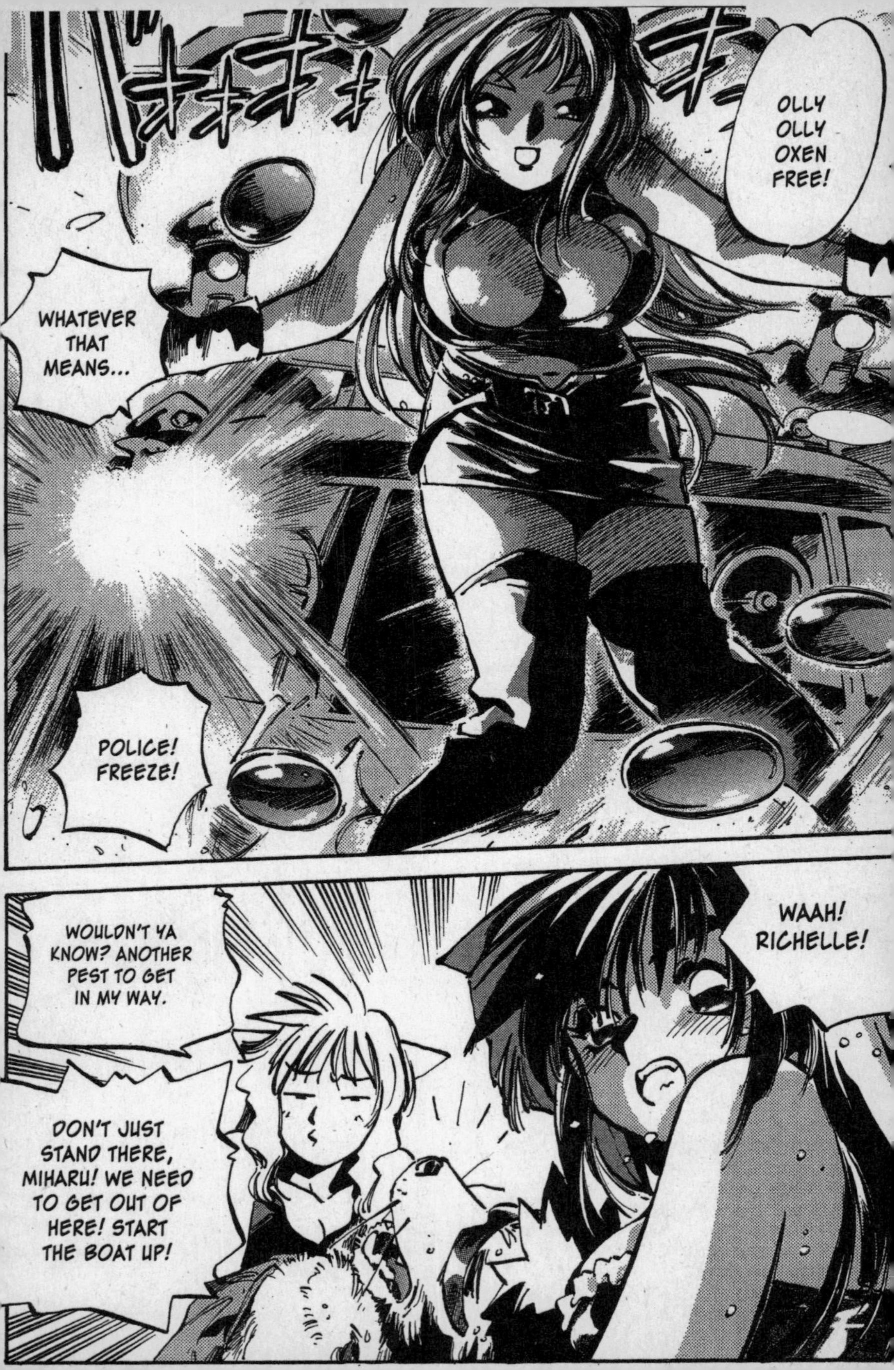
OLLY OLLY OXEN FREE!
WHATEVER THAT MEANS...
POLICE! FREEZE!
WAAH! RICHELLE!
WOULDN'T YA KNOW? ANOTHER PEST TO GET IN MY WAY.
DON'T JUST STAND THERE, MIHARU! WE NEED TO GET OUT OF HERE! START THE BOAT UP!

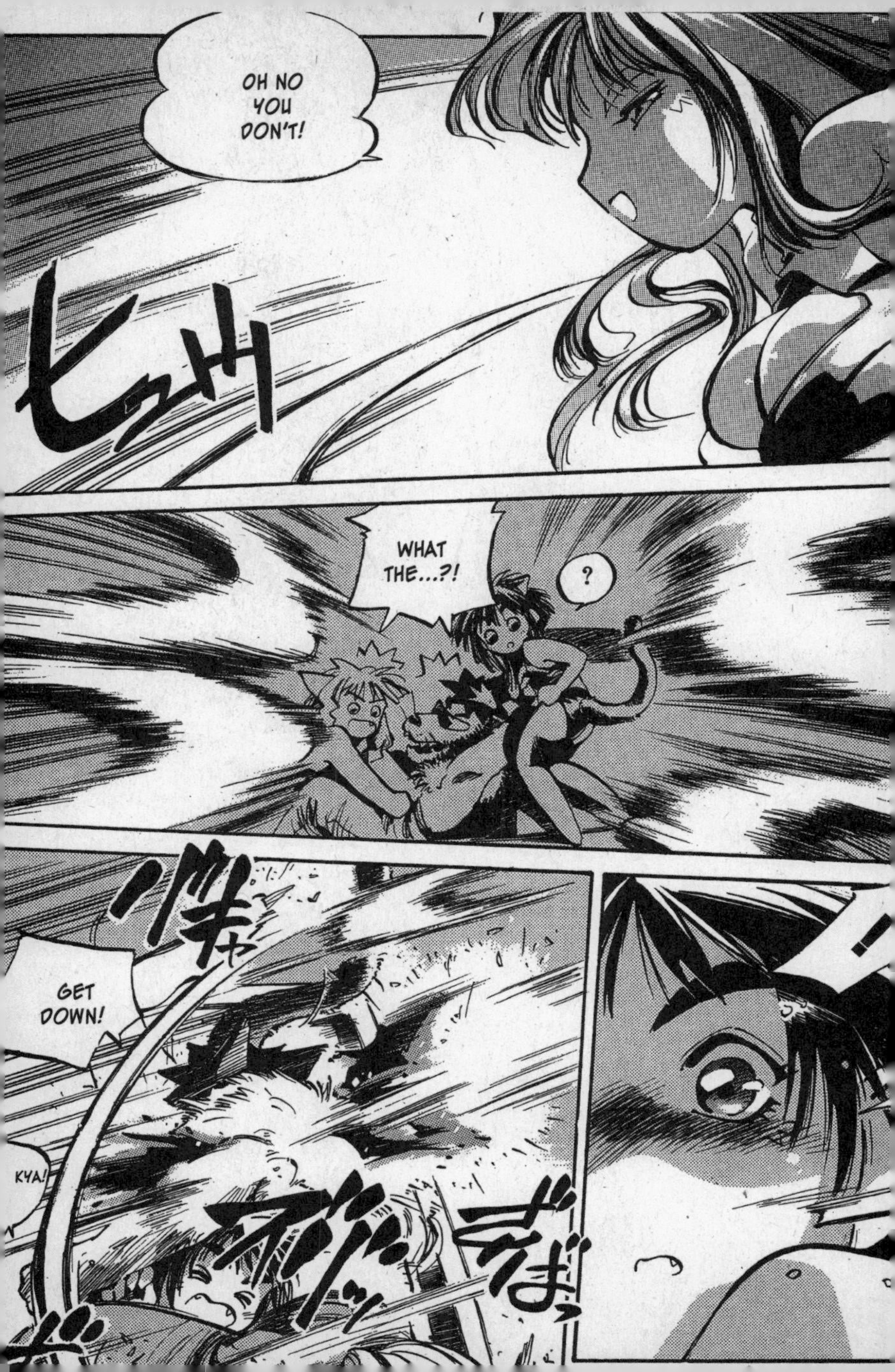
OH NO YOU DON'T!
?
WHAT THE...?!
GET DOWN!
KYA!

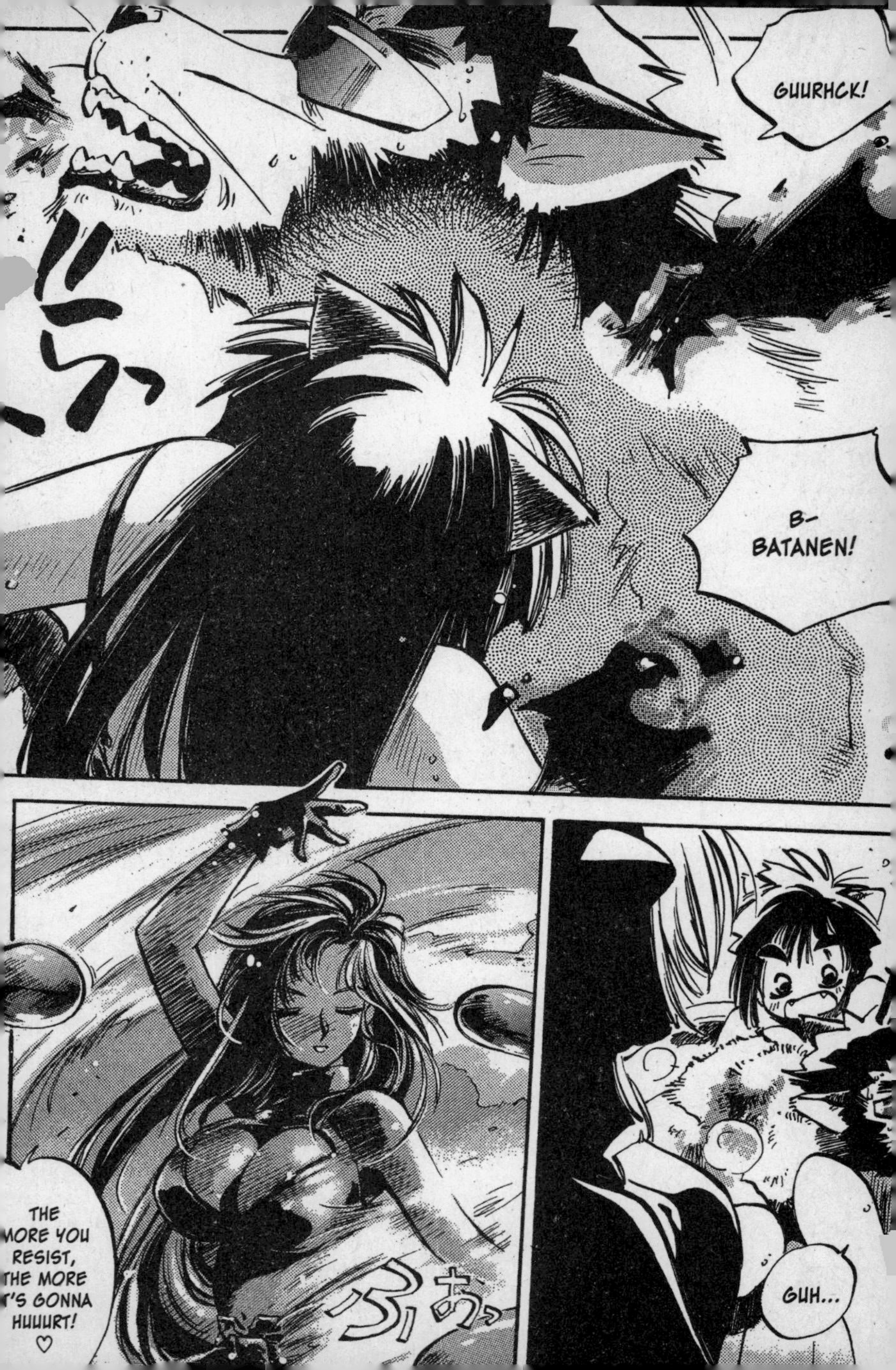
GUURHCK!
B- BATANEN!
GUH...
THE MORE YOU RESIST, THE MORE IT'S GONNA HUUURT! ♡
ふあっ

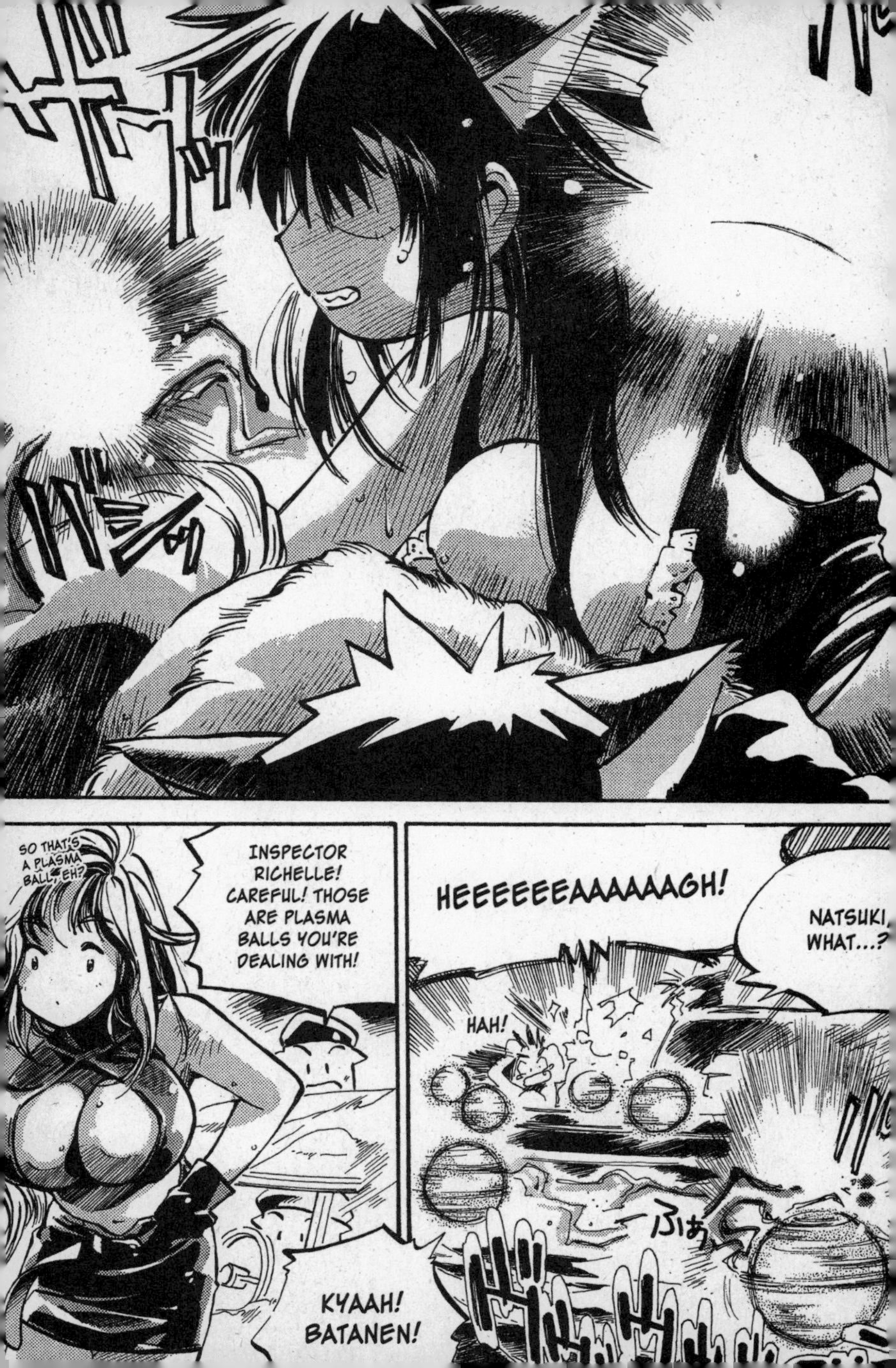
NATSUKI, WHAT...?
HEEEEEEAAAAAAGH!
HAH!
ふあ
INSPECTOR RICHELLE! CAREFUL! THOSE ARE PLASMA BALLS YOU'RE DEALING WITH!
SO THAT'S A PLASMA BALL, EH?
KYAAH! BATANEN!

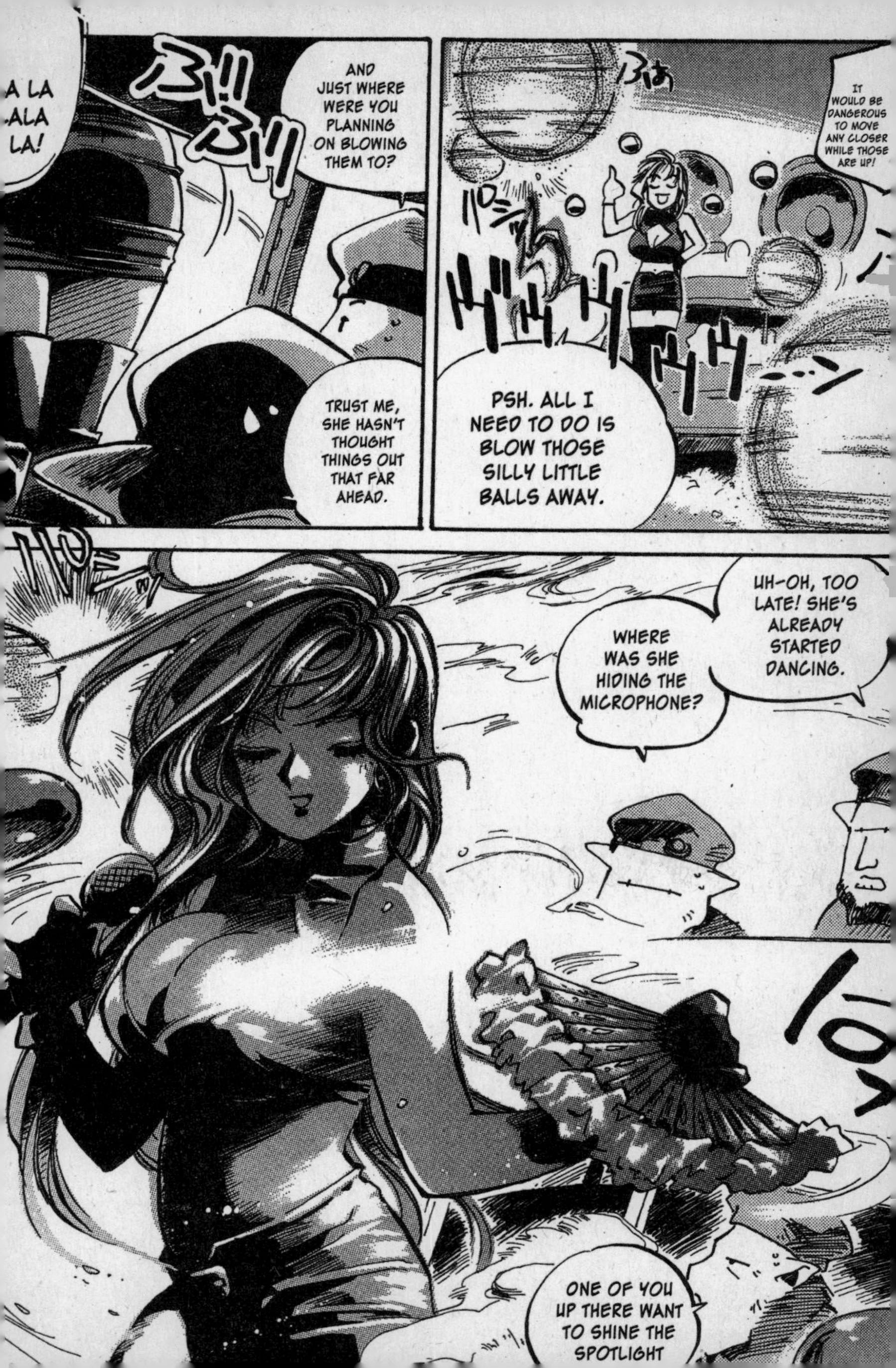
ふぁ
IT WOULD BE DANGEROUS TO MOVE ANY CLOSER WHILE THOSE ARE UP!
PSH. ALL I NEED TO DO IS BLOW THOSE SILLY LITTLE BALLS AWAY.
AND JUST WHERE WERE YOU PLANNING ON BLOWING THEM TO?
TRUST ME, SHE HASN'T THOUGHT THINGS OUT THAT FAR AHEAD.
A LA -ALA LA!
UH-OH, TOO LATE! SHE'S ALREADY STARTED DANCING.
WHERE WAS SHE HIDING THE MICROPHONE?
ONE OF YOU UP THERE WANT TO SHINE THE SPOTLIGHT

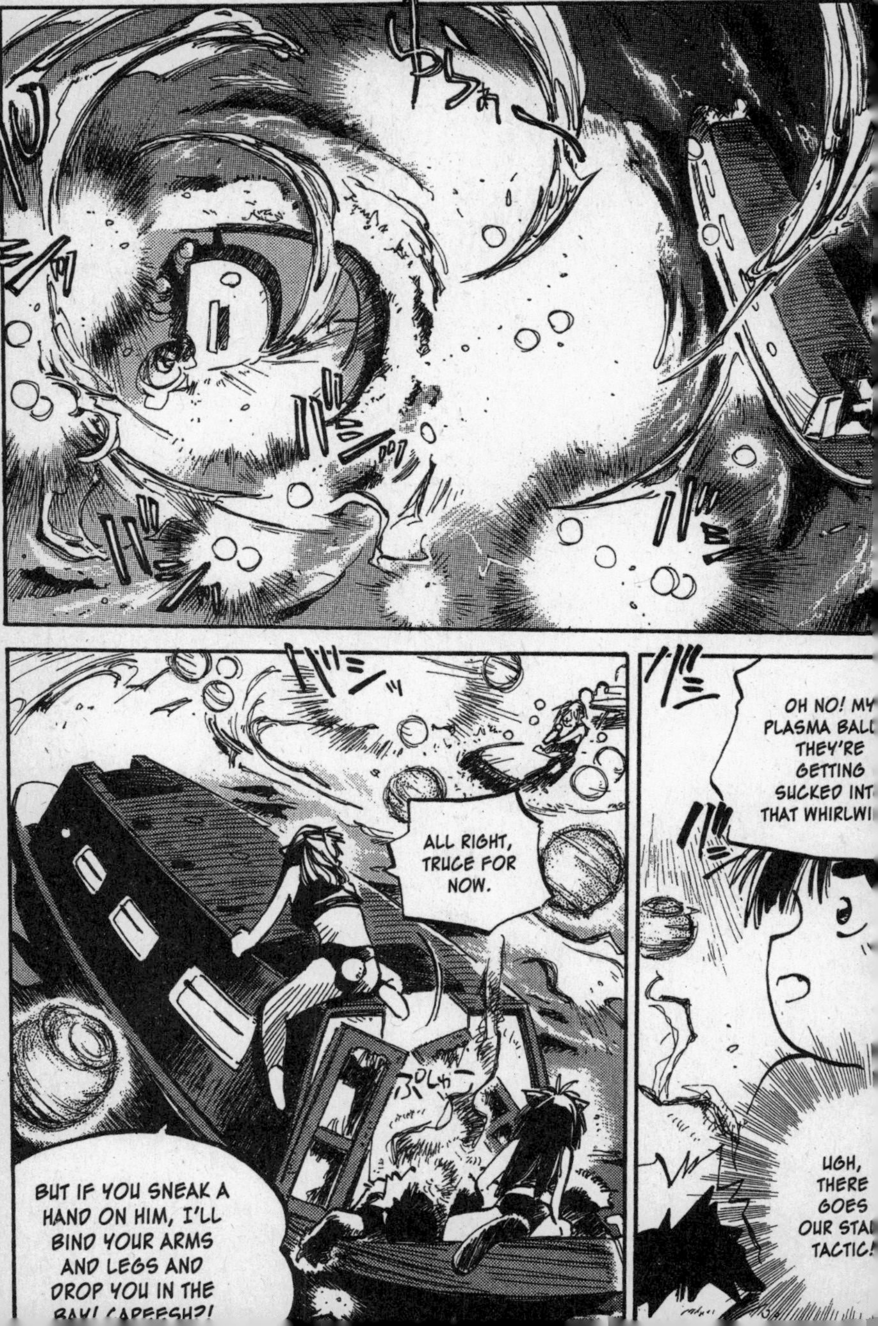
OH NO! MY PLASMA BALL THEY'RE GETTING SUCKED INT THAT WHIRLWI
UGH, THERE GOES OUR STA TACTIC!
ALL RIGHT, TRUCE FOR NOW.
BUT IF YOU SNEAK A HAND ON HIM, I'LL BIND YOUR ARMS AND LEGS AND DROP YOU IN THE BAY! CAPEESH?!

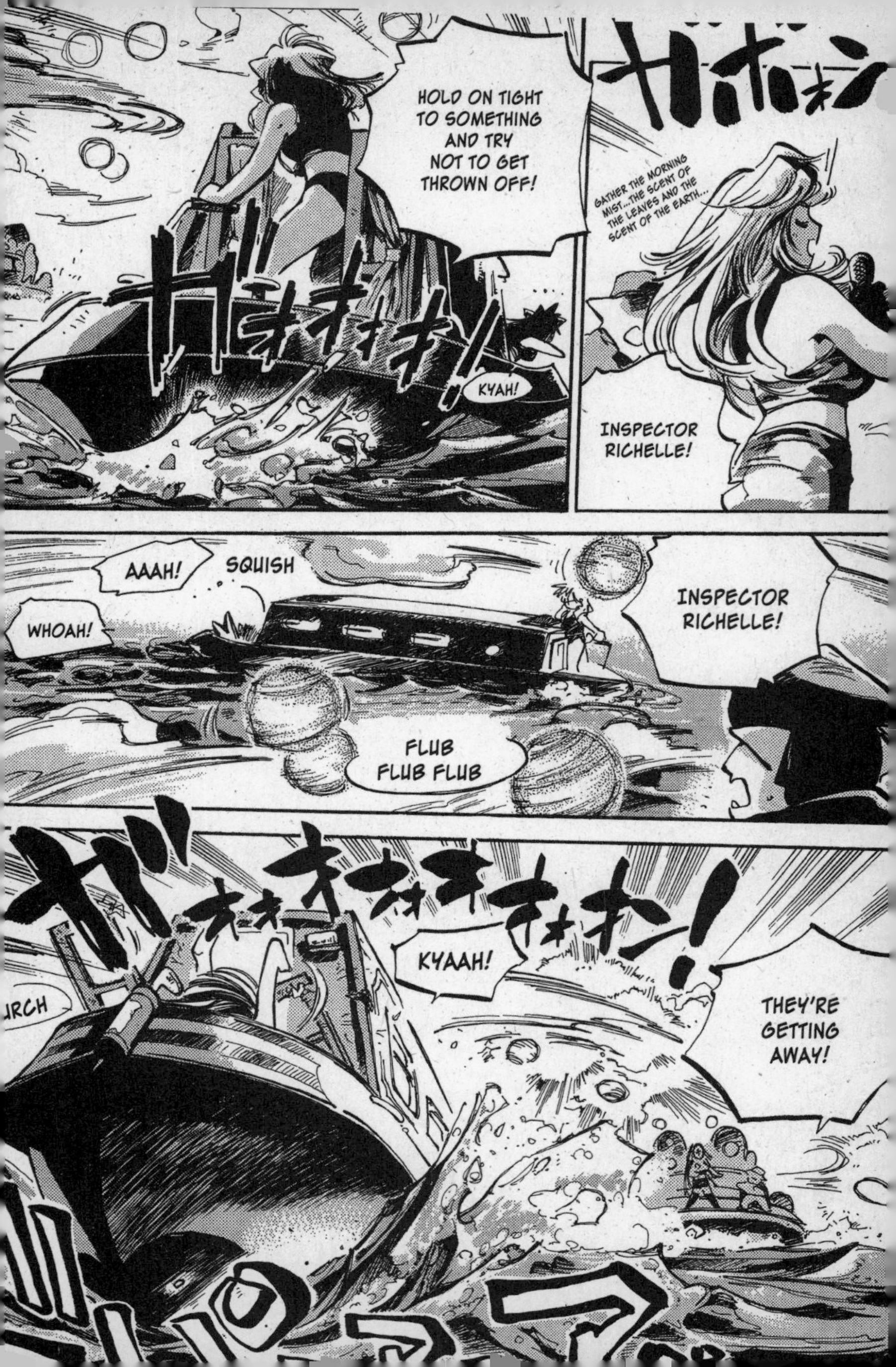
GATHER THE MORNING MIST...THE SCENT OF THE LEAVES AND THE SCENT OF THE EARTH...
INSPECTOR RICHELLE!
HOLD ON TIGHT TO SOMETHING AND TRY NOT TO GET THROWN OFF!
KYAH!
INSPECTOR RICHELLE!
FLUB FLUB FLUB
SQUISH
AAAH!
WHOAH!
THEY'RE GETTING AWAY!
KYAAH!
URCH

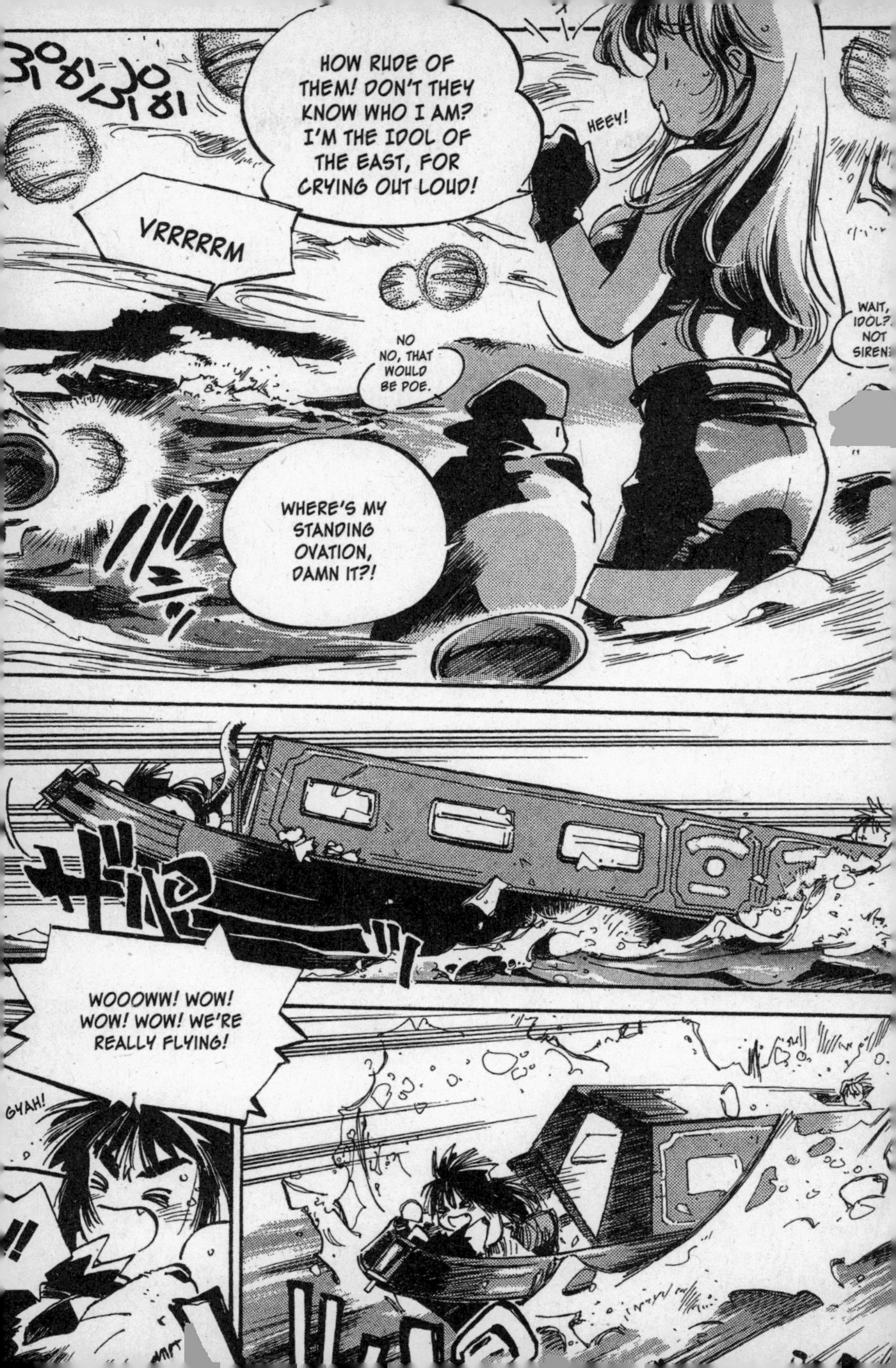
HOW RUDE OF THEM! DON'T THEY KNOW WHO I AM? I'M THE IDOL OF THE EAST, FOR CRYING OUT LOUD!
HEEY!
VRRRRRM
WAIT, IDOL?. NOT SIREN
NO NO, THAT WOULD BE POE.
WHERE'S MY STANDING OVATION, DAMN IT?!
WOOOWW! WOW! WOW! WOW! WE'RE REALLY FLYING!
GYAH!

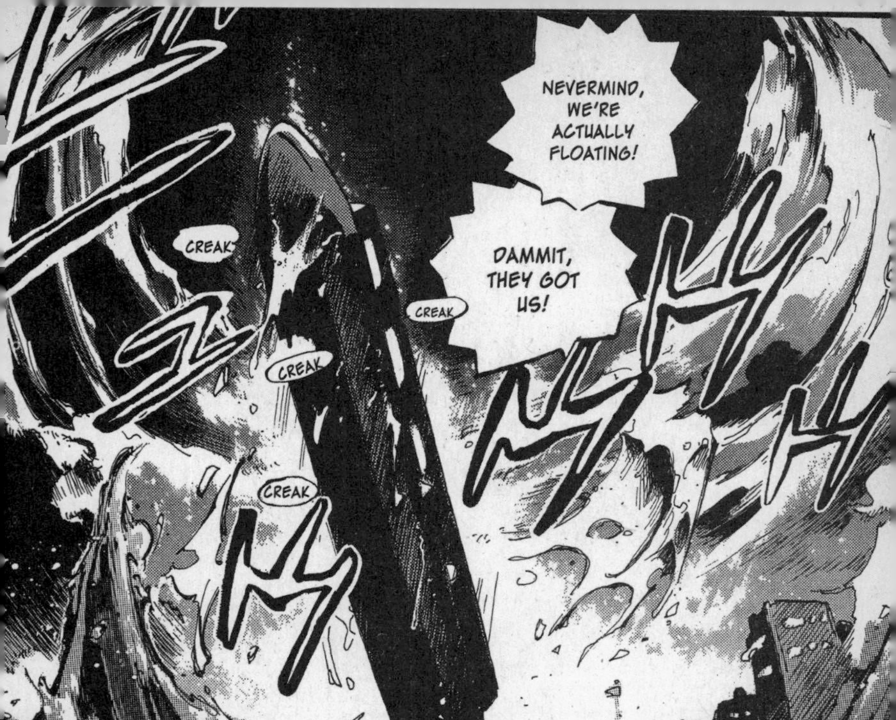
NEVERMIND, WE'RE ACTUALLY FLOATING!
DAMMIT, THEY GOT US!
CREAK
CREAK
CREAK
CREAK
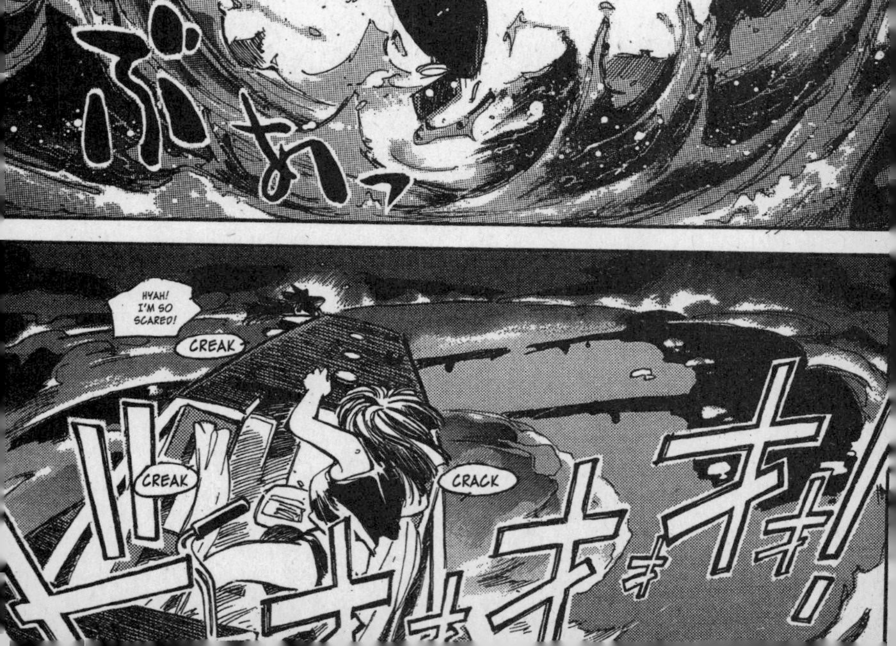
HYAH! I'M SO SCARED!
CREAK
CRACK
CREAK

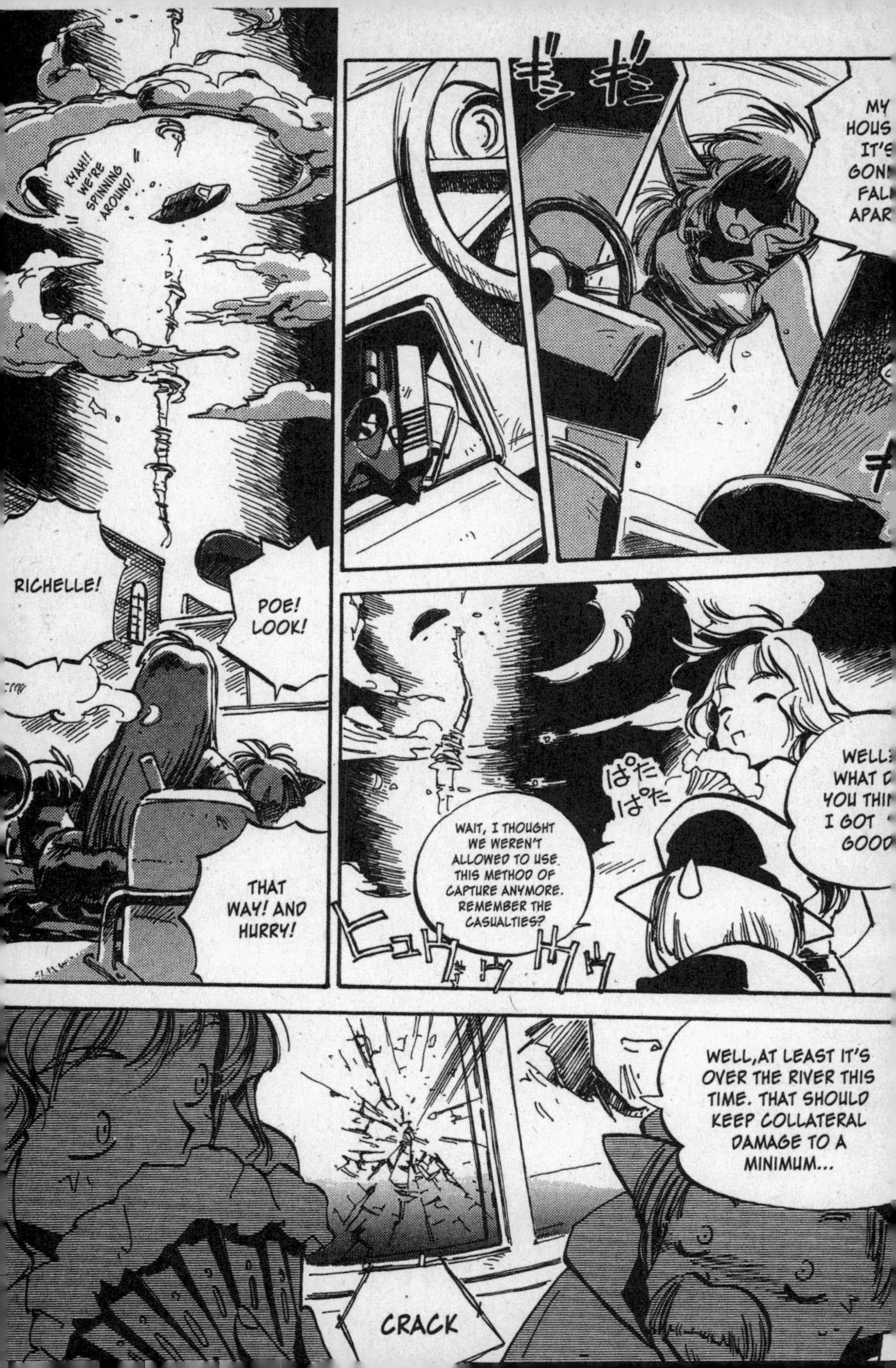

ギシ ギシ
MY HOUS IT'S GONI FAL APAR
KYAH!! WE'RE SPINNING AROUND!
WELL: WHAT D YOU THIN I GOT GOOD
ぱた ぱた
WAIT, I THOUGHT WE WEREN'T ALLOWED TO USE THIS METHOD OF CAPTURE ANYMORE. REMEMBER THE CASUALTIES?
POE! LOOK!
RICHELLE!
THAT WAY! AND HURRY!
WELL, AT LEAST IT'S OVER THE RIVER THIS TIME. THAT SHOULD KEEP COLLATERAL DAMAGE TO A MINIMUM...
CRACK

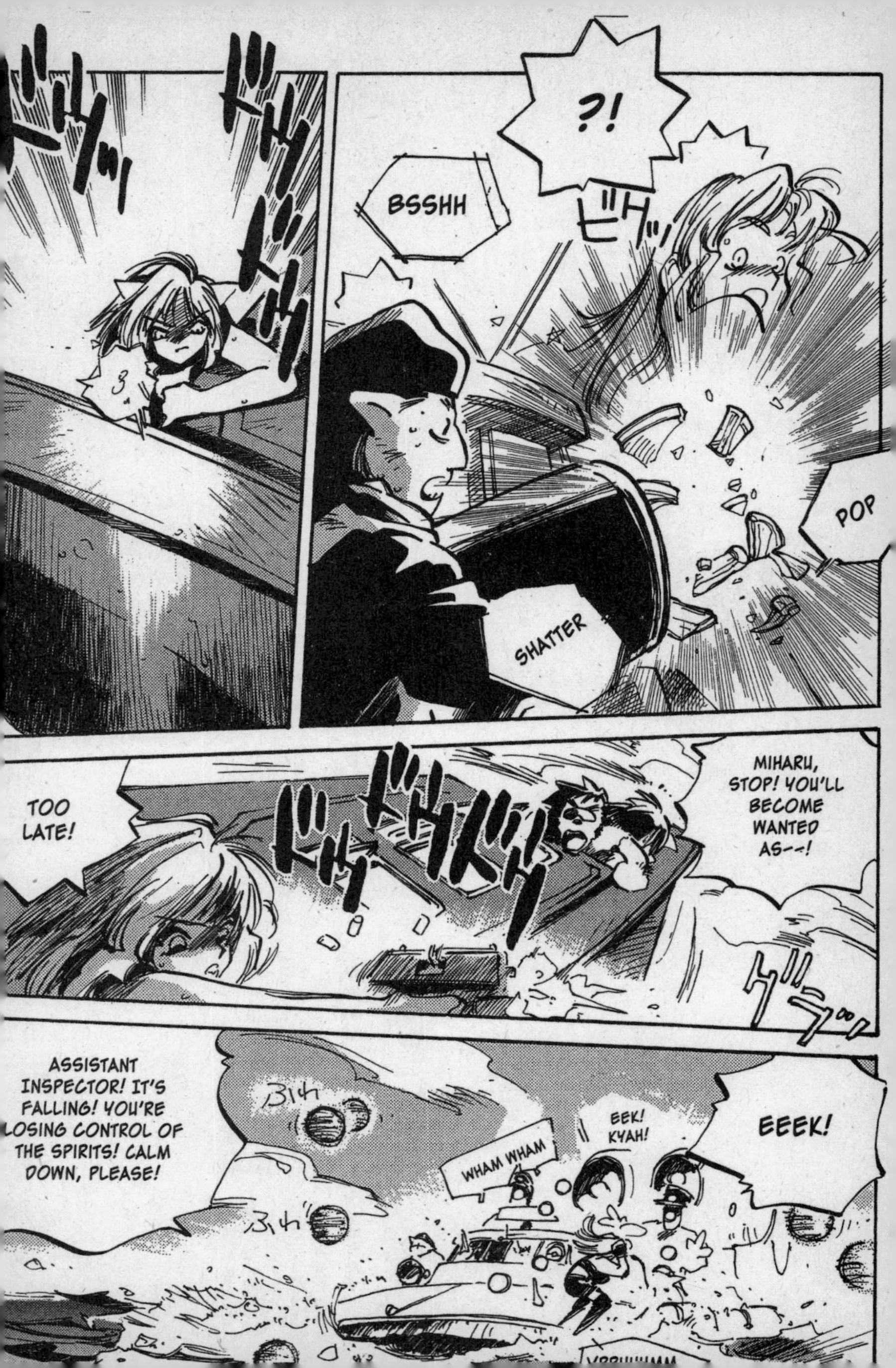

?!
BSSHH
POP
SHATTER
MIHARU, STOP! YOU'LL BECOME WANTED AS--!
TOO LATE!
EEEK!
EEK! KYAH!
WHAM WHAM
ASSISTANT INSPECTOR! IT'S FALLING! YOU'RE LOSING CONTROL OF THE SPIRITS! CALM DOWN, PLEASE!

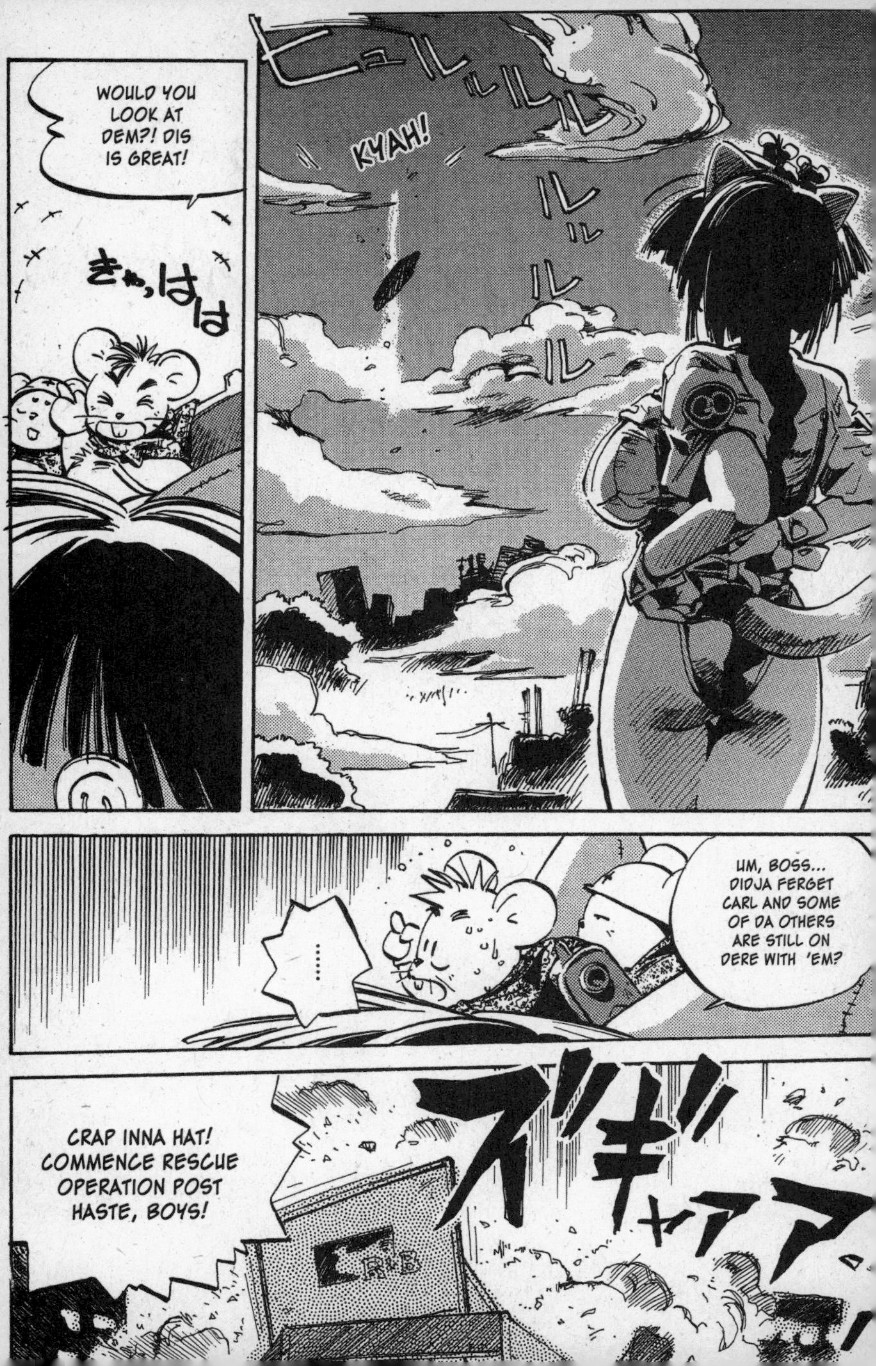
KYAH!
WOULD YOU LOOK AT DEM?! DIS IS GREAT!
きゃっはは
UM, BOSS... DIDJA FERGET CARL AND SOME OF DA OTHERS ARE STILL ON DERE WITH 'EM?
......
CRAP INNA HAT! COMMENCE RESCUE OPERATION POST HASTE, BOYS!

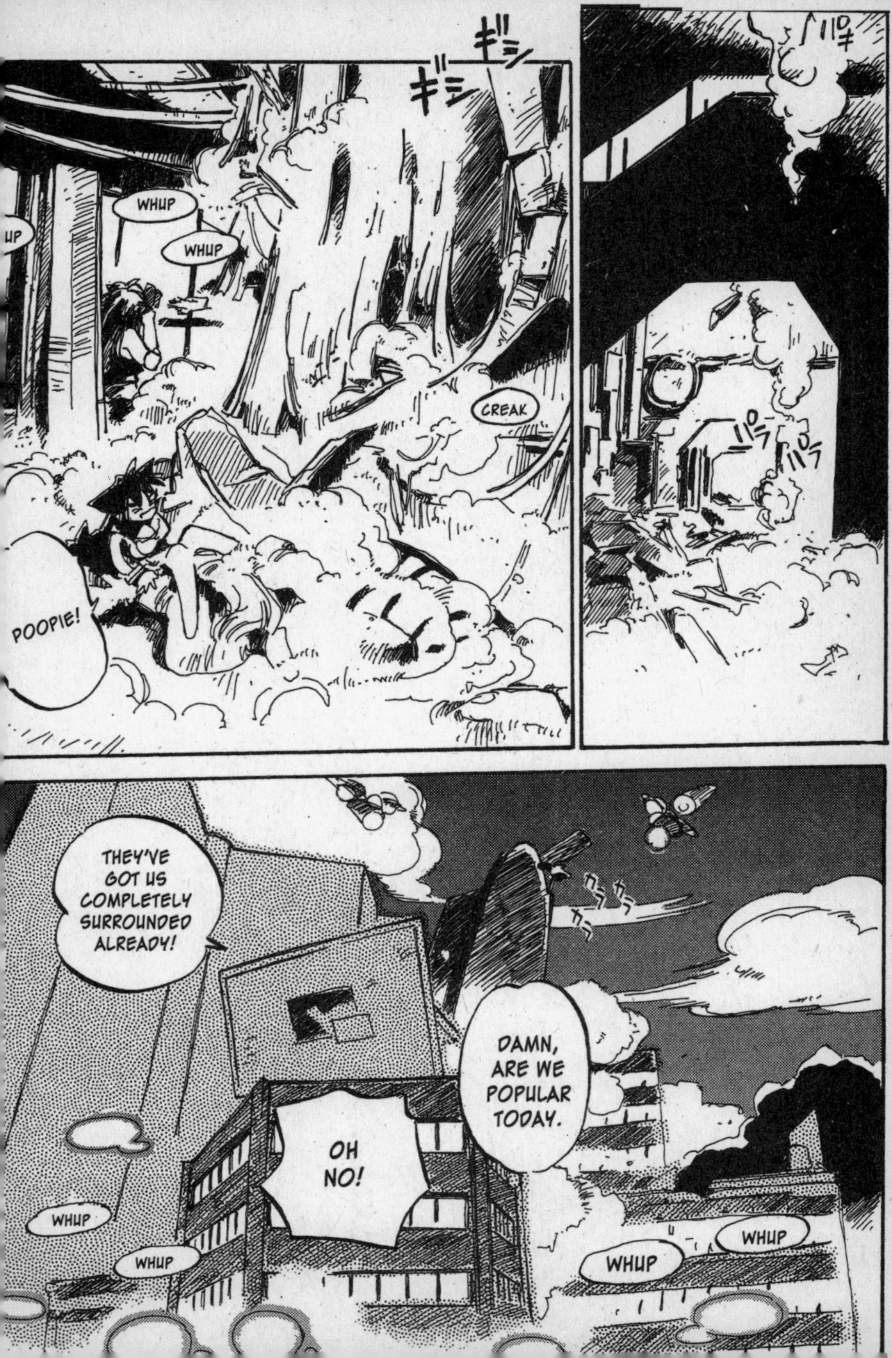
パラ
パラ
ギシ
ギシ
WHUP
UP
WHUP
CREAK
POOPIE!
THEY'VE GOT US COMPLETELY SURROUNDED ALREADY!
DAMN, ARE WE POPULAR TODAY.
OH NO!
WHUP
WHUP
WHUP
WHUP

Report #70
A New Rival

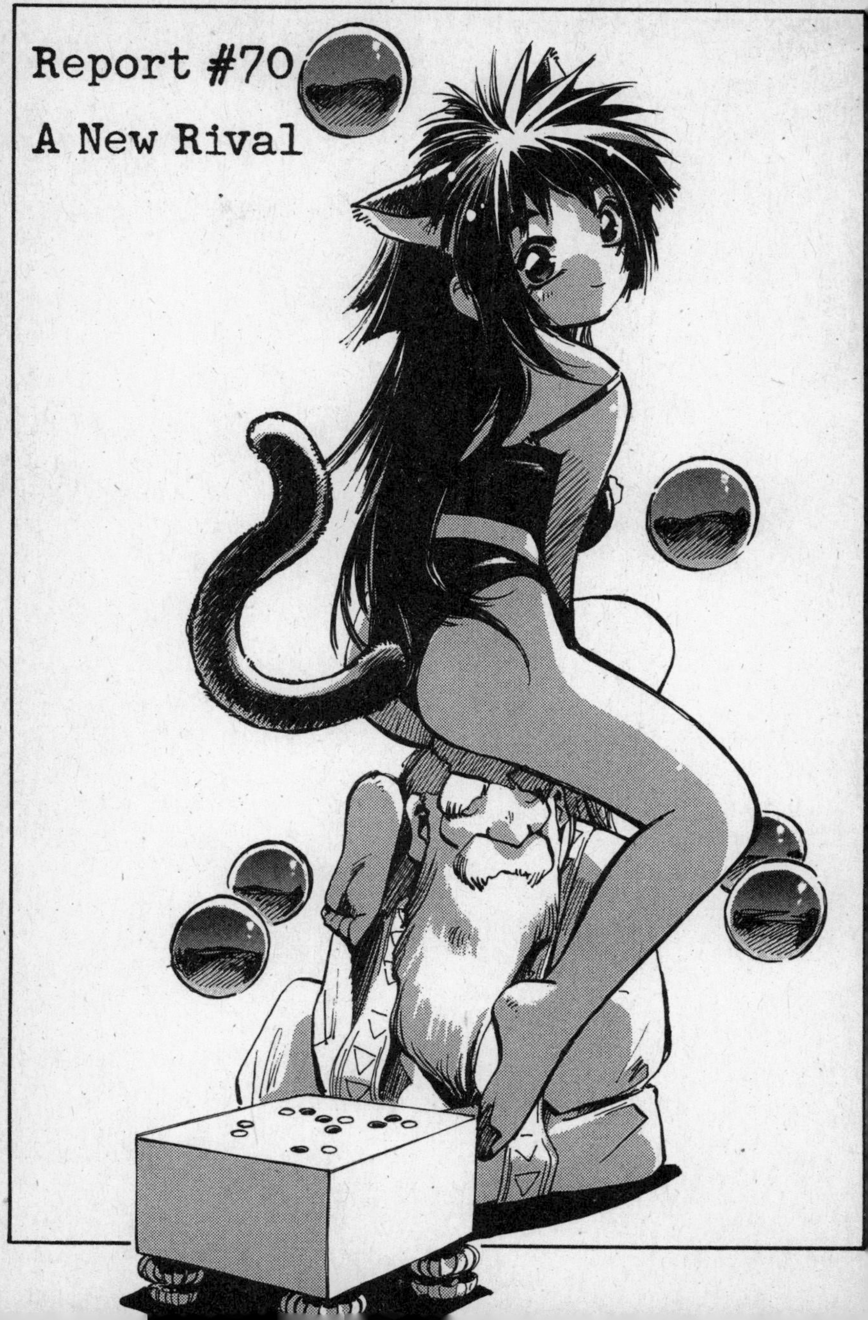

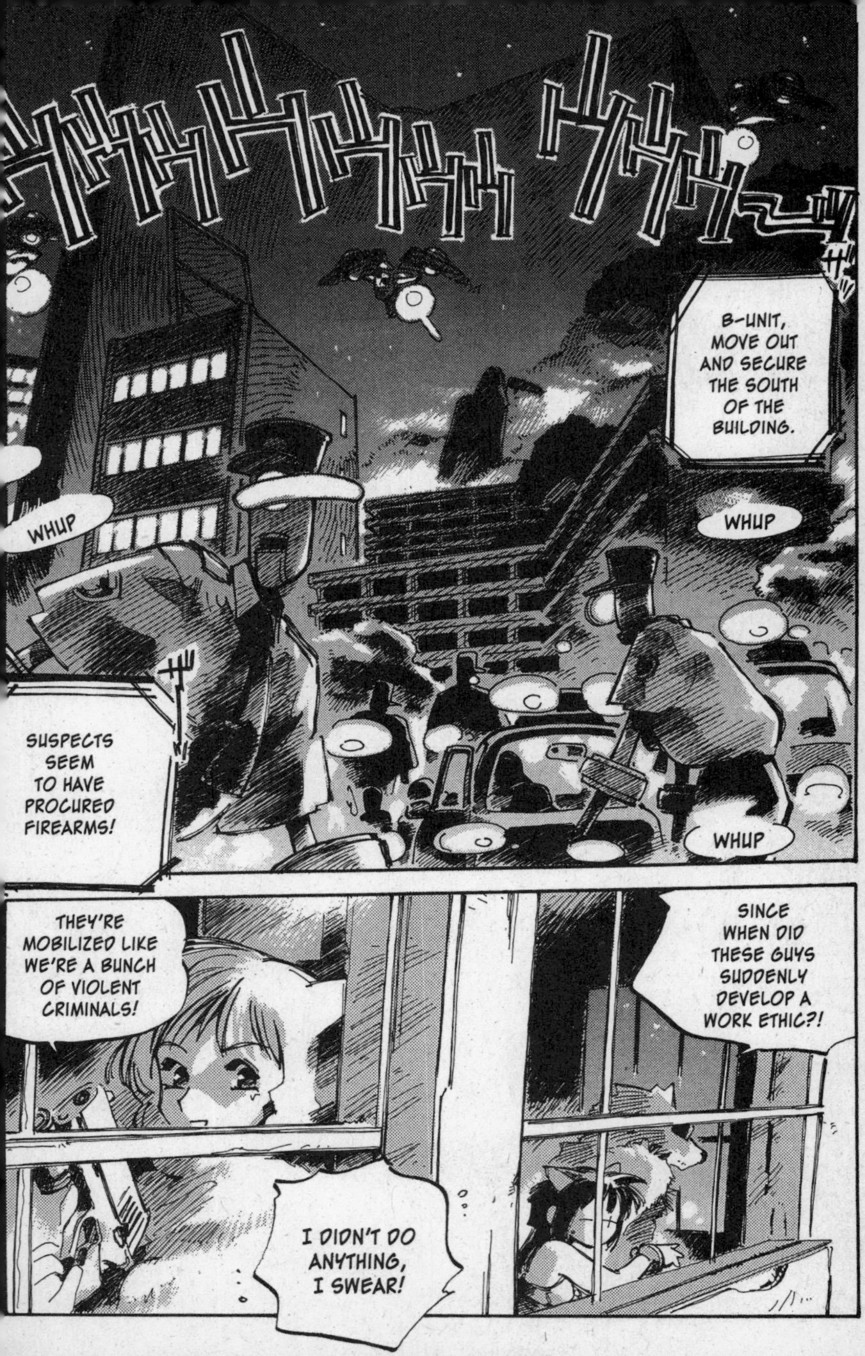
B-UNIT, MOVE OUT AND SECURE THE SOUTH OF THE BUILDING.
WHUP
WHUP
SUSPECTS SEEM TO HAVE PROCURED FIREARMS!
WHUP
SINCE WHEN DID THESE GUYS SUDDENLY DEVELOP A WORK ETHIC?!
THEY'RE MOBILIZED LIKE WE'RE A BUNCH OF VIOLENT CRIMINALS!
I DIDN'T DO ANYTHING, I SWEAR!

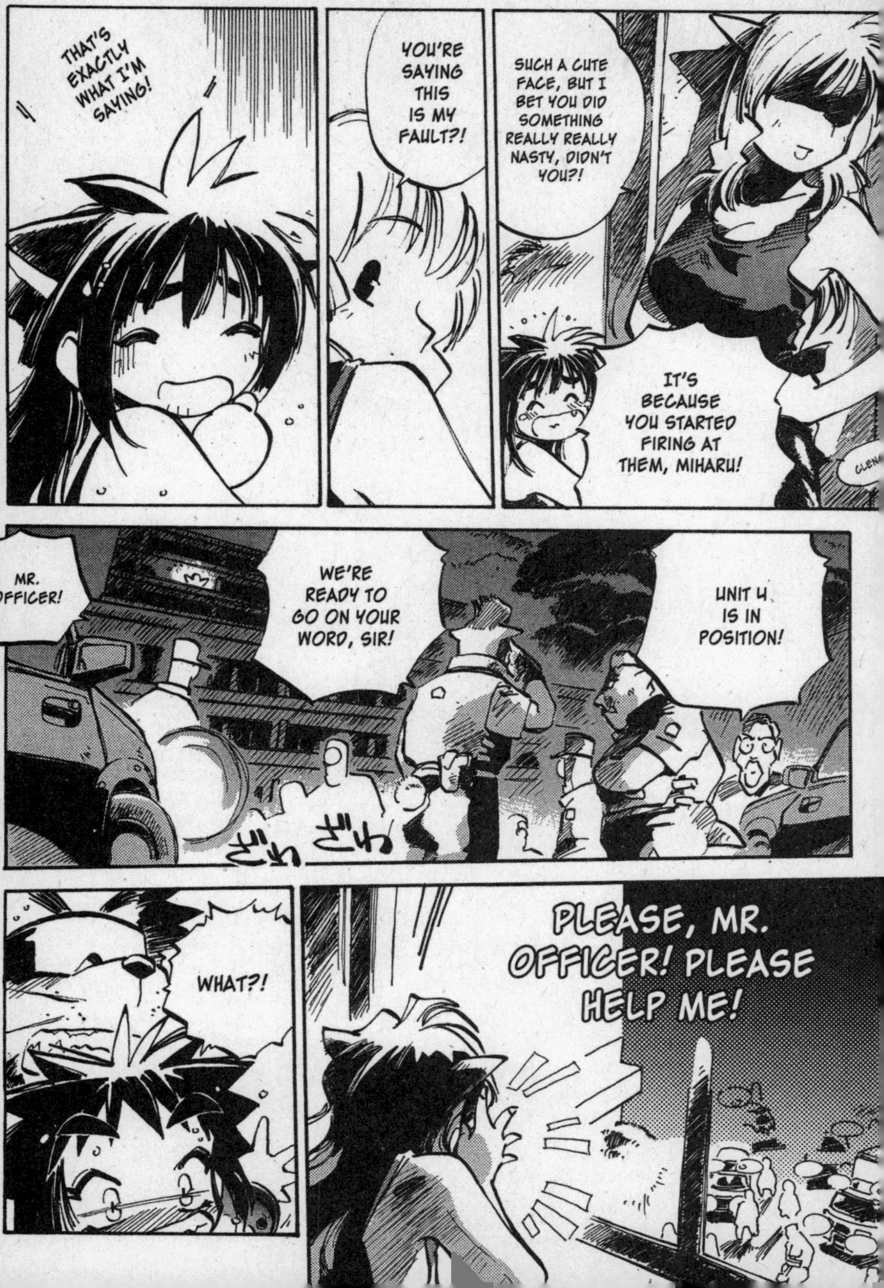
SUCH A CUTE FACE, BUT I BET YOU DID SOMETHING REALLY REALLY NASTY, DIDN'T YOU?!
IT'S BECAUSE YOU STARTED FIRING AT THEM, MIHARU!
YOU'RE SAYING THIS IS MY FAULT?!
THAT'S EXACTLY WHAT I'M SAYING!
UNIT 4 IS IN POSITION!
WE'RE READY TO GO ON YOUR WORD, SIR!
MR. OFFICER!
ざわ ざわ
PLEASE, MR. OFFICER! PLEASE HELP ME!
WHAT?!

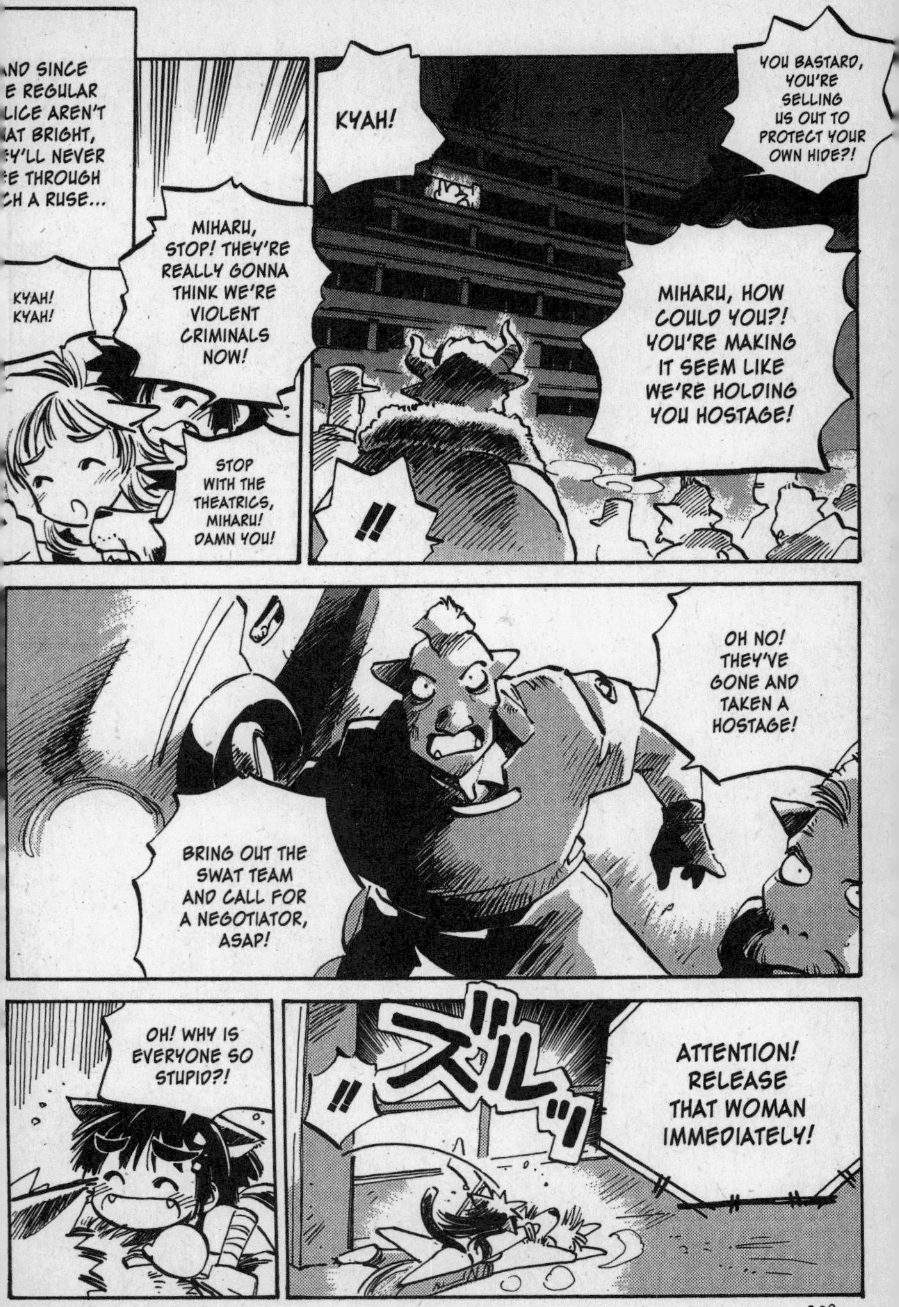
YOU BASTARD, YOU'RE SELLING US OUT TO PROTECT YOUR OWN HIDE?!
KYAH!
MIHARU, HOW COULD YOU?! YOU'RE MAKING IT SEEM LIKE WE'RE HOLDING YOU HOSTAGE!
!!
ND SINCE E REGULAR LICE AREN'T AT BRIGHT, EY'LL NEVER E THROUGH CH A RUSE...
MIHARU, STOP! THEY'RE REALLY GONNA THINK WE'RE VIOLENT CRIMINALS NOW!
KYAH! KYAH!
STOP WITH THE THEATRICS, MIHARU! DAMN YOU!
OH NO! THEY'VE GONE AND TAKEN A HOSTAGE!
BRING OUT THE SWAT TEAM AND CALL FOR A NEGOTIATOR, ASAP!
ズルッ
!!
ATTENTION! RELEASE THAT WOMAN IMMEDIATELY!
OH! WHY IS EVERYONE SO STUPID?!

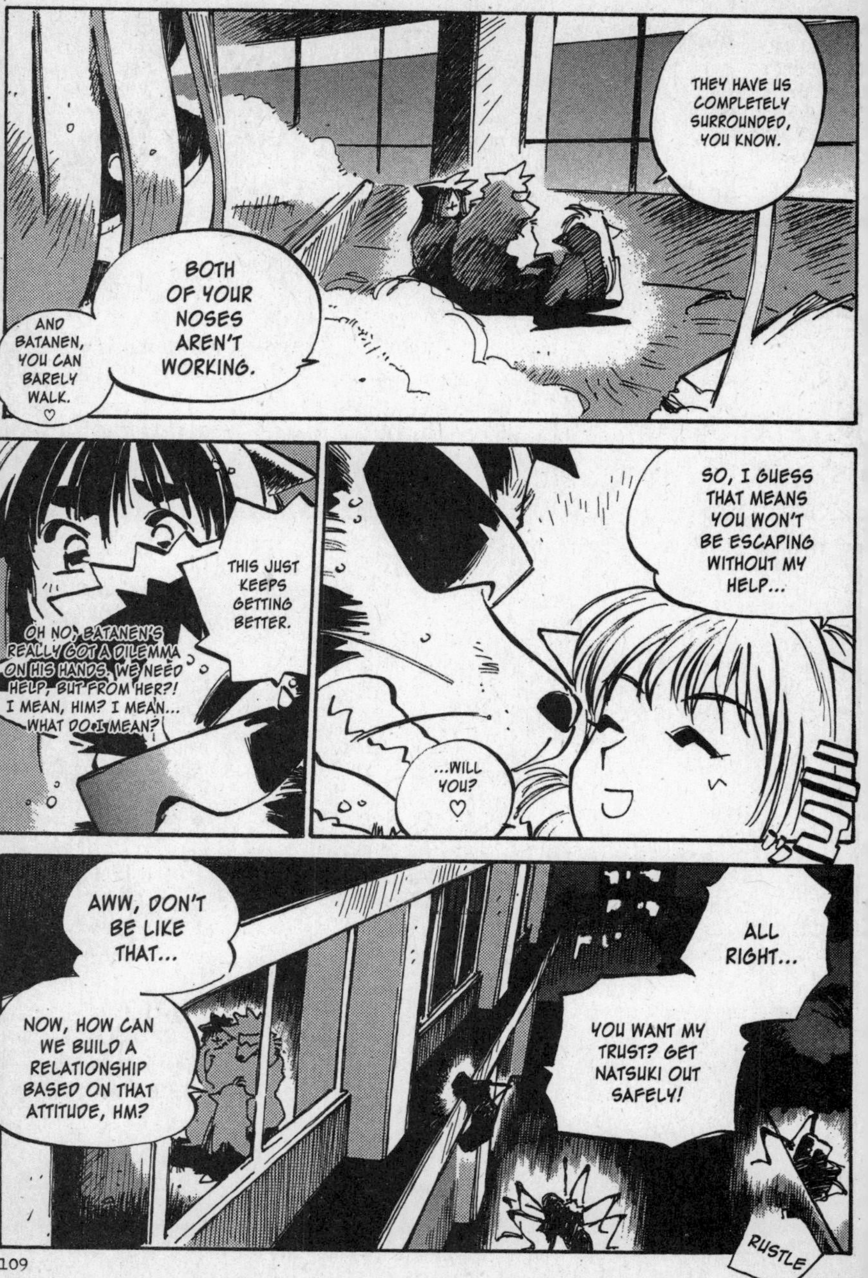

THEY HAVE US COMPLETELY SURROUNDED, YOU KNOW.
BOTH OF YOUR NOSES AREN'T WORKING.
AND BATANEN, YOU CAN BARELY WALK. ♡
SO, I GUESS THAT MEANS YOU WON'T BE ESCAPING WITHOUT MY HELP...
...WILL YOU? ♡
THIS JUST KEEPS GETTING BETTER.
OH NO, BATANEN'S REALLY GOT A DILEMMA ON HIS HANDS. WE NEED HELP, BUT FROM HER?! I MEAN, HIM? I MEAN... WHAT DO I MEAN?
ALL RIGHT...
YOU WANT MY TRUST? GET NATSUKI OUT SAFELY!
RUSTLE
AWW, DON'T BE LIKE THAT...
NOW, HOW CAN WE BUILD A RELATIONSHIP BASED ON THAT ATTITUDE, HM?

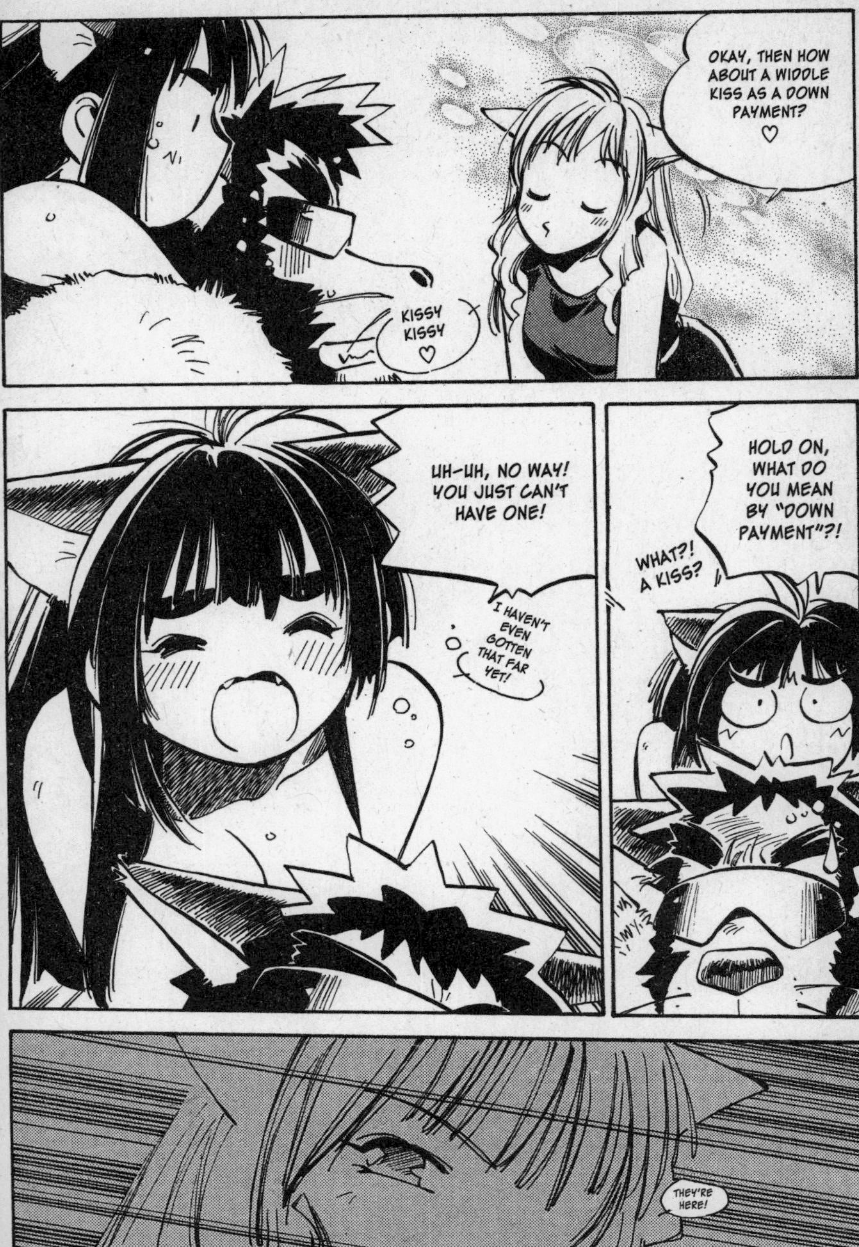
OKAY, THEN HOW ABOUT A WIDDLE KISS AS A DOWN PAYMENT? ♡
KISSY KISSY ♡
HOLD ON, WHAT DO YOU MEAN BY "DOWN PAYMENT"?!
WHAT?! A KISS?
UH-UH, NO WAY! YOU JUST CAN'T HAVE ONE!
I HAVEN'T EVEN GOTTEN THAT FAR YET!
THEY'RE HERE!

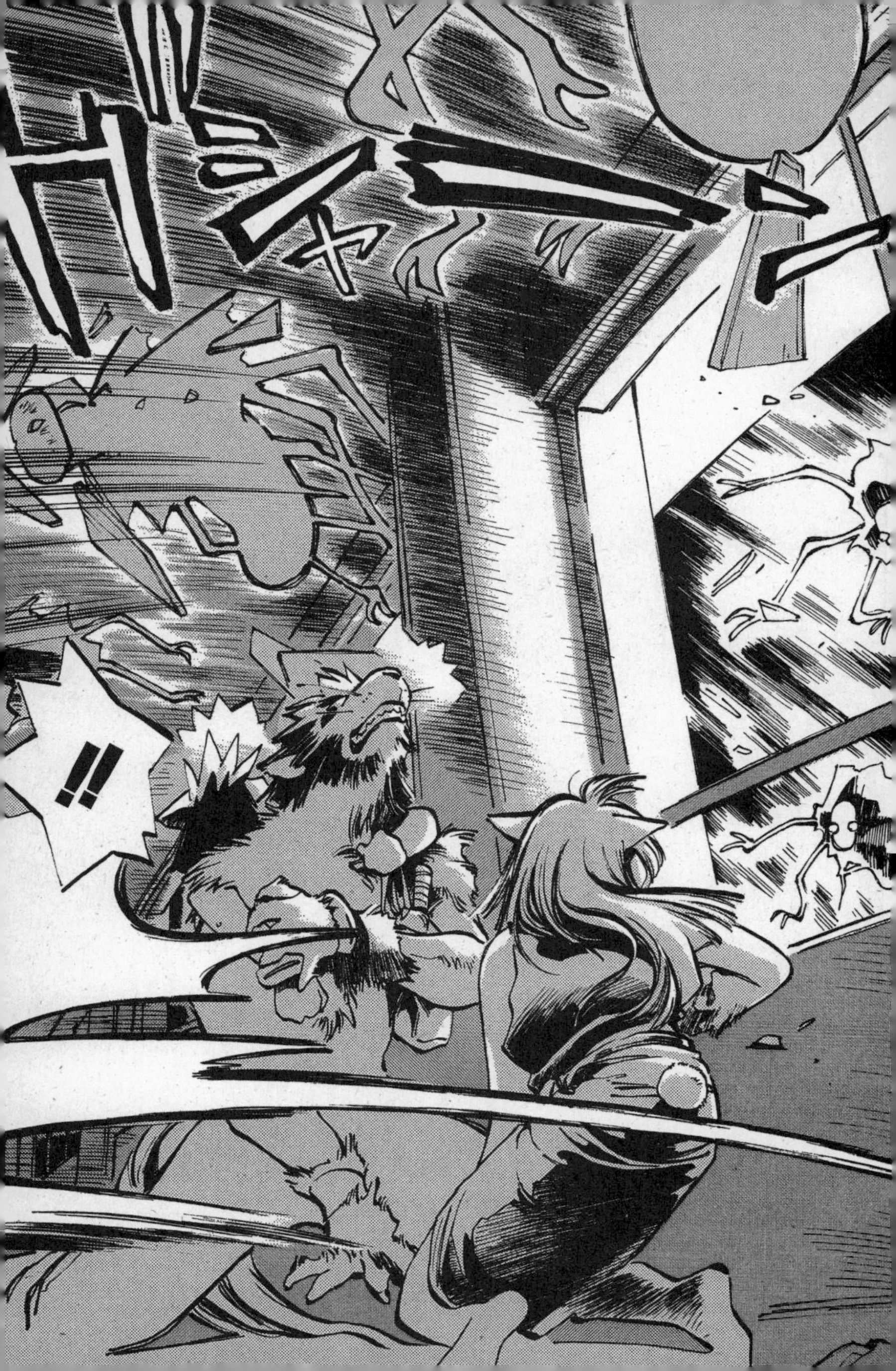
!!

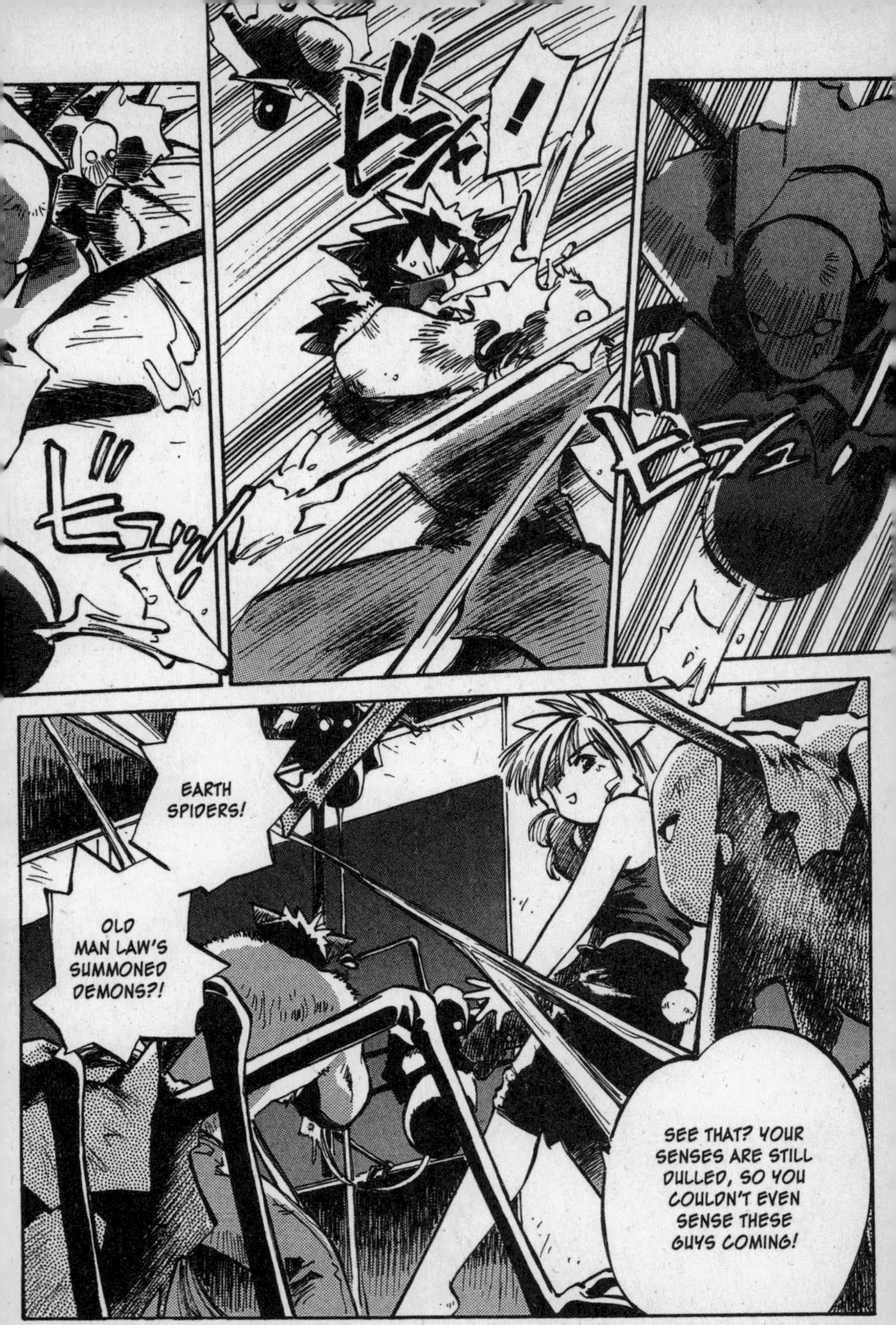
!
SEE THAT? YOUR SENSES ARE STILL DULLED, SO YOU COULDN'T EVEN SENSE THESE GUYS COMING!
EARTH SPIDERS!
OLD MAN LAW'S SUMMONED DEMONS?!

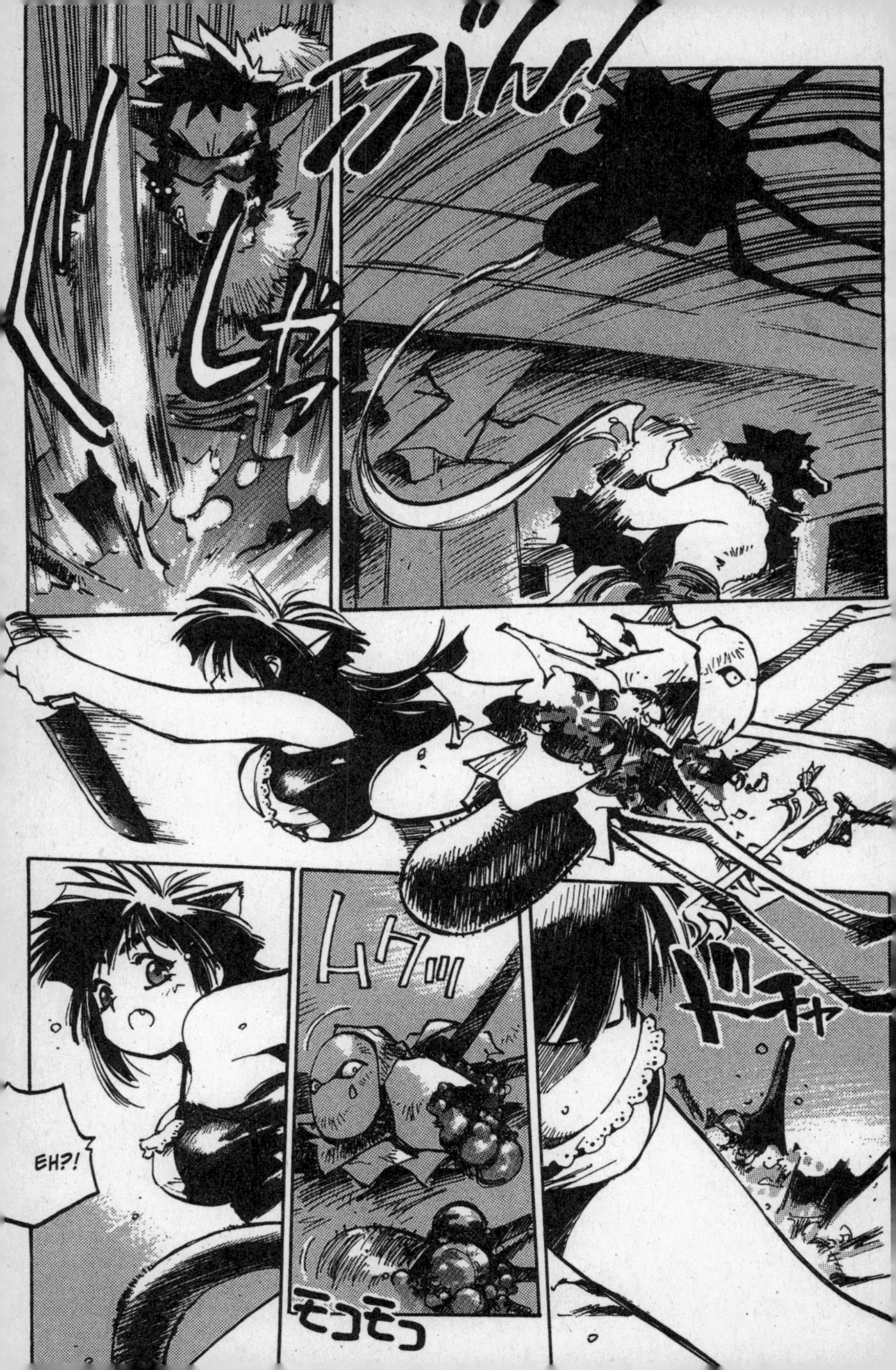
ムクッ
EH?!

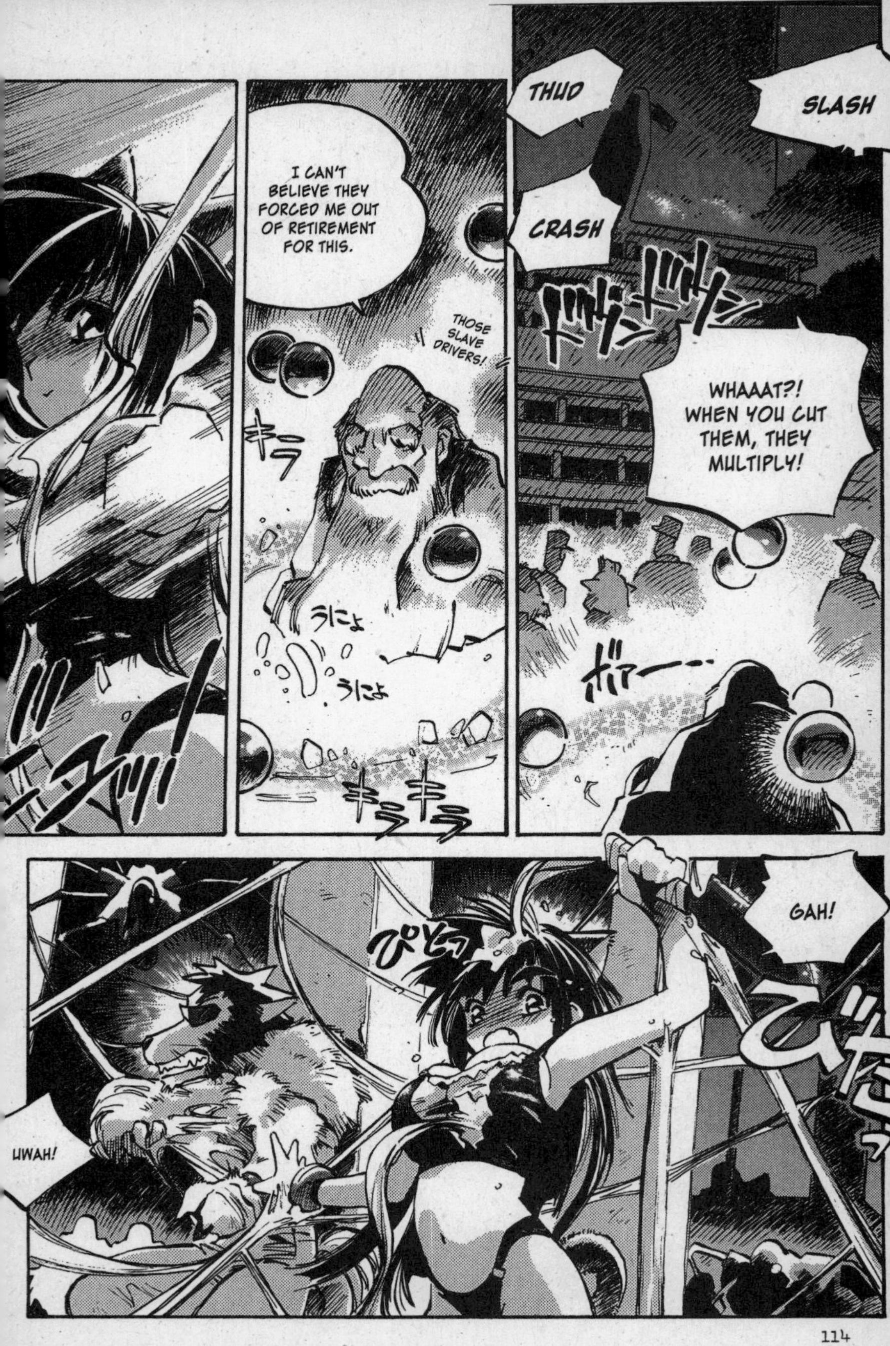
SLASH
THUD
CRASH
WHAAAT?! WHEN YOU CUT THEM, THEY MULTIPLY!
I CAN'T BELIEVE THEY FORCED ME OUT OF RETIREMENT FOR THIS.
THOSE SLAVE DRIVERS!
キラ
うにょ
うにょ
キラキラ
GAH!
UWAH!

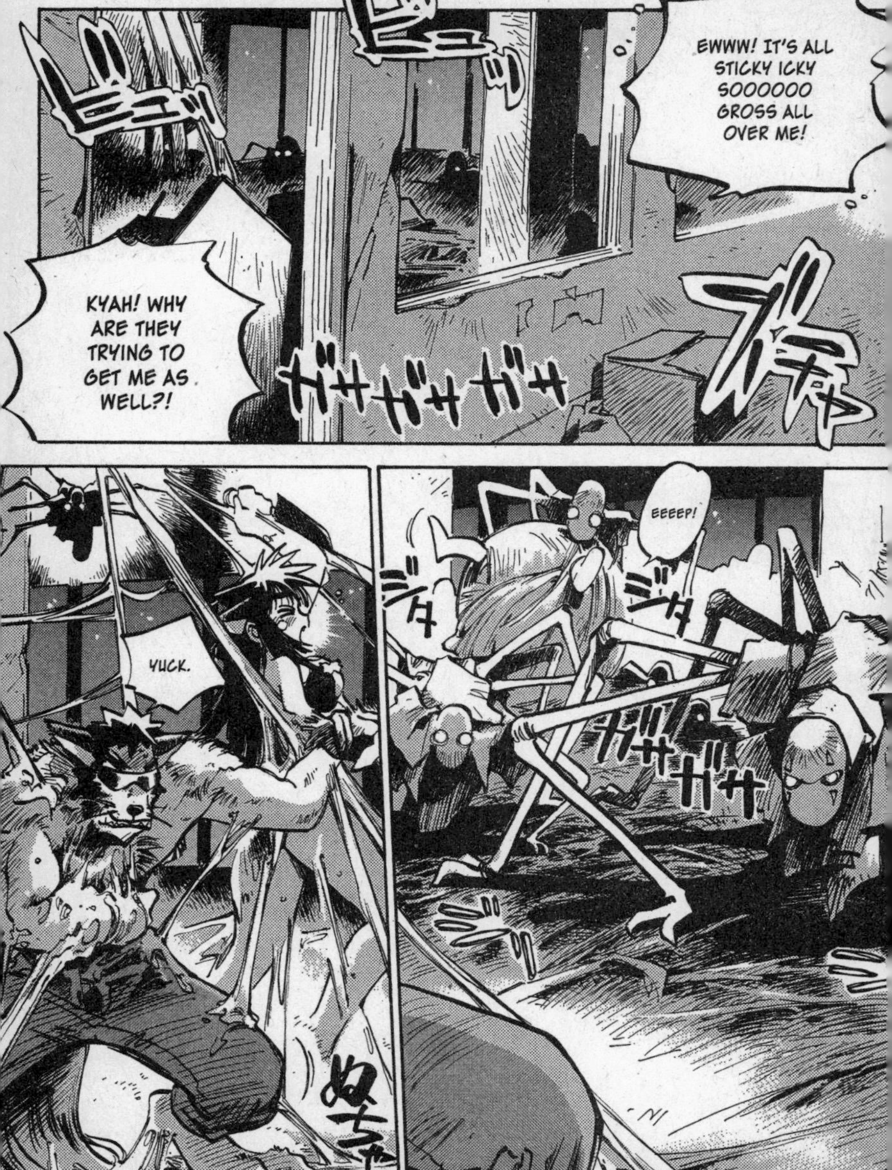
EWWW! IT'S ALL STICKY ICKY SOOOOOO GROSS ALL OVER ME!
KYAH! WHY ARE THEY TRYING TO GET ME AS WELL?!
EEEEP!
YUCK.

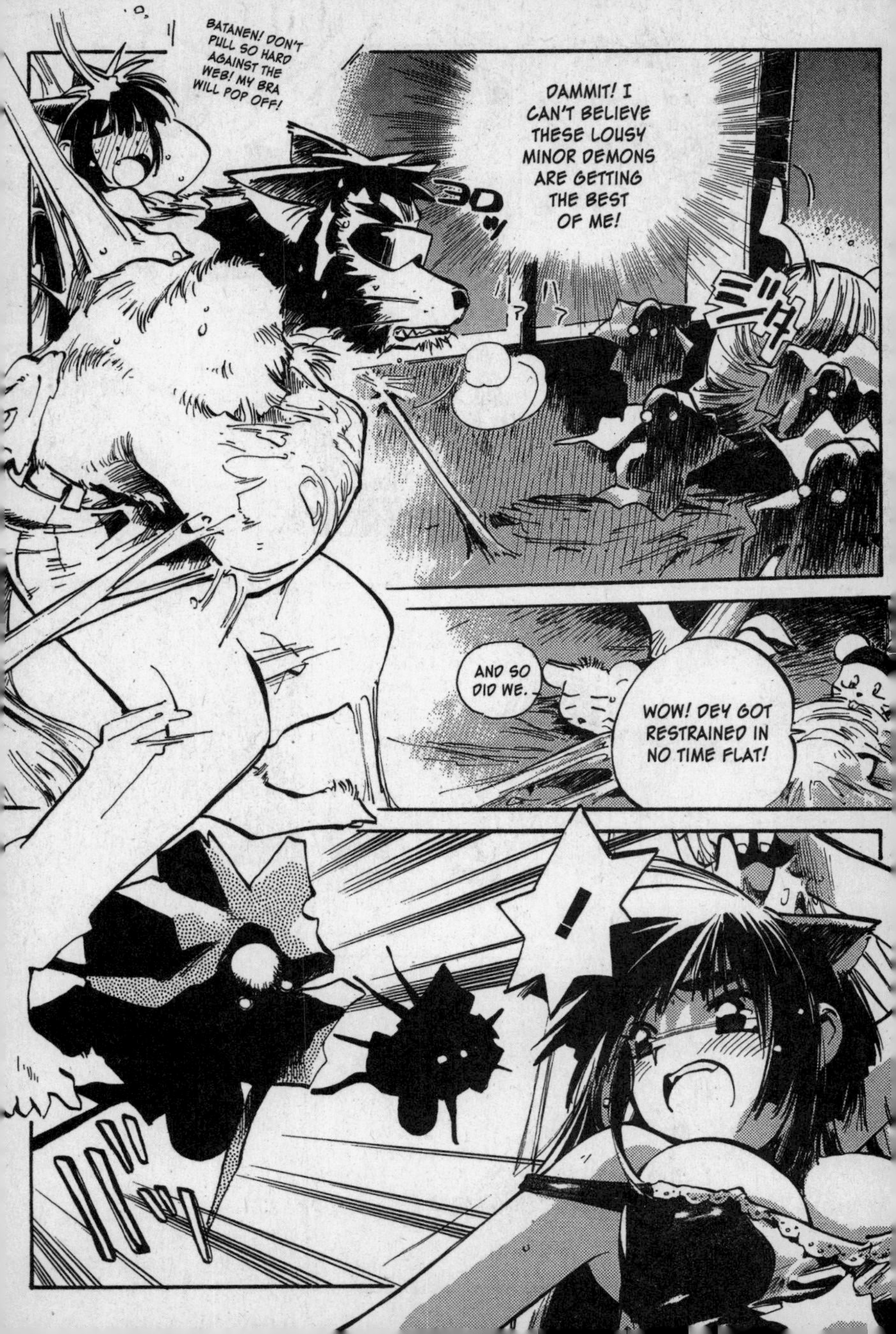

DAMMIT! I CAN'T BELIEVE THESE LOUSY MINOR DEMONS ARE GETTING THE BEST OF ME!
WOW! DEY GOT RESTRAINED IN NO TIME FLAT!
AND SO DID WE.
BATANEN! DON'T PULL SO HARD AGAINST THE WEB! MY BRA WILL POP OFF!
!

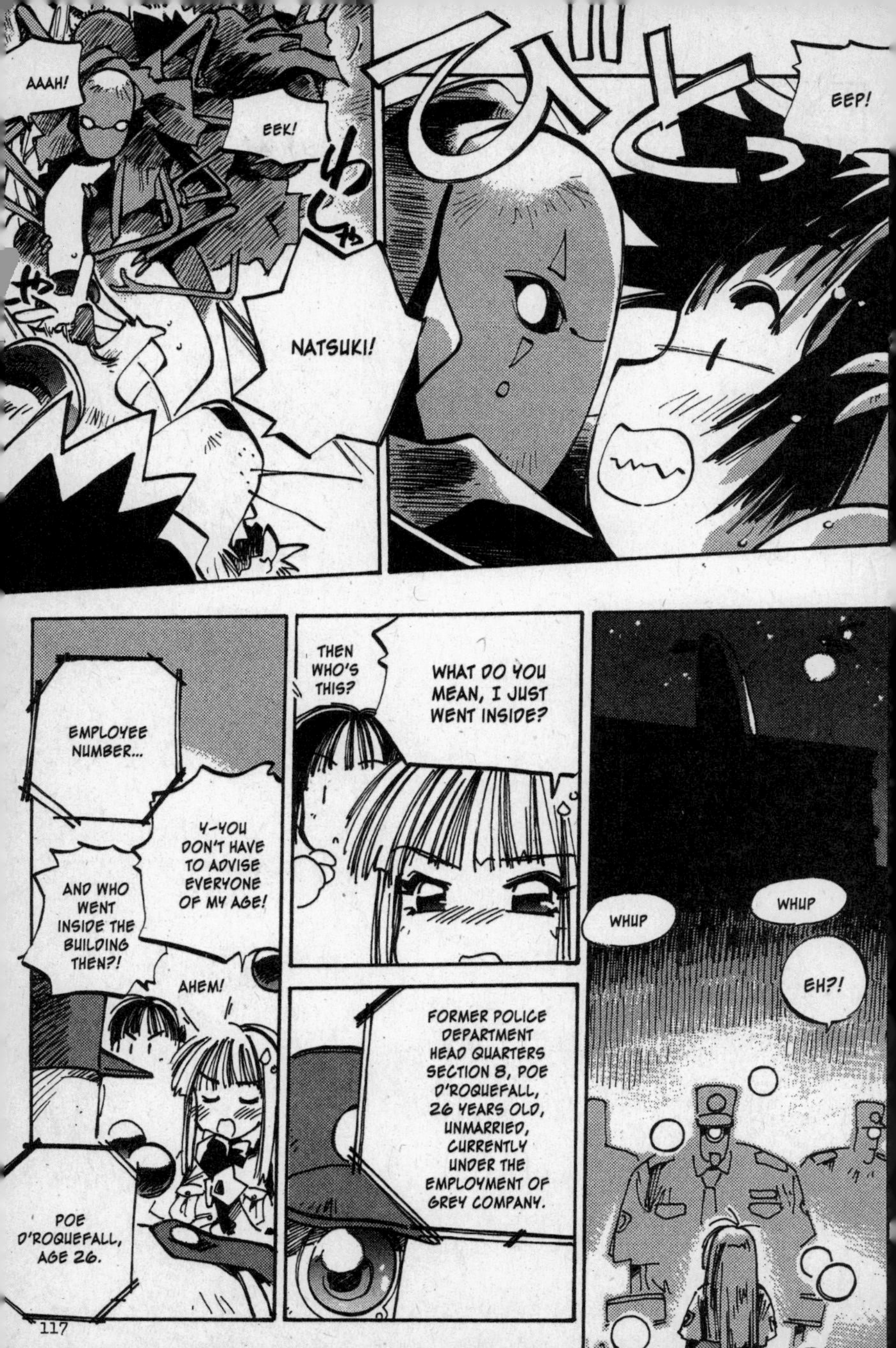
EEP!
EEK!
AAAH!
NATSUKI!
WHUP
WHUP
EH?!
WHAT DO YOU MEAN, I JUST WENT INSIDE?
THEN WHO'S THIS?
FORMER POLICE DEPARTMENT HEAD QUARTERS SECTION 8, POE D'ROQUEFALL, 26 YEARS OLD, UNMARRIED, CURRENTLY UNDER THE EMPLOYMENT OF GREY COMPANY.
EMPLOYEE NUMBER...
Y-YOU DON'T HAVE TO ADVISE EVERYONE OF MY AGE!
AND WHO WENT INSIDE THE BUILDING THEN?!
AHEM!
POE D'ROQUEFALL, AGE 26.

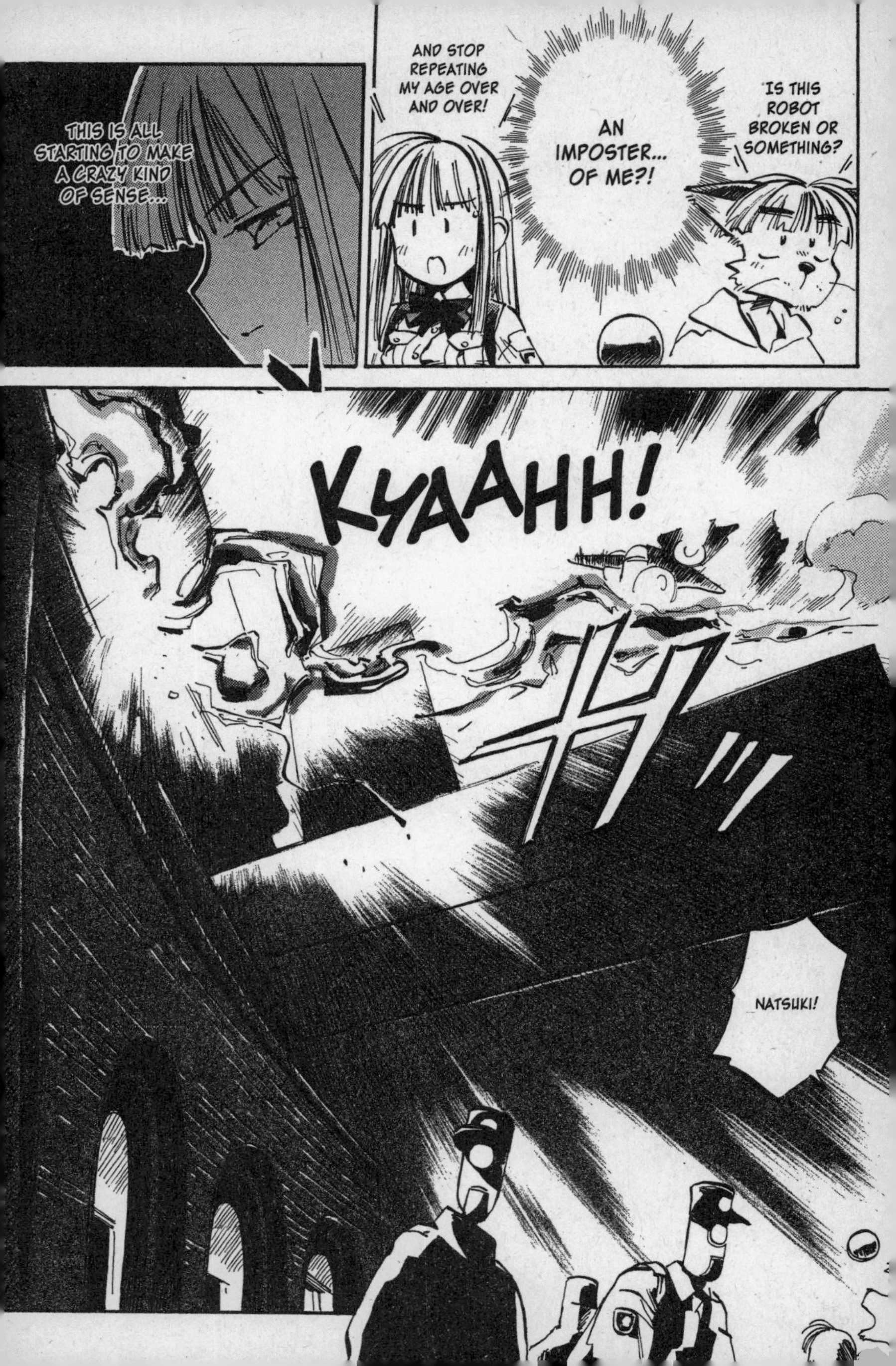
IS THIS ROBOT BROKEN OR SOMETHING?
AN IMPOSTER... OF ME?!
AND STOP REPEATING MY AGE OVER AND OVER!
THIS IS ALL STARTING TO MAKE A CRAZY KIND OF SENSE...
KYAAHH!
NATSUKI!

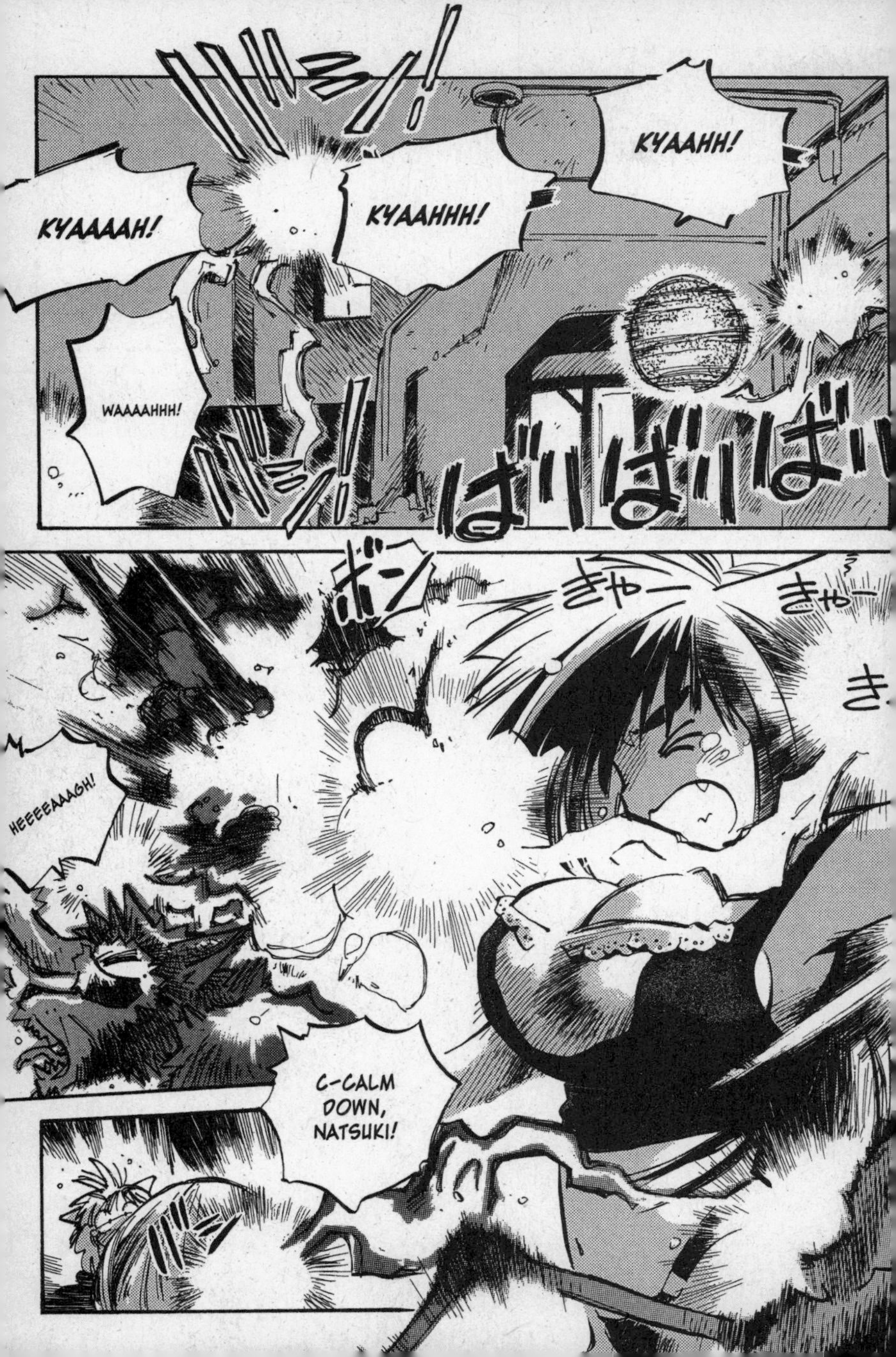

KYAAHH!
KYAAHHH!
KYAAAAH!
WAAAAHHH!
きゃー
きゃー
ボン
HEEEEAAAGH!
C-CALM DOWN, NATSUKI!

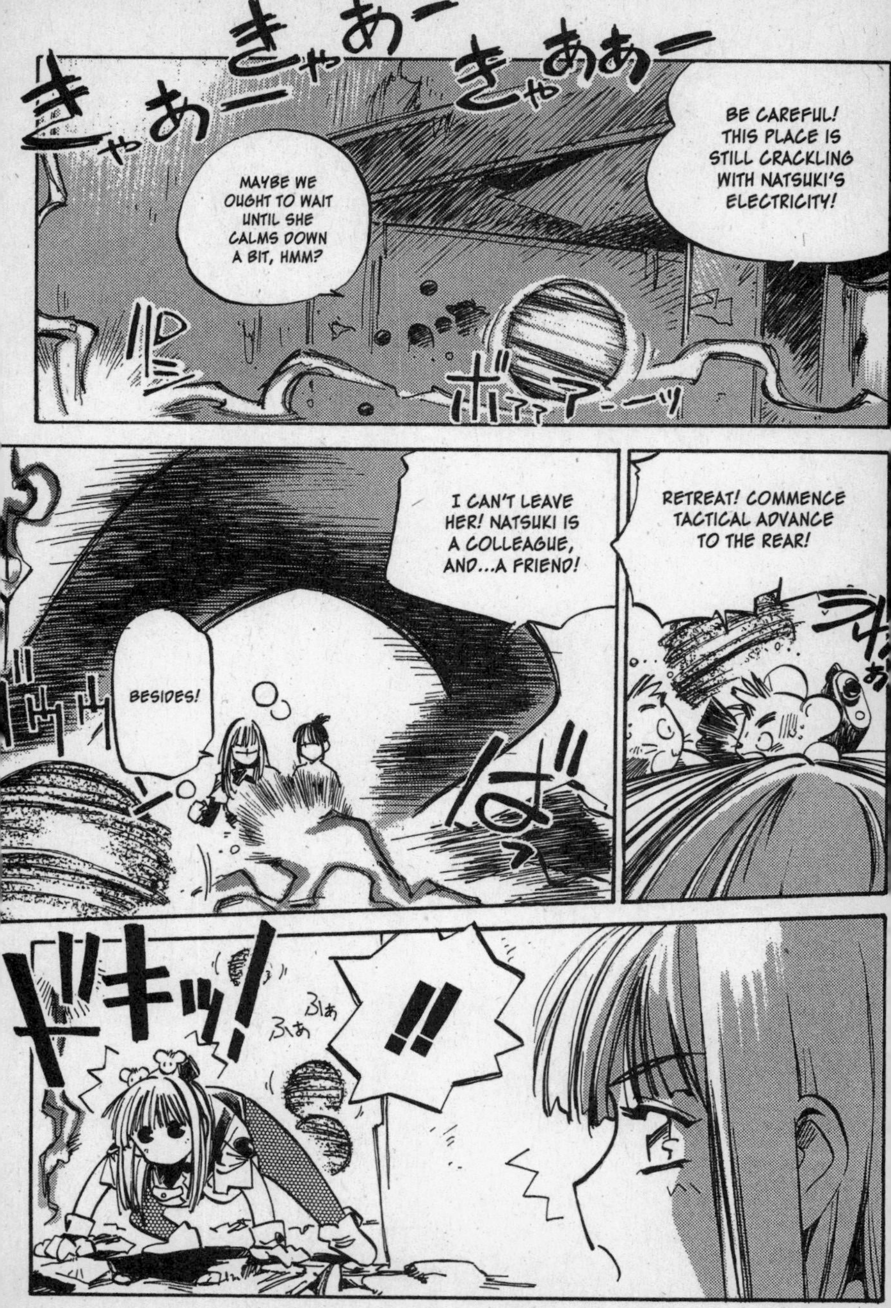

BE CAREFUL! THIS PLACE IS STILL CRACKLING WITH NATSUKI'S ELECTRICITY!
MAYBE WE OUGHT TO WAIT UNTIL SHE CALMS DOWN A BIT, HMM?
RETREAT! COMMENCE TACTICAL ADVANCE TO THE REAR!
I CAN'T LEAVE HER! NATSUKI IS A COLLEAGUE, AND...A FRIEND!
BESIDES!
!!
ふあ ふあ

HYPER POLICE™

ハイパーポリス

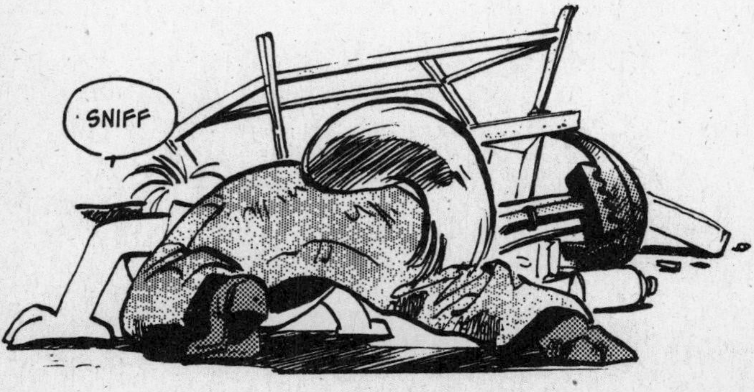
SNIFF

HYPER POLICE™

ハイパーポリス

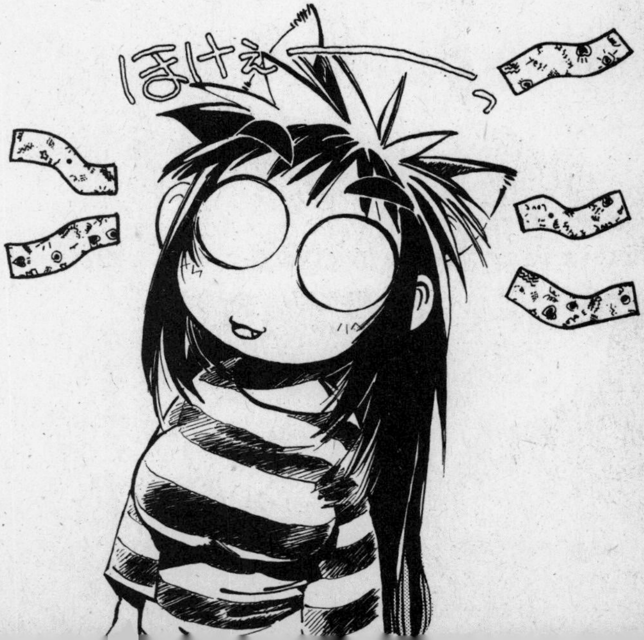
ほけぇーーっ

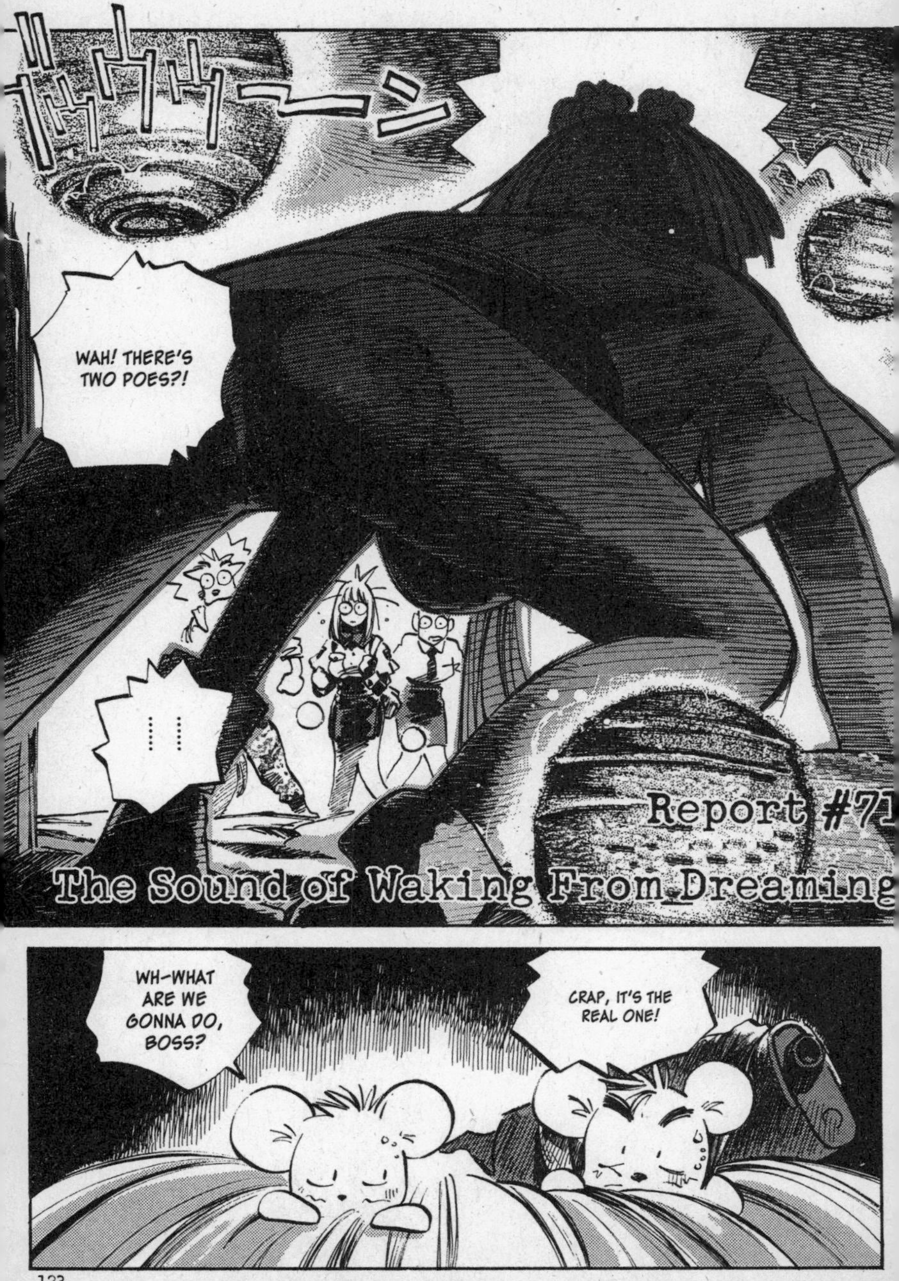
WAH! THERE'S TWO POES?!
......
Report #71
The Sound of Waking From Dreaming
CRAP, IT'S THE REAL ONE!
WH-WHAT ARE WE GONNA DO, BOSS?

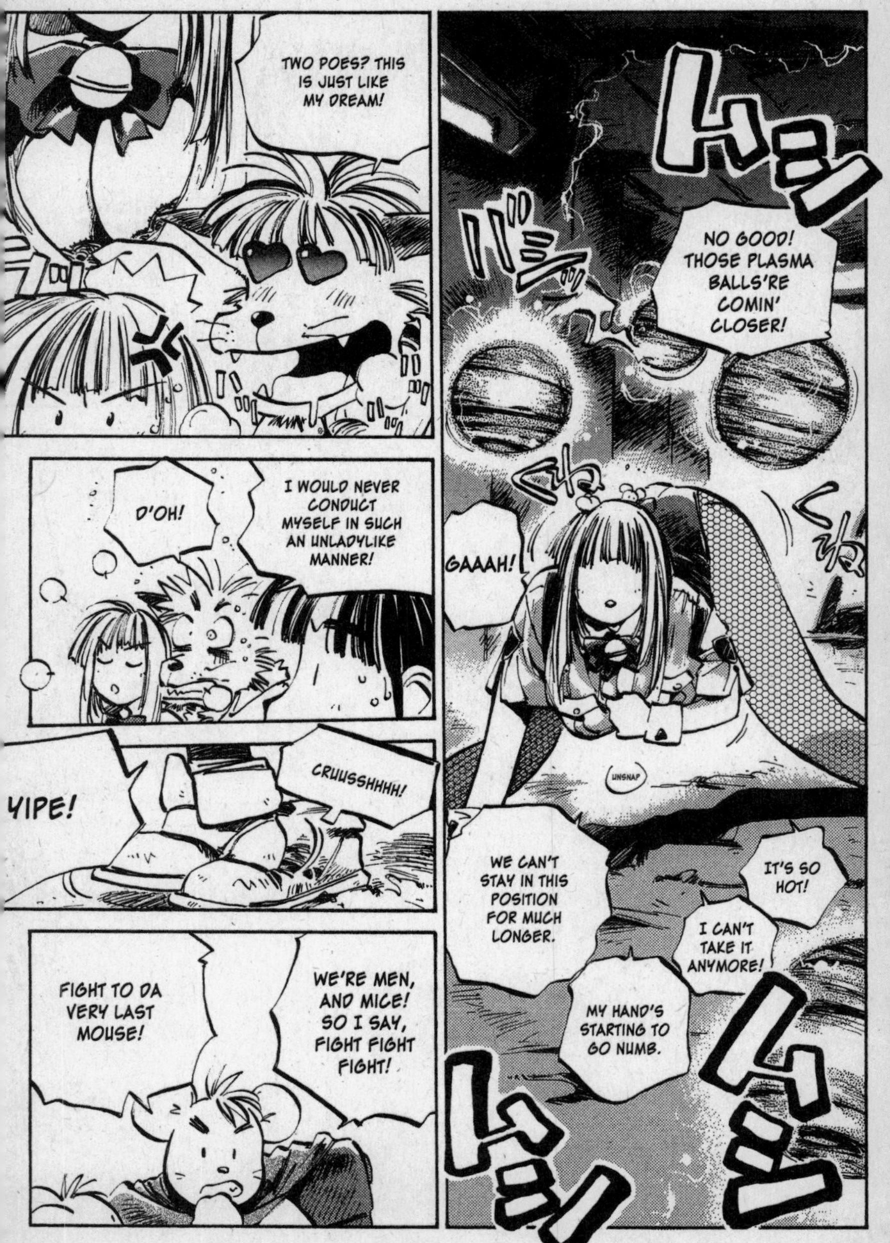
NO GOOD! THOSE PLASMA BALLS'RE COMIN' CLOSER!
GAAAH!
UNSNAP
IT'S SO HOT!
WE CAN'T STAY IN THIS POSITION FOR MUCH LONGER.
I CAN'T TAKE IT ANYMORE!
MY HAND'S STARTING TO GO NUMB.
TWO POES? THIS IS JUST LIKE MY DREAM!
I WOULD NEVER CONDUCT MYSELF IN SUCH AN UNLADYLIKE MANNER!
D'OH!
CRUUSSHHHH!
YIPE!
WE'RE MEN, AND MICE! SO I SAY, FIGHT FIGHT FIGHT!
FIGHT TO DA VERY LAST MOUSE!

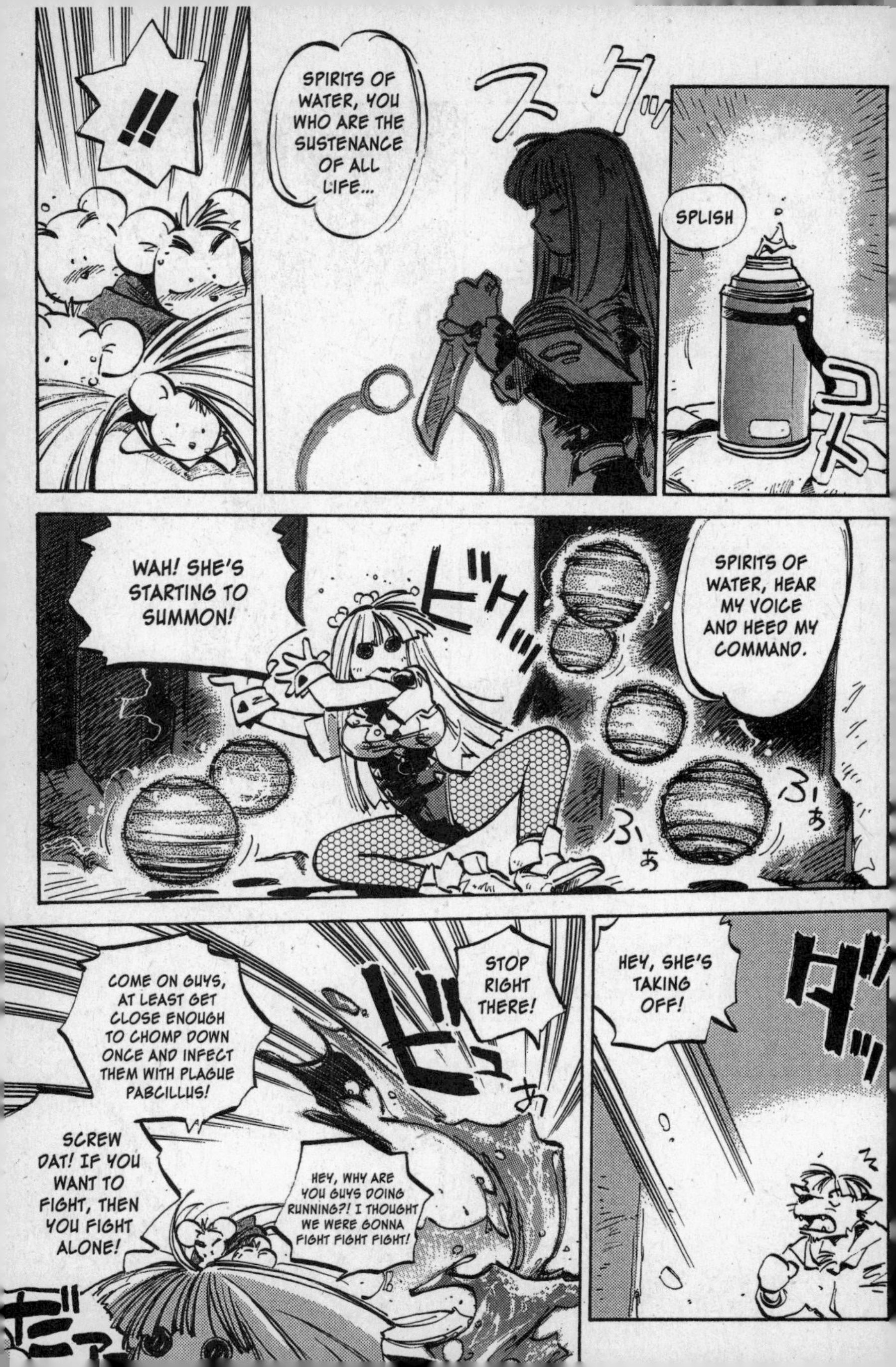
SPLISH
SPIRITS OF WATER, YOU WHO ARE THE SUSTENANCE OF ALL LIFE...
!!
SPIRITS OF WATER, HEAR MY VOICE AND HEED MY COMMAND.
WAH! SHE'S STARTING TO SUMMON!
HEY, SHE'S TAKING OFF!
STOP RIGHT THERE!
COME ON GUYS, AT LEAST GET CLOSE ENOUGH TO CHOMP DOWN ONCE AND INFECT THEM WITH PLAGUE PABCILLUS!
HEY, WHY ARE YOU GUYS DOING RUNNING?! I THOUGHT WE WERE GONNA FIGHT FIGHT FIGHT!
SCREW DAT! IF YOU WANT TO FIGHT, THEN YOU FIGHT ALONE!

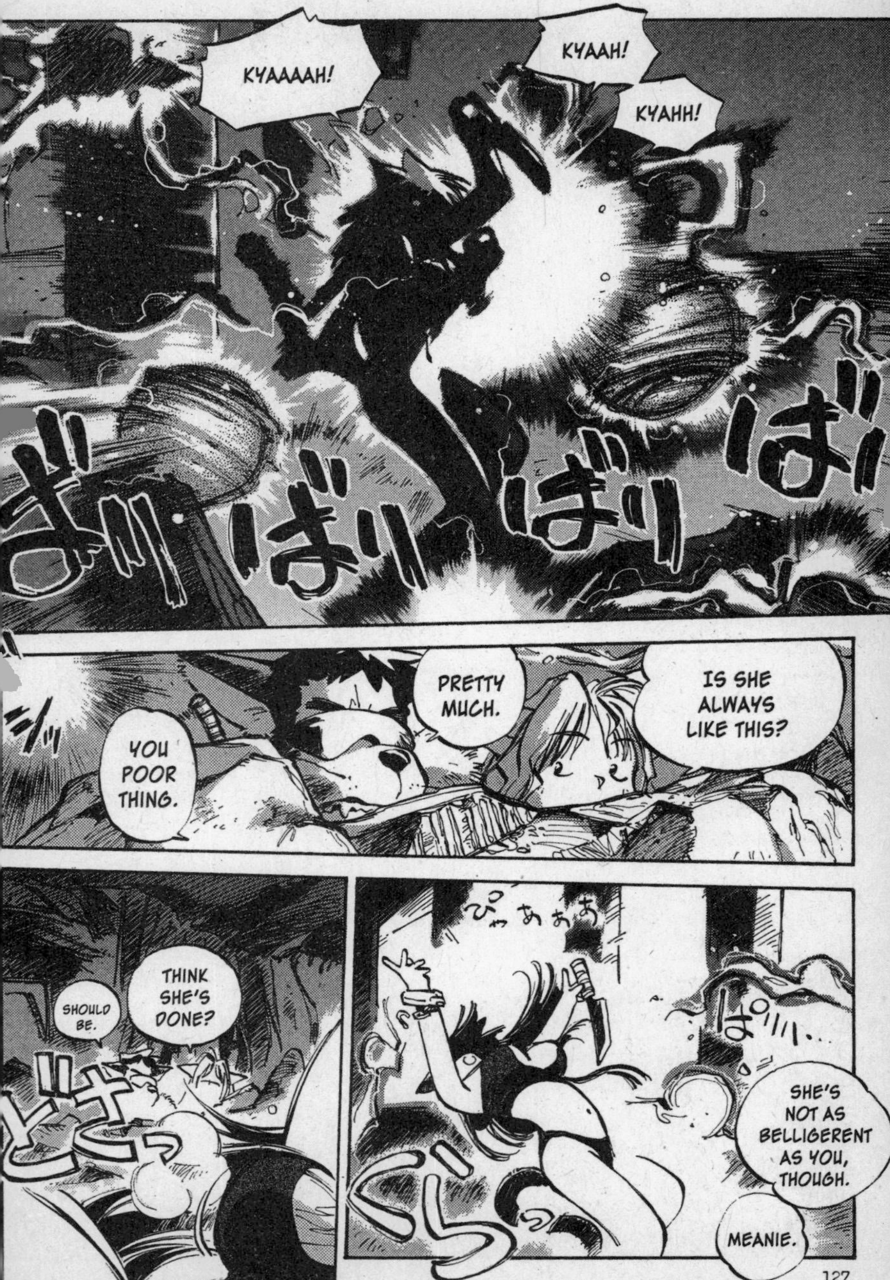
KYAAH!
KYAHH!
KYAAAAH!
IS SHE ALWAYS LIKE THIS?
PRETTY MUCH.
YOU POOR THING.
ぴゃあぁあ
SHE'S NOT AS BELLIGERENT AS YOU, THOUGH.
MEANIE.
THINK SHE'S DONE?
SHOULD BE.

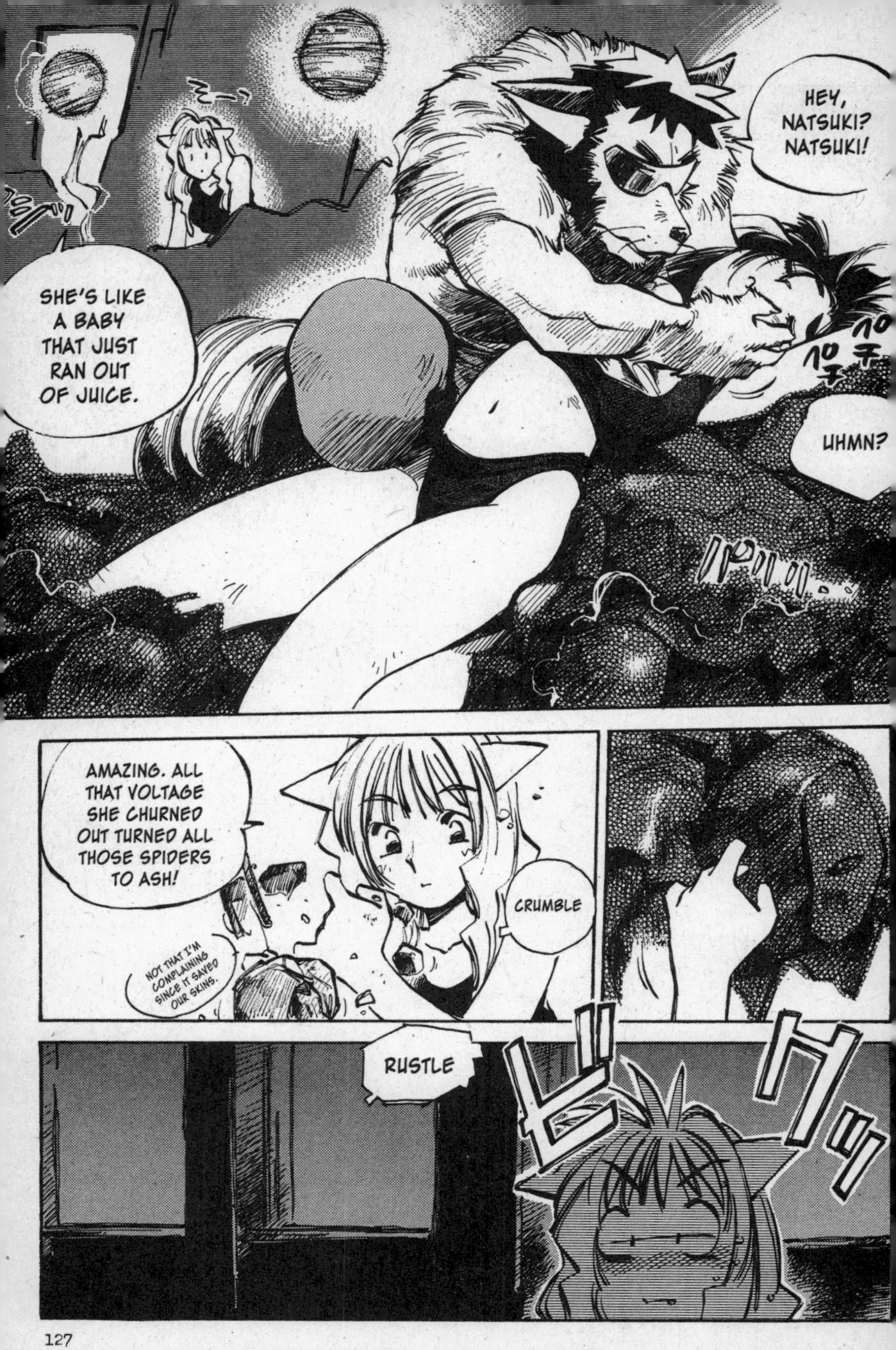
HEY, NATSUKI? NATSUKI!
UHMN?
SHE'S LIKE A BABY THAT JUST RAN OUT OF JUICE.
AMAZING. ALL THAT VOLTAGE SHE CHURNED OUT TURNED ALL THOSE SPIDERS TO ASH!
CRUMBLE
NOT THAT I'M COMPLAINING SINCE IT SAVED OUR SKINS.
RUSTLE

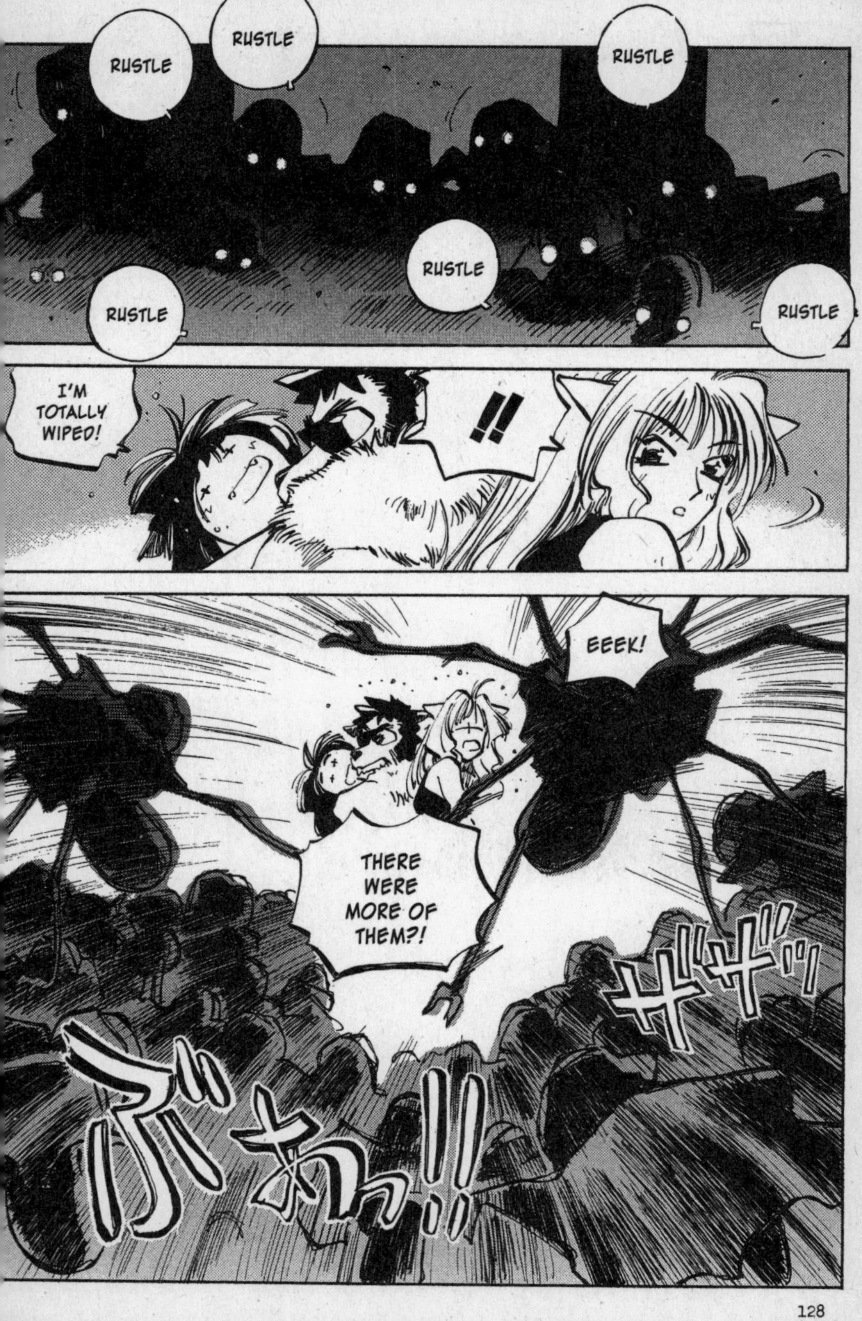
RUSTLE
RUSTLE
RUSTLE
RUSTLE
RUSTLE
RUSTLE
!!
I'M TOTALLY WIPED!
EEEK!
THERE WERE MORE OF THEM?!
ザザッ
ぶぁっ!!

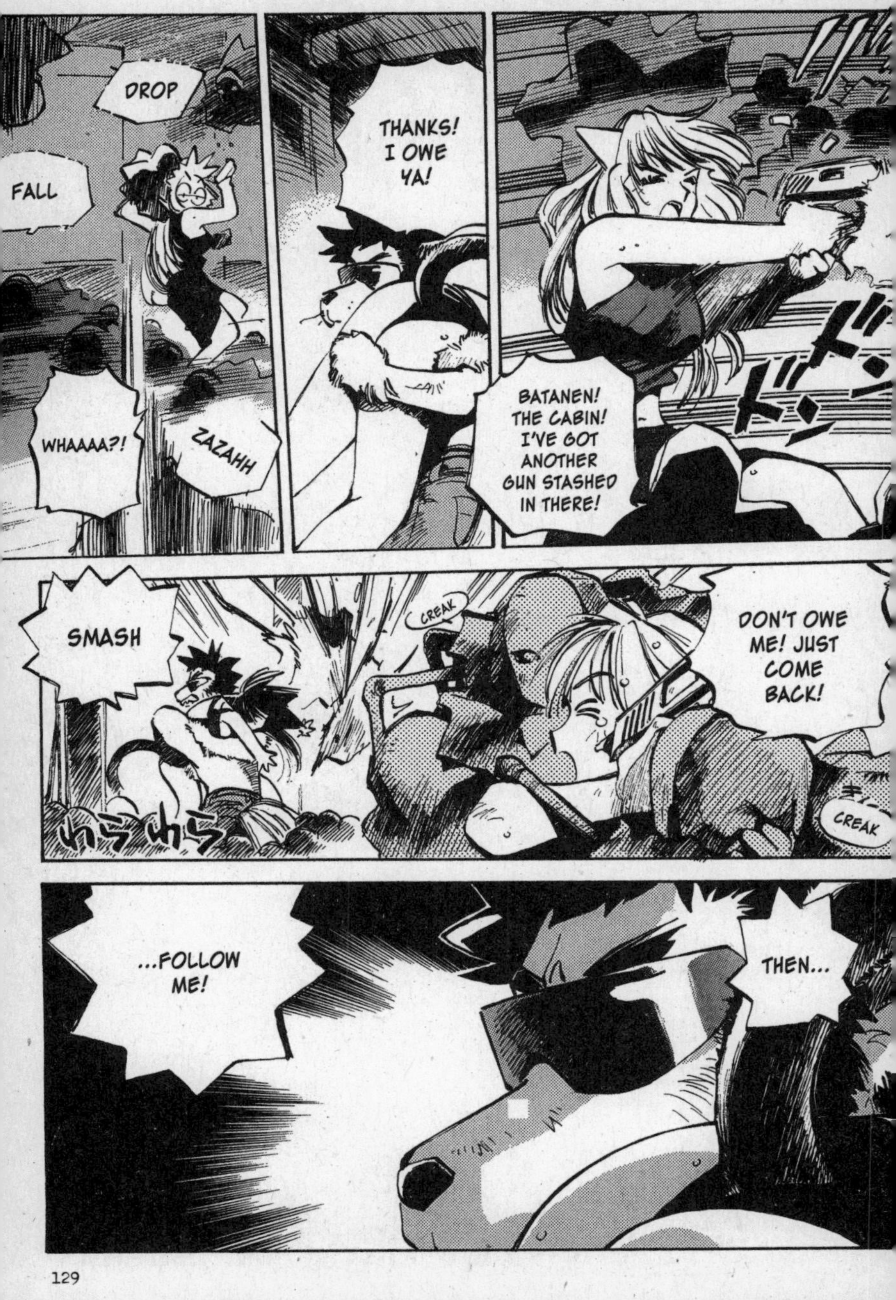
BATANEN! THE CABIN! I'VE GOT ANOTHER GUN STASHED IN THERE!
THANKS! I OWE YA!
DROP
FALL
WHAAAA?!
ZAZAHH
DON'T OWE ME! JUST COME BACK!
CREAK
CREAK
SMASH
THEN...
...FOLLOW ME!

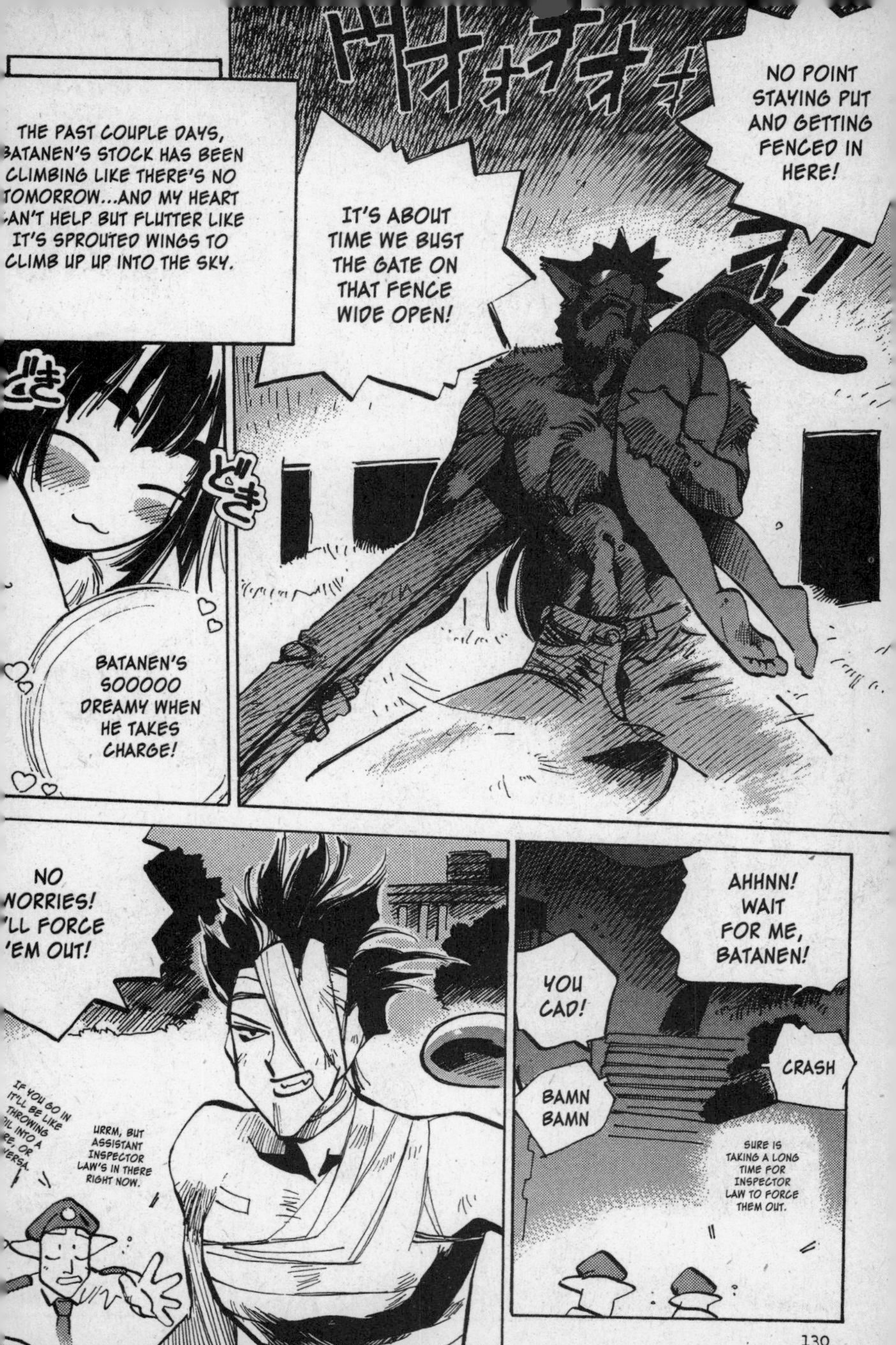
NO POINT STAYING PUT AND GETTING FENCED IN HERE!
IT'S ABOUT TIME WE BUST THE GATE ON THAT FENCE WIDE OPEN!
THE PAST COUPLE DAYS, BATANEN'S STOCK HAS BEEN CLIMBING LIKE THERE'S NO TOMORROW...AND MY HEART CAN'T HELP BUT FLUTTER LIKE IT'S SPROUTED WINGS TO CLIMB UP UP INTO THE SKY.
どき
どき
BATANEN'S SOOOOO DREAMY WHEN HE TAKES CHARGE!
AHHNN! WAIT FOR ME, BATANEN!
YOU CAD!
CRASH
BAMN BAMN
SURE IS TAKING A LONG TIME FOR INSPECTOR LAW TO FORCE THEM OUT.
NO WORRIES! I'LL FORCE 'EM OUT!
URRM, BUT ASSISTANT INSPECTOR LAW'S IN THERE RIGHT NOW.
IF YOU GO IN IT'LL BE LIKE THROWING OIL INTO A FIRE, OR VERSA.

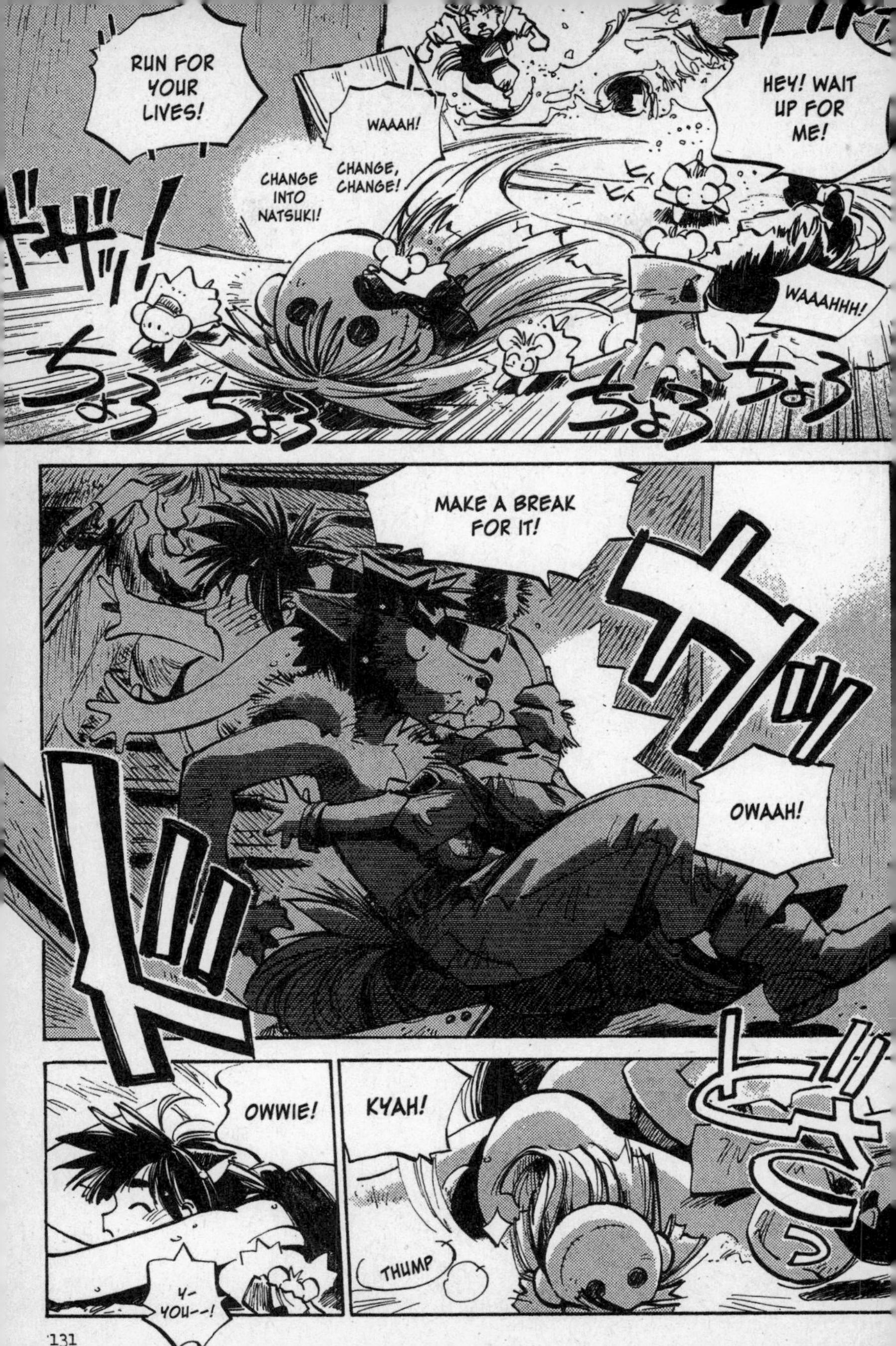
HEY! WAIT UP FOR ME!
WAAAHHH!
WAAAH!
CHANGE, CHANGE!
CHANGE INTO NATSUKI!
RUN FOR YOUR LIVES!
ちょろ ちょろ
ちょろ ちょろ
MAKE A BREAK FOR IT!
OWAAH!
KYAH!
THUMP
OWWIE!
Y-YOU--!

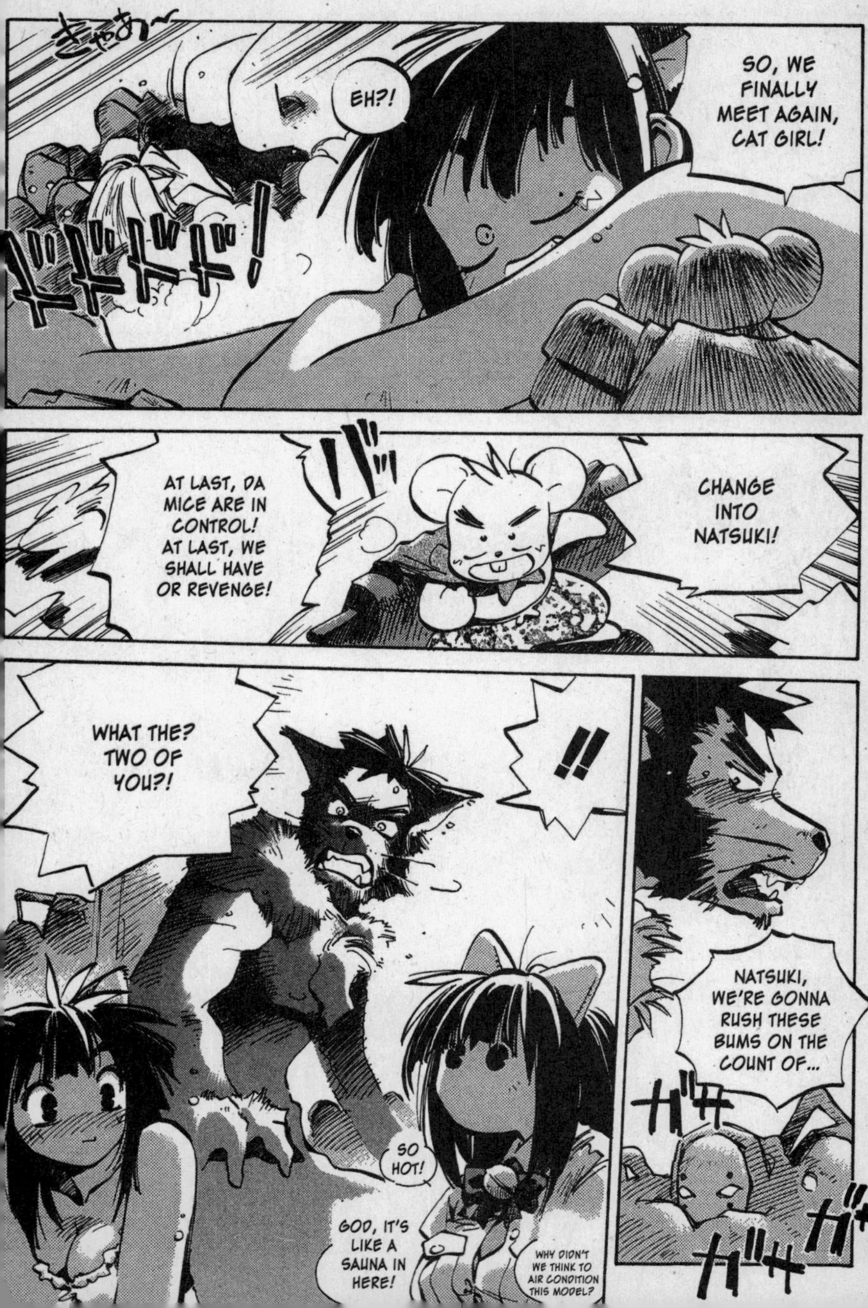

SO, WE FINALLY MEET AGAIN, CAT GIRL!
EH?!
きゃあ～
ドドドドド!
CHANGE INTO NATSUKI!
AT LAST, DA MICE ARE IN CONTROL! AT LAST, WE SHALL HAVE OR REVENGE!
NATSUKI, WE'RE GONNA RUSH THESE BUMS ON THE COUNT OF...
ガサ
ガサ
ガサ
!!
WHAT THE? TWO OF YOU?!
SO HOT!
GOD, IT'S LIKE A SAUNA IN HERE!
WHY DIDN'T WE THINK TO AIR CONDITION THIS MODEL?

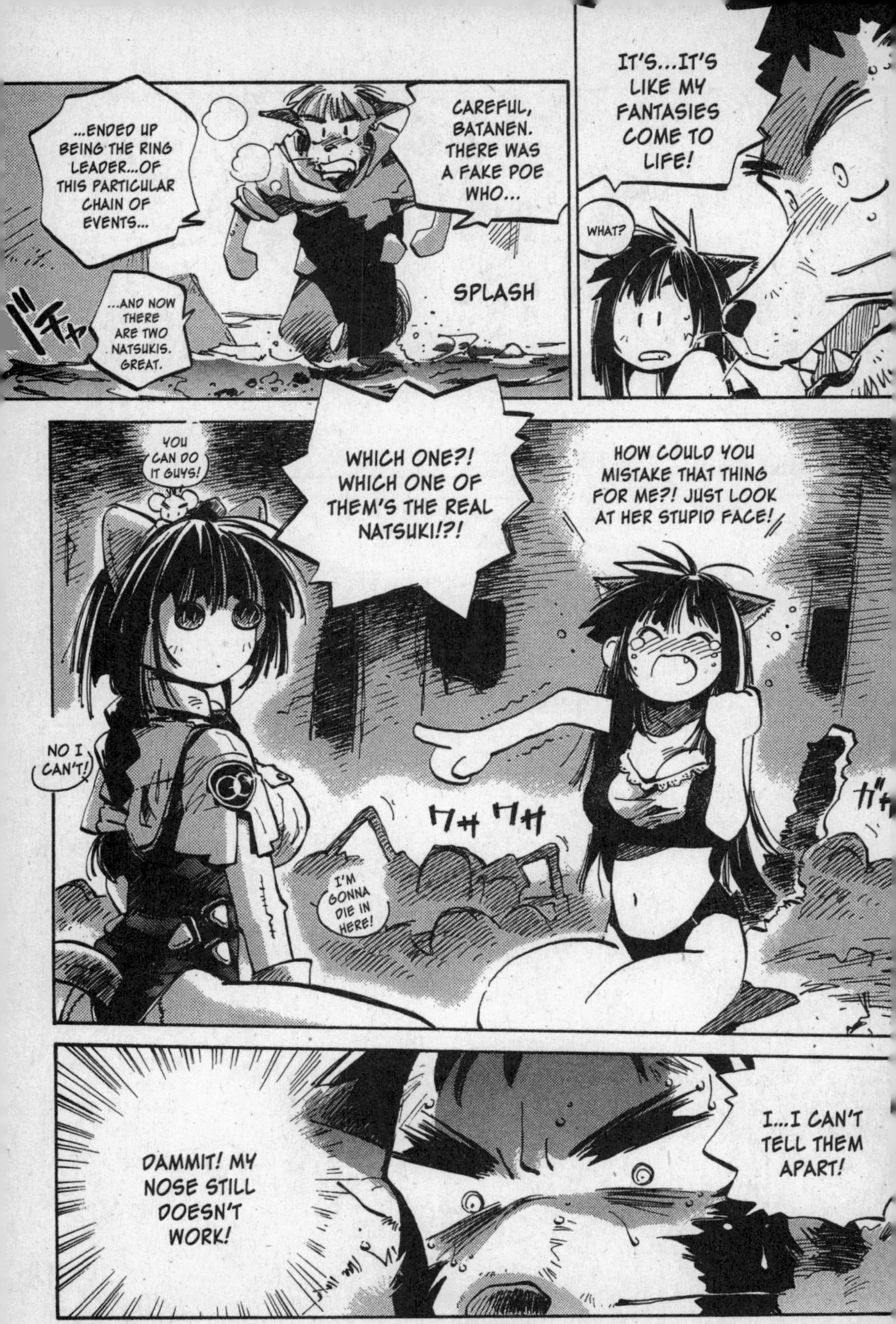
IT'S...IT'S LIKE MY FANTASIES COME TO LIFE!
WHAT?
CAREFUL, BATANEN. THERE WAS A FAKE POE WHO...
SPLASH
...ENDED UP BEING THE RING LEADER...OF THIS PARTICULAR CHAIN OF EVENTS...
...AND NOW THERE ARE TWO NATSUKIS. GREAT.
HOW COULD YOU MISTAKE THAT THING FOR ME?! JUST LOOK AT HER STUPID FACE!
WHICH ONE?! WHICH ONE OF THEM'S THE REAL NATSUKI!?!
YOU CAN DO IT GUYS!
NO I CAN'T!
I'M GONNA DIE IN HERE!
I...I CAN'T TELL THEM APART!
DAMMIT! MY NOSE STILL DOESN'T WORK!

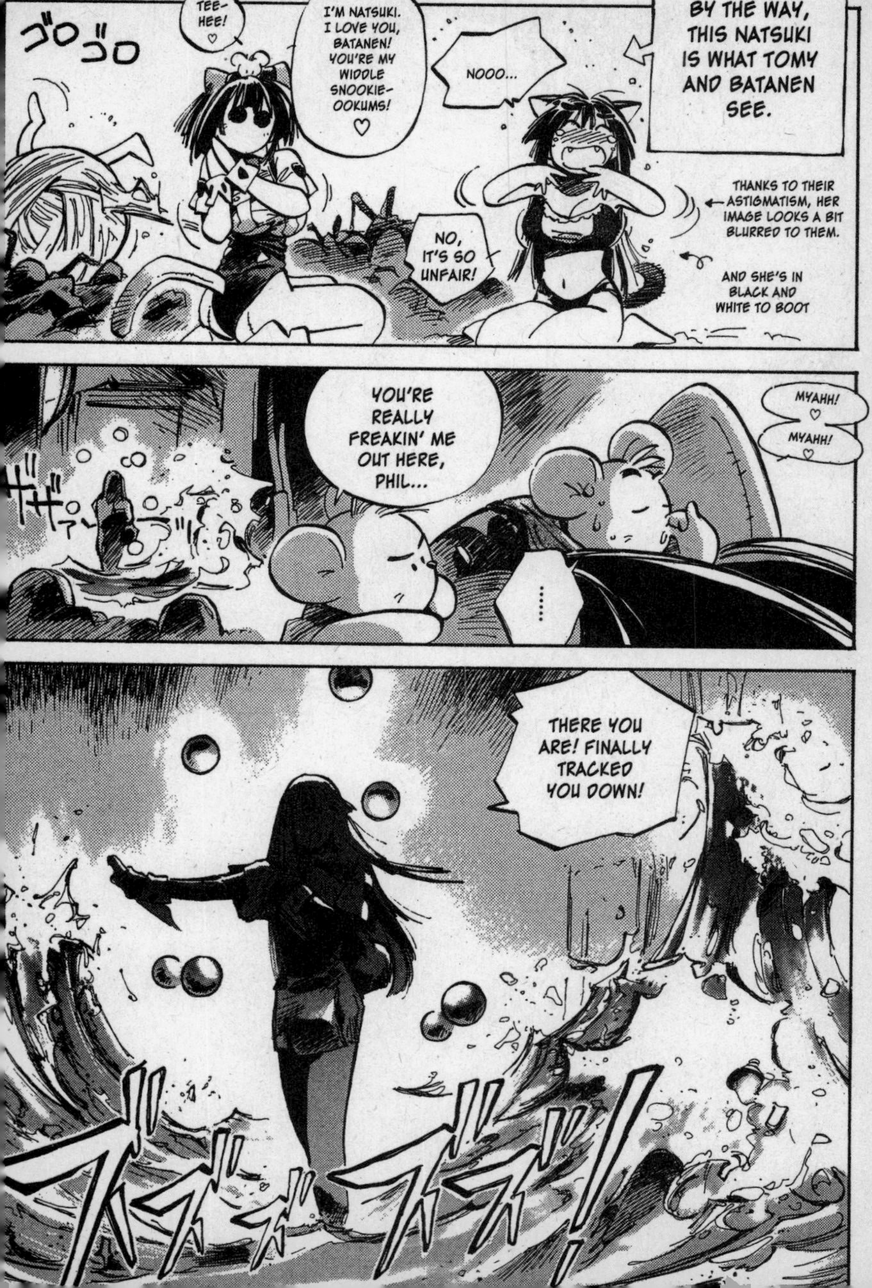
BY THE WAY, THIS NATSUKI IS WHAT TOMY AND BATANEN SEE.
THANKS TO THEIR ASTIGMATISM, HER IMAGE LOOKS A BIT BLURRED TO THEM.
AND SHE'S IN BLACK AND WHITE TO BOOT
NOOO...
NO, IT'S SO UNFAIR!
I'M NATSUKI. I LOVE YOU, BATANEN! YOU'RE MY WIDDLE SNOOKIE-OOKUMS! ♡
TEE-HEE! ♡
ゴロゴロ
MYAHH! ♡
MYAHH! ♡
......
YOU'RE REALLY FREAKIN' ME OUT HERE, PHIL...
ザザァ
THERE YOU ARE! FINALLY TRACKED YOU DOWN!

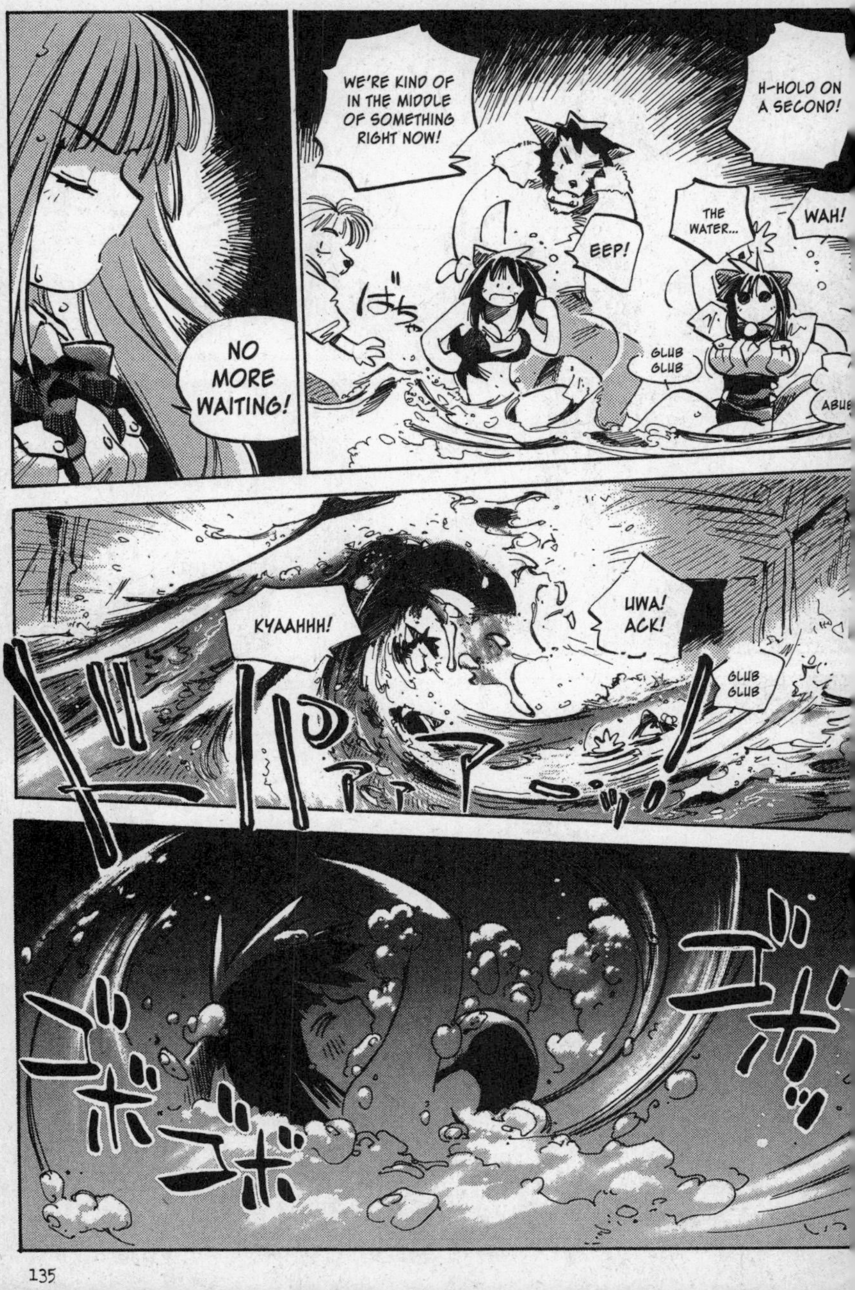
H-HOLD ON A SECOND!
WE'RE KIND OF IN THE MIDDLE OF SOMETHING RIGHT NOW!
WAH!
THE WATER...
EEP!
ばちゃ
ABUB
GLUB GLUB
NO MORE WAITING!
GLUB GLUB
UWA! ACK!
KYAAHHH!
ドバァァァーッ!
ゴボッ
ゴボゴボ

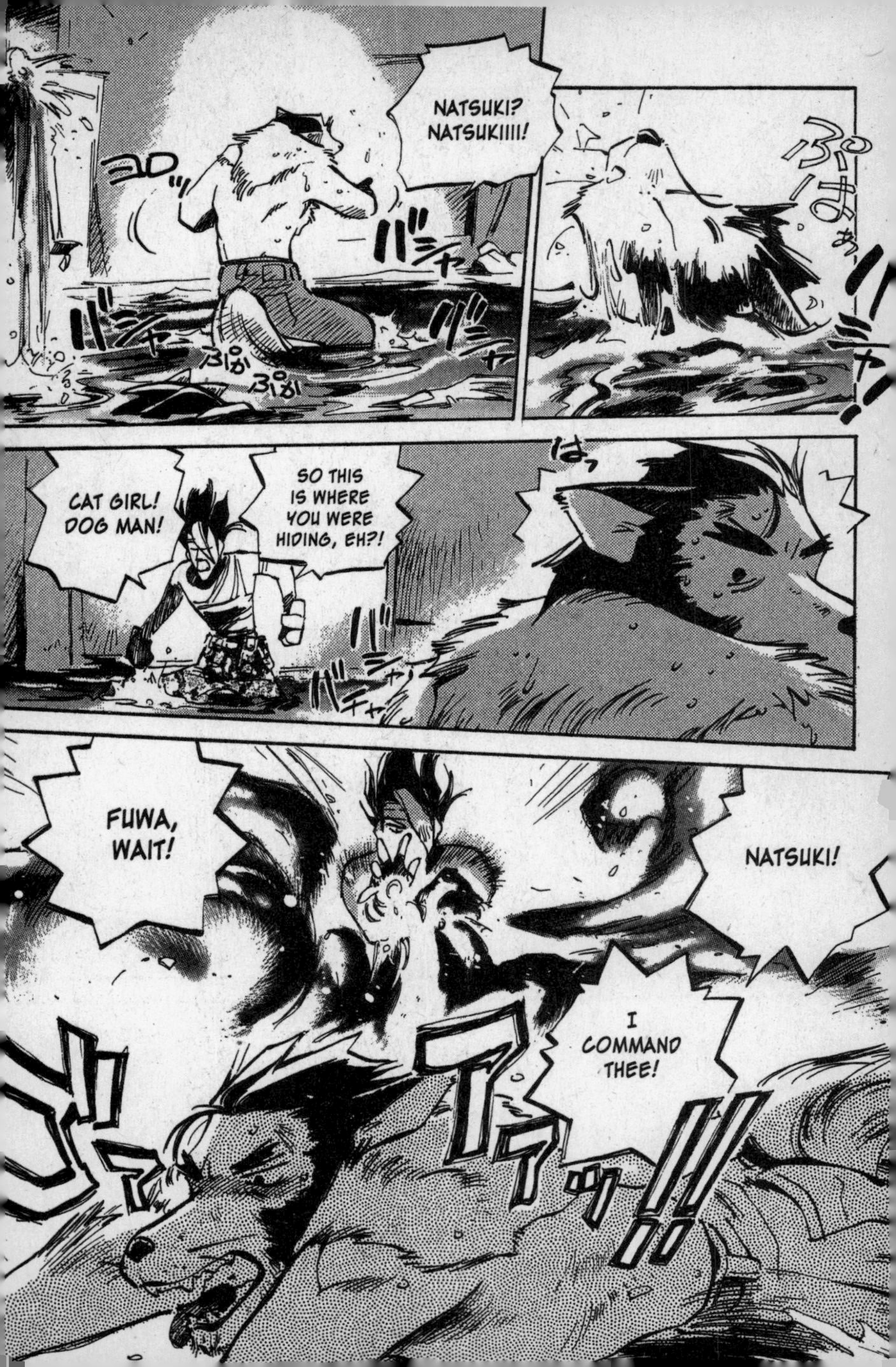

ぷはぁ
NATSUKI?
NATSUKIIII!
SO THIS IS WHERE YOU WERE HIDING, EH?!
CAT GIRL! DOG MAN!
NATSUKI!
FUWA, WAIT!
I COMMAND THEE!

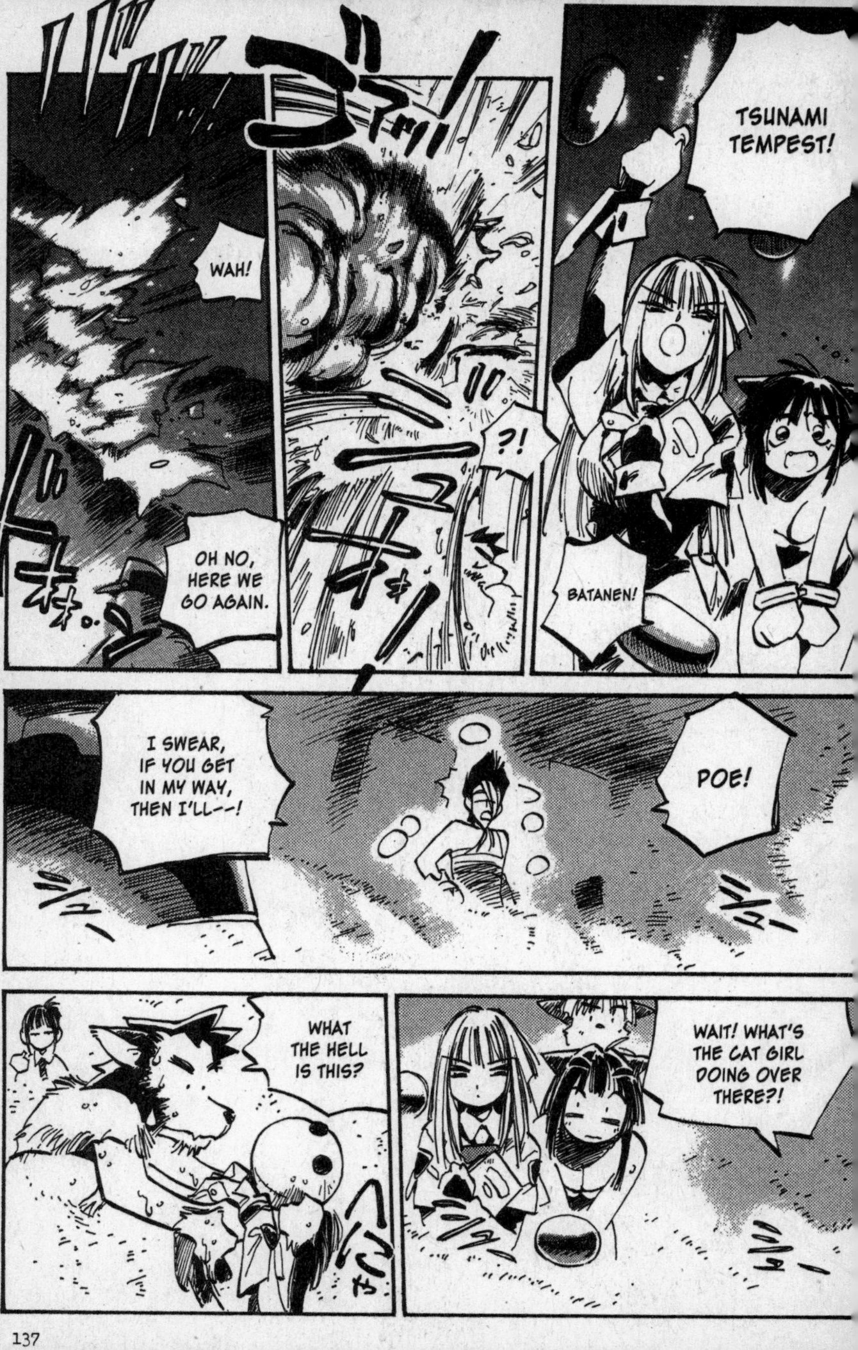
TSUNAMI TEMPEST!
BATANEN!
?!
WAH!
OH NO, HERE WE GO AGAIN.
POE!
I SWEAR, IF YOU GET IN MY WAY, THEN I'LL--!
WAIT! WHAT'S THE CAT GIRL DOING OVER THERE?!
WHAT THE HELL IS THIS?

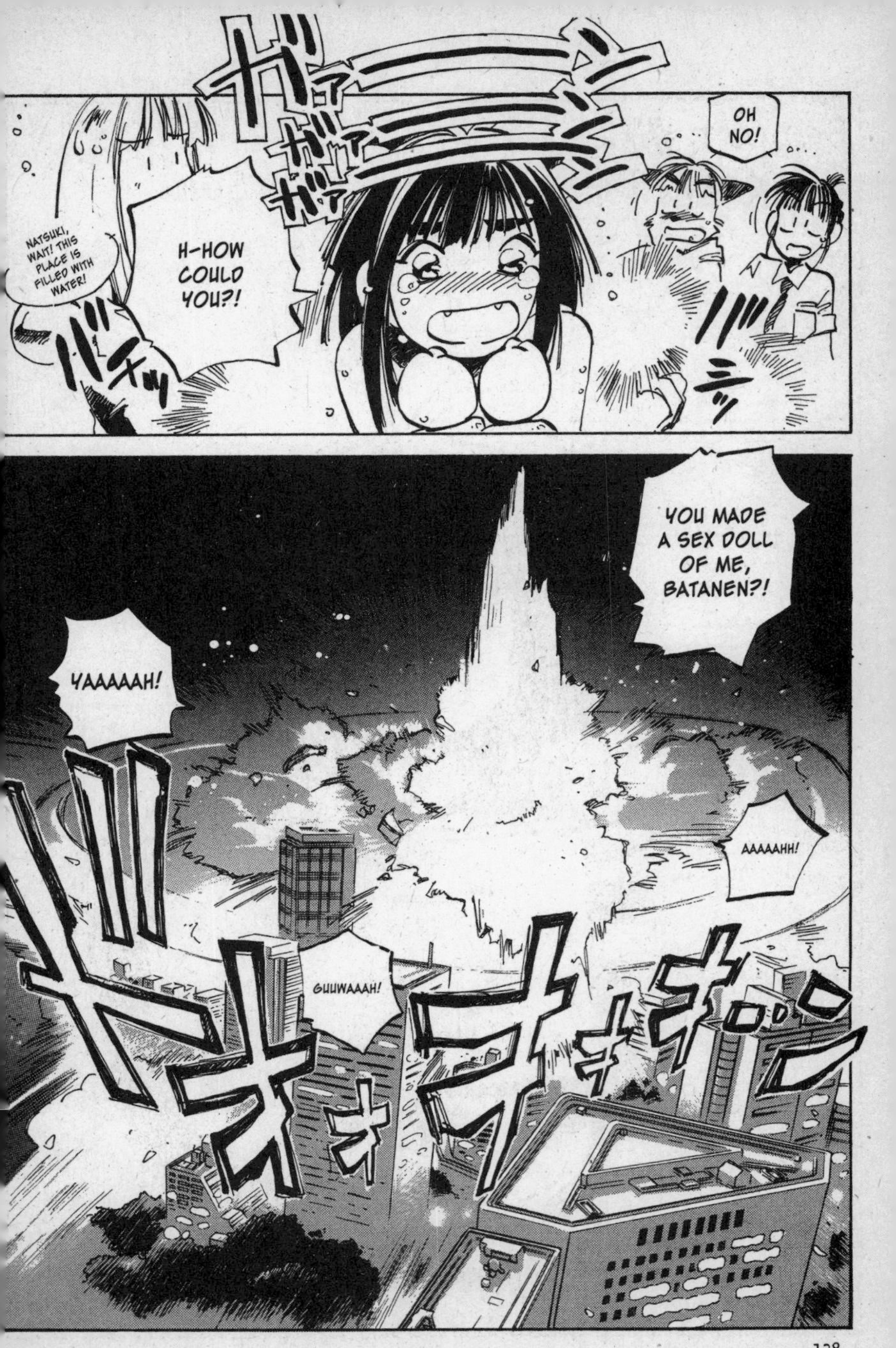
OH NO!
H-HOW COULD YOU?!
NATSUKI, WAIT! THIS PLACE IS FILLED WITH WATER!
YOU MADE A SEX DOLL OF ME, BATANEN?!
YAAAAAH!
AAAAAHH!
GUUWAAAH!

Report #72
Regrets, Deeper than the Sea

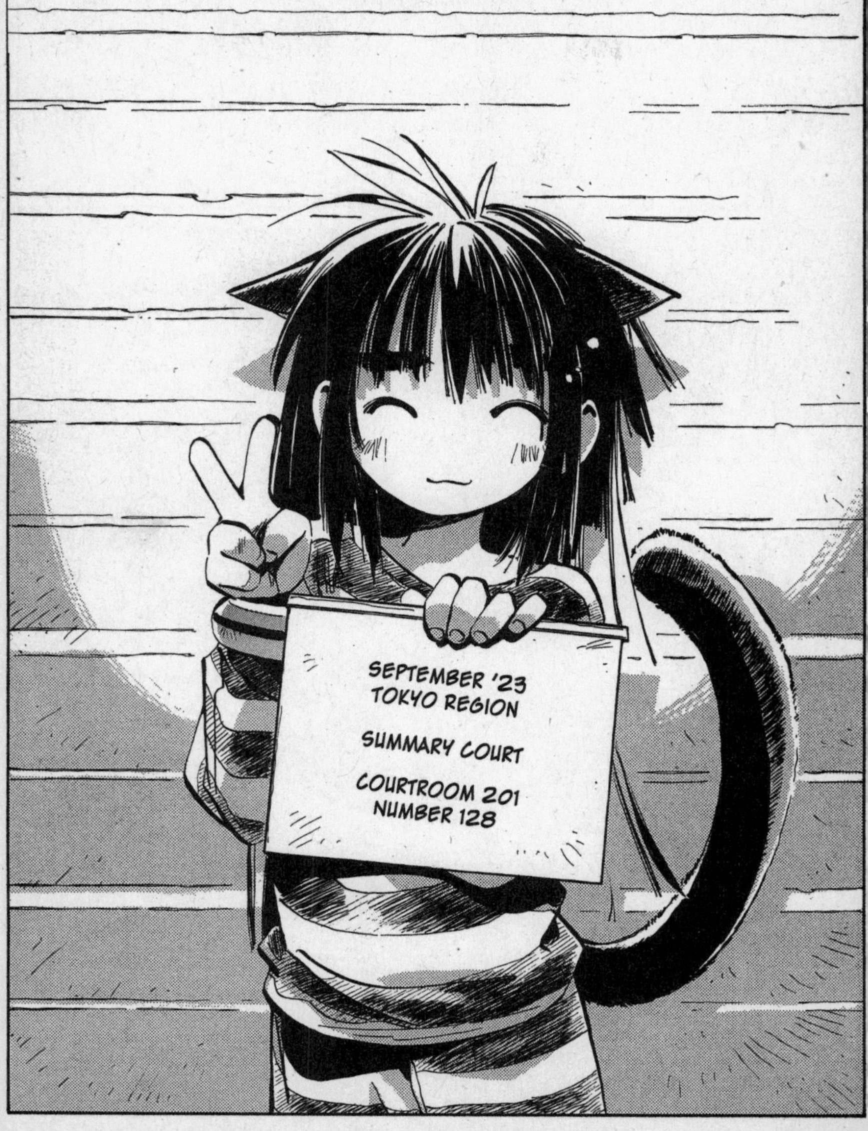
SEPTEMBER '23
TOKYO REGION
SUMMARY COURT
COURTROOM 201
NUMBER 128

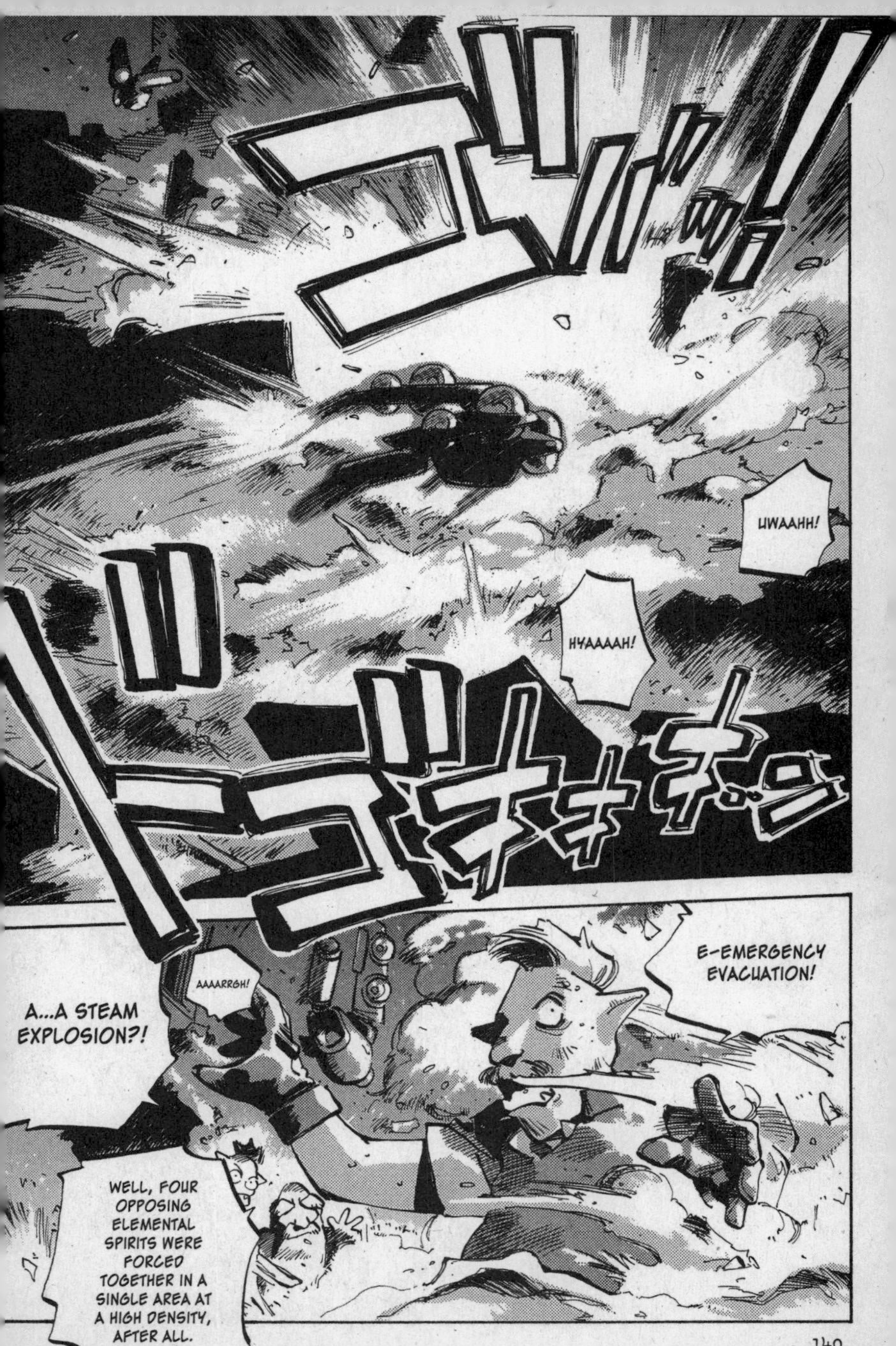
UWAAHH!
HYAAAAH!
E-EMERGENCY EVACUATION!
AAAARRGH!
A...A STEAM EXPLOSION?!
WELL, FOUR OPPOSING ELEMENTAL SPIRITS WERE FORCED TOGETHER IN A SINGLE AREA AT A HIGH DENSITY, AFTER ALL.

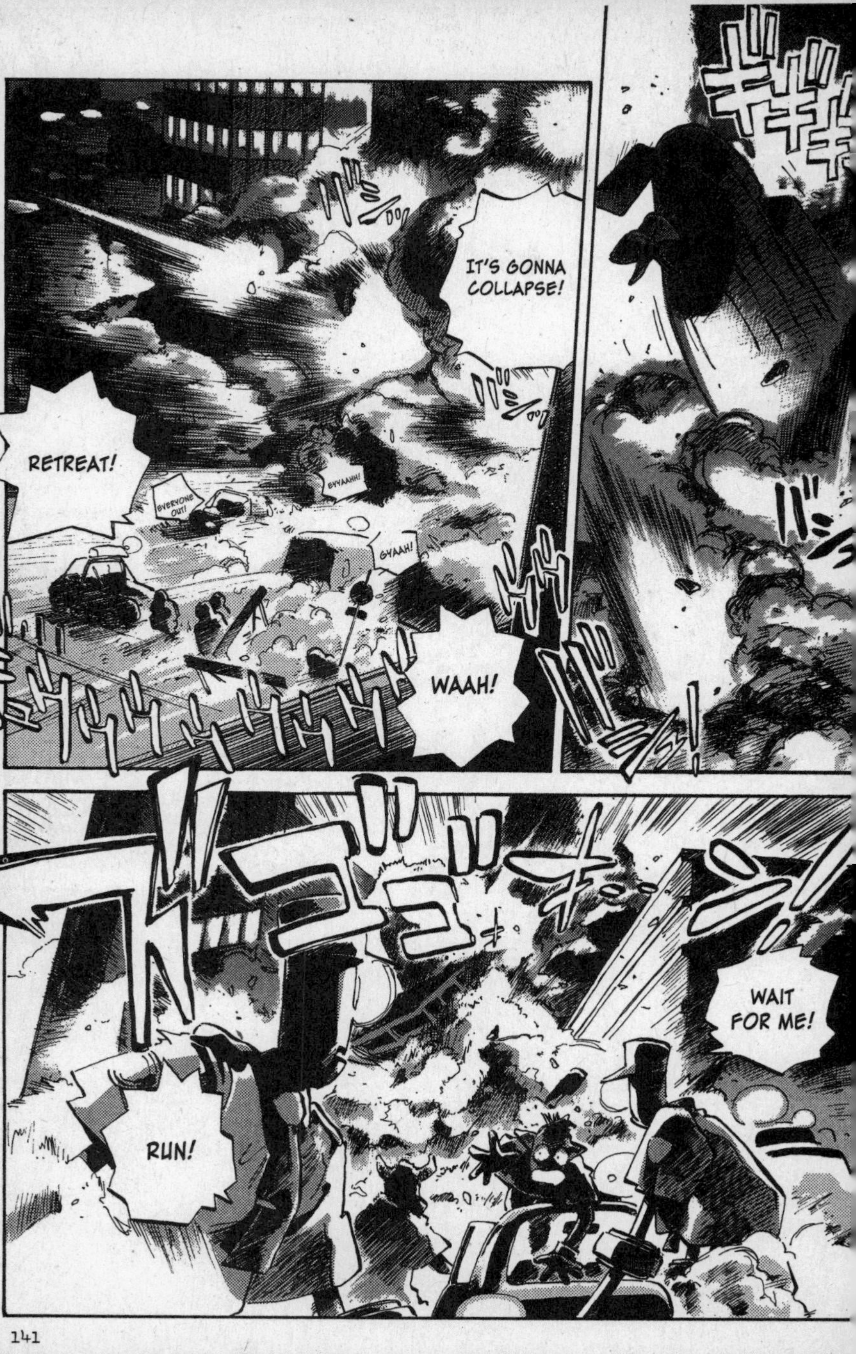
IT'S GONNA COLLAPSE!
GYYAAHH!
RETREAT!
EVERYONE OUT!
GYAAH!
WAAH!
WAIT FOR ME!
RUN!

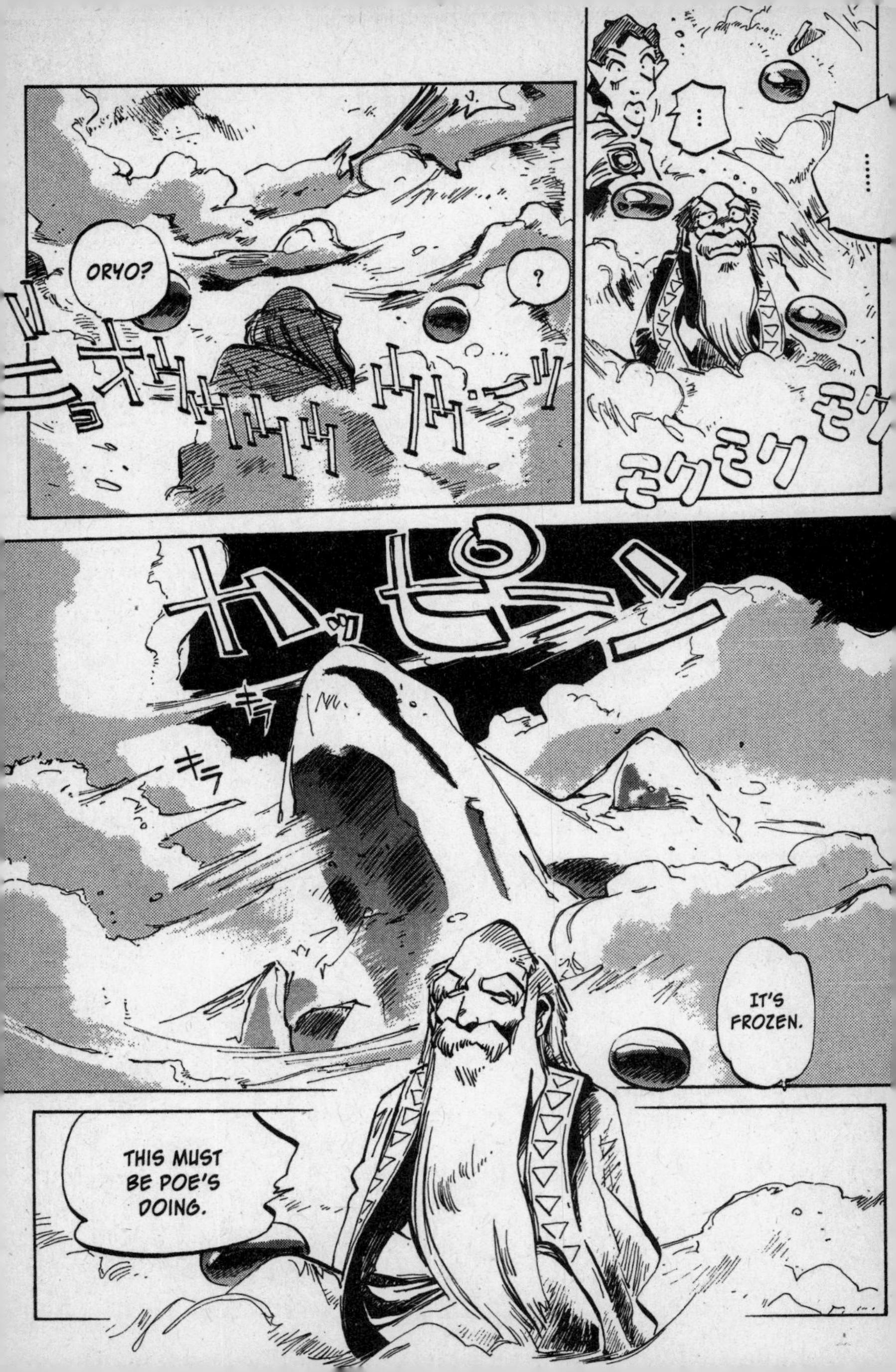
…
…
モクモク
モクモク
ORYO?
?
カッピーン
キラ
キラ
IT'S FROZEN.
THIS MUST BE POE'S DOING.

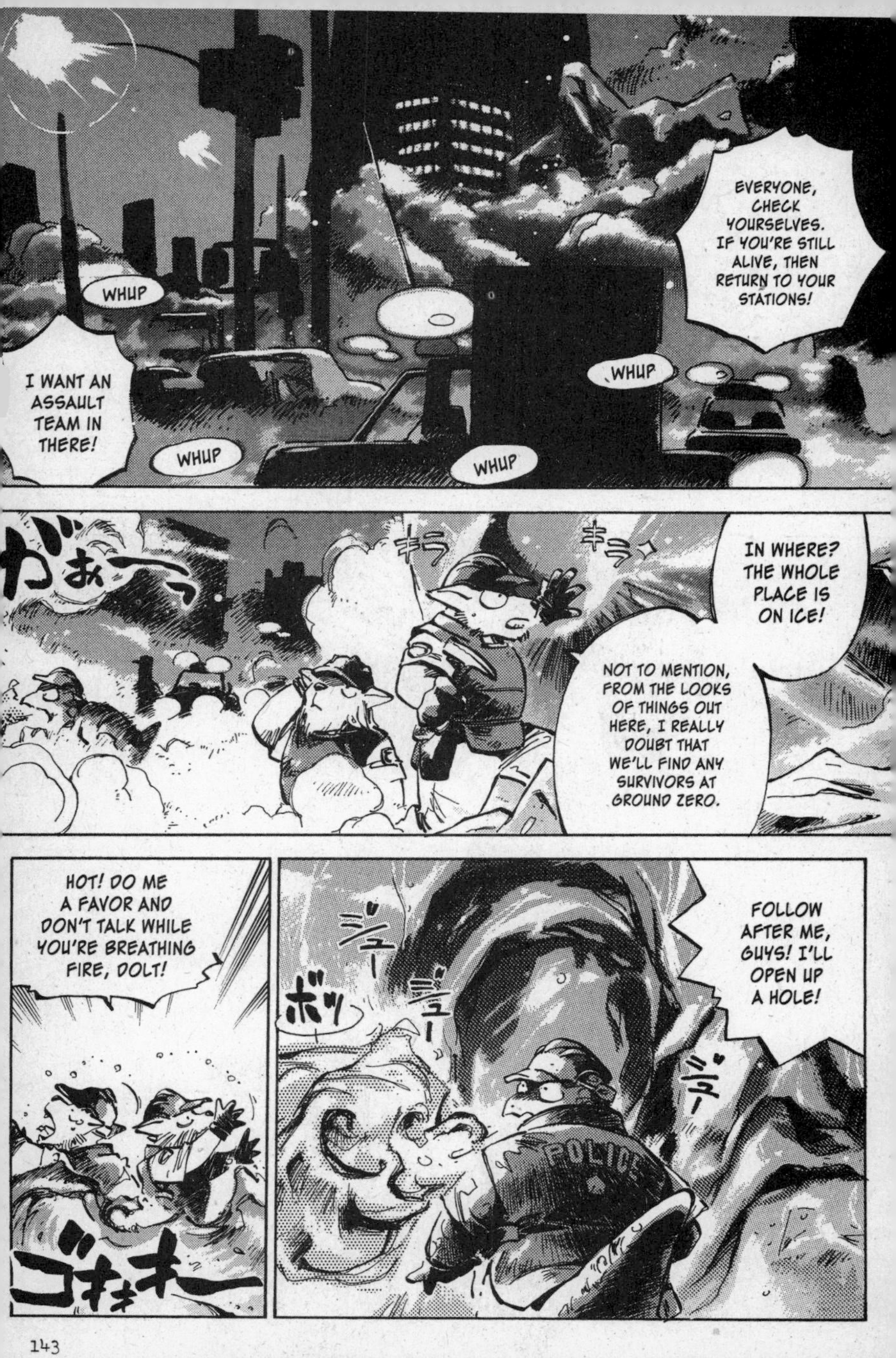
EVERYONE, CHECK YOURSELVES. IF YOU'RE STILL ALIVE, THEN RETURN TO YOUR STATIONS!
WHUP
WHUP
I WANT AN ASSAULT TEAM IN THERE!
WHUP
WHUP
キラ
キラ
IN WHERE? THE WHOLE PLACE IS ON ICE!
NOT TO MENTION, FROM THE LOOKS OF THINGS OUT HERE, I REALLY DOUBT THAT WE'LL FIND ANY SURVIVORS AT GROUND ZERO.
FOLLOW AFTER ME, GUYS! I'LL OPEN UP A HOLE!
ジュー
ジュー
ボッ
POLICE
HOT! DO ME A FAVOR AND DON'T TALK WHILE YOU'RE BREATHING FIRE, DOLT!

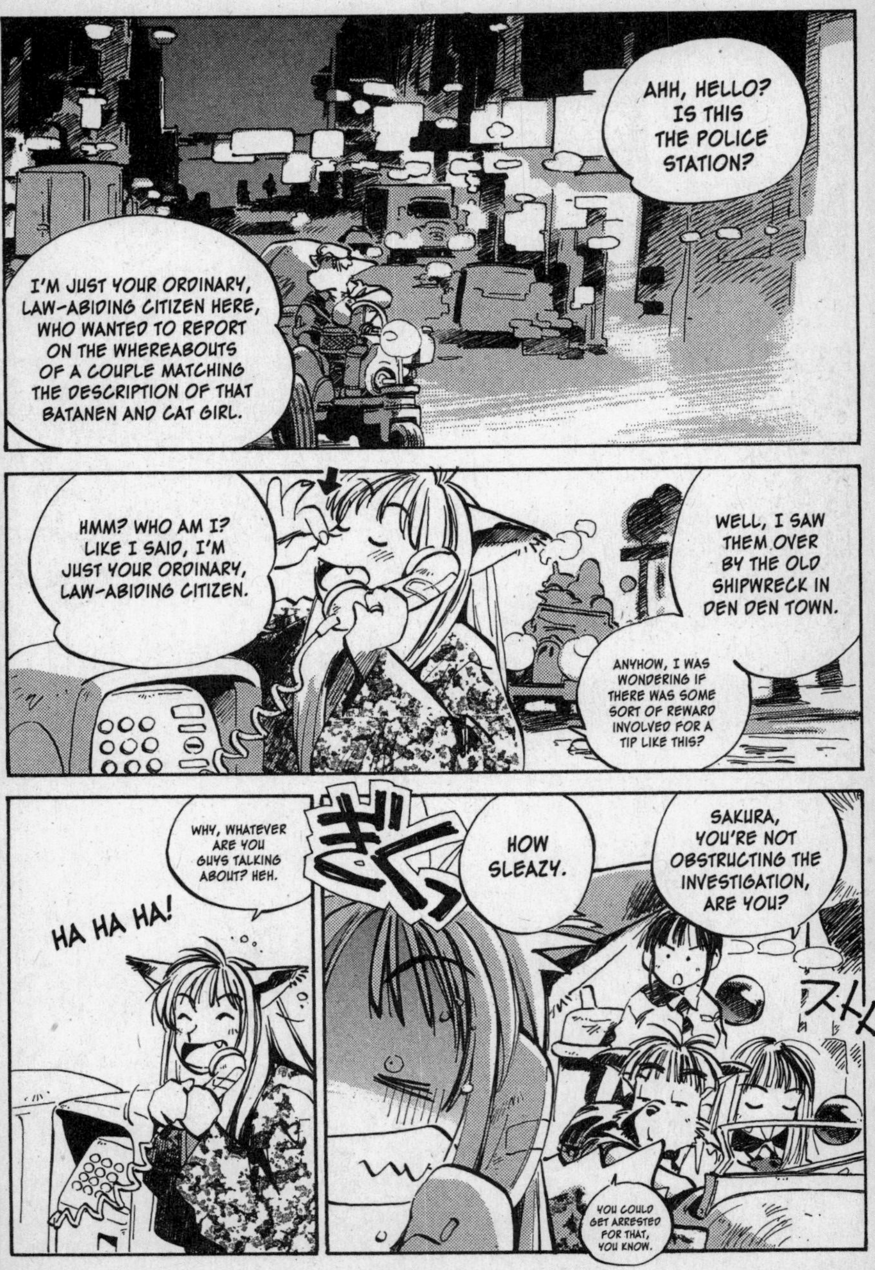

AHH, HELLO? IS THIS THE POLICE STATION?
I'M JUST YOUR ORDINARY, LAW-ABIDING CITIZEN HERE, WHO WANTED TO REPORT ON THE WHEREABOUTS OF A COUPLE MATCHING THE DESCRIPTION OF THAT BATANEN AND CAT GIRL.
WELL, I SAW THEM OVER BY THE OLD SHIPWRECK IN DEN DEN TOWN.
HMM? WHO AM I? LIKE I SAID, I'M JUST YOUR ORDINARY, LAW-ABIDING CITIZEN.
ANYHOW, I WAS WONDERING IF THERE WAS SOME SORT OF REWARD INVOLVED FOR A TIP LIKE THIS?
SAKURA, YOU'RE NOT OBSTRUCTING THE INVESTIGATION, ARE YOU?
HOW SLEAZY.
ぎくっ
YOU COULD GET ARRESTED FOR THAT, YOU KNOW.
WHY, WHATEVER ARE YOU GUYS TALKING ABOUT? HEH.
HA HA HA!

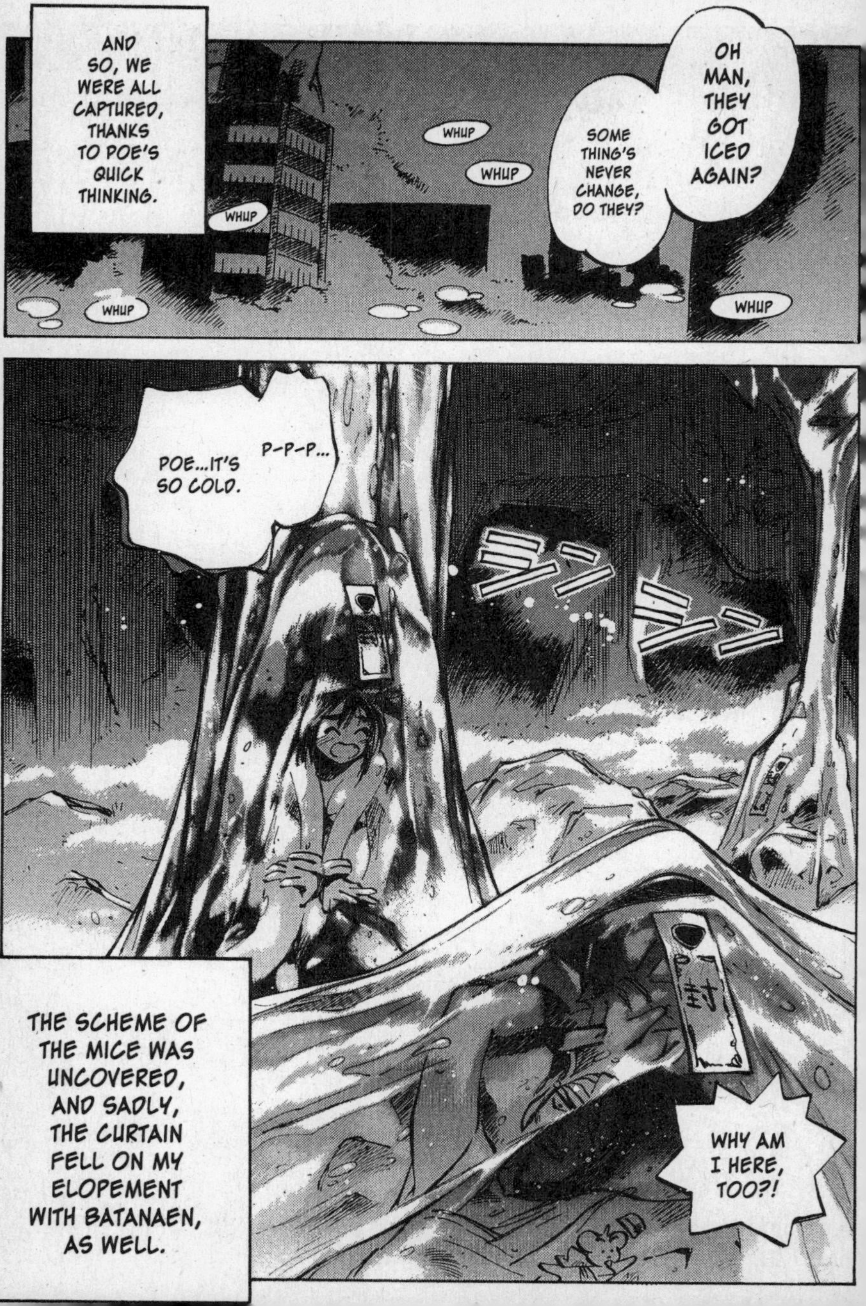
OH MAN, THEY GOT ICED AGAIN?
SOME THING'S NEVER CHANGE, DO THEY?
WHUP
WHUP
WHUP
WHUP
WHUP
AND SO, WE WERE ALL CAPTURED, THANKS TO POE'S QUICK THINKING.
P-P-P...
POE...IT'S SO COLD.
WHY AM I HERE, TOO?!
THE SCHEME OF THE MICE WAS UNCOVERED, AND SADLY, THE CURTAIN FELL ON MY ELOPEMENT WITH BATANAEN, AS WELL.

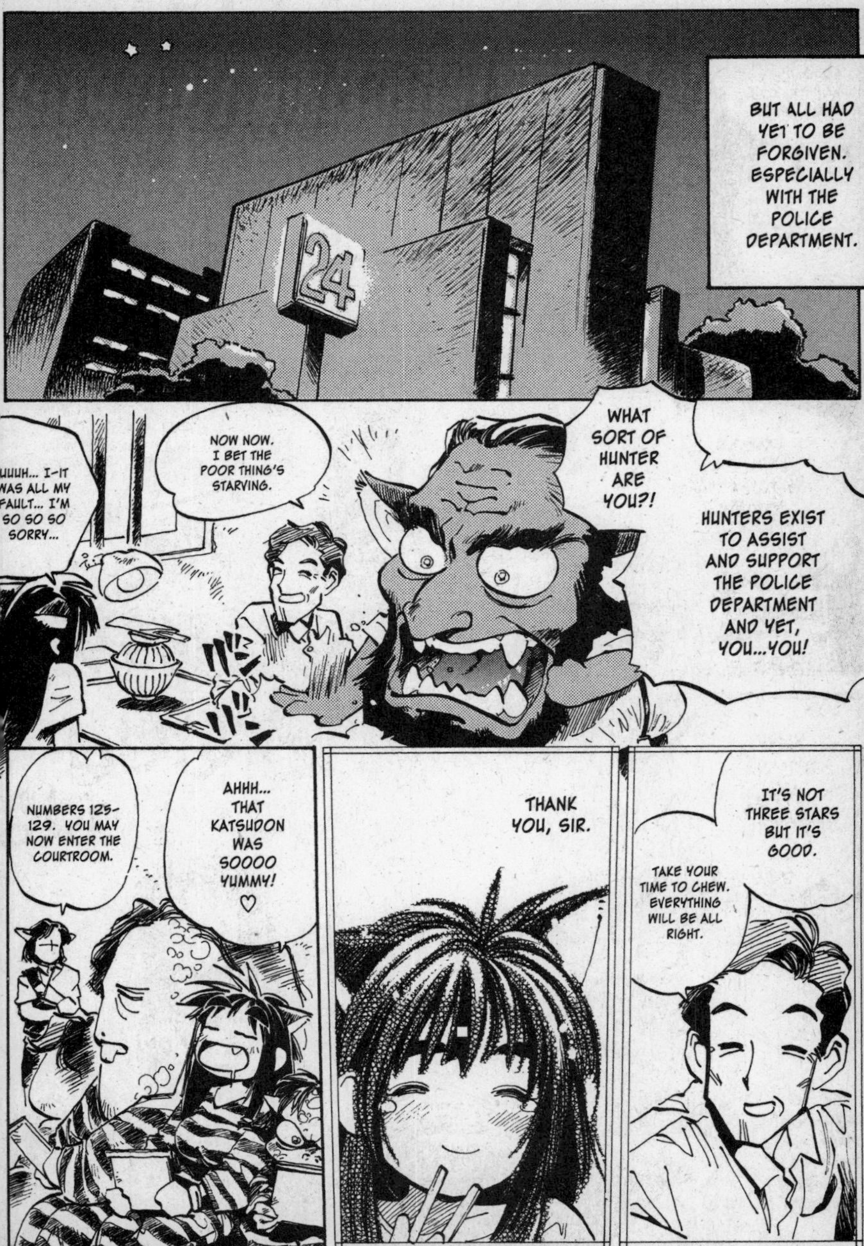
BUT ALL HAD YET TO BE FORGIVEN. ESPECIALLY WITH THE POLICE DEPARTMENT.
WHAT SORT OF HUNTER ARE YOU?!
HUNTERS EXIST TO ASSIST AND SUPPORT THE POLICE DEPARTMENT AND YET, YOU...YOU!
NOW NOW. I BET THE POOR THING'S STARVING.
UUUH... I-IT WAS ALL MY FAULT... I'M SO SO SO SORRY...
IT'S NOT THREE STARS BUT IT'S GOOD.
TAKE YOUR TIME TO CHEW. EVERYTHING WILL BE ALL RIGHT.
THANK YOU, SIR.
AHHH... THAT KATSUDON WAS SOOOO YUMMY! ♡
NUMBERS 125-129. YOU MAY NOW ENTER THE COURTROOM.

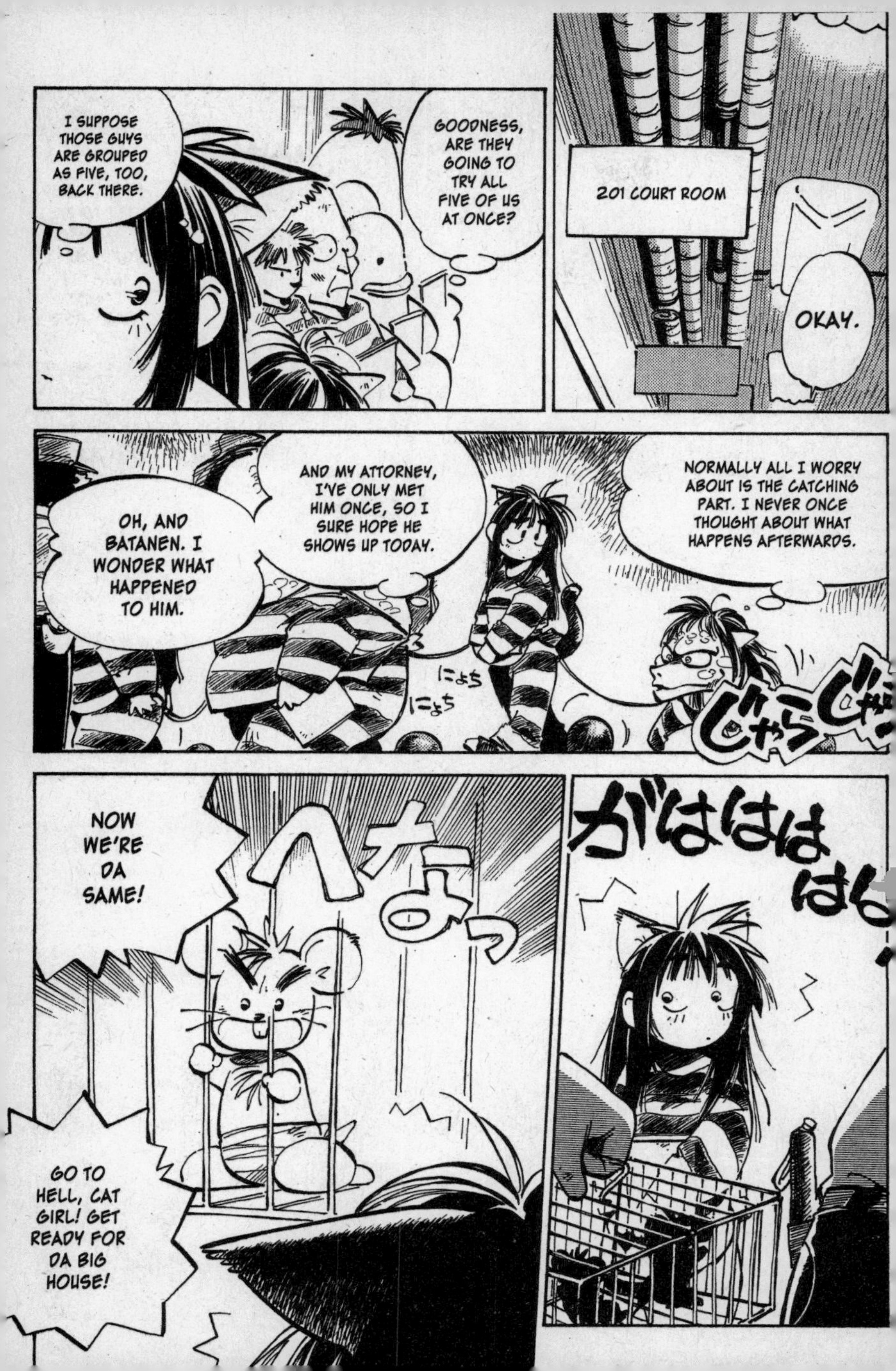

201 COURT ROOM
OKAY.
GOODNESS, ARE THEY GOING TO TRY ALL FIVE OF US AT ONCE?
I SUPPOSE THOSE GUYS ARE GROUPED AS FIVE, TOO, BACK THERE.
NORMALLY ALL I WORRY ABOUT IS THE CATCHING PART. I NEVER ONCE THOUGHT ABOUT WHAT HAPPENS AFTERWARDS.
じゃら
にょち
にょち
AND MY ATTORNEY, I'VE ONLY MET HIM ONCE, SO I SURE HOPE HE SHOWS UP TODAY.
OH, AND BATANEN. I WONDER WHAT HAPPENED TO HIM.
がははは
へよっ
NOW WE'RE DA SAME!
GO TO HELL, CAT GIRL! GET READY FOR DA BIG HOUSE!

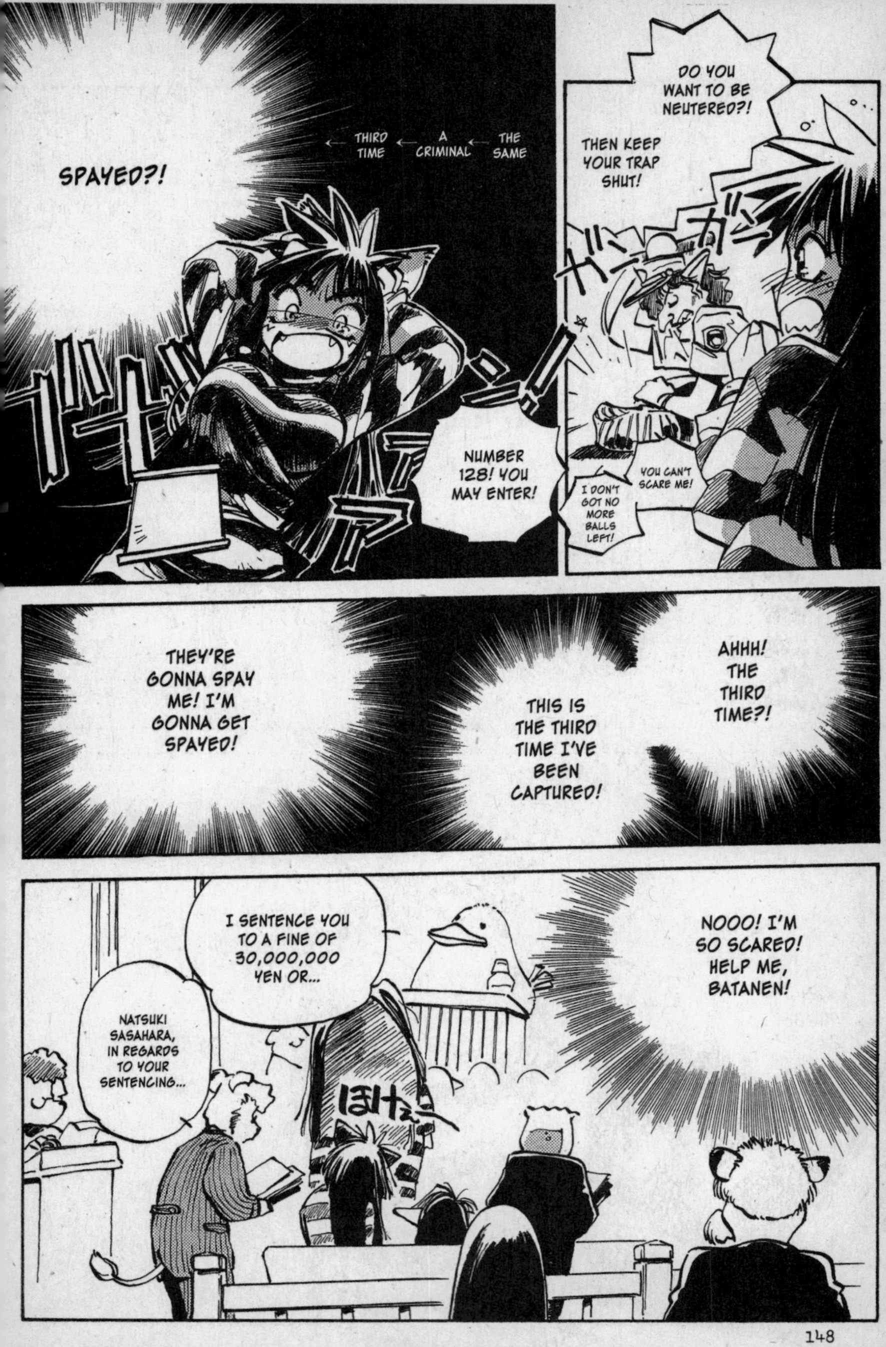
DO YOU WANT TO BE NEUTERED?!
THEN KEEP YOUR TRAP SHUT!
YOU CAN'T SCARE ME!
I DON'T GOT NO MORE BALLS LEFT!
THE SAME ← A CRIMINAL ← THIRD TIME
SPAYED?!
NUMBER 128! YOU MAY ENTER!
AHHH! THE THIRD TIME?!
THIS IS THE THIRD TIME I'VE BEEN CAPTURED!
THEY'RE GONNA SPAY ME! I'M GONNA GET SPAYED!
NOOO! I'M SO SCARED! HELP ME, BATANEN!
I SENTENCE YOU TO A FINE OF 30,000,000 YEN OR...
NATSUKI SASAHARA, IN REGARDS TO YOUR SENTENCING...

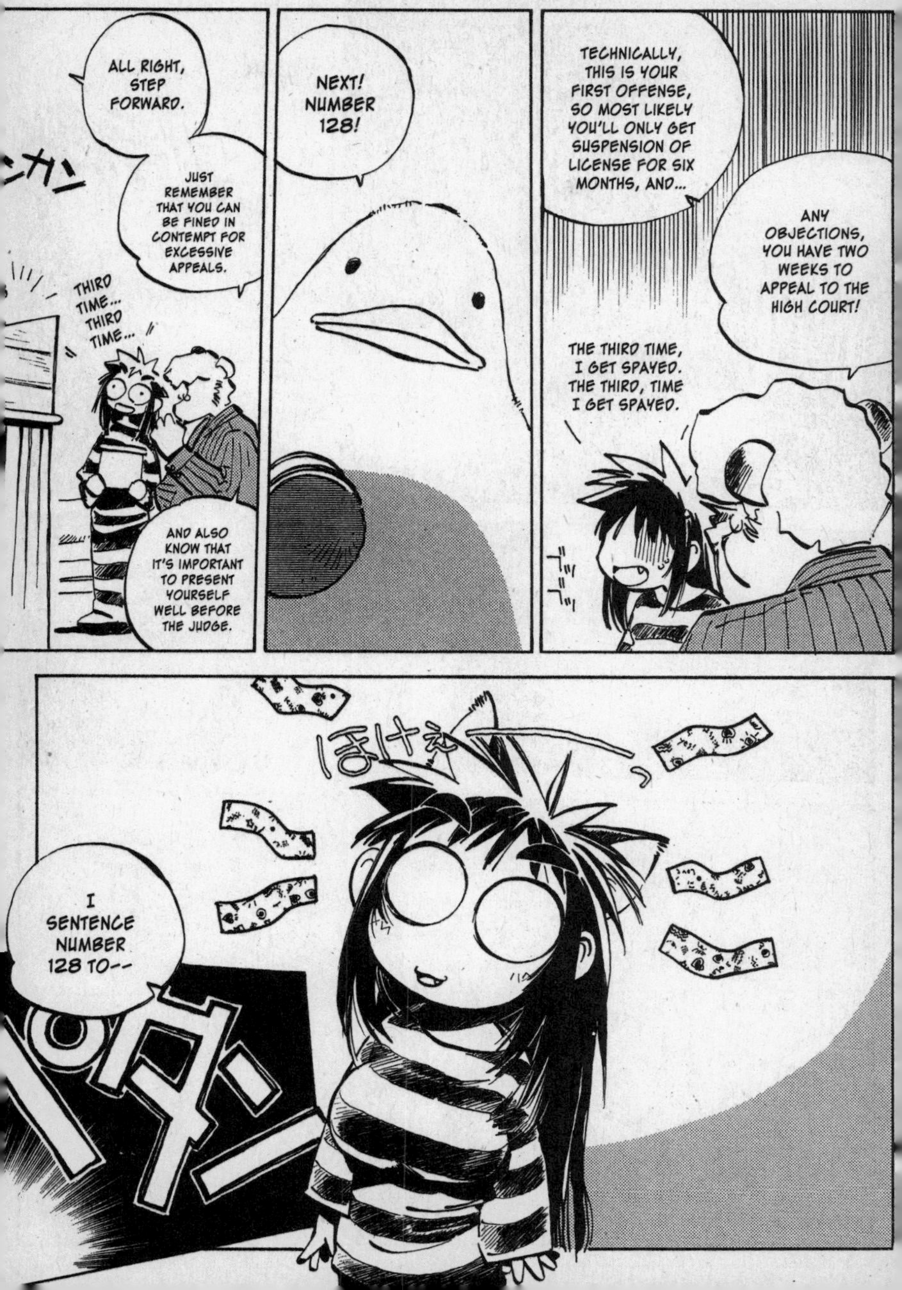

TECHNICALLY, THIS IS YOUR FIRST OFFENSE, SO MOST LIKELY YOU'LL ONLY GET SUSPENSION OF LICENSE FOR SIX MONTHS, AND...
ANY OBJECTIONS, YOU HAVE TWO WEEKS TO APPEAL TO THE HIGH COURT!
THE THIRD TIME, I GET SPAYED. THE THIRD, TIME I GET SPAYED.
NEXT! NUMBER 128!
ALL RIGHT, STEP FORWARD.
JUST REMEMBER THAT YOU CAN BE FINED IN CONTEMPT FOR EXCESSIVE APPEALS.
THIRD TIME... THIRD TIME...
AND ALSO KNOW THAT IT'S IMPORTANT TO PRESENT YOURSELF WELL BEFORE THE JUDGE.
I SENTENCE NUMBER 128 TO--

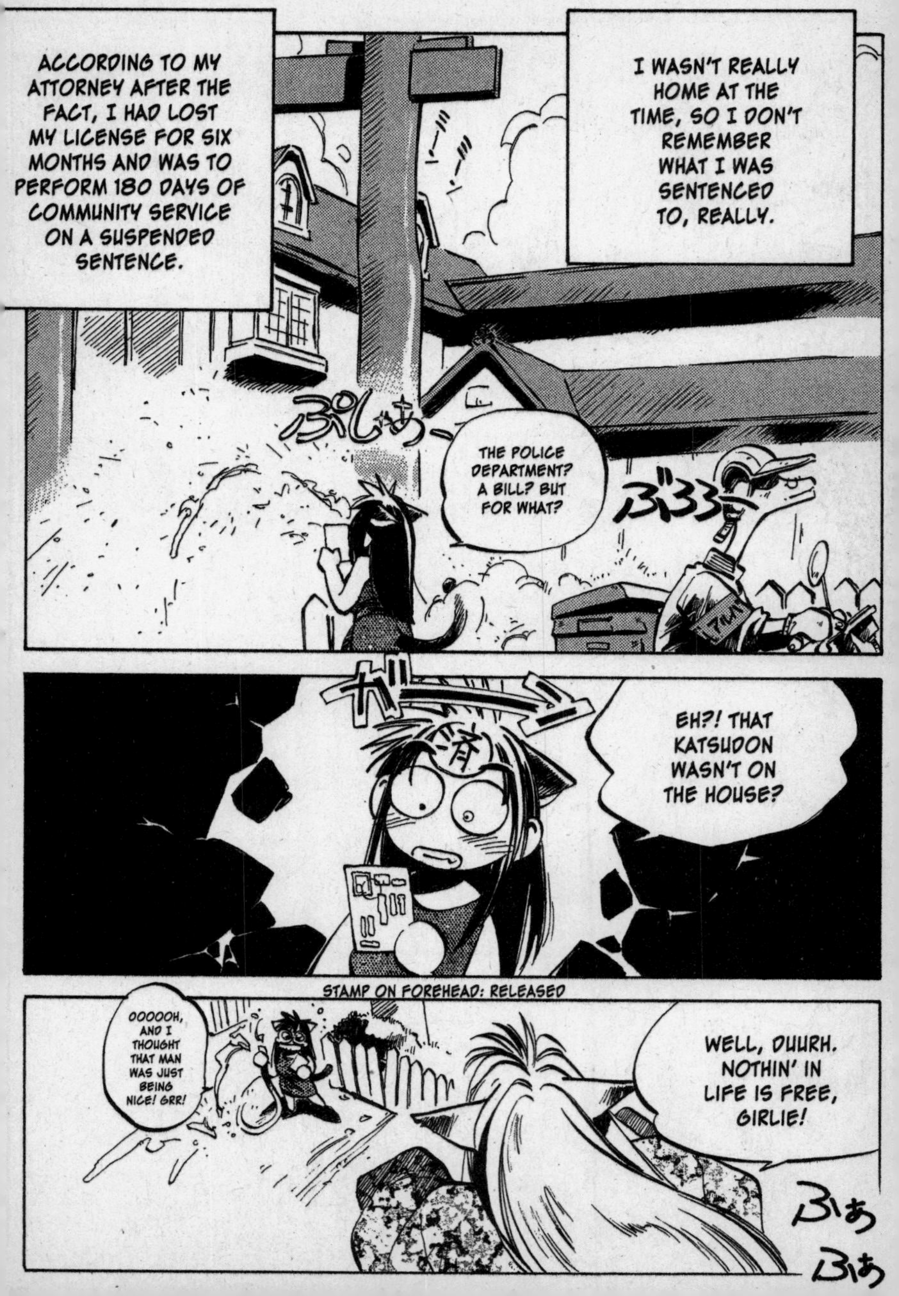
I WASN'T REALLY HOME AT THE TIME, SO I DON'T REMEMBER WHAT I WAS SENTENCED TO, REALLY.
ACCORDING TO MY ATTORNEY AFTER THE FACT, I HAD LOST MY LICENSE FOR SIX MONTHS AND WAS TO PERFORM 180 DAYS OF COMMUNITY SERVICE ON A SUSPENDED SENTENCE.
THE POLICE DEPARTMENT? A BILL? BUT FOR WHAT?
EH?! THAT KATSUDON WASN'T ON THE HOUSE?
STAMP ON FOREHEAD: RELEASED
WELL, DUURH. NOTHIN' IN LIFE IS FREE, GIRLIE!
OOOOOH, AND I THOUGHT THAT MAN WAS JUST BEING NICE! GRR!
ふあ
ふあ

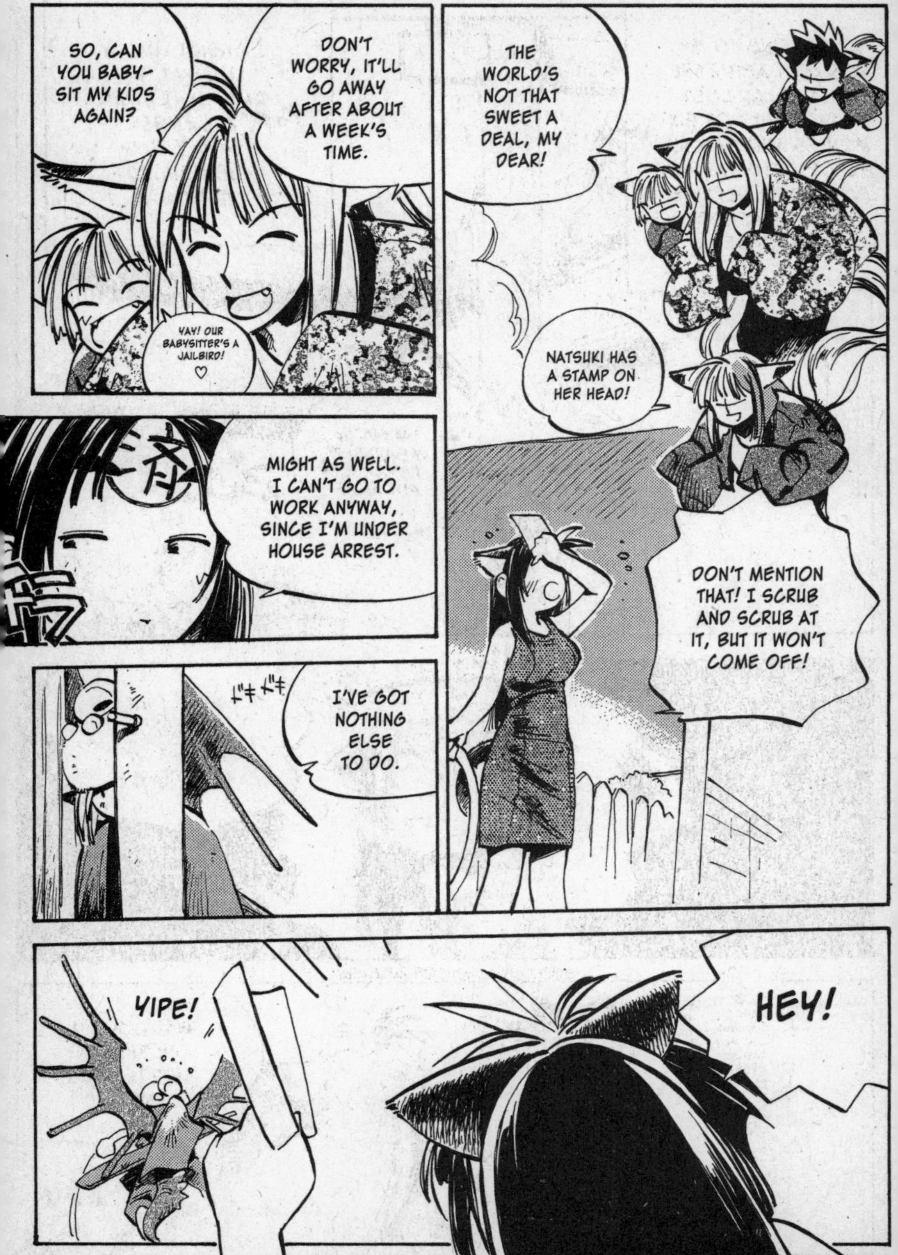
THE WORLD'S NOT THAT SWEET A DEAL, MY DEAR!
NATSUKI HAS A STAMP ON HER HEAD!
DON'T MENTION THAT! I SCRUB AND SCRUB AT IT, BUT IT WON'T COME OFF!
DON'T WORRY, IT'LL GO AWAY AFTER ABOUT A WEEK'S TIME.
SO, CAN YOU BABY-SIT MY KIDS AGAIN?
YAY! OUR BABYSITTER'S A JAILBIRD! ♡
MIGHT AS WELL. I CAN'T GO TO WORK ANYWAY, SINCE I'M UNDER HOUSE ARREST.
I'VE GOT NOTHING ELSE TO DO.
HEY!
YIPE!

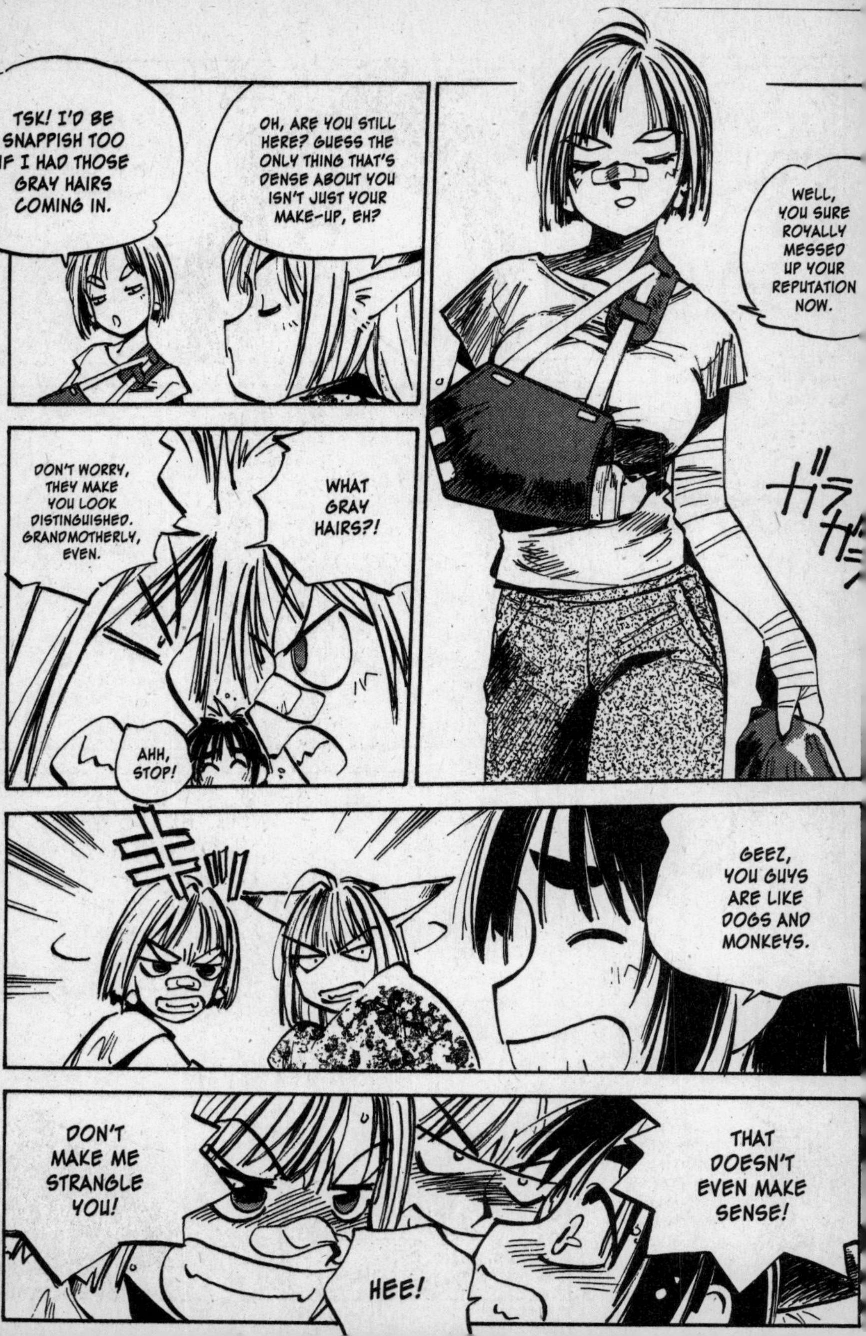
WELL, YOU SURE ROYALLY MESSED UP YOUR REPUTATION NOW.
OH, ARE YOU STILL HERE? GUESS THE ONLY THING THAT'S DENSE ABOUT YOU ISN'T JUST YOUR MAKE-UP, EH?
TSK! I'D BE SNAPPISH TOO IF I HAD THOSE GRAY HAIRS COMING IN.
WHAT GRAY HAIRS?!
DON'T WORRY, THEY MAKE YOU LOOK DISTINGUISHED. GRANDMOTHERLY, EVEN.
AHH, STOP!
GEEZ, YOU GUYS ARE LIKE DOGS AND MONKEYS.
THAT DOESN'T EVEN MAKE SENSE!
DON'T MAKE ME STRANGLE YOU!
HEE!

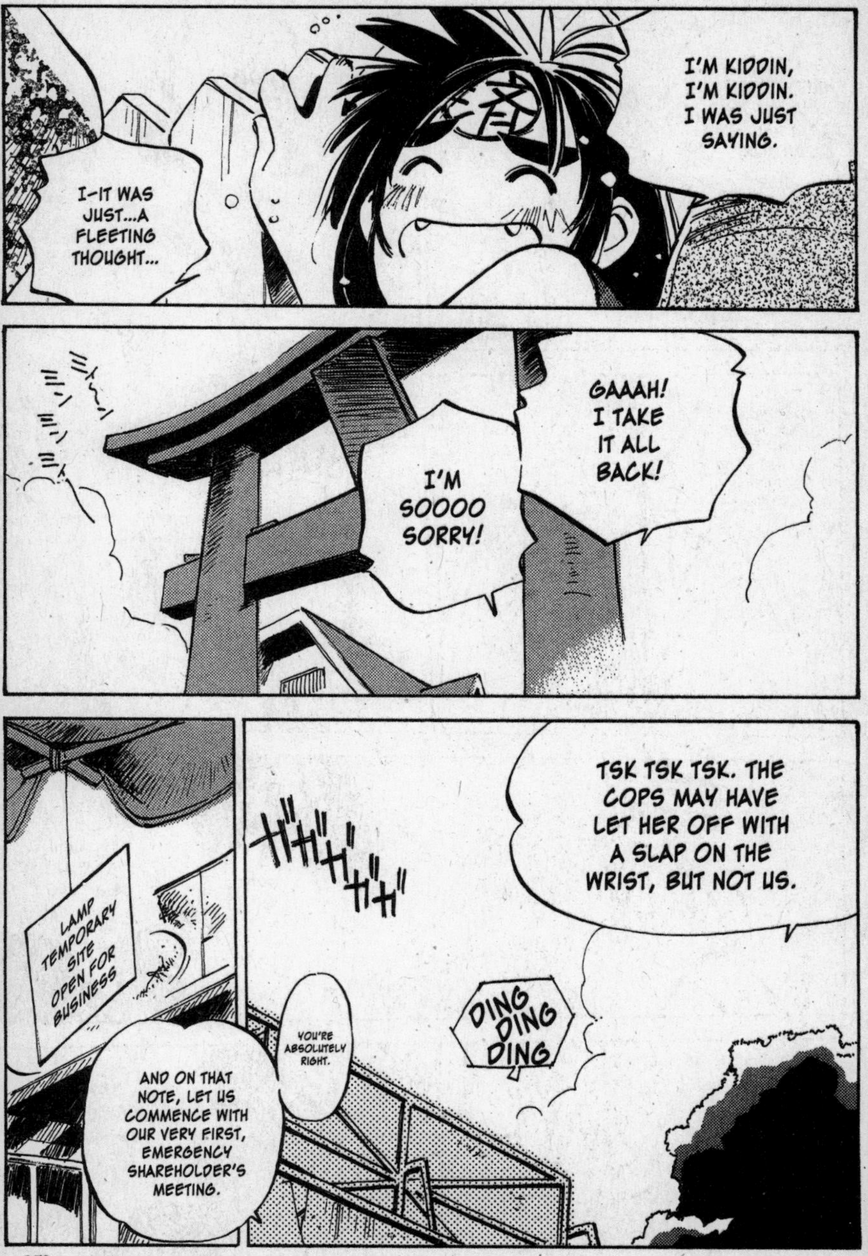
I'M KIDDIN, I'M KIDDIN. I WAS JUST SAYING.
I-IT WAS JUST...A FLEETING THOUGHT...
GAAAH! I TAKE IT ALL BACK!
I'M SOOOO SORRY!
TSK TSK TSK. THE COPS MAY HAVE LET HER OFF WITH A SLAP ON THE WRIST, BUT NOT US.
DING DING DING
LAMP TEMPORARY SITE OPEN FOR BUSINESS
YOU'RE ABSOLUTELY RIGHT.
AND ON THAT NOTE, LET US COMMENCE WITH OUR VERY FIRST, EMERGENCY SHAREHOLDER'S MEETING.

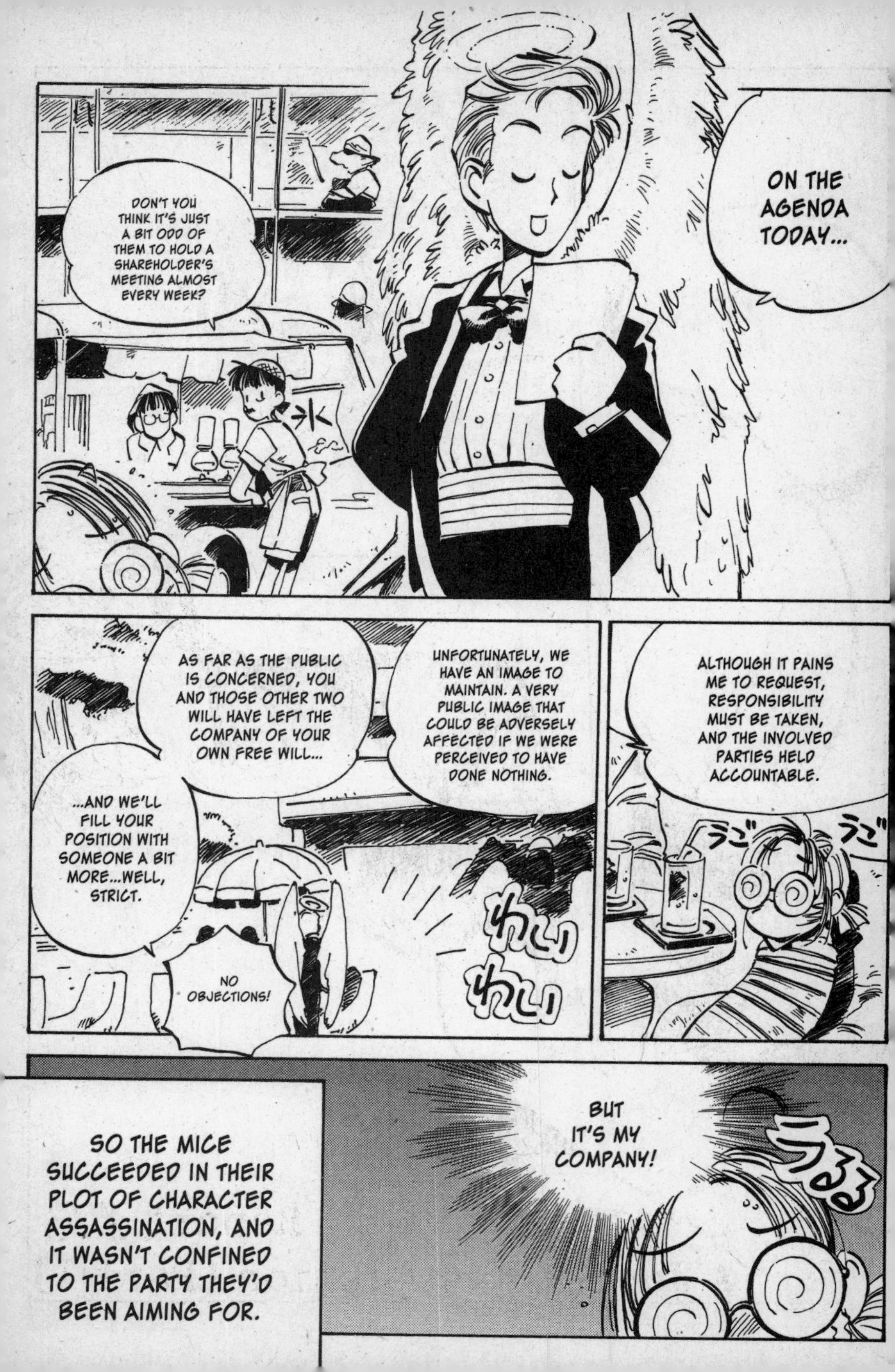

ON THE AGENDA TODAY...
DON'T YOU THINK IT'S JUST A BIT ODD OF THEM TO HOLD A SHAREHOLDER'S MEETING ALMOST EVERY WEEK?
ALTHOUGH IT PAINS ME TO REQUEST, RESPONSIBILITY MUST BE TAKEN, AND THE INVOLVED PARTIES HELD ACCOUNTABLE.
UNFORTUNATELY, WE HAVE AN IMAGE TO MAINTAIN. A VERY PUBLIC IMAGE THAT COULD BE ADVERSELY AFFECTED IF WE WERE PERCEIVED TO HAVE DONE NOTHING.
AS FAR AS THE PUBLIC IS CONCERNED, YOU AND THOSE OTHER TWO WILL HAVE LEFT THE COMPANY OF YOUR OWN FREE WILL...
...AND WE'LL FILL YOUR POSITION WITH SOMEONE A BIT MORE...WELL, STRICT.
わいわい
NO OBJECTIONS!
うるる
BUT IT'S MY COMPANY!
SO THE MICE SUCCEEDED IN THEIR PLOT OF CHARACTER ASSASSINATION, AND IT WASN'T CONFINED TO THE PARTY THEY'D BEEN AIMING FOR.

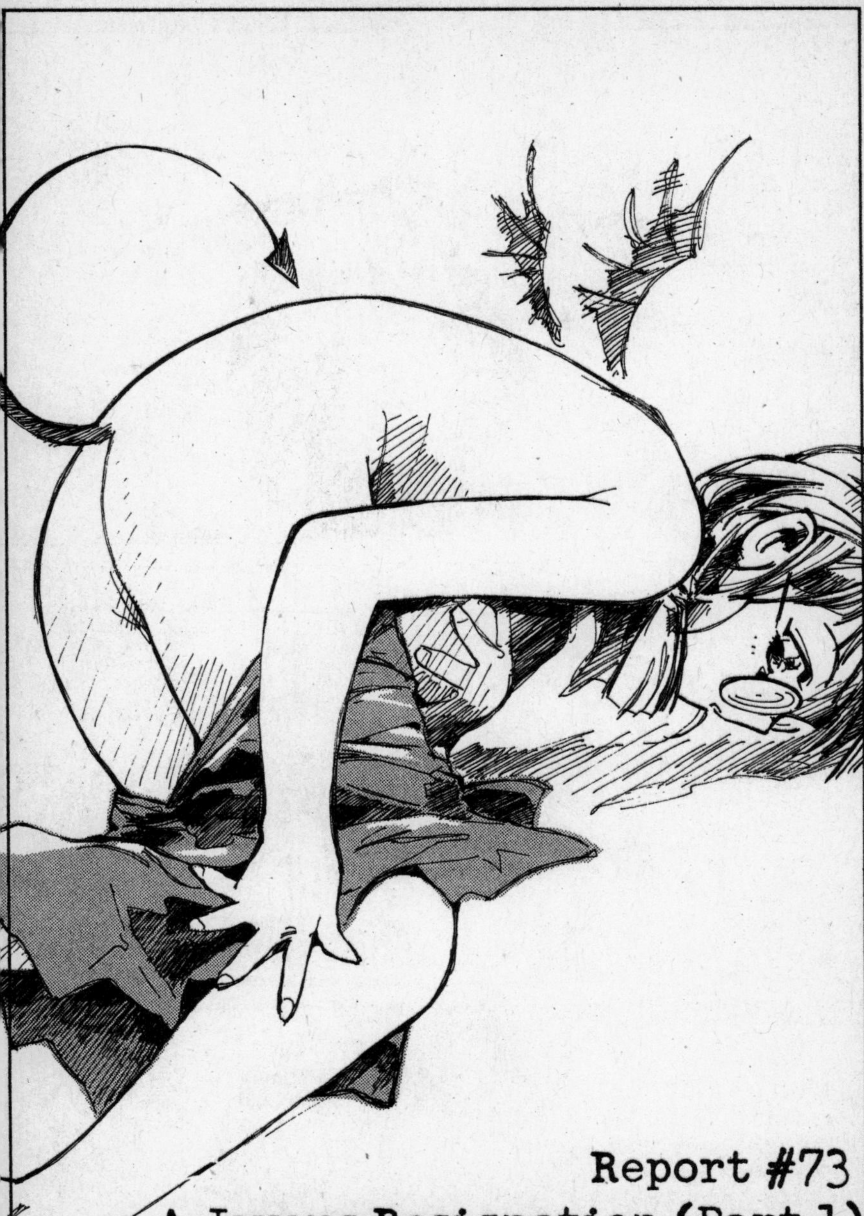
Report #73
A Joyous Resignation (Part 1)

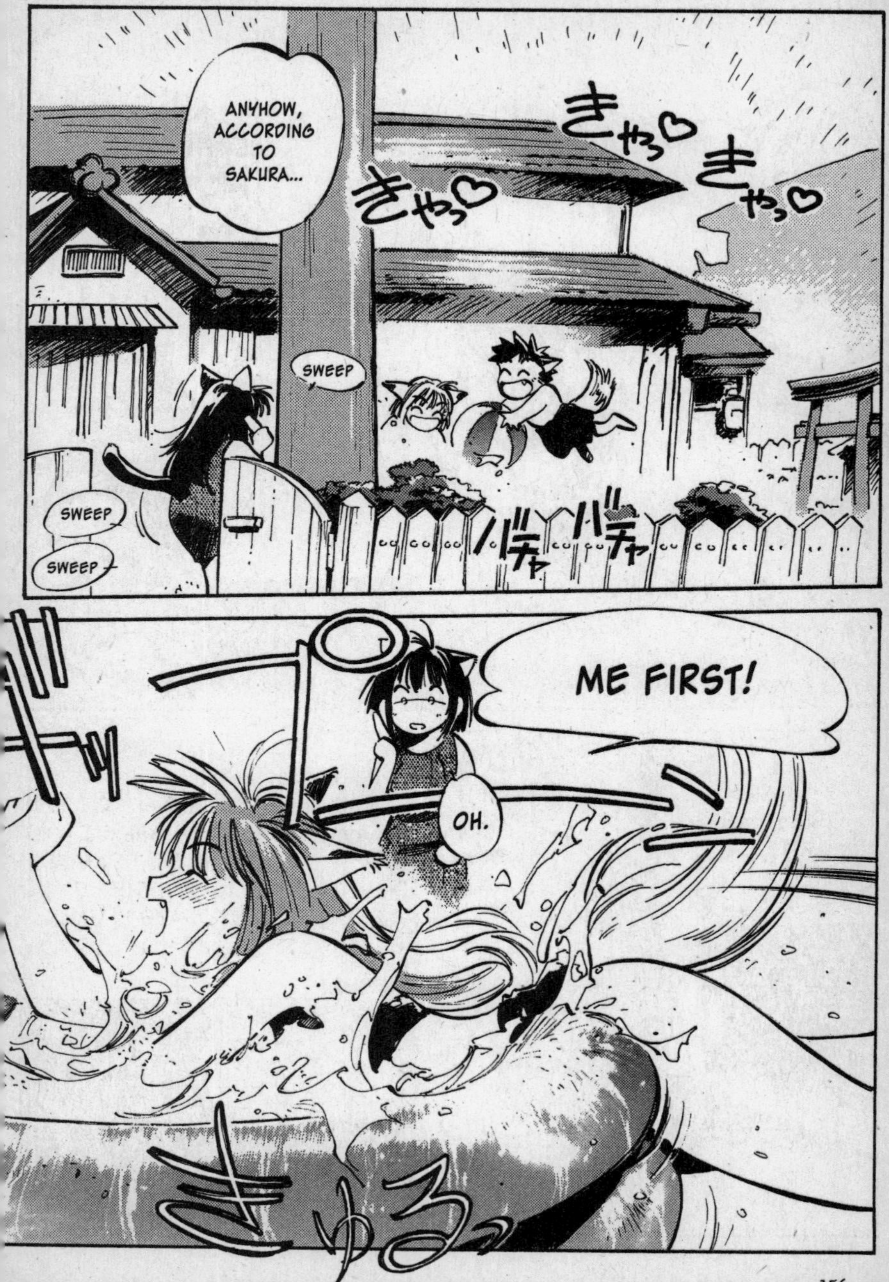
きゃっ♡
きゃっ♡
ANYHOW, ACCORDING TO SAKURA...
きゃっ♡
SWEEP
バチャ
バチャ
SWEEP
SWEEP
ME FIRST!
OH.
きゅるっ

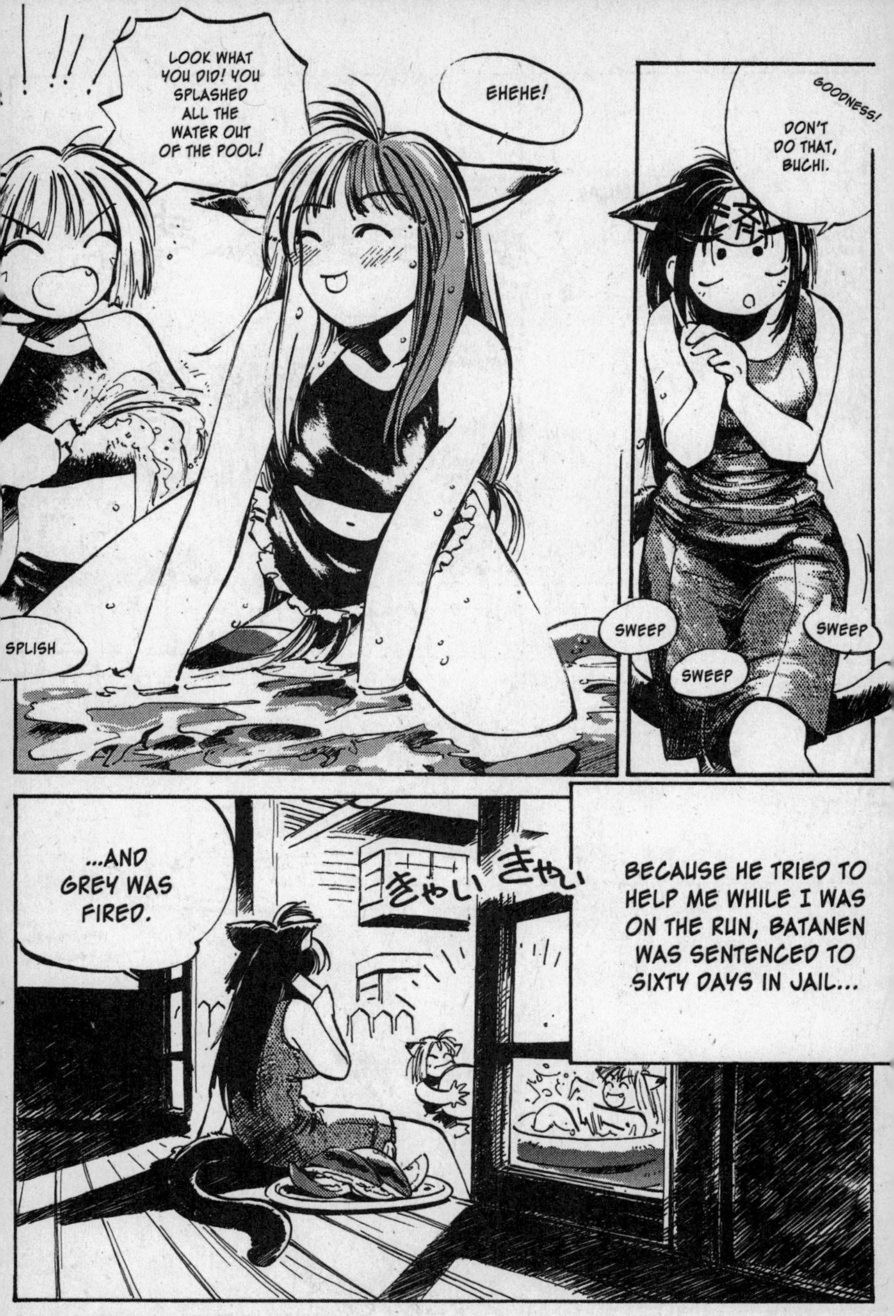
GOODNESS!
DON'T DO THAT, BUCHI.
SWEEP
SWEEP
SWEEP
!!!
LOOK WHAT YOU DID! YOU SPLASHED ALL THE WATER OUT OF THE POOL!
EHEHE!
SPLISH
BECAUSE HE TRIED TO HELP ME WHILE I WAS ON THE RUN, BATANEN WAS SENTENCED TO SIXTY DAYS IN JAIL...
きゃい きゃい
...AND GREY WAS FIRED.

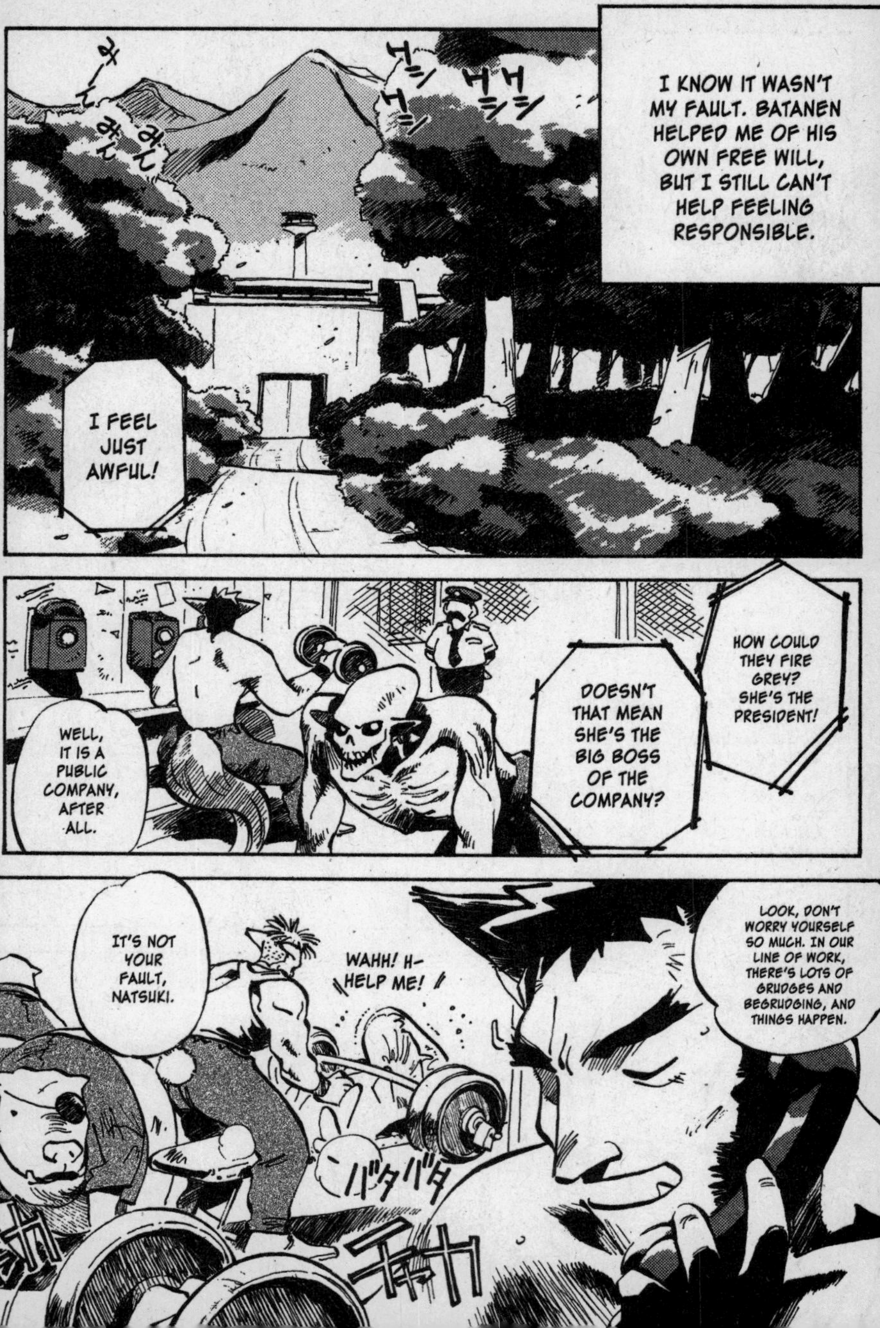
I KNOW IT WASN'T MY FAULT. BATANEN HELPED ME OF HIS OWN FREE WILL, BUT I STILL CAN'T HELP FEELING RESPONSIBLE.
みーん
みんみん
I FEEL JUST AWFUL!
HOW COULD THEY FIRE GREY? SHE'S THE PRESIDENT!
DOESN'T THAT MEAN SHE'S THE BIG BOSS OF THE COMPANY?
WELL, IT IS A PUBLIC COMPANY, AFTER ALL.
LOOK, DON'T WORRY YOURSELF SO MUCH. IN OUR LINE OF WORK, THERE'S LOTS OF GRUDGES AND BEGRUDGING, AND THINGS HAPPEN.
WAHH! H-HELP ME!
バタバタ
IT'S NOT YOUR FAULT, NATSUKI.

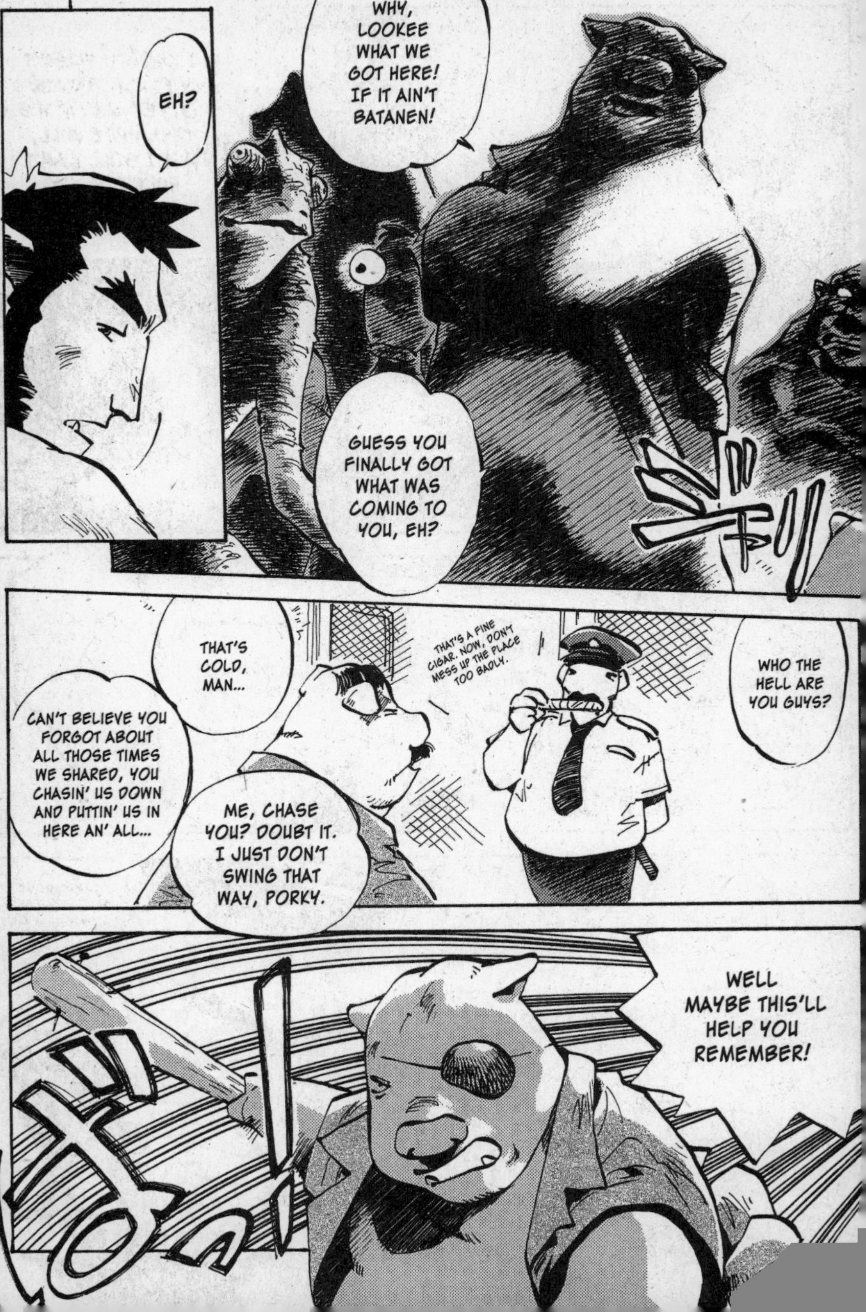
WHY, LOOKEE WHAT WE GOT HERE! IF IT AIN'T BATANEN!
GUESS YOU FINALLY GOT WHAT WAS COMING TO YOU, EH?
EH?
WHO THE HELL ARE YOU GUYS?
THAT'S A FINE CIGAR. NOW, DON'T MESS UP THE PLACE TOO BADLY.
THAT'S COLD, MAN...
CAN'T BELIEVE YOU FORGOT ABOUT ALL THOSE TIMES WE SHARED, YOU CHASIN' US DOWN AND PUTTIN' US IN HERE AN' ALL...
ME, CHASE YOU? DOUBT IT. I JUST DON'T SWING THAT WAY, PORKY.
WELL MAYBE THIS'LL HELP YOU REMEMBER!

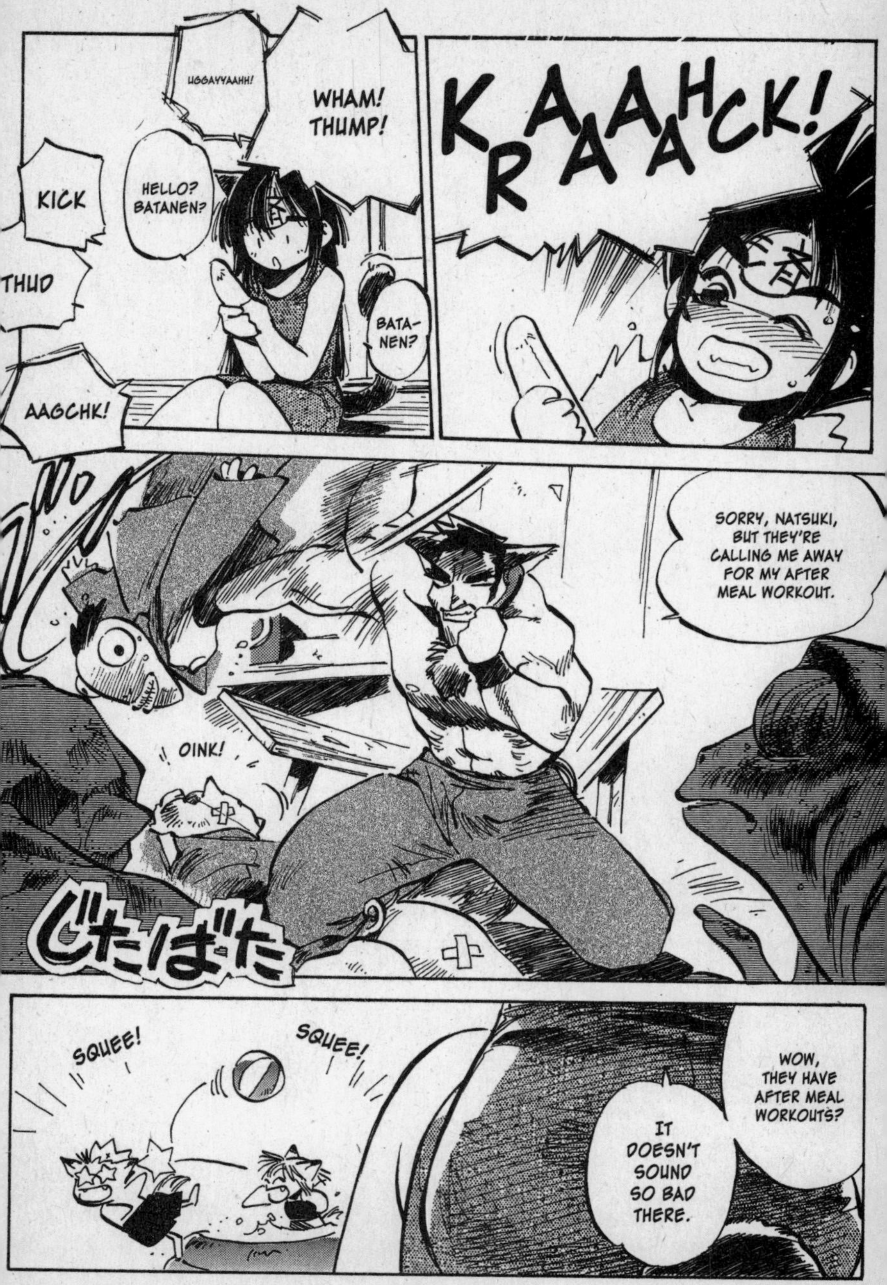

KRAAAAHCK!
UGGAYYAAHH!
WHAM! THUMP!
HELLO? BATANEN?
BATA-NEN?
KICK
THUD
AAGCHK!
SORRY, NATSUKI, BUT THEY'RE CALLING ME AWAY FOR MY AFTER MEAL WORKOUT.
OINK!
じたばた
WOW, THEY HAVE AFTER MEAL WORKOUTS?
IT DOESN'T SOUND SO BAD THERE.
SQUEE!
SQUEE!

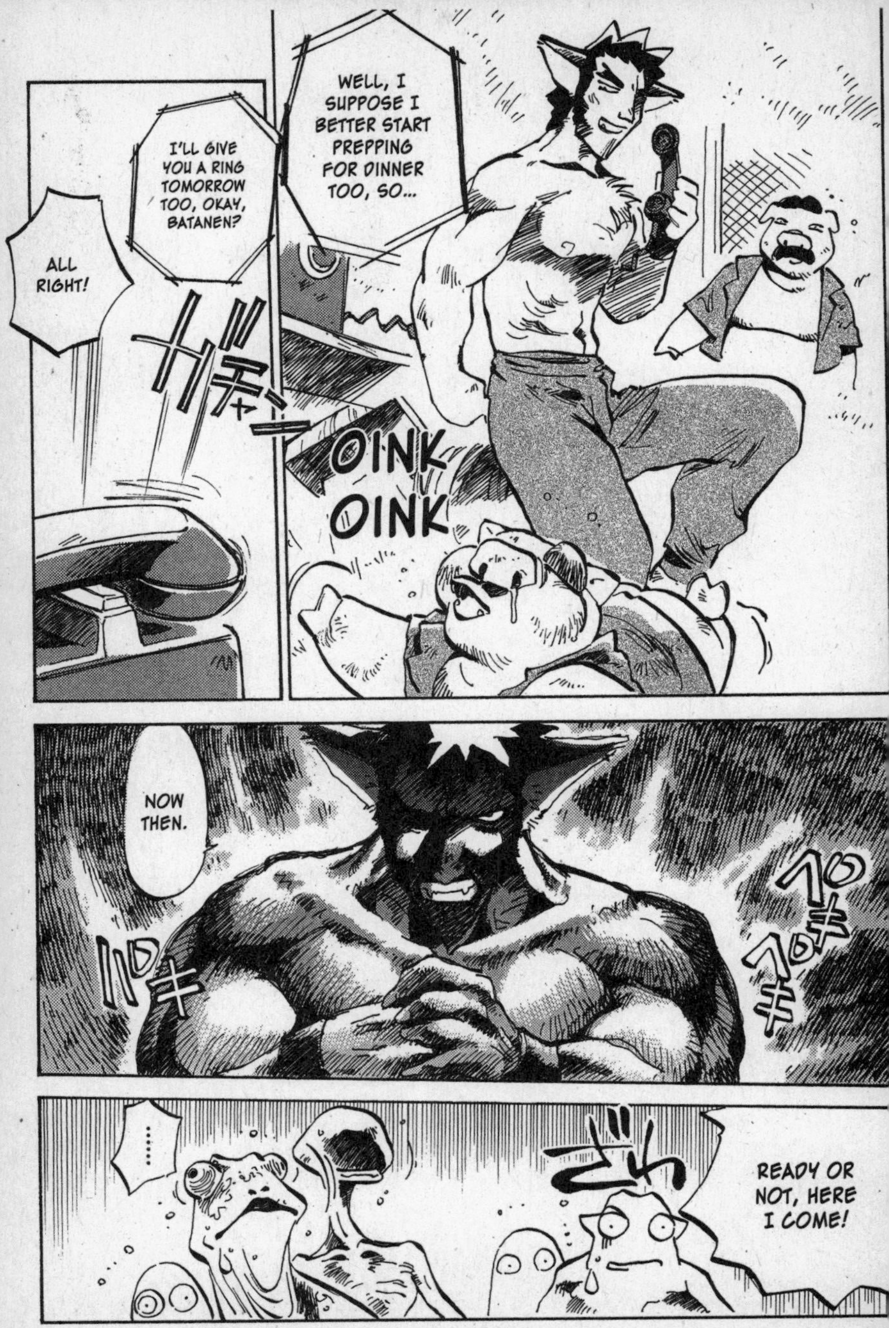
WELL, I SUPPOSE I BETTER START PREPPING FOR DINNER TOO, SO...
OINK OINK
I'LL GIVE YOU A RING TOMORROW TOO, OKAY, BATANEN?
ALL RIGHT!
NOW THEN.
READY OR NOT, HERE I COME!
......

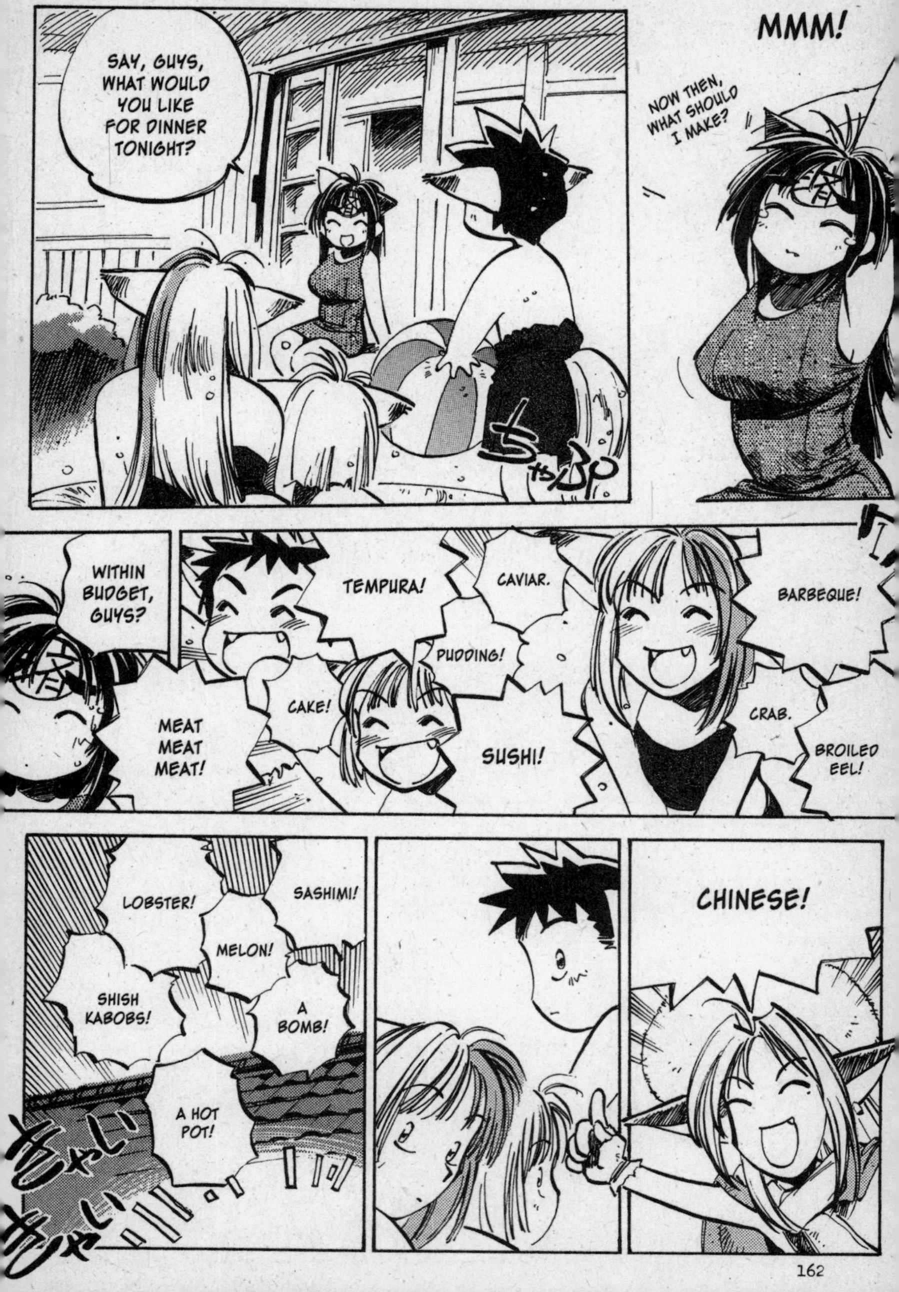
MMM!
NOW THEN, WHAT SHOULD I MAKE?
SAY, GUYS, WHAT WOULD YOU LIKE FOR DINNER TONIGHT?
BARBEQUE!
CAVIAR.
TEMPURA!
PUDDING!
CRAB.
BROILED EEL!
SUSHI!
CAKE!
MEAT MEAT MEAT!
WITHIN BUDGET, GUYS?
CHINESE!
SASHIMI!
LOBSTER!
MELON!
A BOMB!
SHISH KABOBS!
A HOT POT!

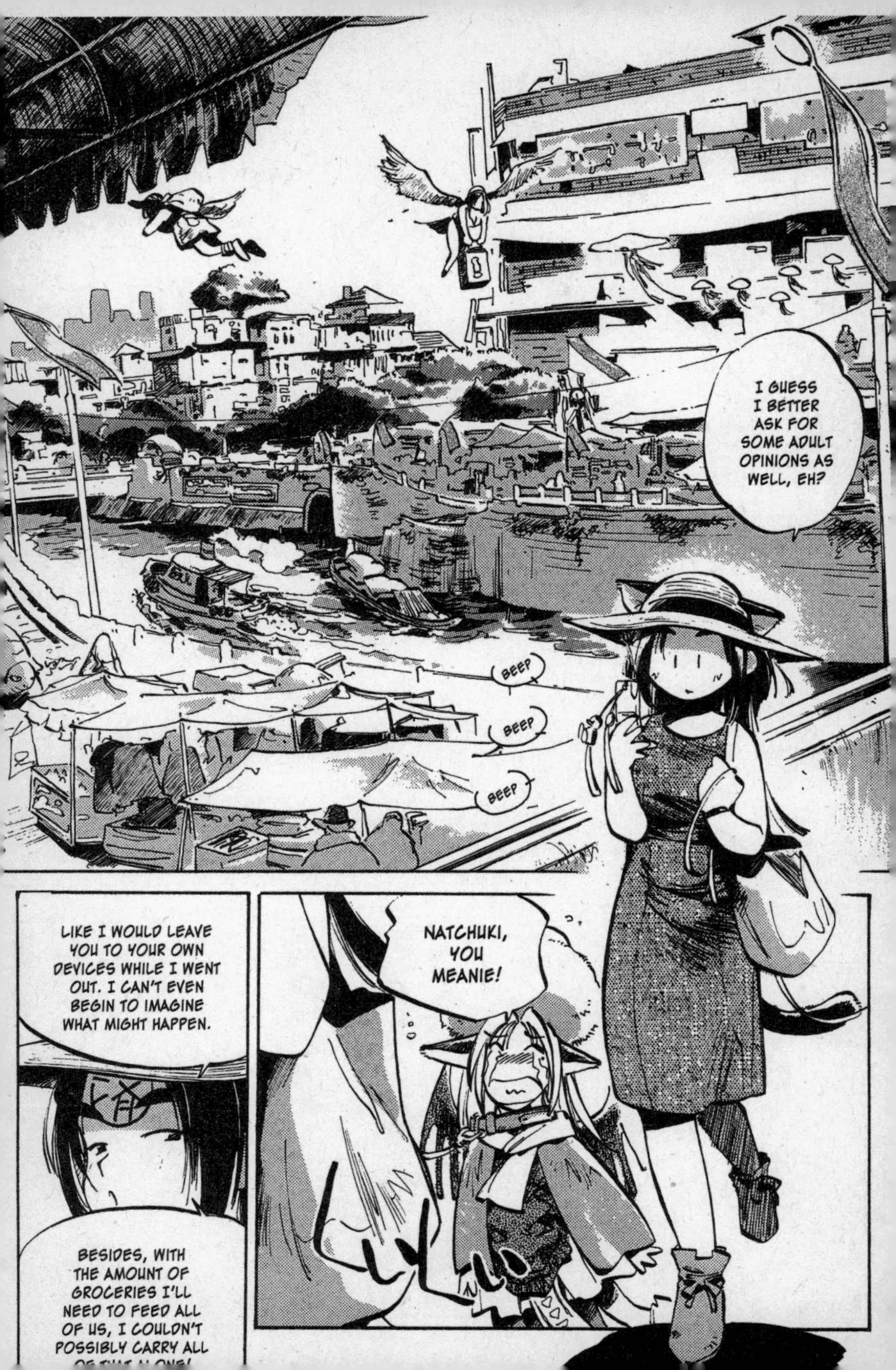
I GUESS I BETTER ASK FOR SOME ADULT OPINIONS AS WELL, EH?
BEEP
BEEP
BEEP
NATCHUKI, YOU MEANIE!
LIKE I WOULD LEAVE YOU TO YOUR OWN DEVICES WHILE I WENT OUT. I CAN'T EVEN BEGIN TO IMAGINE WHAT MIGHT HAPPEN.
BESIDES, WITH THE AMOUNT OF GROCERIES I'LL NEED TO FEED ALL OF US, I COULDN'T POSSIBLY CARRY ALL

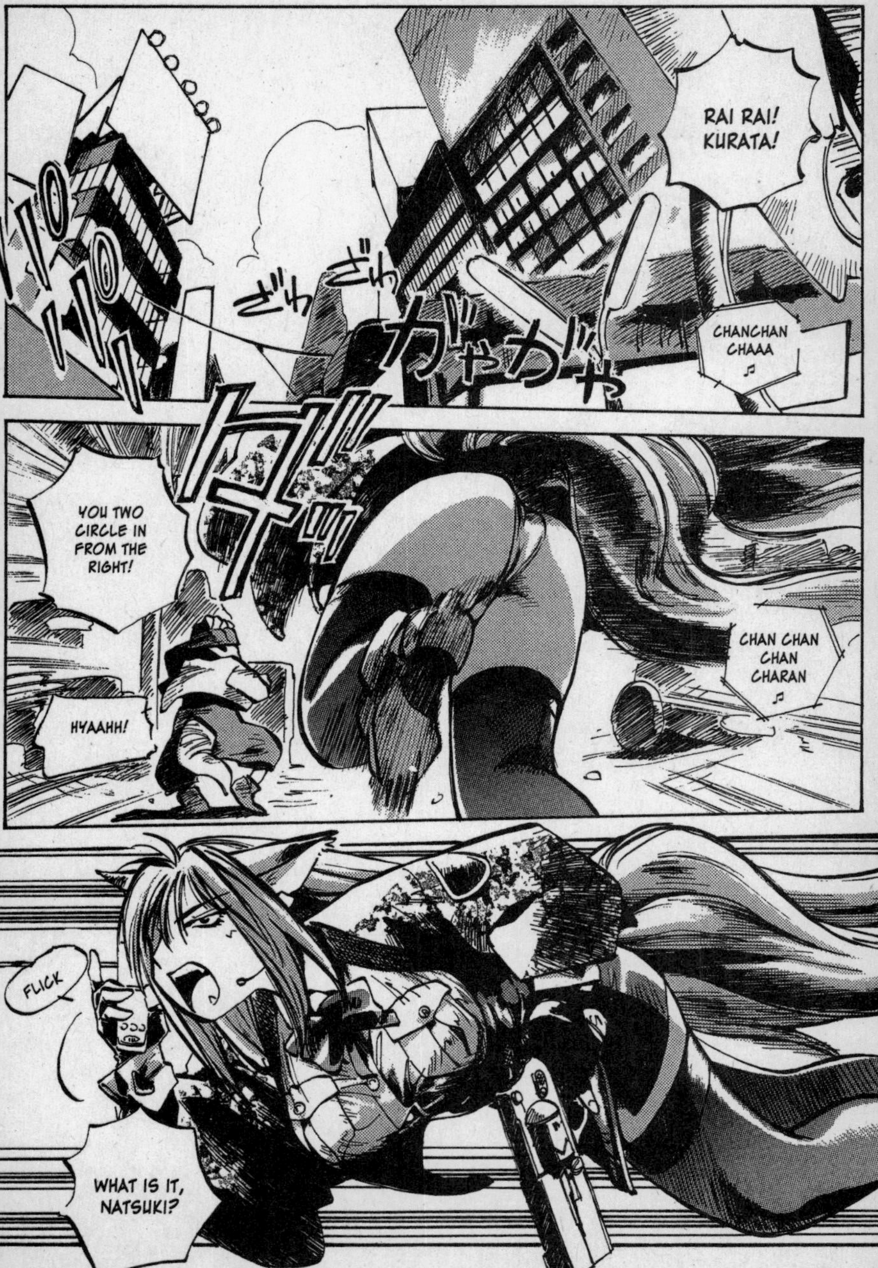
RAI RAI! KURATA!
CHANCHAN CHAAA ♪
ざわ ざわ
CHAN CHAN CHAN CHARAN ♪
YOU TWO CIRCLE IN FROM THE RIGHT!
HYAAHH!
FLICK
WHAT IS IT, NATSUKI?

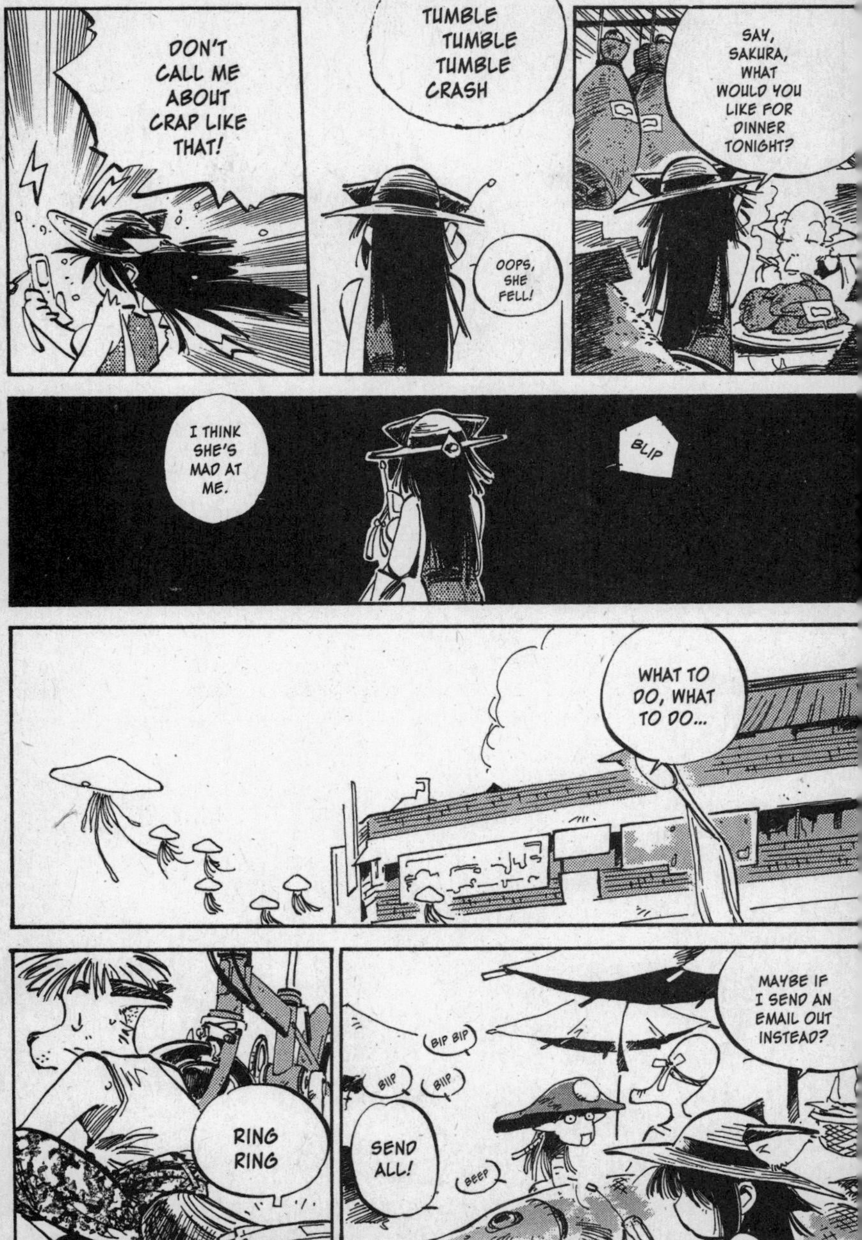
SAY, SAKURA, WHAT WOULD YOU LIKE FOR DINNER TONIGHT?
TRIP TUMBLE TUMBLE TUMBLE CRASH
OOPS, SHE FELL!
DON'T CALL ME ABOUT CRAP LIKE THAT!
BLIP
I THINK SHE'S MAD AT ME.
WHAT TO DO, WHAT TO DO...
MAYBE IF I SEND AN EMAIL OUT INSTEAD?
BIP BIP
BIIP
BIIP
SEND ALL!
BEEP
RING RING

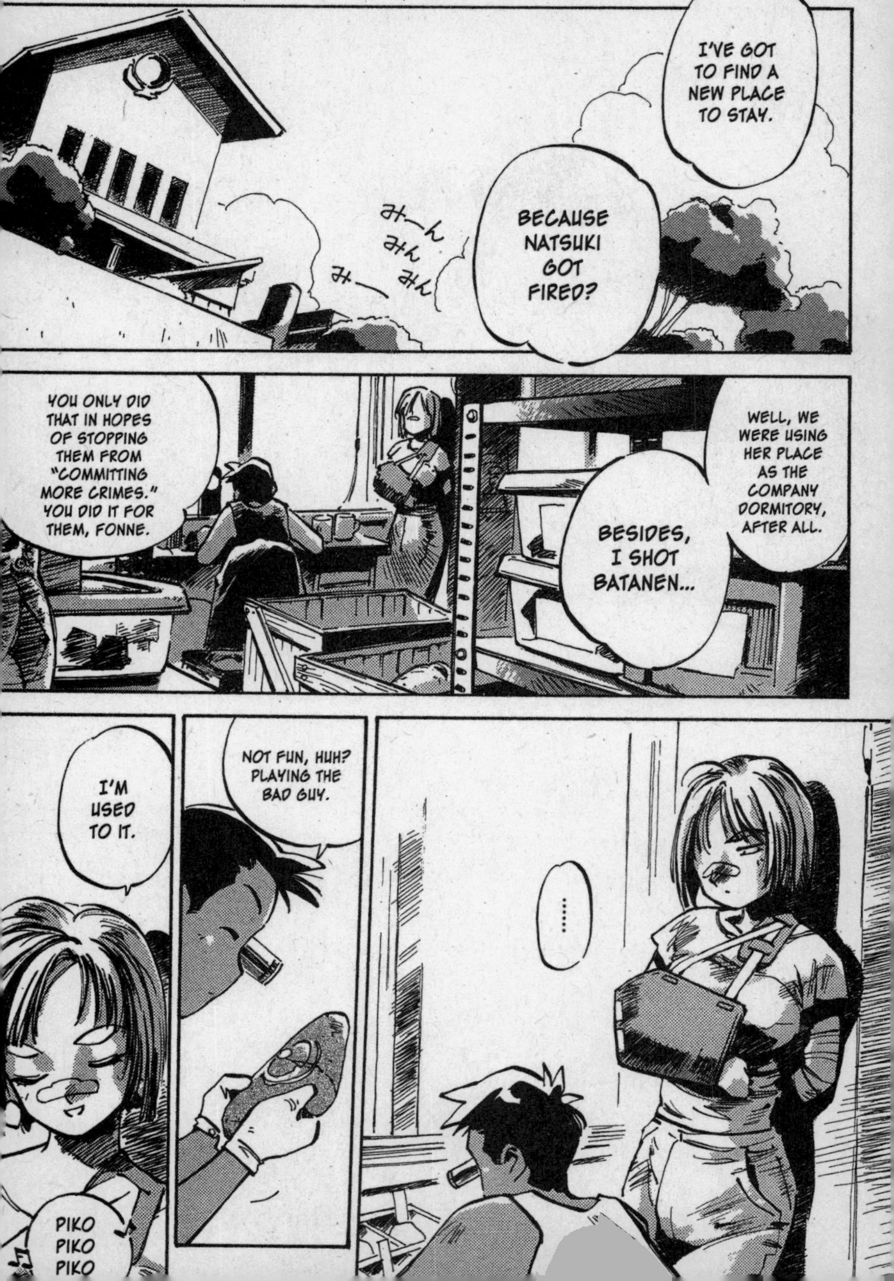
I'VE GOT TO FIND A NEW PLACE TO STAY.
BECAUSE NATSUKI GOT FIRED?
みーん みん みん みー
WELL, WE WERE USING HER PLACE AS THE COMPANY DORMITORY, AFTER ALL.
BESIDES, I SHOT BATANEN...
YOU ONLY DID THAT IN HOPES OF STOPPING THEM FROM "COMMITTING MORE CRIMES." YOU DID IT FOR THEM, FONNE.
......
NOT FUN, HUH? PLAYING THE BAD GUY.
I'M USED TO IT.
PIKO PIKO PIKO

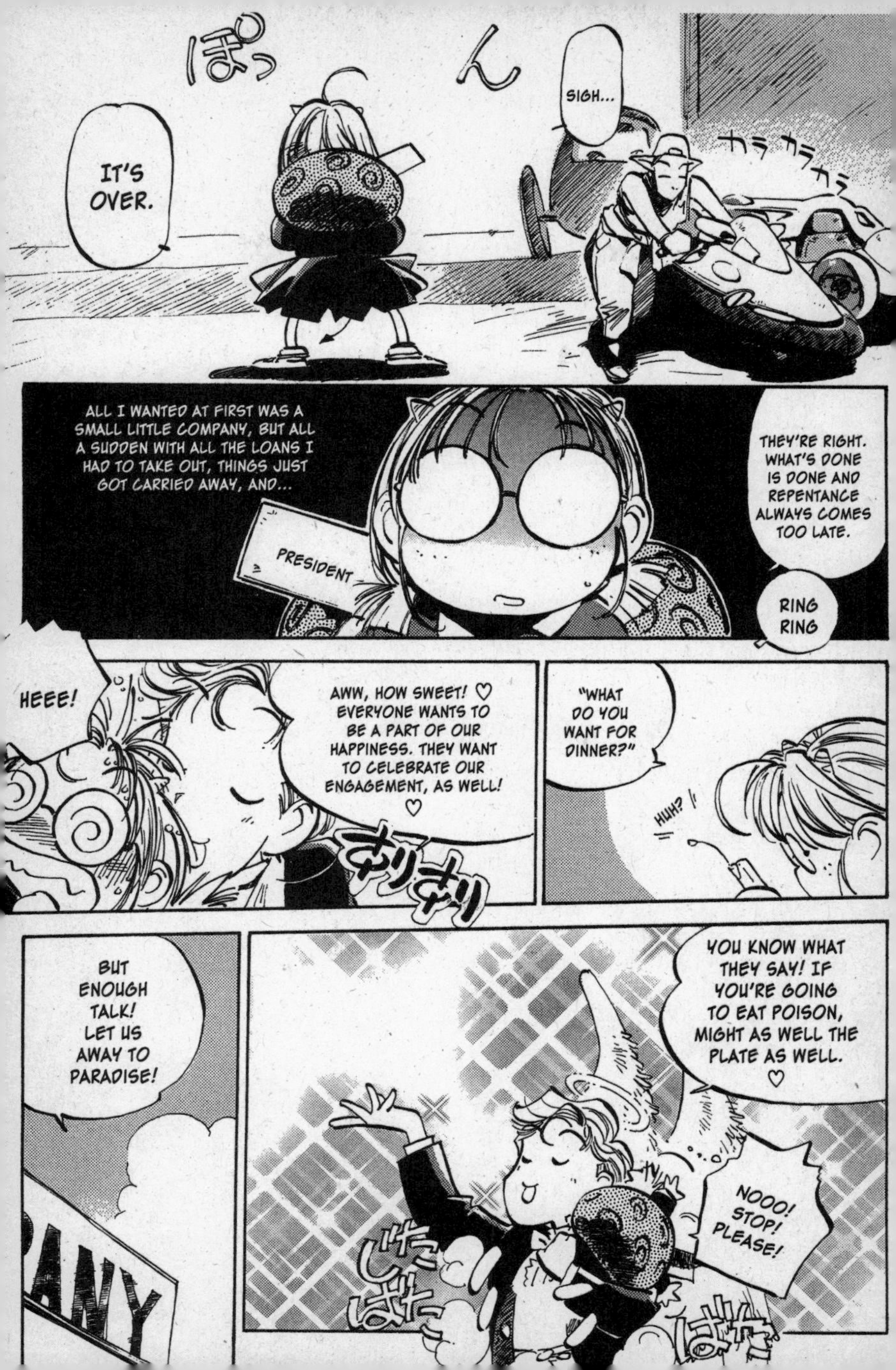
SIGH...
カラカラカラ
ぽっ ん
IT'S OVER.
THEY'RE RIGHT. WHAT'S DONE IS DONE AND REPENTANCE ALWAYS COMES TOO LATE.
RING RING
ALL I WANTED AT FIRST WAS A SMALL LITTLE COMPANY, BUT ALL A SUDDEN WITH ALL THE LOANS I HAD TO TAKE OUT, THINGS JUST GOT CARRIED AWAY, AND...
PRESIDENT
"WHAT DO YOU WANT FOR DINNER?"
HUH?
AWW, HOW SWEET! ♡ EVERYONE WANTS TO BE A PART OF OUR HAPPINESS. THEY WANT TO CELEBRATE OUR ENGAGEMENT, AS WELL! ♡
HEEE!
すりすり
YOU KNOW WHAT THEY SAY! IF YOU'RE GOING TO EAT POISON, MIGHT AS WELL THE PLATE AS WELL. ♡
NOOO! STOP! PLEASE!
じたばた
ばた
BUT ENOUGH TALK! LET US AWAY TO PARADISE!
ANY

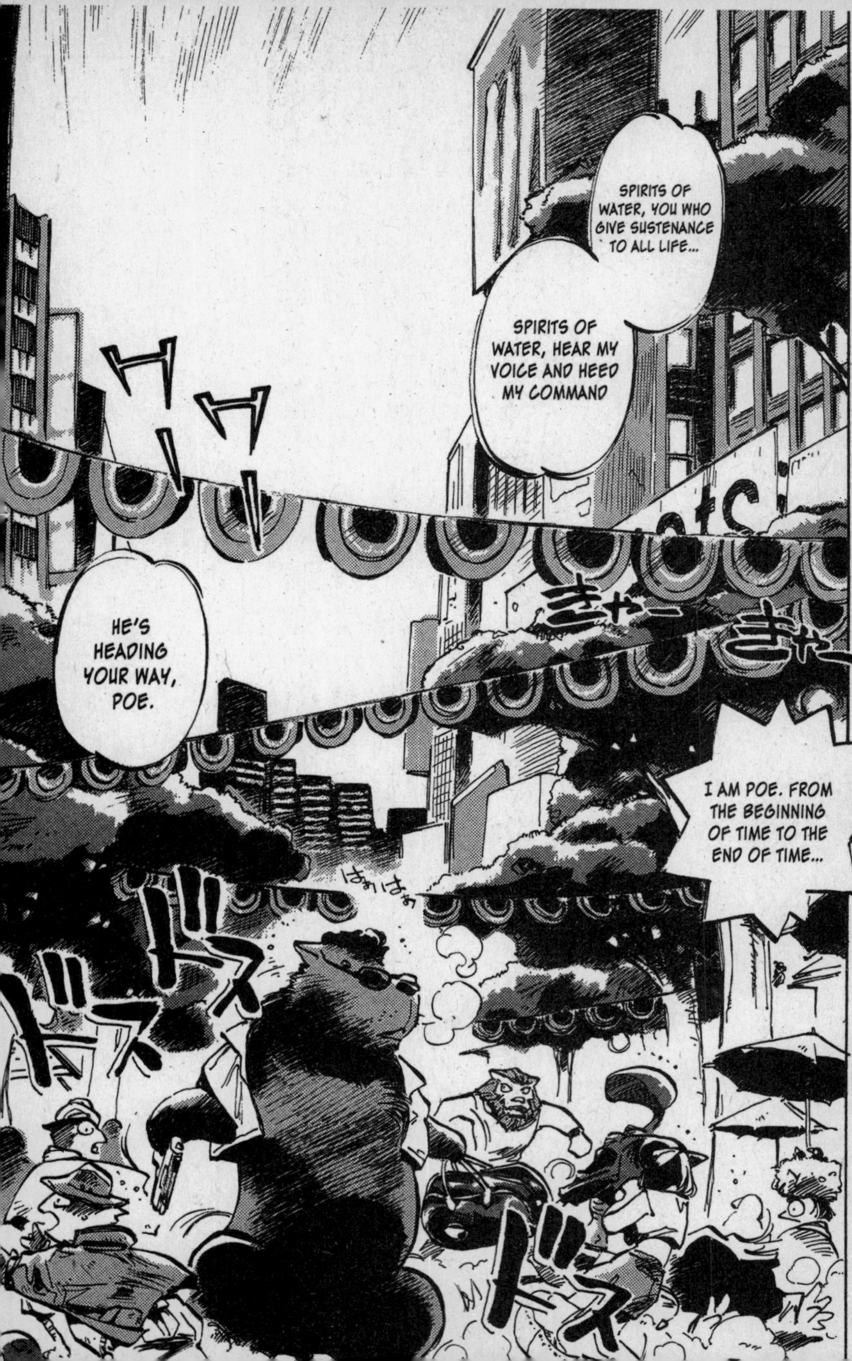
SPIRITS OF WATER, YOU WHO GIVE SUSTENANCE TO ALL LIFE...
SPIRITS OF WATER, HEAR MY VOICE AND HEED MY COMMAND
HE'S HEADING YOUR WAY, POE.
I AM POE. FROM THE BEGINNING OF TIME TO THE END OF TIME...

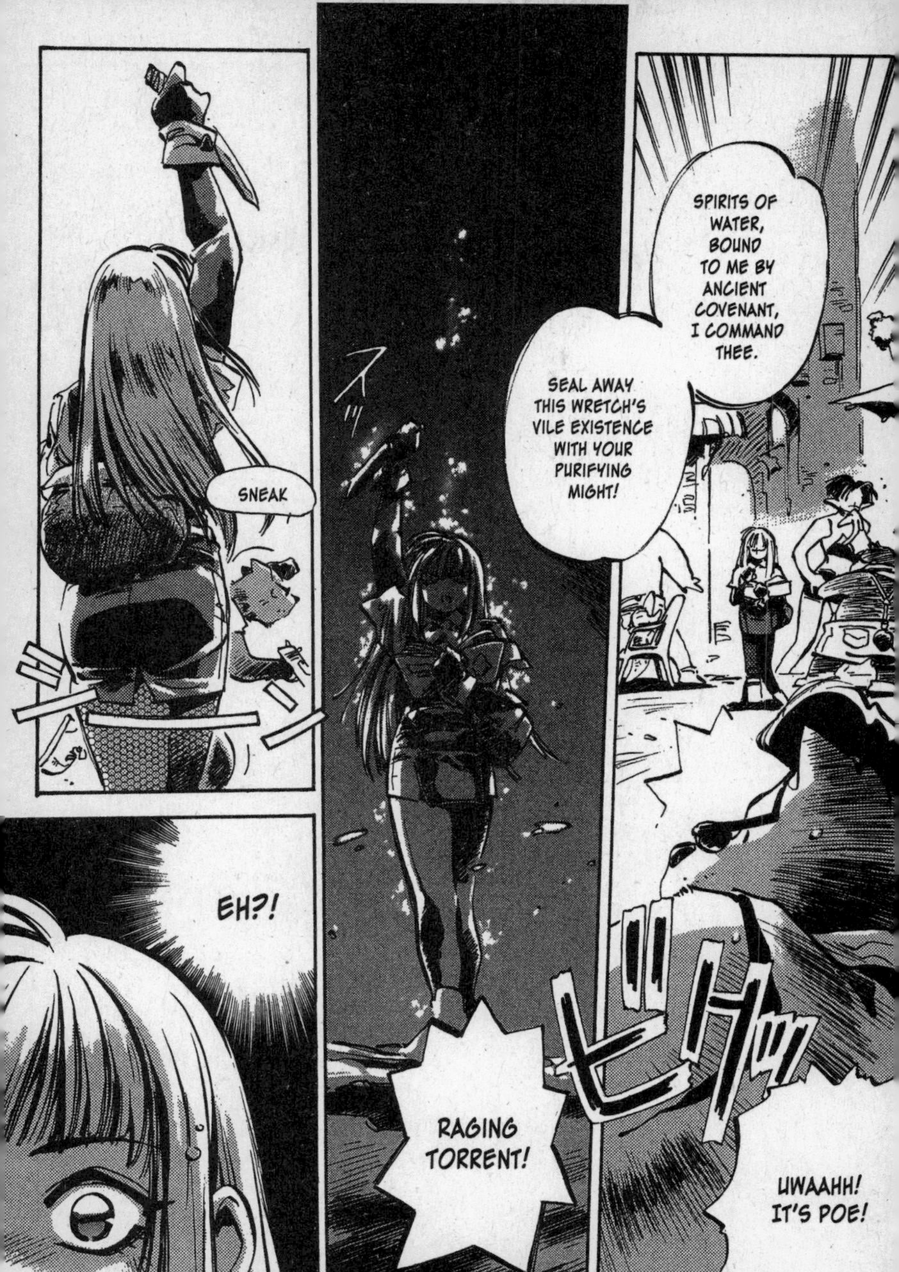
SPIRITS OF WATER, BOUND TO ME BY ANCIENT COVENANT, I COMMAND THEE.
SEAL AWAY THIS WRETCH'S VILE EXISTENCE WITH YOUR PURIFYING MIGHT!
UWAAHH! IT'S POE!
RAGING TORRENT!
SNEAK
EH?!

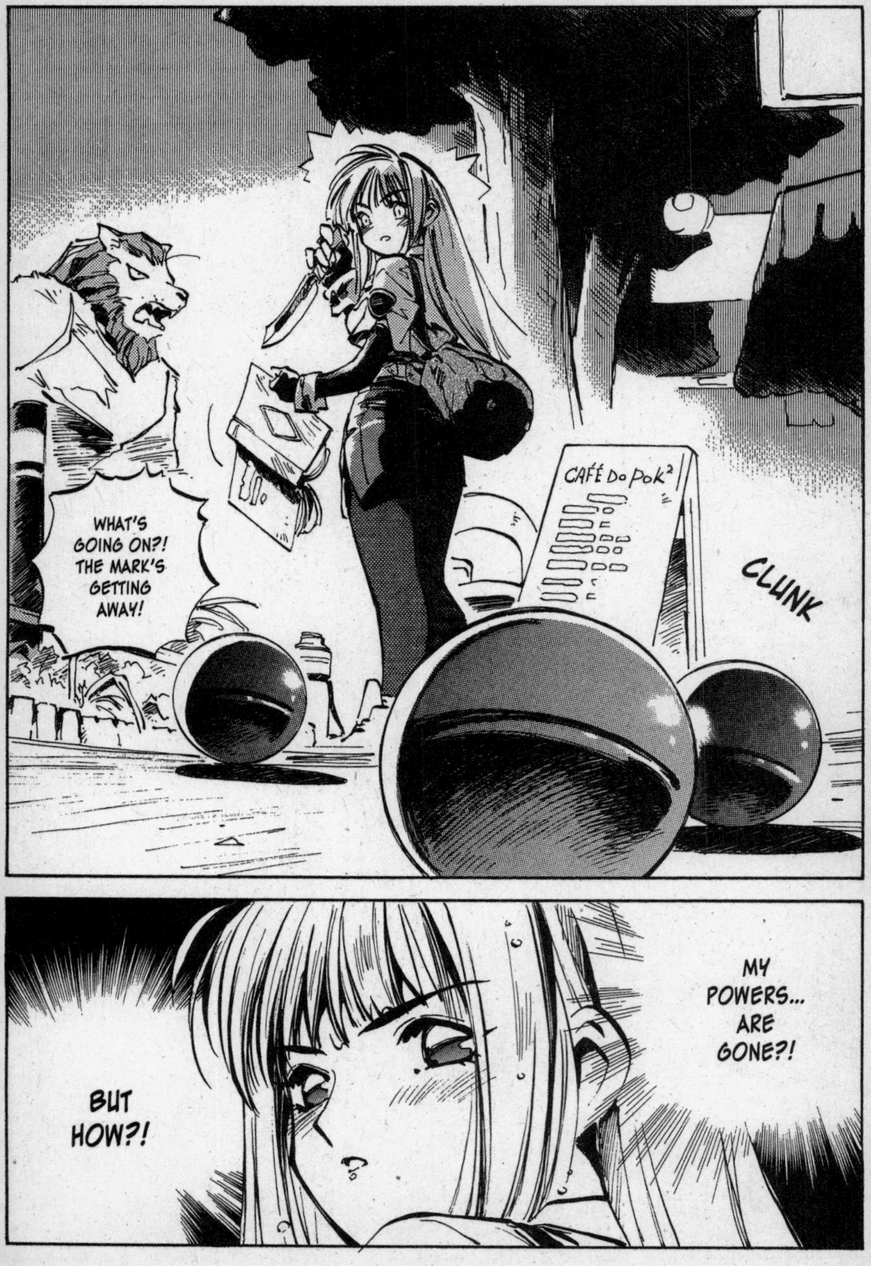
CAFÉ Do Pok²
CLUNK
WHAT'S GOING ON?! THE MARK'S GETTING AWAY!
MY POWERS... ARE GONE?!
BUT HOW?!

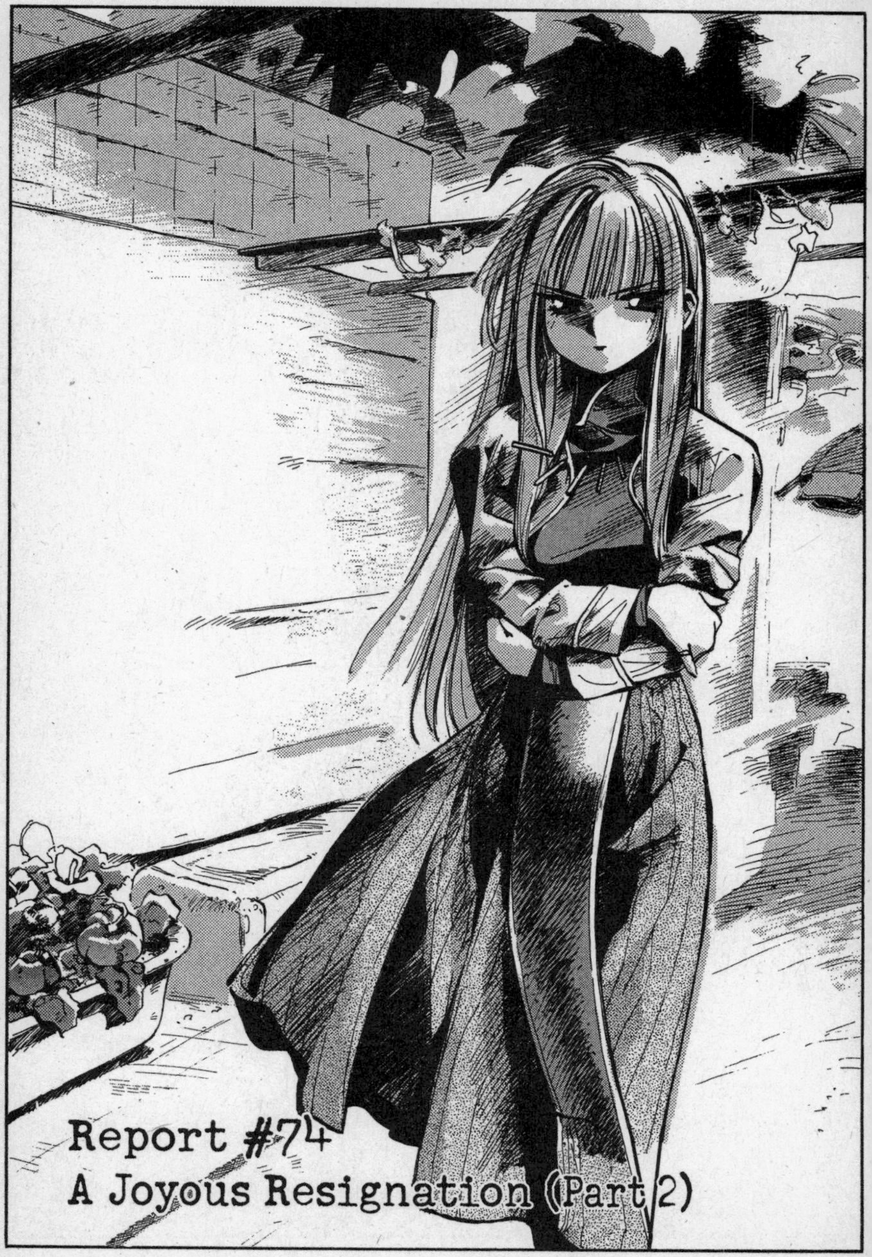
Report #74
A Joyous Resignation (Part 2)

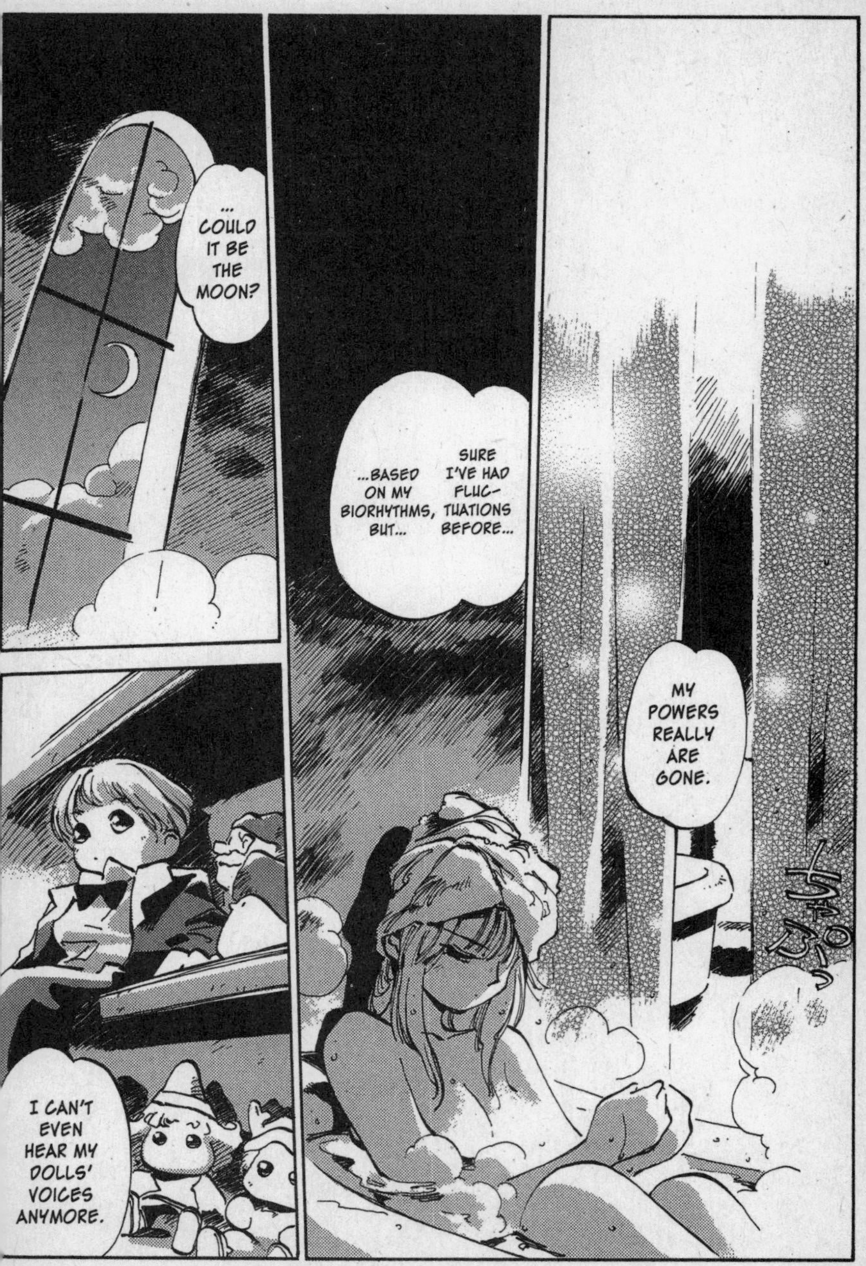
MY POWERS REALLY ARE GONE.
ちゃぷっ
SURE I'VE HAD FLUC-TUATIONS BEFORE...
...BASED ON MY BIORHYTHMS, BUT...
...COULD IT BE THE MOON?
I CAN'T EVEN HEAR MY DOLLS' VOICES ANYMORE.

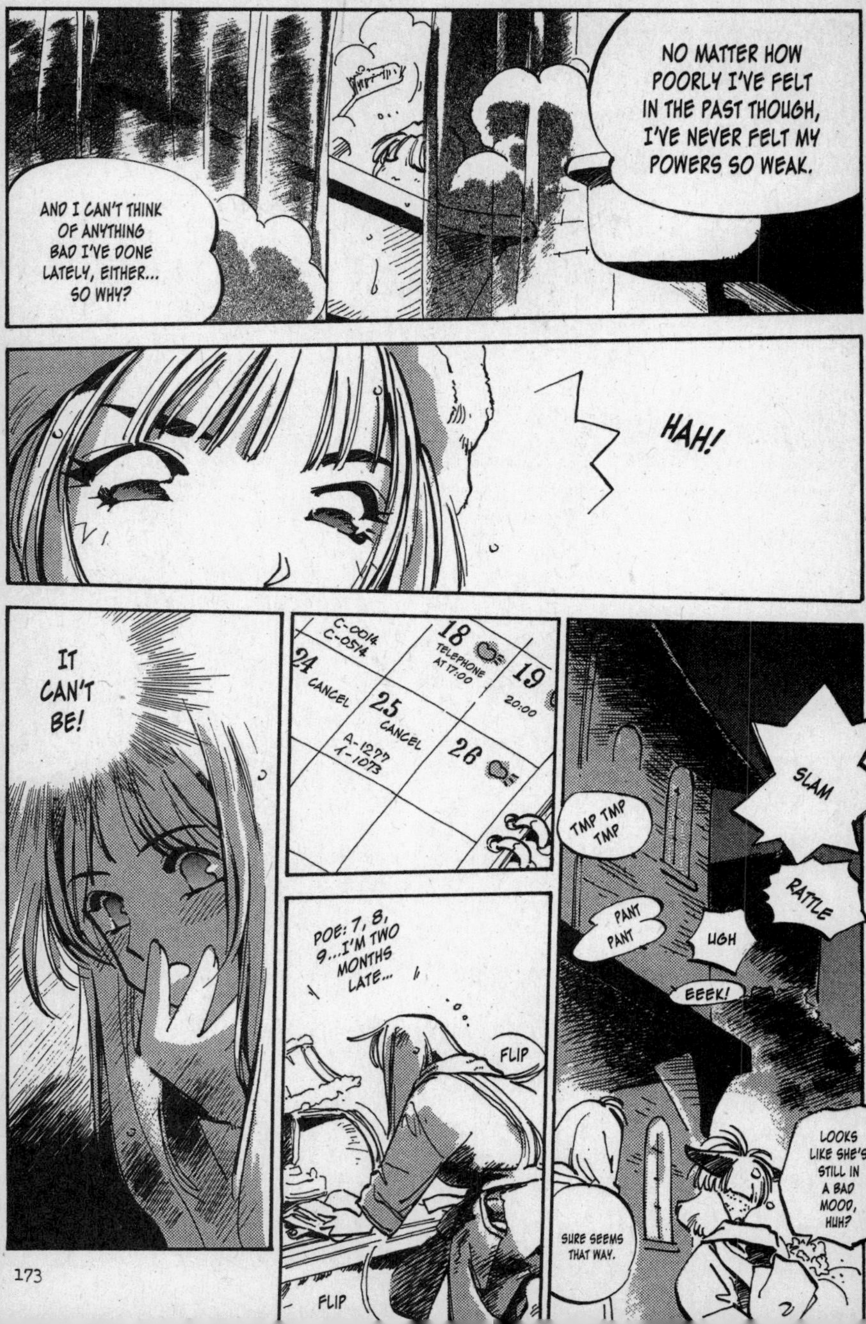
NO MATTER HOW POORLY I'VE FELT IN THE PAST THOUGH, I'VE NEVER FELT MY POWERS SO WEAK.
AND I CAN'T THINK OF ANYTHING BAD I'VE DONE LATELY, EITHER... SO WHY?
HAH!
SLAM
TMP TMP TMP
RATTLE
UGH
PANT PANT
EEEK!
LOOKS LIKE SHE'S STILL IN A BAD MOOD, HUH?
SURE SEEMS THAT WAY.
C-0014
C-0514
18
TELEPHONE AT 17:00
19
20:00
24
CANCEL
25
CANCEL
A-1277
1-1073
26
POE: 7, 8, 9...I'M TWO MONTHS LATE...
FLIP
FLIP
IT CAN'T BE!

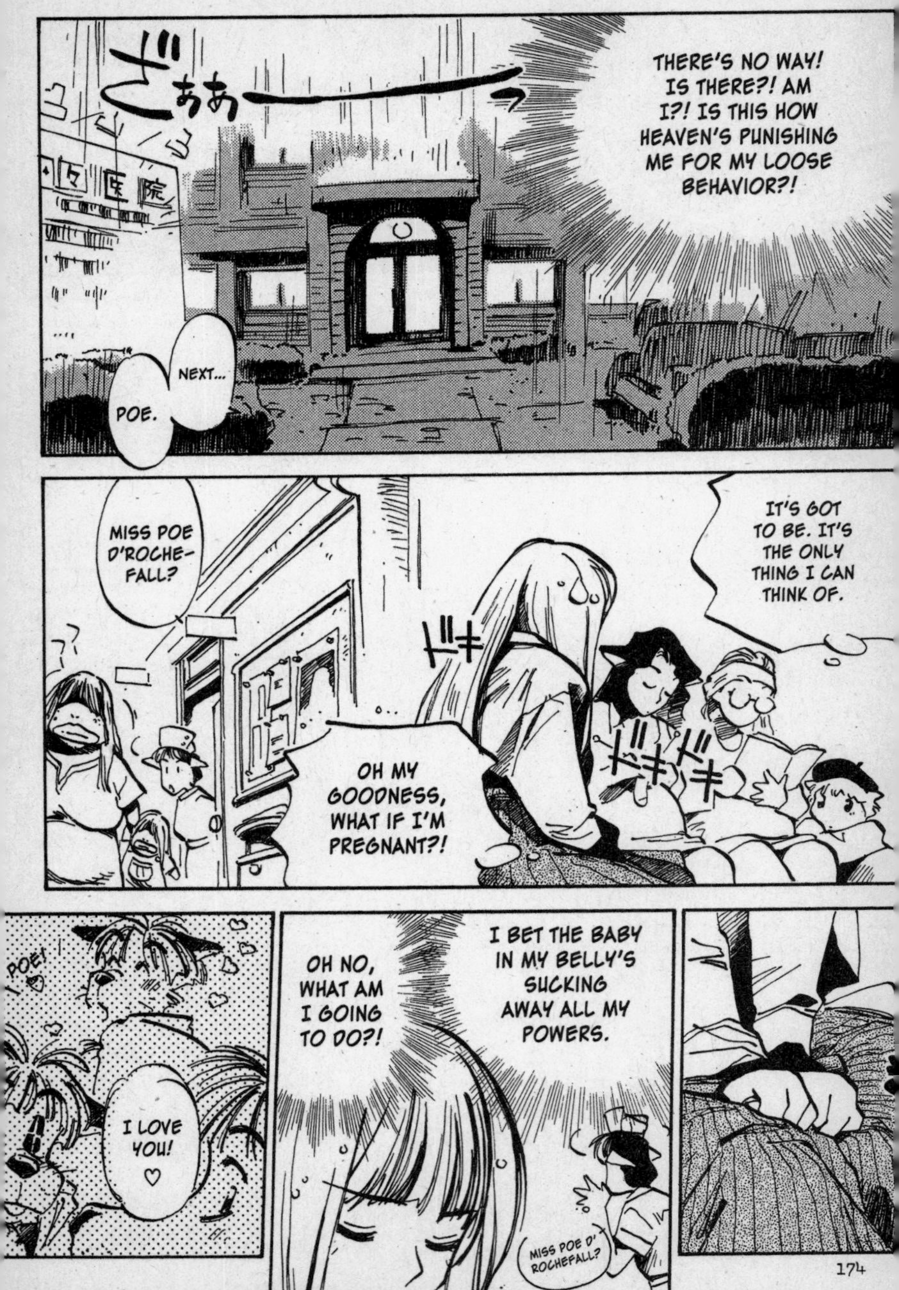
THERE'S NO WAY! IS THERE?! AM I?! IS THIS HOW HEAVEN'S PUNISHING ME FOR MY LOOSE BEHAVIOR?!
ざあー
NEXT...
POE.
IT'S GOT TO BE. IT'S THE ONLY THING I CAN THINK OF.
MISS POE D'ROCHE-FALL?
ドキ
ドキドキ
OH MY GOODNESS, WHAT IF I'M PREGNANT?!
I BET THE BABY IN MY BELLY'S SUCKING AWAY ALL MY POWERS.
OH NO, WHAT AM I GOING TO DO?!
MISS POE D' ROCHEFALL?
I POE!
I LOVE YOU! ♡

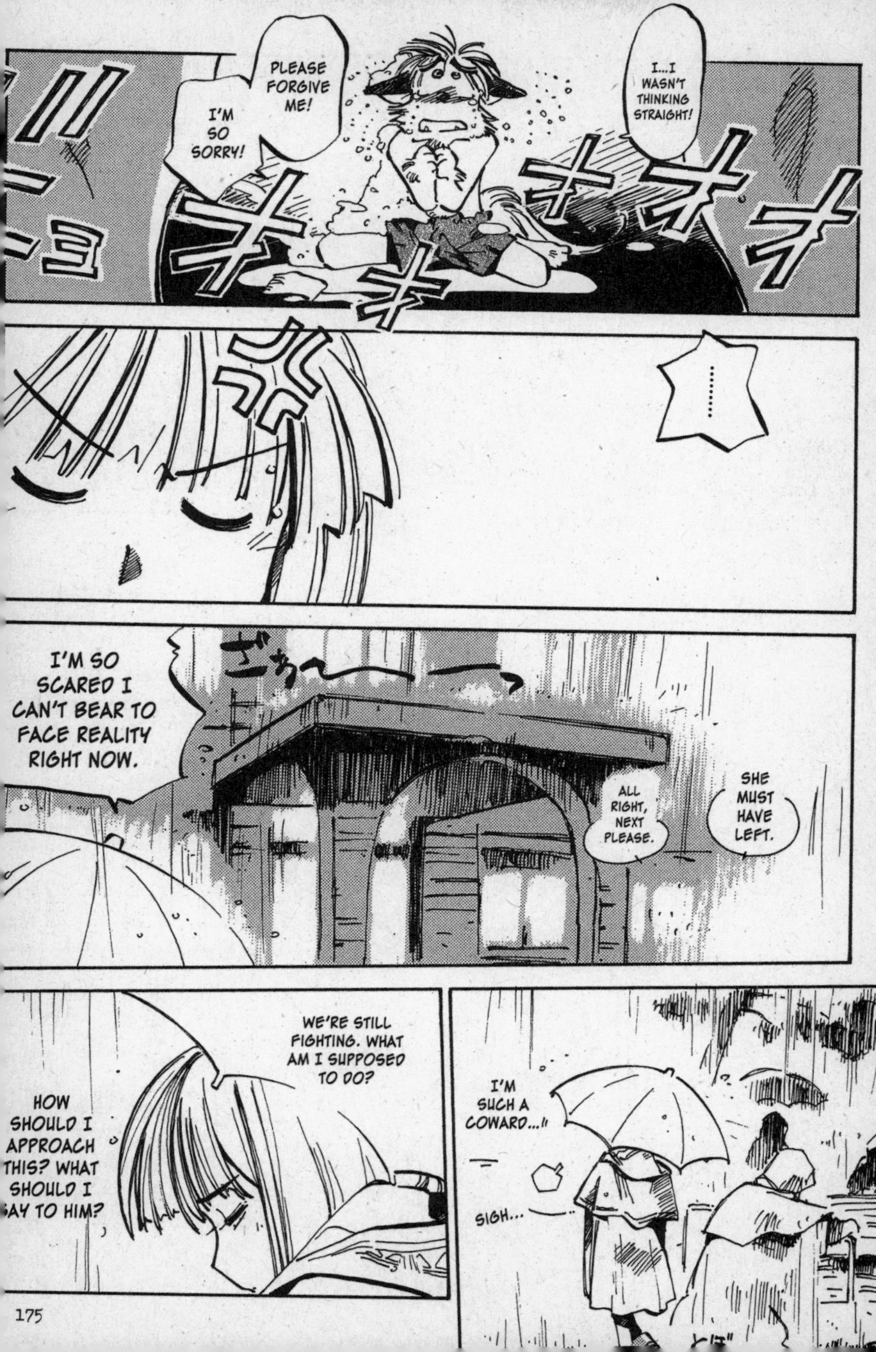

I...I WASN'T THINKING STRAIGHT!
PLEASE FORGIVE ME!
I'M SO SORRY!
....
SHE MUST HAVE LEFT.
ALL RIGHT, NEXT PLEASE.
I'M SO SCARED I CAN'T BEAR TO FACE REALITY RIGHT NOW.
I'M SUCH A COWARD...
SIGH...
WE'RE STILL FIGHTING. WHAT AM I SUPPOSED TO DO?
HOW SHOULD I APPROACH THIS? WHAT SHOULD I SAY TO HIM?

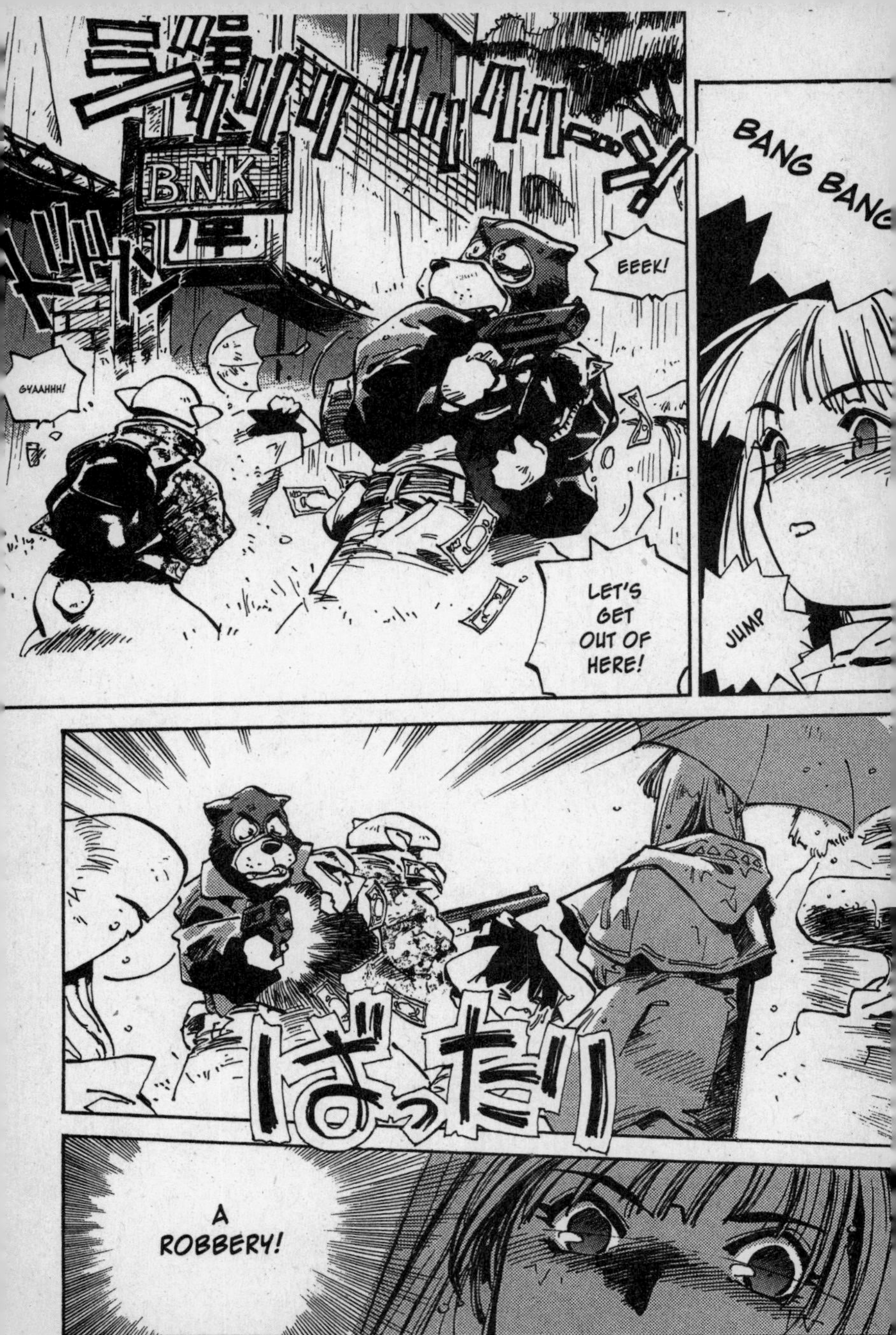
BANG BANG
JUMP
EEEK!
BNK
GYAAHHH!
LET'S GET OUT OF HERE!
A ROBBERY!

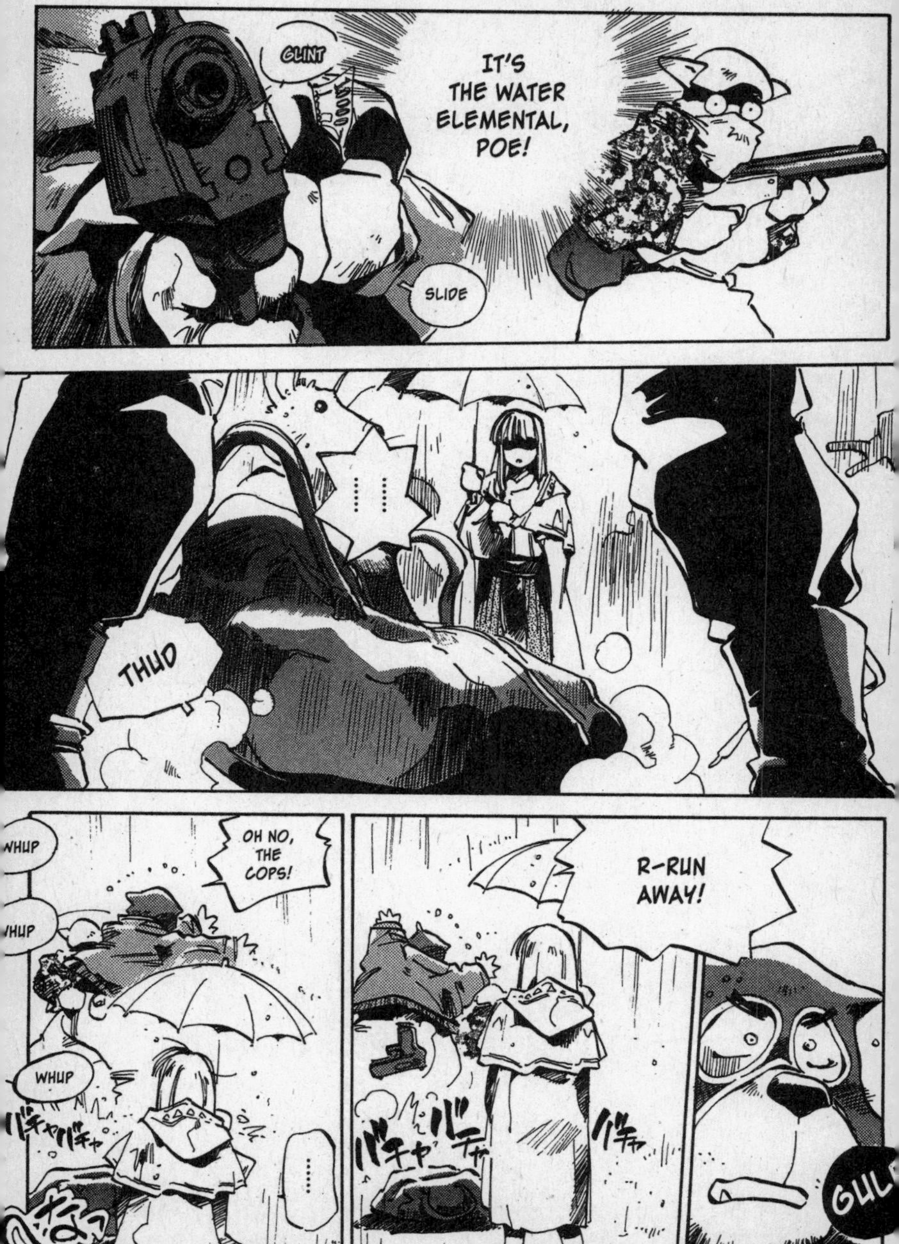
IT'S THE WATER ELEMENTAL, POE!
GLINT
SLIDE
......
THUD
R-RUN AWAY!
GUL
バチャ
バチャ
バチャ
OH NO, THE COPS!
WHUP
WHUP
WHUP
......
バチャバチャ

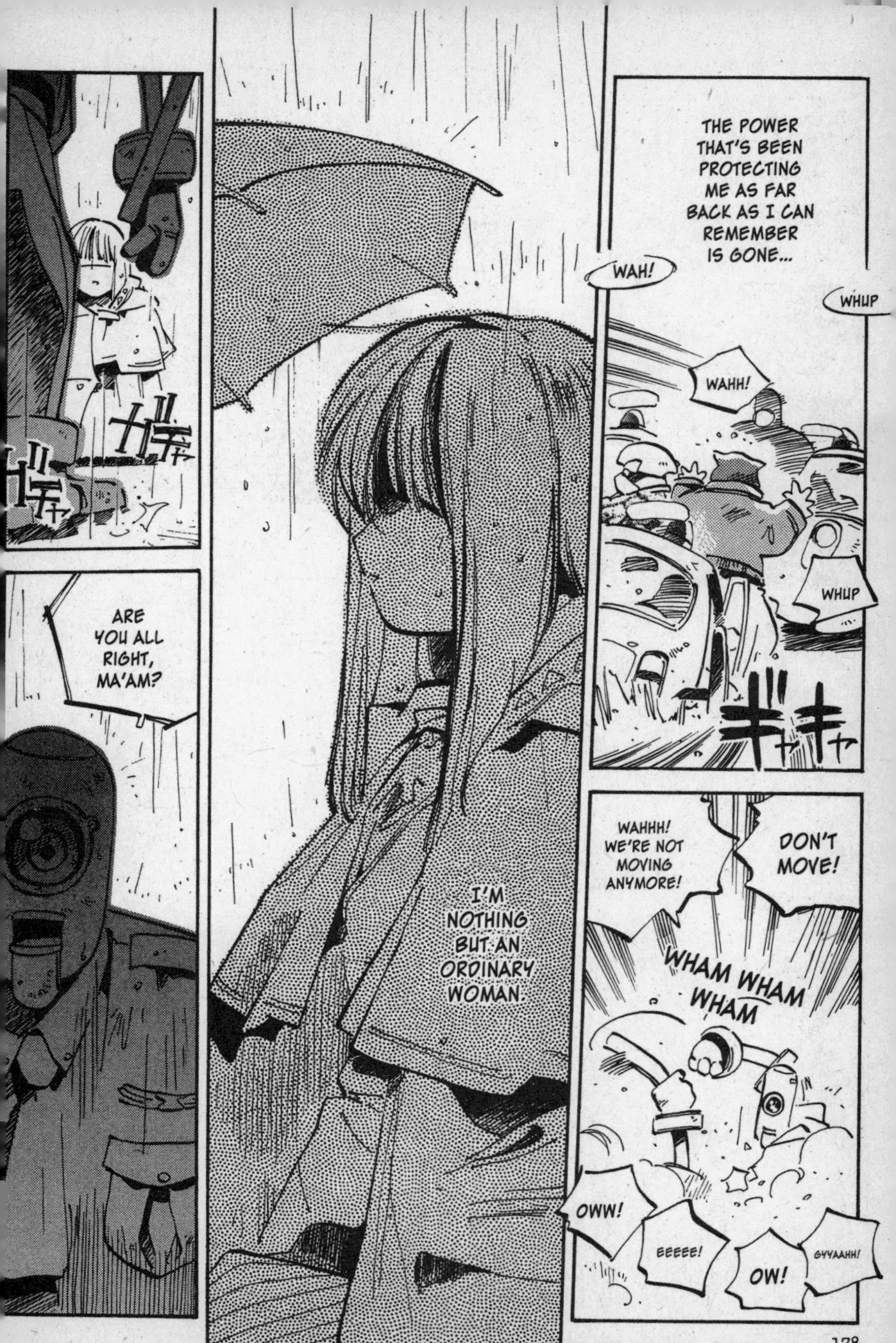
THE POWER THAT'S BEEN PROTECTING ME AS FAR BACK AS I CAN REMEMBER IS GONE...
WAH!
WHUP
WAHH!
WHUP
DON'T MOVE!
WAHHH! WE'RE NOT MOVING ANYMORE!
WHAM WHAM WHAM
OWW!
EEEEE!
GYYAAHH!
OW!
I'M NOTHING BUT AN ORDINARY WOMAN.
ARE YOU ALL RIGHT, MA'AM?

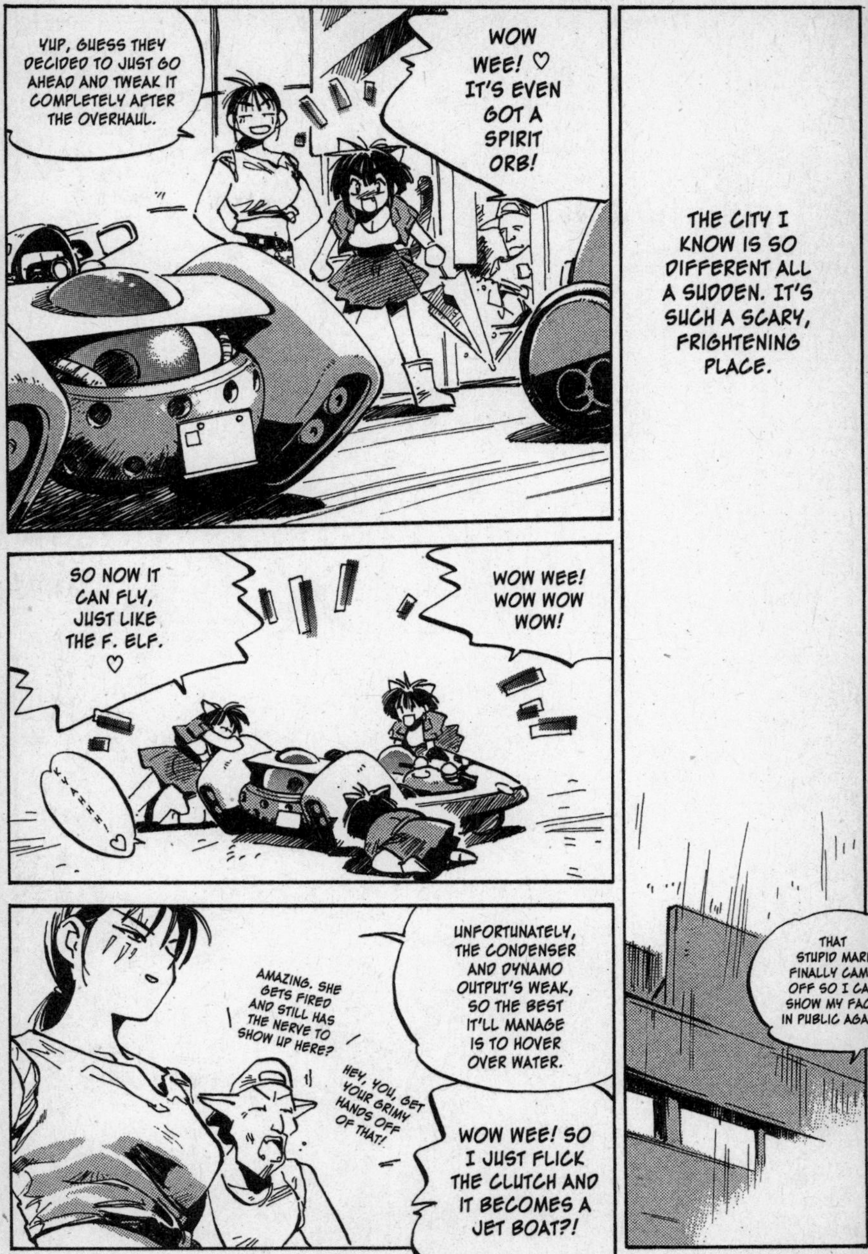
THE CITY I KNOW IS SO DIFFERENT ALL A SUDDEN. IT'S SUCH A SCARY, FRIGHTENING PLACE.
THAT STUPID MAR FINALLY CAM OFF SO I CA SHOW MY FAC IN PUBLIC AGA
WOW WEE! ♡ IT'S EVEN GOT A SPIRIT ORB!
YUP, GUESS THEY DECIDED TO JUST GO AHEAD AND TWEAK IT COMPLETELY AFTER THE OVERHAUL.
WOW WEE! WOW WOW WOW!
SO NOW IT CAN FLY, JUST LIKE THE F. ELF. ♡
UNFORTUNATELY, THE CONDENSER AND DYNAMO OUTPUT'S WEAK, SO THE BEST IT'LL MANAGE IS TO HOVER OVER WATER.
AMAZING. SHE GETS FIRED AND STILL HAS THE NERVE TO SHOW UP HERE?
HEY, YOU, GET YOUR GRIMY HANDS OFF OF THAT!
WOW WEE! SO I JUST FLICK THE CLUTCH AND IT BECOMES A JET BOAT?!

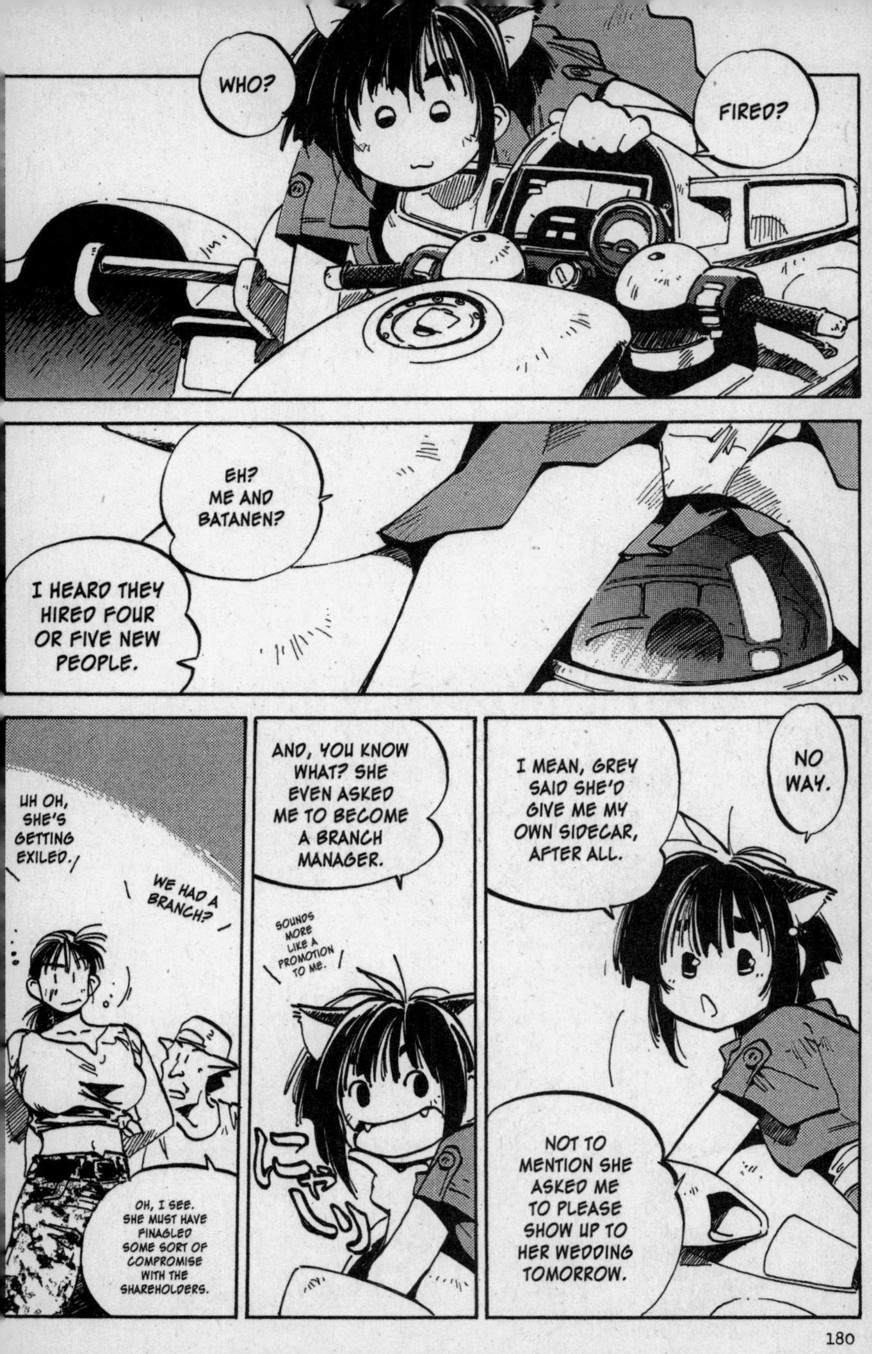
FIRED?
WHO?
EH? ME AND BATANEN?
I HEARD THEY HIRED FOUR OR FIVE NEW PEOPLE.
NO WAY.
I MEAN, GREY SAID SHE'D GIVE ME MY OWN SIDECAR, AFTER ALL.
NOT TO MENTION SHE ASKED ME TO PLEASE SHOW UP TO HER WEDDING TOMORROW.
AND, YOU KNOW WHAT? SHE EVEN ASKED ME TO BECOME A BRANCH MANAGER.
SOUNDS MORE LIKE A PROMOTION TO ME.
WE HAD A BRANCH?
UH OH, SHE'S GETTING EXILED.
OH, I SEE. SHE MUST HAVE FINAGLED SOME SORT OF COMPROMISE WITH THE SHAREHOLDERS.

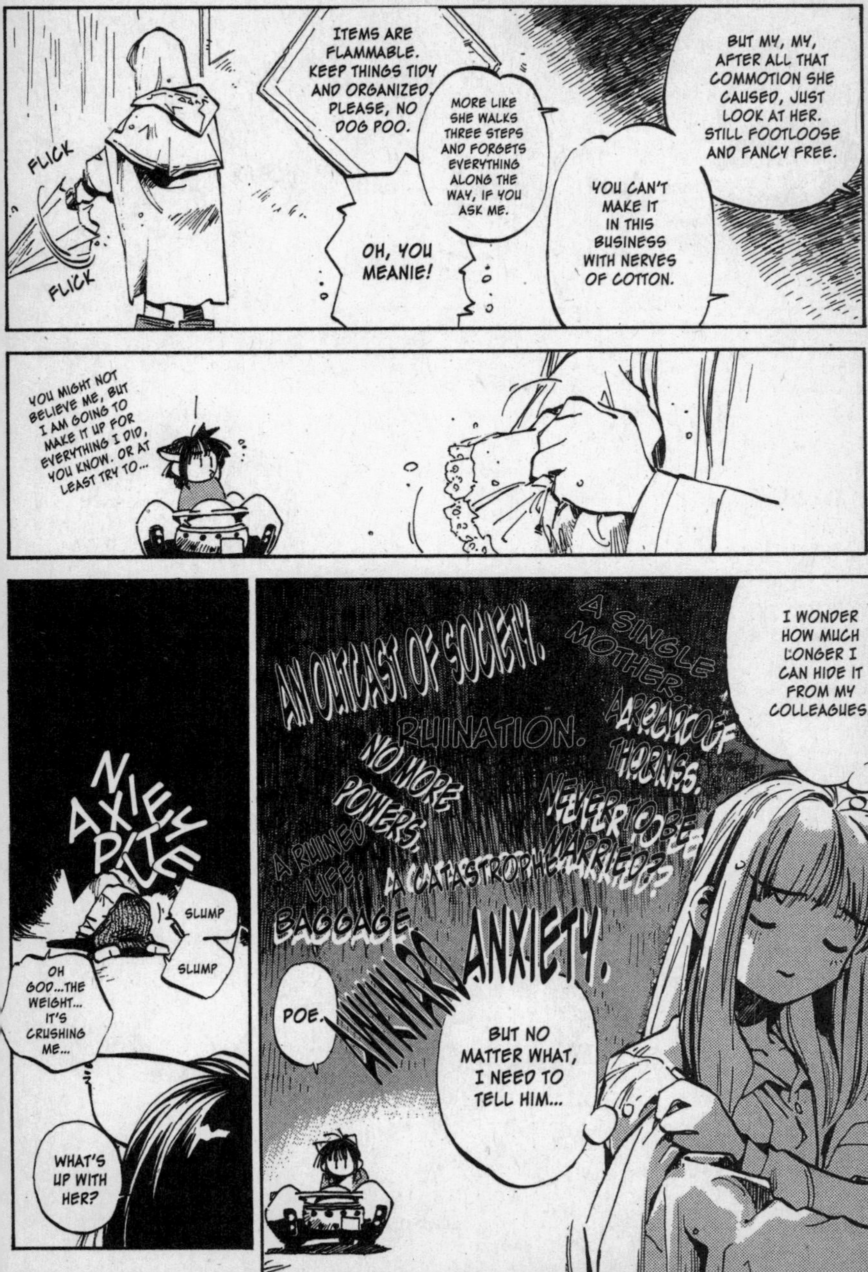

BUT MY, MY, AFTER ALL THAT COMMOTION SHE CAUSED, JUST LOOK AT HER. STILL FOOTLOOSE AND FANCY FREE.
YOU CAN'T MAKE IT IN THIS BUSINESS WITH NERVES OF COTTON.
MORE LIKE SHE WALKS THREE STEPS AND FORGETS EVERYTHING ALONG THE WAY, IF YOU ASK ME.
OH, YOU MEANIE!
ITEMS ARE FLAMMABLE. KEEP THINGS TIDY AND ORGANIZED. PLEASE, NO DOG POO.
FLICK
FLICK
YOU MIGHT NOT BELIEVE ME, BUT I AM GOING TO MAKE IT UP FOR EVERYTHING I DID, YOU KNOW. OR AT LEAST TRY TO...
I WONDER HOW MUCH LONGER I CAN HIDE IT FROM MY COLLEAGUES.
A SINGLE MOTHER.
AN OUTCAST OF SOCIETY.
RUINATION.
NO MORE POWERS.
NEVER TO BE MARRIED?
A RUINED LIFE.
BAGGAGE.
ANXIETY.
BUT NO MATTER WHAT, I NEED TO TELL HIM...
POE.
SLUMP
SLUMP
OH GOD...THE WEIGHT... IT'S CRUSHING ME...
WHAT'S UP WITH HER?

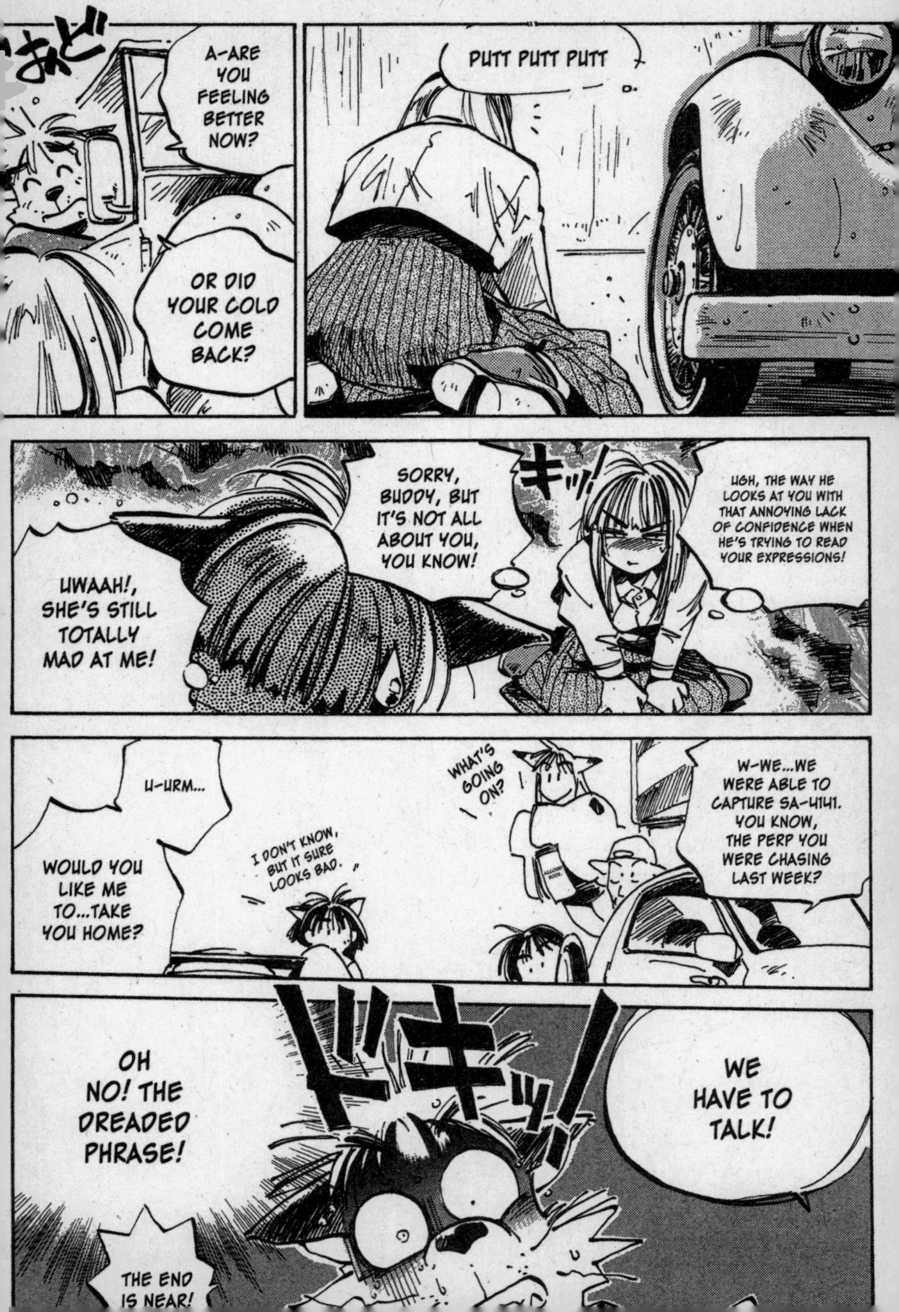
PUTT PUTT PUTT
おど
A-ARE YOU FEELING BETTER NOW?
OR DID YOUR COLD COME BACK?
UGH, THE WAY HE LOOKS AT YOU WITH THAT ANNOYING LACK OF CONFIDENCE WHEN HE'S TRYING TO READ YOUR EXPRESSIONS!
キッ!
SORRY, BUDDY, BUT IT'S NOT ALL ABOUT YOU, YOU KNOW!
UWAAH!, SHE'S STILL TOTALLY MAD AT ME!
W-WE...WE WERE ABLE TO CAPTURE SA-4141. YOU KNOW, THE PERP YOU WERE CHASING LAST WEEK?
WHAT'S GOING ON?
I DON'T KNOW, BUT IT SURE LOOKS BAD.
U-URM...
WOULD YOU LIKE ME TO...TAKE YOU HOME?
WE HAVE TO TALK!
ドキッ!
OH NO! THE DREADED PHRASE!
THE END IS NEAR!

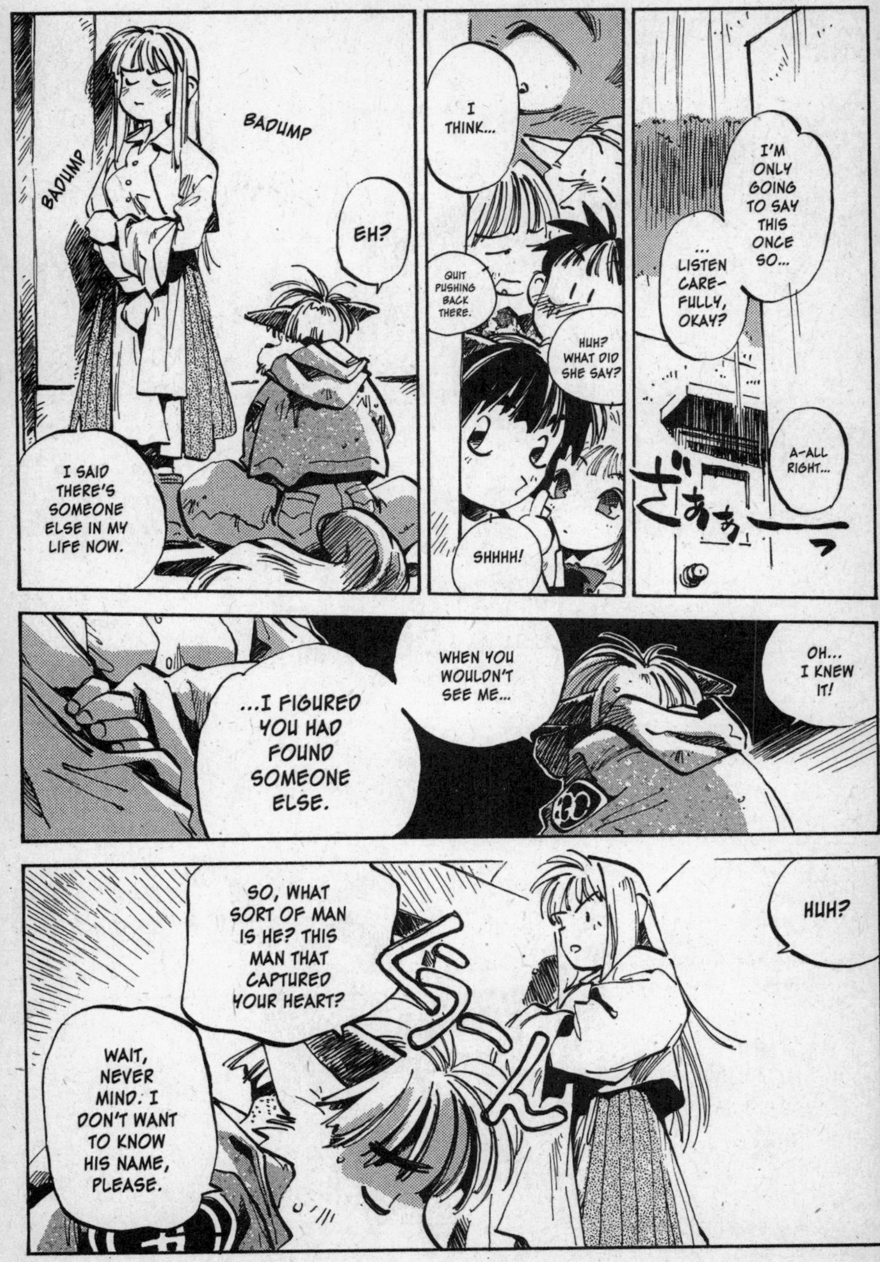
I'M ONLY GOING TO SAY THIS ONCE SO...
...LISTEN CARE-FULLY, OKAY?
A-ALL RIGHT...
ざあぁーっ
I THINK...
QUIT PUSHING BACK THERE.
HUH? WHAT DID SHE SAY?
SHHHH!
EH?
BADUMP
BADUMP
I SAID THERE'S SOMEONE ELSE IN MY LIFE NOW.
OH... I KNEW IT!
WHEN YOU WOULDN'T SEE ME...
...I FIGURED YOU HAD FOUND SOMEONE ELSE.
HUH?
SO, WHAT SORT OF MAN IS HE? THIS MAN THAT CAPTURED YOUR HEART?
WAIT, NEVER MIND. I DON'T WANT TO KNOW HIS NAME, PLEASE.

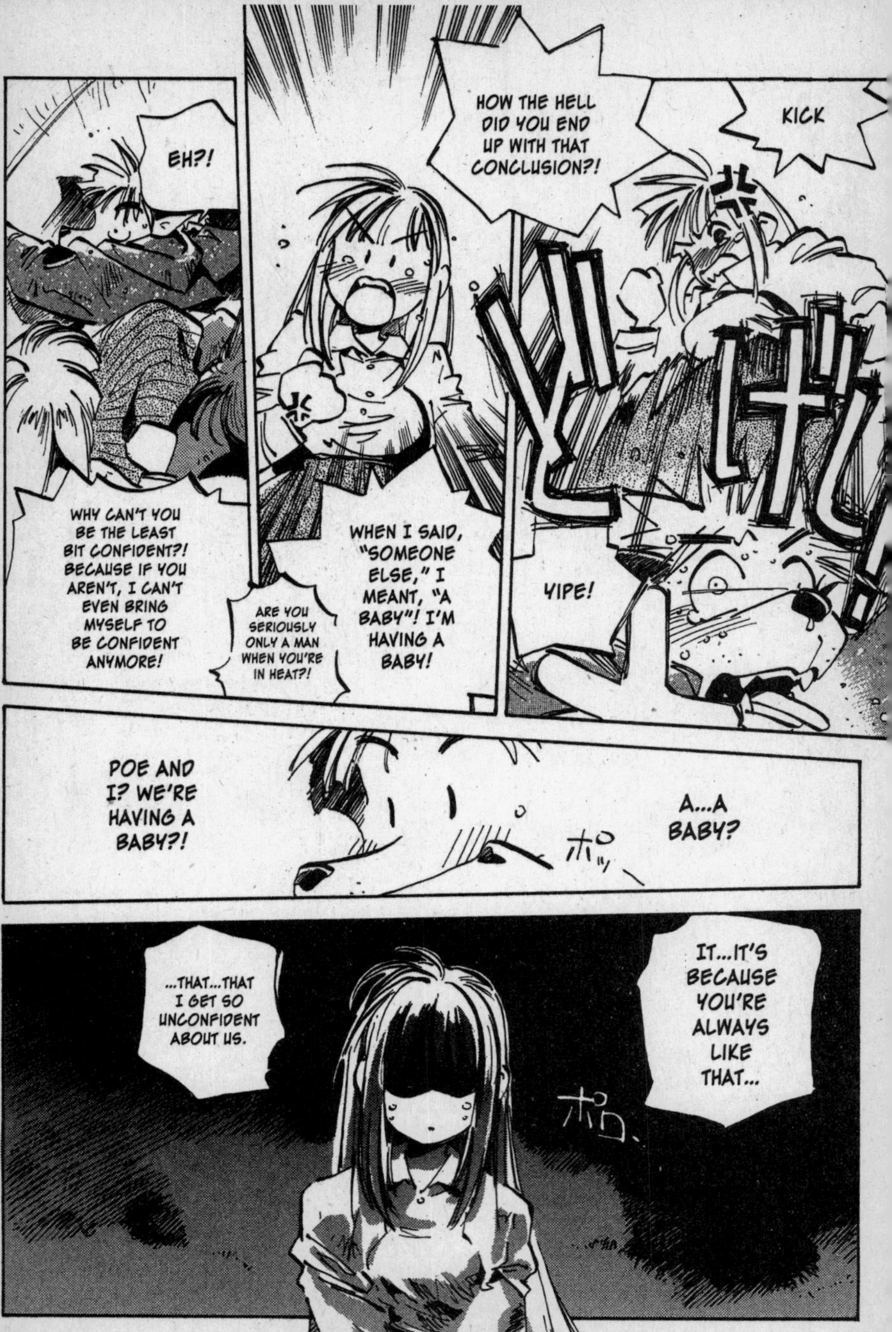
HOW THE HELL DID YOU END UP WITH THAT CONCLUSION?!
KICK
YIPE!
WHEN I SAID, "SOMEONE ELSE," I MEANT, "A BABY"! I'M HAVING A BABY!
ARE YOU SERIOUSLY ONLY A MAN WHEN YOU'RE IN HEAT?!
EH?!
WHY CAN'T YOU BE THE LEAST BIT CONFIDENT?! BECAUSE IF YOU AREN'T, I CAN'T EVEN BRING MYSELF TO BE CONFIDENT ANYMORE!
A...A BABY?
ポッ
POE AND I? WE'RE HAVING A BABY?!
IT...IT'S BECAUSE YOU'RE ALWAYS LIKE THAT...
ポロ
...THAT...THAT I GET SO UNCONFIDENT ABOUT US.

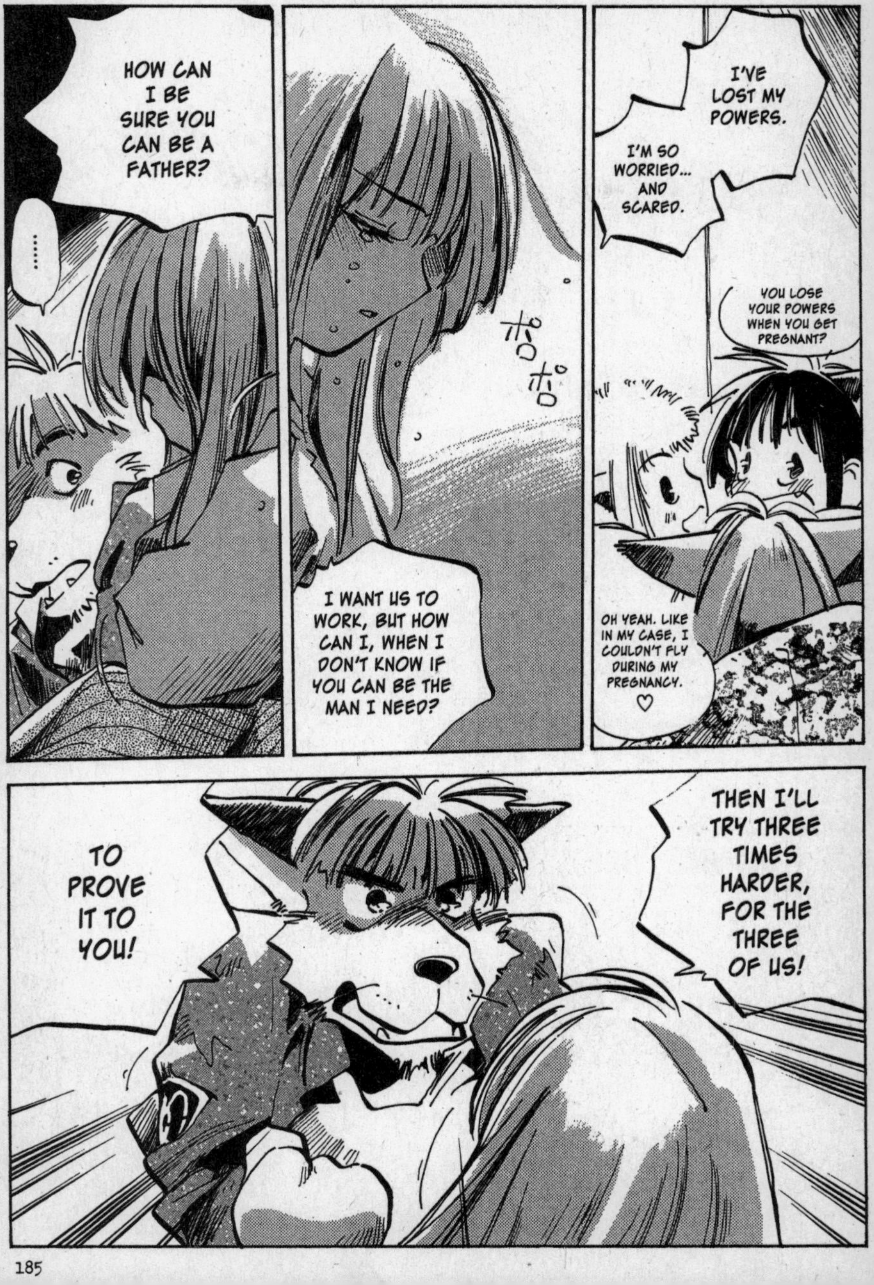
I'VE LOST MY POWERS.
I'M SO WORRIED... AND SCARED.
YOU LOSE YOUR POWERS WHEN YOU GET PREGNANT?
OH YEAH. LIKE IN MY CASE, I COULDN'T FLY DURING MY PREGNANCY. ♡
ポロ ポロ
I WANT US TO WORK, BUT HOW CAN I, WHEN I DON'T KNOW IF YOU CAN BE THE MAN I NEED?
HOW CAN I BE SURE YOU CAN BE A FATHER?
......
THEN I'LL TRY THREE TIMES HARDER, FOR THE THREE OF US!
TO PROVE IT TO YOU!

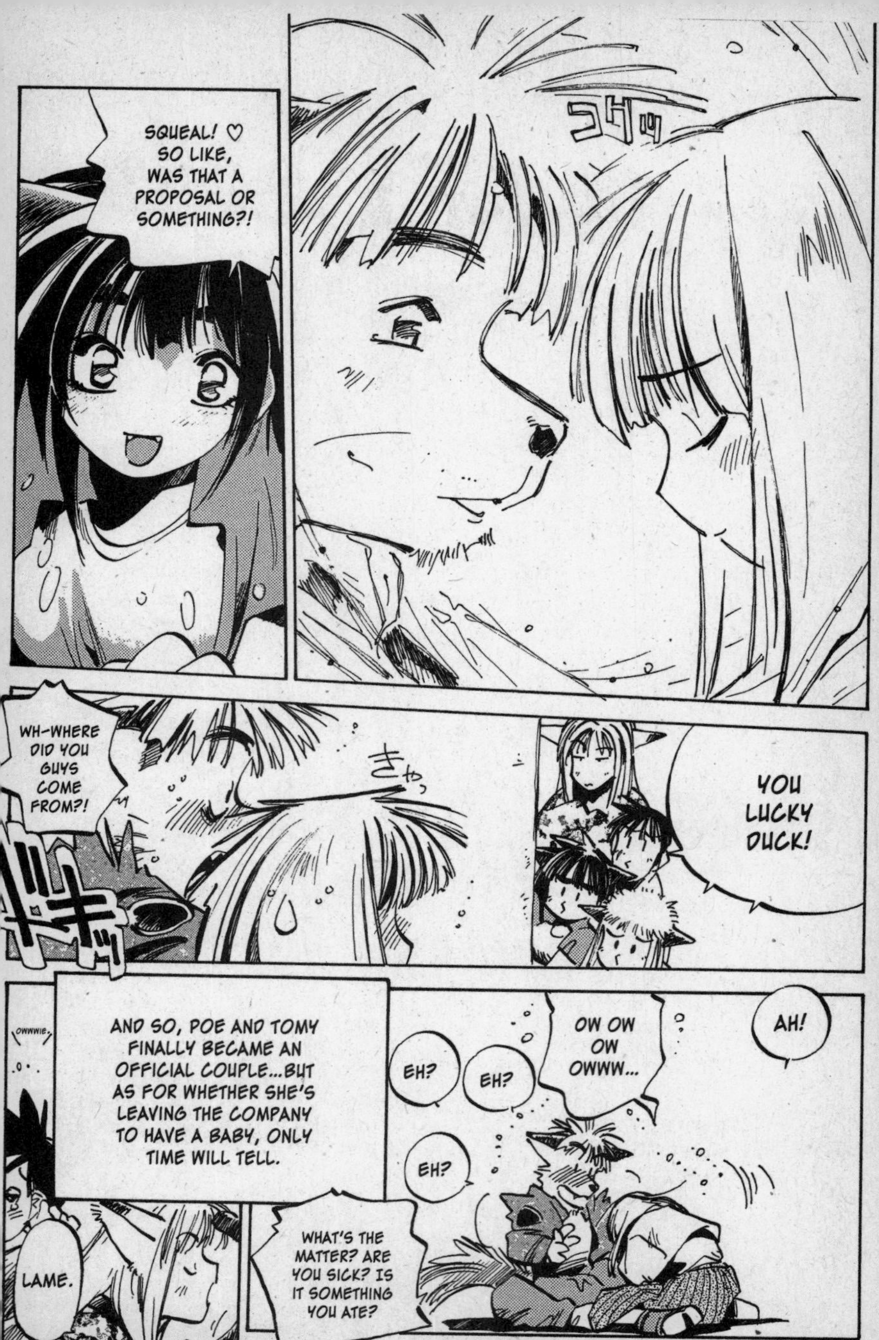
コクッ
SQUEAL! ♡ SO LIKE, WAS THAT A PROPOSAL OR SOMETHING?!
YOU LUCKY DUCK!
きゃっ
WH-WHERE DID YOU GUYS COME FROM?!
ドキッ
AH!
OW OW OW OWWW...
EH?
EH?
EH?
WHAT'S THE MATTER? ARE YOU SICK? IS IT SOMETHING YOU ATE?
AND SO, POE AND TOMY FINALLY BECAME AN OFFICIAL COUPLE...BUT AS FOR WHETHER SHE'S LEAVING THE COMPANY TO HAVE A BABY, ONLY TIME WILL TELL.
OWWWIE
LAME.

End of Volume 8

WANTED

MEE

FOR THE PERPETRATION AND SALE OF TRULY TWISTED MANGA FEATURING FURRY FEMME FATALES.

A PRODUCT OF YANAGAWA IN THE FUKUOKA PREFECTURE, MEE WAS BORN ON JUNE 24 IN 1963. PAST ACTIVITY HAS INCLUDED WRITING AND ILLUSTRATING KOTETSU NO DAIBOKEN (KOTETETSU'S GREAT ADVENTURES) FOR WANI MAGAZINE COMICS. CURRENTLY BELIEVED TO BE WORKING ON THE HYPER POLICE MANGA (THOUGH THIS INFORMATION MAY BE OUT OF DATE).

SUSPECT HAS ISSUED THE FOLLOWING STATEMENT TO POLICE COMPANY: "I WOULD LIKE TO HOOK SAKURA UP WITH A BOYFRIEND AND NATSUKI WITH A FIANCE, BUT IT LOOKS LIKE THIS MAY TAKE A WHILE. NEVERTHELESS, I THANK YOU FOR YOUR SUPPORT."

POLICE COMPANY
UNSOLVED CASE REPORT

GENERAL INFORMATION	
Case file number: 122507 - XMS	

Investigation status:

Attention All Units: The case of the fake Natsuki Sasahara has finally been solved, but when our favorite cat girl decides to go on a luxurious vacation to the tropics, she finds it's not all it's cracked up to be. Two of our lovely ladies are stranded, akin to Cast Away, where they must learn to survive the untamed wild. As like all of our exceptional Units, Natsuki's ready to kick it into high gear to prove her worth to the team, only adding fuel to the flame -- literally! It's only when she stumbles upon her ability to produce time-and-space-bending vortexes that she gets her second chance.

But while vortexes may be Natsuki's ticket to a promotion, it seems that the authorities from another dimension don't appreciate it too much...and are willing to lay down their alternative-dimensional laws!

PD-292 (Rev. 2-99) This information is available in alternative formats upon request. Printed on Recycled Paper

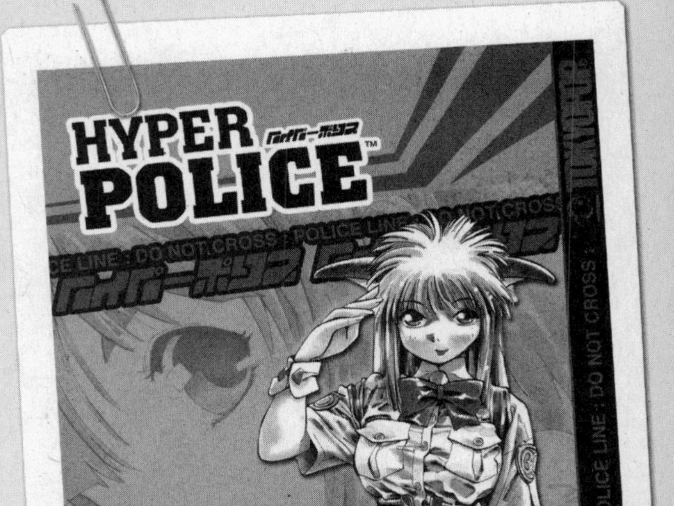

HYPER POLICE™
ハイパーポリス
POLICE LINE : DO NOT CROSS : POLICE LINE : DO NOT CROSS
VOLUME 09 • STORY & ART BY MEE

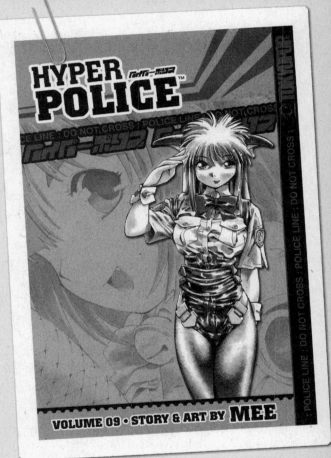

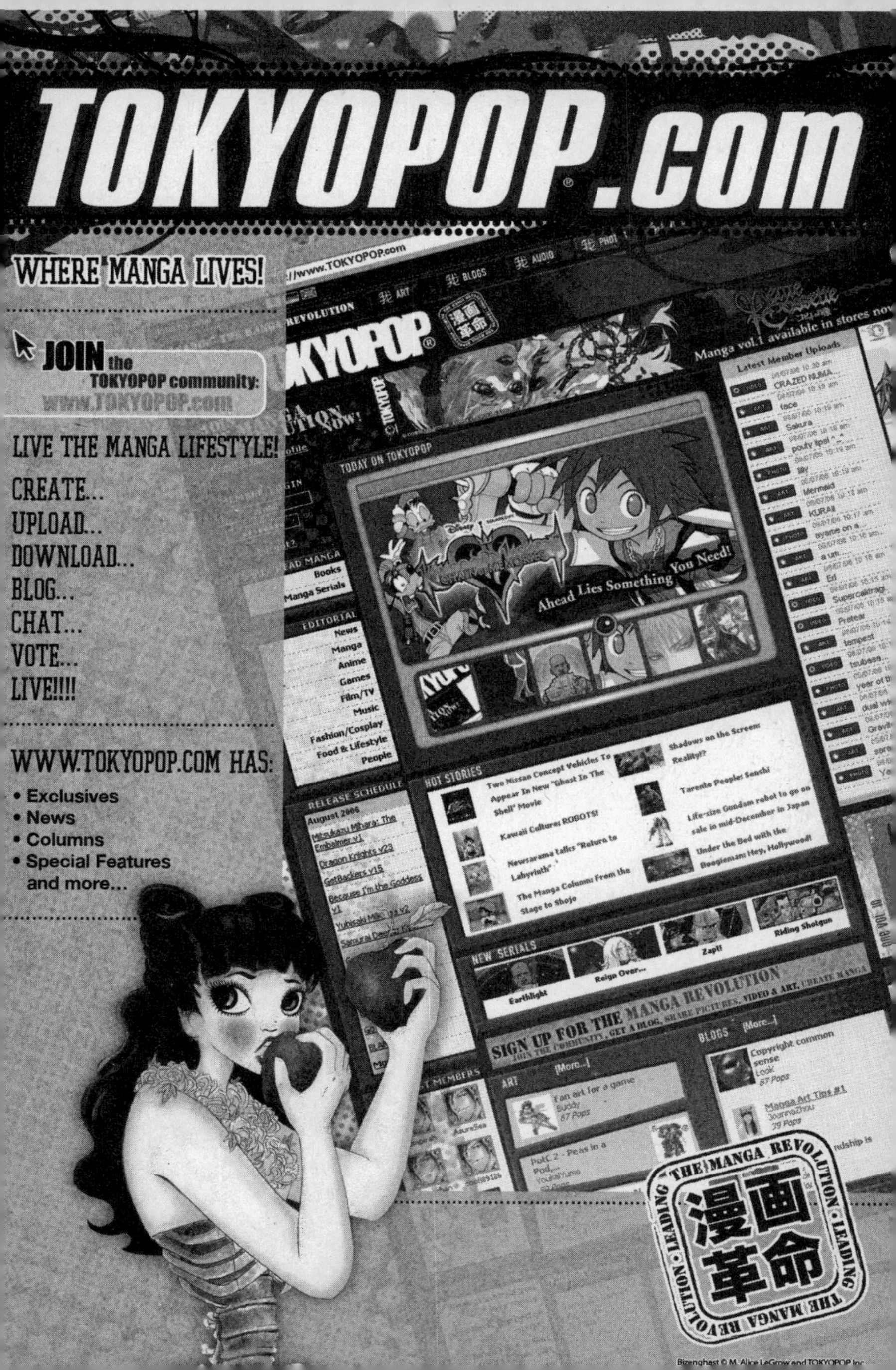
TOKYOPOP®.com
WHERE MANGA LIVES!
JOIN the TOKYOPOP community:
www.TOKYOPOP.com
LIVE THE MANGA LIFESTYLE!
CREATE...
UPLOAD...
DOWNLOAD...
BLOG...
CHAT...
VOTE...
LIVE!!!!
WWW.TOKYOPOP.COM HAS:
• Exclusives
• News
• Columns
• Special Features and more...
THE MANGA REVOLUTION
漫画革命
LEADING THE MANGA REVOLUTION
Bizenghast © M. Alice LeGrow and TOKYOPOP Inc.

STOP!

This is the back of the book. You wouldn't want to spoil a great ending!

This book is printed "manga-style," in the authentic Japanese right-to-left format. Since none of the artwork has been flipped or altered, readers get to experience the story just as the creator intended. You've been asking for it, so TOKYOPOP® delivered: authentic, hot-off-the-press, and far more fun!

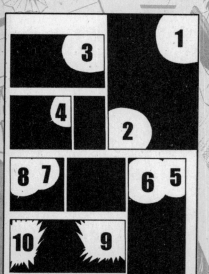

DIRECTIONS

1
2
3
4
5
6
7
8
9
10

If this is your first time reading manga-style, here's a quick guide to help you understand how it works.

It's easy... just start in the top right panel and follow the numbers. Have fun, and look for more 100% authentic manga from TOKYOPOP®!

THE MANGA REVOLUTION · LEADING 漫画革命

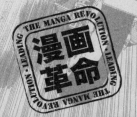